DAYS OF
OUR LIVES

DAYS OF OUR LIVES

A Complete History of the Long-Running Soap Opera

MAUREEN RUSSELL

McFarland and Company, Publishers, Inc.
Jefferson, North Carolina, and London

The present work is a reprint of the library bound edition of Days of Our Lives: A Complete History of the Long-Running Soap Opera, first published in 1995 by McFarland.

LIBRARY OF CONGRESS CATALOGUING-IN-PUBLICATION DATA

Russell, Maureen.
   Days of our lives : a complete history of the long-running soap opera / by Maureen Russell.
      p.   cm.
   Includes bibliographical references and index.

   ISBN 978-0-7864-5983-4
   softcover : 50# alkaline paper ∞

   1. Days of our lives (Television program)   I. Title.
PN1992.77.D38R87   2010
791.45'72—dc20   95-35873

British Library cataloguing data are available

Cover image ©2010 Shutterstock

Manufactured in the United States of America

McFarland & Company, Inc., Publishers
   Box 611, Jefferson, North Carolina 28640
   www.mcfarlandpub.com

For Ted, Betty, Jack and Mac

ACKNOWLEDGMENTS

First and foremost, I want to thank Ken Corday; without his assistance I would have been unable to bring this story to you. I also give my most heartfelt appreciation to the cast, crew, writers, and production staff of *Days of Our Lives*, both past and present, for their generosity of time and spirit. I could not have done it without them: Matthew Ashford, Debbie Ware Barrows, Joe Behar, Bill Bell, Lee Phillip Bell, Richard Bloore, Lester Borden, Macdonald Carey, Crystal Chappell, Ken Corday, Mason Dickson, Chip Dox, Gary Fogel, Don Frabotta, Joe Gallison, Becky Greenlaw, Mike Grigaliunas, Sheryl Harmon, Elizabeth Harrower, Bill Hayes, Susan Seaforth Hayes, Wayne Heffley, Jack Herzberg, Terry Ann Holst, Roger Inman, George Jenesky, Kathy Kelly, H. Wes Kenney, Wally Kurth, Nancy Lewis, Rick Lorentz, Ed Mallory, Greg Meng, Dusty Morales, Frank Parker, Linda Poindexter, Quinn Redeker, Suzanne Rogers, Charlotte Ross, Pat Schultz, Camilla Scott, Margaret Scully, Charles Shaughnessy, Pat Falken Smith, Stephen Wyman, Ed Zimmerman.

Thanks to Paul Camp, Brigitte Kueppers, and Ray Soto of the UCLA Theater Arts Library for all their help. Thanks to Shirley Kennedy at the Academy of Television Arts and Sciences Library. Thanks to Norma Jane Russell for listening to my *Days* tales. Thanks to *Days* fans everywhere, but especially Julie, Laura, the Peel sisters and Joanna. And special thanks to Wanda Bryant and her red pen; I could not have done it without her.

CONTENTS

PREFACE

When I began writing this book, Macdonald Carey (*Tom Horton*), Joy Garrett (*Jo Johnson*), Jack Herzberg, producer, John Lupton (*Tommy Horton*), and Mark Tapscott (*Bob Anderson*) were still with us. Now they are gone.

I had the pleasure of interviewing both Mac and Jack for this book, and I would like to briefly share my experience with these two special men.

Jack Herzberg and I exchanged several letters before he called one day and asked, "Why don't you come down to Temecula and visit? I'll fix you lunch." How could I refuse? I drove down to his home. Good to his word, he had lunch ready and waiting. A shrimp salad, made with tomatoes and cucumbers, he proudly explained, from his own garden. Lunch turned into dinner as Jack and I talked for nearly six hours. We watched videotapes of *Days* past. We watched Emmy ceremonies from days past. Jack talked about *Days* with great love and affection. We chatted about chili cook-offs and his judging beauty pageants (pictures from which he had proudly displayed on his office wall). As I left his house that day, I never suspected that only a few months later, he would be gone. Thanks for the memories, Jack.

When Mac called me, I was stunned. Here was *Tom Horton*, everyone's surrogate grandfather, on the phone. He was as nice and charming and wonderful as any fan would have ever dreamed. He invited me to his home. When I arrived that evening, Mac gave me a tour. First, he showed me his beloved rose garden. Then, back inside the house, he led me to his library, where his treasured collection of first editions was displayed. We talked for nearly two hours. I thanked him and left. Disaster. Much to my chagrin, my car would not start. Mac lived high in the hills, so I had no choice but to walk back to the house, knock on the door and explain my problem. After I called the Auto Club, Mac, ever chivalrous, invited me to dinner. Then he apologized: would microwave lo-cal dinners be all right? As an actor, he always had to watch his weight. Smiling, he teased, maybe he'd have to do a love scene in the near future, and he wanted to look his best. What could I say? I was overwhelmed. Then Mac asked if we could watch his favorite show, *Jeopardy*. It was just about to begin. Of course. I spent the next hour with Mac, simply enjoying his gracious hospitality. Eventually, the car was repaired, and I was on my way. I will never forget Mac's kindness, his wit, his easy charm or his style.

Good night, sweet prince, and flights of angels sing thee to thy rest.

MAUREEN RUSSELL, *December 1994*

INTRODUCTION

I am an historian and a fan of *Days of Our Lives*. The initial idea for this book was almost a joke. A friend and I were discussing our life-long love affair with *Days of Our Lives*. My friend said to me, "You know so much about this show, you should write a book." I felt a little bit like Andy Hardy: "Hey, kids, let's put on a show." But I could not get the idea out of my mind. Why not write a book? I had the credentials, I had the desire. I wrote a letter to *Days'* executive producer and owner, Ken Corday. I cannot describe the shock and delight that I felt when he called and asked to meet with me. When he gave the book the go-ahead, I felt like a child let loose in a candy store. What could be more wonderful than being allowed to write a book about one of my favorite subjects and in the bargain getting to meet so many wonderful people? And thus I came to write this book combining two of my most cherished interests: history and *Days*.

This book does not contain an in-depth analysis of the demographics, economics, or viewing patterns of the daytime viewer because my concern is not social science. Nor does it include discussions of content analysis, textual criticism, or varying philosophies of knowledge. My goal is to write a narrative history and reference guide to *Days of Our Lives* that will be of interest to both the devoted fan and the casual viewer. I have used two primary research tools: archival research and oral history.

I am indebted to a great number of people for allowing me access to their files and granting me interviews. They are all gratefully recognized in the Acknowledgments. Some people may feel that I rely too heavily on quotations. But it was my feeling that readers would prefer to "hear" an anecdote in the storyteller's own words, rather than to read my summary.

To begin the story at the beginning of the story (to paraphrase Dickens),

I began watching *Days* when I was a child. My best friend's mother got me hooked the show's very first year, 1965. Since then I have followed the vicissitudes of the *Hortons, Bradys, DiMeras, Johnsons,* and all the other families of *Days*. I decided to write this book when I realized that some viewers did not know the back story or character history needed to make sense of the current story. Besides, I wanted to know how *Days* was born and was surprised to learn that no complete history of *Days* existed. My goal was immediate: to write such a history.

   Days is the longest-running daytime drama produced by a single family, the Cordays.[1] It began with Ted Corday, passed to his wife, Betty Corday, and now rests with their son Ken Corday. Ted and Betty Corday died years ago, but I interviewed Ken Corday as well as the original director, Joe Behar, and producer, Jack Herzberg[2]; first-year producer, Wes Kenney; and early writers Bill Bell and Pat Falken Smith. The birth of *Days*, its rocky beginnings, and its 30-year legacy are chronicled in Chapter 1.

   Once I knew how the show originated, I wanted to know how it continued. Daytime drama is, after all, a never-ending tale, the ultimate in serial format. *Days* has been seen Monday through Friday for over 30 years. Barring preemptions, it has never missed a day, never missed an episode. *Days* produces a one-hour television program five days a week, 52 weeks a year. That is over 260 shows a year, more than 7,800 episodes in 30 years. I knew I must include an in-depth description of this Herculean task. I have visited the set time and time again and marvelled as the cast, crew, and production people performed their magic. I interviewed actors, writers, producers, directors, production designers, costume designers, camera operators, sound experts, editors, stage managers; I talked to almost everyone who helps put this show on the air. I wanted to demonstrate what a true group effort *Days of Our Lives* represents and exactly how a show is created, from the time the actors, production staff, crew, and directors get a script to the time it is videotaped, edited, and finally sent to NBC to air. This overall production picture is Chapter 2.

   The written word is obviously the backbone of the show. Thirty years have produced over 7,800 scripts, over 700,000 pages of dialogue! Writing for daytime television is unlike writing for any other medium. Daytime writing has been compared to an assembly line, what with its head writers, break-down writers, script writers, and all manner of story consultants. Some of the best writers in the business have written for *Days*; their story is told in Chapter 3.

   Days has often been credited with having the best cast in daytime. The actors who bring the characters to life and the characters created by the combined talents of the writers and actors are discussed in Chapter 4.

   No daytime drama could exist without the fans, and *Days of Our Lives* has probably the most devoted fans in daytime. The fans, fan gatherings, fan clubs, the appeal of the show and of certain characters and actors to the fans are the focus of Chapter 5.

Producer Jack Herzberg on the set with Susan Seaforth Hayes (c. 1971). Jack proudly proclaimed this his favorite *Days'* photo. Courtesy Susan Seaforth Hayes and Monty Sherman.

The complete story history of *Days* is presented in Chapter 6. In trying to convey 30 years of story, I have had to condense story line. But, with apologies to writers past and present for possibly losing intricacies and nuance of story, I have tried to make it as current and coherent as possible.

History, production, and writing are all necessary discussions, but I also felt that separate appendices would provide easy reference. The complete family trees pictured in Appendix A are presented so that all the marriages, remarriages, divorces, affairs, and children produced might have some coherent genealogy. As the family trees indicate, hundreds of characters have appeared on *Days*, and a panoply of actors have passed through Salem in 30 years to bring these characters to life. I have tried to give them all credit. The complete cast and character lists that appear in Appendices B and C were compiled from cast sheets graciously supplied to me by Corday Productions. "Principals," "recurrings," and "under-fives" are those primarily listed, but when the information is available, I credit "extras" as well. Appendix D lists all Emmy nominations and

Emmys garnered by the show. Appendix E lists all *Days'* "Soap Opera Award" winners. Finally, I close with a complete bibliography. It is directed at both the student interested in daytime television and fans looking for further information on their favorite actors. The general materials listed discuss both soap opera in general and *Days* specifically. The articles cited that appear in publications devoted exclusively to soap opera (*Soap Opera Digest, Soap Opera Magazine, Soap Opera Update, Soap Opera Weekly*) deal solely with *Days of Our Lives*.

While this book is dedicated especially to *Days of Our Lives*, I think a few words about the beginning of "soap opera" are in order. The genre as we know it today, is said to have gotten its name from the prevalence of soap companies among early sponsors.[3]

However, the continuing story or serial is not a new dramatic form. Writers from Dickens to Balzac had published their novels serially. Local movie houses ran serials that hooked moviegoers to Pauline's perils or Helen's hazards. But it was not until the 1930s that the serial format came to radio.

In 1922 the American Telephone & Telegraph Company (AT&T) announced that it was making available radio air-time for anyone who wanted to buy it. AT&T had 16 sponsors within six months. However, radio was still a new medium, and it had hours of programming to fill each day. This meant that many new types of programming could be tried, as long as there was a sponsor, and that anything successful would be endlessly copied.

Radio drama debuted as early as 1922, but it was not a huge success until 1928 and CBS's *True Story*. And the notion of *serial* drama was considered risky. Would listeners tune in to a story that was not resolved in a single episode? The answer was a resounding "yes" as the evening serial comedy *Amos 'n' Andy* attracted 40 million listeners in its heyday. *Amos 'n' Andy* was the first radio show to use the serial format, the continuing narrative, that never-ending tale where the story unfolds and the plot situations are resolved over a period of weeks, months, and years. *Amos 'n' Andy* became a national institution and sold a lot of toothpaste for its sponsor, Pepsodent.

Despite the seeming success of the serial format, programmers were hesitant to try it in the daytime. They feared that their audiences would be primarily "housewives" without buying power. In fact, advertising rates charged for daytime were half that of nighttime. However, advertisers soon realized that they had a "captive" audience and that homemakers were a good listening demographic. Though they did not compete directly in the labor force, they often controlled the household budget and made the purchases.

Shortly, the sponsors replaced the networks as the producers of the programs. The sponsors, in turn, looked to their advertising agencies to come up with program ideas that would draw big audiences. Soon the agencies began creating ideas of their own, rather than waiting for a sponsor to ask. One such idea was the continuing daytime serial, 15 minutes in length, based on the problems faced by contemporary men and women. While it would be impossible to credit a single individual with this idea, two names stand at the forefront: Hummert and Phillips.

Before I discuss the Hummerts and Irna Phillips, I must remind the reader of the decade. It was the early 1930s, post–Depression America. Jobs and money were scarce, pessimism was rampant. Where could you turn for some comfort and understanding, escape and entertainment? How about your radio and the small friendly community to be found on your favorite serial?

Soap opera as we know it today began with Frank and Anne Hummert and Irna Phillips. The Hummerts were advertising executives at the agency Glackett, Sample and Hummert.[4] The Hummerts built on existing models like *Amos 'n' Andy* when they proposed the idea of a continuing daytime drama, but they revolutionized the writing process. Realizing that one soap opera would not make them rich, they organized a machine for the generation of serials. The Hummerts would create the story and show it to a sponsor. If the sponsor signed on, the Hummerts would give them outlines to make sure the episodes conformed to the sponsor's expectations. Then the Hummerts would pay "dialoguers" or script writers to write the actual scripts. Thus the Hummerts kept control of character, plot, and the rights to the shows. Between 1932 and 1940 the Hummerts created more than 30 soap operas.

The Hummerts located all their soaps in the Midwest; Chicago was their home base. They chose all their actors from that area, thus creating a more accurate Midwest drama. They felt that the Midwest represented an ideal of American values and attitudes that would appeal to their audience. They had a basic formula: good against evil, fantasies of romance combined with a familiar environment and an identifiable heroine. The "Hummert formula" was always the same: people share common needs, values, and problems, and the listeners quickly identified with their faithful radio heroes and heroines.

The other major name in the field of early daytime drama was Irna Phillips. Irna was hired as an actress by radio station WGN in Chicago in 1929 to host a talk show, *Thought for the Day*. In 1930 she either suggested or was asked to submit an idea for a new drama, *Painted Dreams*, which is usually credited as the "first" daytime soap opera.[5] Irna's formula was different from the Hummerts. She focused on characterization more than plot line. Her characterizations were simple and straightforward, more "realistic." In the 1930s the Hummert fantasies were more popular, but by the forties, the war years, Irna's more "realistic" vision was preferred. Her characters found themselves in situations that were identifiable to her listeners. Her stories usually centered around strong female characters. She was the first to introduce the professional woman. She was also the first to make amnesia respectable as a plot device, and she invented the medical soap; the first was *The Road to Life*.

The move from radio to television came slowly. RCA began selling televisions in 1946; by 1952, 15 million U.S. homes had television sets. Soaps were slow to move to television because of their cost. Actors and writers were needed for radio soaps, but television soaps required actors, writers, sound and lighting technicians, sets and designers, costumes and makeup, directors and assistants, plus studio space. In other words, it cost a great deal more money to produce. In 1946 there was a one-day TV broadcast of the radio soap *Big Sister*. It failed. In 1950 CBS got Procter & Gamble to sponsor a network television soap, *The First Hundred Years*. It lasted barely two years. In 1952 Irna Phillips' *Guiding Light* became the first radio soap opera to make a successful move to television. And, in conjunction with an overall expansion of daytime, three television serials premiered in the 1951-52 season for CBS: *Search for Tomorrow*, *Love of Life*, and *The Egg and I*. The first two were very popular, establishing CBS' lead in daytime and proving to advertisers that the daytime serial drama was indeed a viable format. If the advertisers knew that the daytime television drama had an audience that would buy its product, they would be more than willing to sponsor daytime drama.

In 1956 another major change took place when the television serial moved from the 15- to 30-minute format. Irna Phillips' innovative *As the World Turns* was the first. Between 1950 and 1960, 41 television soap operas went into production. Of those, two remain today, *Guiding Light* and *As the World Turns*. By 1960 CBS, ABC, and NBC had dropped all radio soap operas from their schedules. But soaps were flourishing on television. In 1963 and 1964 NBC challenged CBS' daytime domination by introducing *The Doctors* and Irna Phillips' *Another World*. In 1965 NBC decided to add another daytime drama to its schedule, one Irna Phillips helped create with Ted Corday. The new soap opera was titled *Days of Our Lives*.

* * *

I want to again thank all of the actors who graciously consented to be interviewed. All contract players who appeared on *Days* between June 1990 and September 1991 were asked for interviews. All who were interviewed are included in the book. Also, all fan club presidents of actors who appeared on the show between June 1990 and September 1991 were contacted. All who responded are included in the book.

Also, a brief stylistic note: character names are printed in *italics* in chapters 1–5 for ease of identification. However, in chapter 6, which deals exclusively with characters and not actors, the names are *not* printed in italics.

CHAPTER 1

BEGINNINGS

Legend has it that one day Irna Phillips, Ted Corday, and Allan Chase were sitting on a porch in Southampton when they came up with the idea for *Days of Our Lives*. The true story is richer, more varied and, like a true soap opera, more complex.

Theodore (Ted) Corday began his career as a lawyer in Canada, but his life-long love of the theater drew him to New York and the Broadway stage. He began his production career, as son Ken Corday says, as a "cable puller." Within three years he was a stage manager and within two years of that, a director. He directed a number of Broadway shows, including *Cabin in the Sky*, *Porgy and Bess*, and *Harvey*. He also directed radio shows such as *Gangbusters*.

In 1941 he married Elizabeth (Betty) Shay. Betty Shay was a graduate of Boston University and performed as an actress with Milton Parson's Shakespearean troupe and in stock productions in New England and on Broadway. She also worked as a production associate on *Cabin in the Sky* and *John Henry*, where she met her husband-to-be. From 1935 to 1940 she worked for the advertising agencies of Young & Rubicam and Benton & Bowles; both owned soap operas. The following decade she produced two soap operas for NBC radio: *Pepper Young's Family* and *Young Doctor Malone*. When her sons were born in 1948 and 1950, she devoted herself to being a full-time wife and mother.

After the war's end in 1945, Ted Corday left the Army Signal Corps and, like Betty, worked solely in radio. He directed a number of radio soap operas, including the Irna Phillips' creation *Guiding Light*. *Guiding Light* was the first radio soap to move to television, and in its first year of production, 1952, it ran on both television and radio. Ted Corday would direct the radio broadcast in the mornings, then walk across the hall in the afternoons to the television stu-

The first family of *Days*, the Hortons: (l-r) (back) *Mickey Horton* (John Clarke), *Tom Horton* (Macdonald Carey), *Tommy Horton* (John Lupton), *Bill Horton* (Ed Mallory), (front) *Addie Horton Olson* (Patricia Barry), *Alice Horton* (Frances Reid), and *Marie Horton* (Maree Cheatham) (c. 1966). Courtesy Ed Mallory.

dio and direct the same script for television. After leaving *Guiding Light*, Ted directed and produced another Irna Phillips' creation, *As the World Turns*. Ken Corday relates the tale of the how that show and two others got their titles.

It was called *As the Earth Turns* basically a year and a half before it went on the air. My mother was a wonderful titler, and she said to Irna before it went on, "Let's call it *As the World Turns*." "Oh, it sounds better." Many years before ... *The Edge of Night* ... was supposed to be called *The Edge of Darkness* ... and the *Young and the Restless* was supposed to be *The Young and Impatient*. [1]

Ken Corday explains his parents' entry into the world of daytime television, their collaboration with Irna Phillips and the conception of *Days of Our Lives*,

The front porch story is a cute story, but there were probably a lot of discussions before and after that. But suffice it to say that in some kind of story discussion, my father, Irna, and my mother, because they were close—as close as anyone could get with Irna Phillips—were sitting around talking about what kind of soap opera there was not on the air in the mid-sixties, the early sixties, that most soap operas at that time were based on the urban hospital situation, and were very urbanized and really could have taken place in any one tall building. So what their concept was, "Let's do one in color," because no one had done color. "Let's do one about a rural kind of middle-class country doctor, who has a larger than two- or three-children family—he had five—and who stands for a real kind of moralism and that love conquers all and morality will win out in the end." And, of course, with that as a background all of the, for lack of a better word, shenanigans and misbehavior by the siblings was created, was enhanced by the strong moral fiber of *Tom* and *Alice* ... It basically was "Let's do a soap that is not like any other" and then the secondary thought was "Let's get a name film star as the starring role." And that was Mac Carey.[2]

Macdonald Carey had starred in a variety of movie roles,[3] but he also had a soap opera connection; he had starred in the Irna Phillips' radio soap opera *Woman in White* in Chicago for WGN in 1937.

Carey says of that first job in soap opera:

I started in Chicago in 1937, and I was put under contract by NBC. I had been with a Shakespearean stock company, and we were flooded out. We were on the road, and a lot of bookings got cancelled. I had to work, and I decided to try radio. My uncle lived in Chicago, and I auditioned and got a job at NBC as part of their stock company. And the first series that I worked on was called *Woman in White*, and it was created by Irna Phillips. That was the first series that I had a contract for, and it was with Irna. So it was probably through Irna that Ted Corday heard of me.[4]

As Carey recalls the job offer, "Ted Corday called me and said, 'How would you like to do a soap opera?' And I said I would like to do anything. And he said, 'Well, it would revolve around you and your family ... you are liable to be stuck ten years doing this show. Are you prepared to face that?' I said 'Sure, let's do it.'"[5] Little did either suspect that *Days of Our Lives* would still be going strong over thirty years later.

Ted Corday said in his initial presentation to the network, "*Days of Our Lives* was created by Irna Phillips, Allan Chase,[6] and me and was designed to bring to the daytime audience a new and vital set of characters, at once identifiable and set on the broadest possible family base. From our years of experience in the daytime serial field, we think we know what will capture the daytime audience ... strong emotional stories that spring from interesting people."[7] As Ted concluded in the presentation program, "The story elements of *Days of Our Lives* are many, our characters varied and abundant, and our canvas large—to make a most exciting picture of life in America today."[8]

For this presentation Ted Corday had created a unique pilot, as he explained,

Bill Horton (Ed Mallory) and his father, *Tom* (Macdonald Carey), share a drink with friend *Bob Anderson* (Mark Tapscott) while watching their favorite sport on the television (c. 1972). Courtesy Corday Productions.

In preparing the pilot for *Days of Our Lives*, we followed a much more challenging course to bring you a new type of pilot presentation. What we have done is take our first major story, which will require perhaps three to six months to play out, and condensed the story into a series of episodic key scenes. In this way you will be able to meet more of our characters and see how they are each involved in the story's development and how each contributes to its complications.[9]

The director of the *Days'* pilot was Joe Behar. Joe Behar had directed radio soap opera in New York, including *From These Roots* for Benton & Bowles and NBC and *The Greatest Gift*. He also directed the pilot for ABC's *General Hospital* in 1963. Although they had not met prior to 1965, Ted Corday was familiar with Joe Behar's New York soap opera work and his direction of NBC's nighttime game show *Let's Make a Deal*. Ted Corday had originally called upon Behar to direct the pilot and part of the first six months' episodes of the other Corday soap opera on NBC, *Morning Star*.[10] When Ted Corday needed a director for the *Days'* pilot he asked Behar to take off a week from *Morning Star* and move to *Days*. The *Days* pilot was written by Charles Gussman and taped at the NBC Burbank Studios on July 13 and 14, 1965, in Studios 1, 2, and 4.

"Each day is a little life. Every waking and rising, a little breath. Every fresh morning, a little youth. Every rest and sleep a little death; and the sands are running through the hourglass."[11] This was the epigraph used for the pilot, although the now-familiar hourglass and title were the same. The cast of the pilot included: Macdonald Carey (*Tom Horton*), Mary Jackson (*Alice Horton*), Maree Cheatham (*Marie Horton*), David McLean (*Craig Merritt*), Ron Husmann (*Tony Merritt*), John Clarke (*Mickey Horton*), Charla Doherty (*Julie Olson*), Burt Douglas (*Jim*), Ed Prentiss (*Narrator* and *Minister*), and Marilyn Fox (*Nurse*). Of the pilot cast only John Clarke remains on the show today.

Joe Behar remembers the pilot presentation: "Jackie Cooper—he was head of Columbia TV—he'd sit at a big desk, and he just said, 'One of our great shows is going to be [*Days of Our Lives*], and you are going to love it.'"[12] Jackie Cooper had obviously always wished the show his best; he sent a telegram to Ted Corday on July 8, 1965, that read, "Please extend my very best wishes to all those working for you and a special good luck to you personally. Jackie Cooper."[13]

Cooper was correct. The pilot was a success, and NBC decided to buy *Days of Our Lives*. The first show was taped November 1, 1965. The script was written by Peggy Phillips and Kenneth M. Rosen. New actors had been brought in to fill two key roles. Frances Reid, with an extensive career on stage, was cast as *Alice Horton*. (She is now one of the two remaining original cast members.) And Dick Colla became *Tony Merritt*.

The familiar hourglass was present,[14] but the epigraph had been changed to "Each moment in life becomes a memory. Each day brings on the next, and tomorrow will soon run its course. This day only is ours."[15] This was the scripted epigraph, but the one that made it to the air was the now familiar, "Like sands through the hourglass, so are the days of our lives," inspired by verse six of the twenty-third Psalm and penned by Ted Corday.[16] As Ed Mallory explains, "Ted always loved the epigraphs. That's why he wrote, 'Like sands through the hourglass...' He loved to hear the intro with the announcer."[17]

The show's producer was Jack Herzberg. Herzberg had been a successful producer in television's early years, producing such shows as *Highway Patrol* and *Science Fiction Theater*. As he likes to say to people regarding *Days*, "I got it born, through puberty, and into adultery, and then I left."[18] He had also been a Staff Sergeant in the Army Signal Corps, making training films during the war, the very same Signal Corps in which Ted Corday served as Captain. As both men were surprised to discover at their initial meeting, Ted Corday had cut all of Jack Herzberg's orders. It seemed that their professional relationship would progress from the Army Signal Corps to daytime television.

Days of Our Lives premiered November 8, 1965. It had been brought in by NBC to fill the 2:00 p.m. time slot formerly held by another soap opera, *Moment of Truth*, which was cancelled. Initial critical reaction to the show was not overwhelming. *Variety*'s review stated, "'*Lives*' on the basis of the opener

Maggie Horton (Suzanne Rogers), center, surrounded by the men of Salem (l-r), "Gets Happy!": *Robert LeClere* (Robert Clary), *Mickey Horton* (John Clarke), *Don Craig* (Jed Allen), *Dr. Greg Peters* (Peter Brown), *Doug Williams* (Bill Hayes), *Mike Horton* (Wesley Eure). Courtesy Suzanne Rogers.

had many warm and winning moments ... the half hour in its unsophisticated way told a pleasant tale of nice people."[19] *Days* needed to be more than "pleasant." It was near cancellation within its first six months. Ted Corday, who had worked so hard to get the show on the air, knew it was in trouble. He also knew that due to his own ill health, he might be unable to save it. Changes needed to be made, and soon. The first change was hiring a new head writer, Bill Bell.

William J. (Bill) Bell had worked with Irna Phillips for years. He had first written scripts for Irna when both worked for WMMB, the CBS affiliate radio station in Chicago. His formal serial writing career began in 1956 when he left the advertising firm of Cunningham and Walsh to begin writing for Phillips' *Guiding Light*. As Bill Bell explains:

She [Irna Phillips] offered me a job doing *Guiding Light*, which was then a 15-minute live show, and I did it for about nine months ... this was just as *As the World Turns* started. *World Turns* started in April, I joined Irna about June or July, *World Turns* was just about three months old. After it was on about a year, Irna, who had been doing the show with Agnes [Aggie] Nixon, who lived in Philadelphia, felt she would be more comfortable doing the show with Bill Bell who lived a block from her on the north side of Chicago. So, in turn, she talked to Aggie, about Aggie taking over *Guiding Light*, and she would just bow out of that altogether. Aggie did [take over *Guiding Light*], so I went with her [Irna] on *As the World Turns*. After about seven years [1964] we created *Another World* together, and subsequently sold it to Procter & Gamble.[20]

Bell's first encounter with *Days* was in an unofficial capacity. Irna Phillips lived in Chicago, and the Cordays had moved to California. As Bill Bell relates, "We [Irna and I] really worked together on everything. I was in on a lot of the meetings when Teddy [Corday] came to Chicago, and they would talk about the show. I am not going to say I was a major force, but I was not an insignificant contributor, just because we were all friends and I was there, never thinking I would be involved with the show."[21]

Irna and Bill Bell occasionally went to California for story meetings, and one of those trips inspired a classic Irna Phillips story.[22] To those who knew her, Irna was both a hypochondriac and accident-prone. When she lived in Chicago the doctor who lived in the apartment beneath hers was called upon to make thrice-daily house calls. She was known to switch seats in restaurants lest she be sitting too near an air conditioner and be chilled. She even stopped trains to summon a doctor. Something always seemed to happen to Irna, whether it was hair spray in her face or ear drops in her eyes.

On one of her first visits to California, Irna attended a story meeting with Ted Corday, Bill Bell, Joe Behar, and a few others. Both Bell and Behar remember the room as small, with nearly barren concrete walls. Halfway through the meeting, a painting, the *only* object on the walls, suddenly fell from its hook and hit Irna squarely on the head! Nurses were summoned, and Irna quickly taken to nearby St. Joseph's Hospital as her stunned companions could only sit and wonder at the seeming impossibility of the accident. Irna was fine, but as Bell attested, "Did she put on a performance." Behar, an obvious master of understatement, concluded, "Boy, was she in a bad mood." As Bill Bell said of life with Irna, "It was quite an adventure."

And the adventure continued. Ted Corday, Irna Phillips, and Bill Bell had worked together for years on *As the World Turns*, so when Ted needed a new head writer for *Days*, he knew whom to call: Bill Bell. Originally, Bill planned to be head writer for *Days* while continuing to work with Irna on *World Turns*. But he soon realized *Days* needed his undivided attention. "The show was in trouble. Larry White, who was in charge of daytime television at that time at NBC said, 'Bill, are you sure you want to do this?' Because at that time *As the World Turns* is getting a 60 share, a 60-plus share ... and *Days* [has] about a 19 share. He said, 'Unless something happens to the show at 13 weeks, it's over, we're dropping it.' So I thought, 'What the hell.' It became a challenge. I lost ten pounds the first week of writing the show."[23]

As Bell said, "These are really the Days of Our Survival."[24] But Bell's writing brought the show a vast improvement in ratings.[25] As Bell himself wrote in 1967, "Ours has now become the quality serial on television. At long last it is a show of which I am tremendously proud. The marriage between writer and production has truly been consummated."[26]

In 1977, *Days* won the *Daytime TV Magazine* Readers' Poll for Best Show, Susan Seaforth Hayes for Best Actress and Bill Hayes for Best Actor. Betty Corday (left) holds the award for Best Show. Courtesy Susan Seaforth Hayes.

Sadly, Ted Corday did not live to see *Days* reach number one. He passed away in July 1966. The show was left to his wife. One of the first things she did was call another producer, H. Wes Kenney. Wes Kenney had known Ted Corday when both were directors in New York. They had been members of the Radio and Television Directors Guild and served on various boards and committees together over the years. Wes Kenney remembers visiting California in 1964 and meeting Ted Corday at Columbia Pictures at the Sunset Gower Studios; they discussed the possibility of directing a show that Ted was planning, but *Days* was not yet on, and Kenney returned to New York to produce and direct *The Doctors.*

But soon after Ted Corday's death, Wes Kenney moved to California and signed to produce and also direct an occasional episode. He likes to tell the story of his first day at NBC. "The first day I drove in, I drove into my parking spot, and there was one with my name on it, and it was spelled 'Kenny.' And my name is Kenney, and, of course, I had fought this all my life. So I walked into the office, and nobody there knew me. 'Yes, may I help you?' 'I'm Wes Kenney. By the way, on my parking spot, the name tag is 'Kenny,' and my name is spelled 'Kenney.' I would appreciate it if you would change it.' 'Yes, we can take care of that.' I said, 'If I drive in tomorrow morning, and it's not changed, I am going to drive out.' I got a smile out of that."[27]

They must have corrected the parking space sign. Wes Kenney stayed with the show on and off until 1979. In 1974 he left to produce the prime-time series, *All in the Family*, for a year for Norman Lear. But Kenney was induced to return to *Days* in 1975 when it made the switch from half-hour to hour.

Bill Hayes recalls Kenney's work as a producer. "Wes Kenney is a bit of a genius. Wes would watch a scene play and then come over and tell you one thing and turn your dial one notch this way and your co-star's dial one notch that way, and the scene would suddenly go 'wham' and just take off. I saw him do it over and over again."[28]

Actor Frank Parker, who currently portrays *Shawn Brady*, remembers auditioning for another part in 1965.

When *Days* first went on the air, I read for the part of *Bill Horton*. Betty and Ted were at the readings at Rene Valenti's office at the old Screen Gems. I went in and I read for it, and they said, "Really good, but I think you might be a bit too young." So I told them, "There is a buddy of mine out here from Pittsburgh. He is a really good actor: Ed Mallory." And they laughed. They said, "Well, he is one of our top choices." And you know what happened there. Ed went on to play the role.[29]

Ed Mallory tells the story of how he got the role of *Bill Horton*.

I started with another show with Ted Corday called *Morning Star*, which ran on NBC for approximately nine months … just enough time for Ted to have his baby, which was *Days of Our Lives*. And we knew we were cancelled, and we were all kind of down in the dumps. And we knew that *Days of Our Lives* had started that November of 1965. And on *Morning Star* I was the only guy under contract at this particular time.…So as we were all kind of celebrating in a sad way our demise and saying, "Well, we'll see each other again" all of a sudden Ted came down and said to me, "How about coming over and playing Bill Horton?" And I said, "Gee…" He said, "He's graduating from medical school and it's overlapping by a week or so of *Morning Star* going off the air and Bill Horton coming on to *Days*." And they were on different shooting schedules, so I was running up and down the hall, being Bill Riley *and* Bill Horton.[30]

Days of Our Lives continued with Bill Bell as head writer until 1973 when he created his own soap opera, *The Young and the Restless*. Pat Falken Smith, who had been Bell's associate writer for many years, took over the head writing duties. Falken Smith had originally come to *Days* in 1965 when her former protege, Peggy Phillips, had called and asked for help. From episode number 65 on, Falken Smith was an integral part of the show.

Falken Smith began her writing career at the Pasadena Playhouse. She was a story consultant for *Playhouse 90*, and story consultant and head writer for the prime-time shows *Bonanza*, *Father of the Bride*, and *National Velvet*. She also wrote episodes of *Perry Mason*, *Shane*, and *Rawhide*.

With story assists from Bill Bell, who remained as a story consultant until 1975 when the show expanded to an hour, Falken Smith took *Days* to even greater heights as the show garnered Emmy nominations for Outstanding Dramatic Series every year from 1973 to 1979, winning for 1977/78. The *Days* writing team also won the Emmy for Outstanding Writing in a Drama Series in 1975/76.

Pat Falken Smith left *Days* in 1977, and the show went through three head writers, Ann Marcus, Ruth Flippen Brooks, and Elizabeth Harrower. Despite some memorable story-telling moments, the show's ratings fell. NBC decided a complete overhaul was in order. Longtime producer Wes Kenney left the show and was replaced by Al Rabin, previously one of the show's directors. Many backstage personnel were phased out by the new producer. New head writer Nina Laemmle eliminated 14 characters and introduced nine new ones in 1980. Some pundits dubbed this reconstruction the "St. Valentine's Day Massacre."

First Laemmle, then Michele Poteet-Lisanti and Gary Tomlin were head writers for the next two years as the show limped along in ratings. Pat Falken Smith returned in 1982, but left the following year, and her associate writer Maggie DePriest took over. From 1985 to 1992 the show again went through a variety of head writers including Thom Racina, Sheri Anderson, Leah Laiman, Anne Howard Bailey, Anne Schoettle, Richard Allen, Beth Milstein, and Gene Palumbo. The show's current [August 1995] head writer is James Reilly. Falken Smith says of the show with which she has been associated for 25 years, "There were good times and bad times, there were dry times, and then the green rains fell."[31]

The single thread of continuity to *Days of Our Lives* in 30 years has been the Corday family. When Ted passed away, Betty took over as Executive Producer. In 1981 their son Ken came in as a producer. Betty Corday semi-retired in 1986 because of ill health and passed away November 17, 1987. Ken Corday became the show's executive producer and the legacy continued. As Ken reveals,

[*Days of Our Lives*] always will be [a Corday family production]. It was an unsaid promise, but a well understood promise between me and my mother before she passed away. There have been offers from the networks and large studios to buy this show from us. We will not sell it. Because I am afraid. I am afraid for the six million fans that have been devoted for 25 years. That in the hands of someone else's sensibilities, not that it is better or worse, the show would change. And it would not necessarily be the show that they have watched for 25 years. And when asked who is going to do it when I am not doing it? Hopefully I will be around long enough to see my children…do it.[32]

Ken Corday reveals that his perception of *Days of Our Lives* as a family legacy has changed over time:

Ted and Betty Corday. Pictured here in New York City, c. 1944. This is their son, Ken's, favorite photo. Courtesy Ken Corday.

I did not really understand full well what it was while my father was alive. We didn't know he had a big hit show. As my mother worked on it for 20 years, I saw that it was more and more important, not only just to this family, but to all the people who watch. And if there is a legacy, specifically and objectively, it is a) that the show is always produced by Corday Productions and really that is "A1."... "A" number one or "A" prime is that the show stands for what it has always stood for and continues to be honest to its principles and its morals...that the family, the concept of the family is very important and the love stories of its children and of all the members of the family are important.[33]

Days of Our Lives is above all a family show about family. Cast, crew, and production staff echo this sentiment. The crew stresses how much they like and respect each other and insisted to me that fact be specifically mentioned. The word "family" pops up again and again. Becky Greenlaw, senior producer[34], says "You talk to the cameramen, you talk to the cast, you talk to the staff, the crew, they all say it's like a family. There is a true family. Betty [Corday] always cared about the people who worked on the show and always took care of them. She was demanding in the good sense of the word. Everybody did their job because they liked working here...Ken has continued in the same vein; he is very supportive, he cares. He cares about not only the show, but the people who work on the show, and it makes it a very pleasant place to work."[35]

Ed Mallory remembers Ted Corday.

Ted was a very hands-on producer. Ted would go through page by page, as we read the script. We'd read the whole thing. We'd block it that day before we left. And Ted would say, for example,"Get under that line, bring something more to it, the writing here isn't really so good, bring your own stuff to this, do that." He was very precise. He was also very innovative. We tried really hard to keep *Morning Star* on the air. And we did a very strange thing... We had a character named Joe Birney who was a crook, but he was kind of a good crook and he ended up kind of heroic. My character, Bill Riley, worked for a magazine and Bill was writing an article, the thrust of which was, "Should Joe Birney get a second chance?" Joe was played by Norman Burton, who was a good character actor. Now Ted wanted to build a mail response to try to keep the show on the air. So I would be playing a scene, for example, with this girl in a hospital room, who's been injured because her apartment lobby has been blown up, because the crooks tried to get Joe. Joe saved her, she's OK. I'm talking to her, "Do you think Joe Birney should be given a second chance?" And she says, "Yes, he's learned his lesson, he's a good man." And I would lift my head from looking at her and look right into the lens and ask, "What about you folks?" And I would talk directly to the audience. And I'd say, "If you think Joe Birney should be given a second chance, send your cards or letters to me, Bill Riley, Box 1234, Glendale, California." We got 85,000 to 90,000 responses, but not enough to keep the show on the air. There was a picture taken in Screen Gems of Ted and me... It was like "Miracle on 34th Street" with all these mail bags dumped out and we were both sitting on this pile of mail. Ted was a character. He was a show biz guy.[36]

Macdonald Carey calls the Cordays the show's "guiding force" and says, "Ted Corday was a very sure hand...Betty Corday was a firm hand [and] a steadying influence."[37]

Bill Bell recalls the Cordays, "They were terribly special, Ted and Betty, they were just the finest people."[38]

Ken Corday says of his parents, "My mother and father, Ted and Betty Corday, instilled in all of us a real heartbeat, a love of family and a love of what that means. It has kept us alive for [30] years and, God willing, it will continue."[39]

As Ted Corday said in 1964, "*Days of Our Lives* is the story of a family...."[40]

CHAPTER 2

ON THE SET

Production

Days of Our Lives has produced over 7,800 episodes in its thirty-year history. That is 260 shows a year for over 30 years. The show ran a half-hour in its first decade, but in 1975 made the switch to a one-hour format. Producing a one-hour television program five days a week is a grueling task. As Ken Corday explains, "We are doing a mini-series every week. We are doing five hours a week, a hundred pages a day. We have had people like Steven Spielberg, Brian De Palma, and Sidney Pollack come in and watch us tape. And each of them said at the end of the week, 'I think it is physically impossible to mount 60 minutes a day on the screen.' Yet we have to do it."[1]

But no one ever said doing it would be easy. Actor and director Ed Mallory reveals, "Daytime can be such a funny medium. It's often a difficult medium. It's tough. There are so many variables. When it's working the way you've envisioned it, it's wonderful. But when nothing is working, you're wondering... Why? Why? Why? It's the agony and ecstasy."[2]

Everyone involved marvels at its creation. Actor Charles Shaughnessy believes,

Daytime is great. It is a very unique medium. I am always amazed that we do a show in a day and that the quality comes out as it does. The mind boggles. And it has been a real privilege to work on the show with the people that I have worked with and in this environment and to see how it is done. They are a very nice bunch of people and real professionals. We have a good time but, by God, we do the work and it is out there on the screen.[3]

This chapter will demonstrate how they do the work and "get it out there on the screen" from the time the actors, crew, and directors get a script to the time it is videotaped, edited, and aired. In addition, differences between taping a half-hour "live tape" show and the current studio practices will be discussed.

19

The Early Years

Days of Our Lives began taping at NBC's Burbank Studio on November 1, 1965. In the early years, when the show ran a half-hour, the director would arrive on the scene at about 4:30 a.m. to set the stage, mark the spots, and make sure everything was in order. Actors would arrive at 7:00 a.m. for blocking, then a run-through, then dress rehearsal, and finally taping.[4] The scenes were shot in the order that they were scripted. Taping for the day would end around 1:00 p.m. and then the actors would begin rehearsing for the next day's shooting. There would be a read-through, dry blocking, and more rehearsal with the director and producer present to discuss the show. Although the show was shot on videotape, the actors were expected to get through a scene with little or no error because few edits were made.

Jack Herzberg describes a typical day in the early years:

We used to start at the top of the show, and we would put in commercials as we went. And it was like a stage play. And it was wonderful because we got something out of the actors that we lost in the hour. We got a tension. And we didn't stop for anything. A tremendous blunder yes, but otherwise, you didn't stop for anything. One day I was in the [control] booth. A character had hurt her leg and the line is: "My doctor told me to stay off my feet a few days." So we were in the booth, at run-through and dress everything is fine. It comes to the taping and the line comes out, in the heat of the drama, "The doctor told me to take my feet off for a couple of days." And I listened and I heard the line and I looked up and down, and the sound man was listening and he looked up at me and said, "no" and went back, he thought it just couldn't be. I could not stop it, I was out of time, I was out of money. I let it go through. Do you know that we never got one letter on that? Ted Corday, who listened at home and on the air, never heard it. And I expected to catch holy hell about that. But we have had other things, where we didn't think it was anything and everybody called.[5]

As Joe Behar describes the early-morning rehearsals that took place while the cast and crews of other shows slept in.

We started doing early rehearsal, we rehearsed earlier than everybody…when it was a half hour show we would start at 7:00 a.m., which was considered early then. Because…when we first started, NBC needed their tape machines for the *Tonight Show*. They had to use those men and those machines and so we had to be finished by a certain time and in order to make sure we were finished, we started early. And after that was not a problem anymore, everybody got so used to that early time, that we kept it…because unless you have an unusually late day, you can have a normal dinner time and see your family.[6]

Days' situation was far from perfect in the early years. As Wes Kenney explains, "NBC had four studios in the main building, and *Days of Our Lives* was shifted from pillar to post. They would give us the studio that was empty…scenery would get broken, props would get lost…but we lived with it. After two or three years NBC finally built us Studio 9, it was a warehouse…and they did a great job. It was a terrific thing."[7]

Bill Hayes describes those early days of taping:

Alice Horton (Frances Reid) as Groucho, *Don Craig* (Jed Allen) as Margaret Dumont, and *Doug Williams* (Bill Hayes) as Chico perform a Marx Brothers' sketch. Courtesy Bill Hayes.

When we did a half-hour, we only used half of one studio. We would have four sets, maybe at the most five, sometimes three in a circle and it was no great distance. I could hear that scene when I was getting ready to do my scene. And we only used three cameras and just as they were winding up that scene, the cameraman would just turn around and focus over here and we were into the scene. And automatically when your mind... just like putting blue next to red, if they were finishing on a very high pitch, then you naturally would start this one on a different feel. You could hear what was going on, everybody was involved in everything.[8]

And how *Days'* plan to get through a scene without an error led a real-life love affair to blossom.

And we did not have editing capabilities then. In fact, if you goofed, you had to go back to a commercial break. You could not pick up in the middle of a scene. In fact, one of the scenes that Susan [Seaforth Hayes] and I recall the most of all is the scene when the stereo would not work. That was real. They had this thing on and you had to turn it a certain way and hold it a certain length of time and if it caught, then it would go. The prop guy, Don, said, "Here's what you do. You turn it like this, and hold it just for a second and then let it go." I said, "I'm trying, I really am." It works, okay, now you set it up again. Put the record on. It was one of those things where you turn it on and it would start and the record would drop and the tone arm would come out and play it. It was playing "The Look of Love." And we did our scene, we did our wonderful kiss, turned on the thing, and it would not go on. We cannot pick it up from here, we have to go back to the commercial break, which was a black slug, and start over, get a running start. And we do the whole scene, come to the kiss and Susan put her heart and soul in that kiss, memorable kiss, four or five times.[9]

Days was never a live show, unlike some of the others shows on which Bill Bell and Irna Phillips collaborated. Joe Gallison started on one such soap: *Another World.* To contrast the live show with the live tape, Gallison explains the excitement and insanity:

There are moments that stick to my mind. There was an actress, who was the star of the show, and they had worked her five days, week in and week out, and she was just exhausted. She was downstage right. I was going on about love and marriage and having patience, and things will work out, all this Pollyanna stuff. I am upstage center and I finish this long speech, two pages, which is outrageously long, walking down to her and finishing. As I walk up to her, well, she is waiting for a bus. I look into those blank eyes and it is her line and it is live. And you could feel the muscles tense in the cameramen. I looked at her and waited, for what seemed an eternity, and nothing, perfectly relaxed, daydreaming. So I grabbed her arm and I said, "Pat, you haven't heard a word I have said!" "No!" So I condensed it and repeated it very quickly, "oh yes" and she picked up her line and we went on with the scene. But it was moments like that. As soon as they cut to her, you could see that she had gone to a faraway place. Then there was another time with the same actress. I used to go up to my dressing room, which was on the second floor. There was a stairway from the second floor to the stage. And after notes, I kicked off my shoes, put my feet up and absorbed the notes into my performance. And one day I fell asleep in my dressing room, trying to absorb these notes. And talk about a relaxed actor. I am very professional. I am always there, to the point that the stage manager doesn't even worry about me, which in this case he should have. And the actress is out watering flowers in her patio and I walk up and we have this scene about something. But I was late. Five, four, three, two, one, and she is out there watering those flowers and nothing. They cue me and I am not there. The stage manager goes crazy, runs into the booth and screams, "He's not there!" So the associate producer rushes upstairs, rips open my dressing room door and shouts, "You're on!" And I was sound asleep. I put on my shoes, rush out the door, go down those steel steps, boom, boom, clunk, clunk, clunk, "Oh, hi Pat." All of America heard me.[10]

Days was not nearly as hectic. Their shooting and rehearsal schedule remained the same until 1975, when it became a one-hour show. The schedule that had worked well for a half-hour show was too much for a one-hour show. Cast and crew alike were coming in at 7:00 a.m. and not leaving until midnight. The situation was becoming intolerable as cast and crew became more and more exhausted. Then recently-returned producer Wes Kenney decided to take action.

First of all, I begin to think back, having come out of theater I was always gung-ho about doing things in sequence because you are building motivation. Then I begin to think… "Listen, Wes, look at the motion picture business. For years they have been doing feature films where they do the last scene first"…and what came out of it was the realization that you have to be flexible. It was a gradual process, but we took out dry blocking for the crew. We would come in and the actors would get blocked dry, but then we would go right on camera and begin the block. And we begin to do things like move into a set and when we were there we would do every scene in that set. Emotionally we found that doing all the scenes in the set worked beautifully for the actors, the scenes were progressive anyway and cut in at different times. We would do this story, this story, this story. Frequently, in the old days, a person would, let us say, be screaming their heart out and then two hours later they would come back, or on taping it would be twenty minutes, but they would be back. Now a person would end up with tears and we would fade to black, beat, beat, beat, and up we would come and the whole emotion was still there.[11]

Bob Anderson (Mark Tapscott) plays the "Sugar Blues." Courtesy Bill Hayes.

The other innovation that came with the switch to the hour-long show was the directors' schedule. For years *Days* had had two directors who alternated days. But when the show went to one hour a third director was hired. A director would work Monday and Thursday the first week, Tuesday and Friday the second week, and Wednesday the third week, then begin the rotation anew. This saved the directors from the crushing schedule of working two to three days every week.

Much the same schedule is still in effect today. Susan Seaforth Hayes, a veteran of the half-hour show as well as a current cast member, describes working in daytime,

The directors work terrible, long hours. The cameramen, the lighting crew, terrible long hours. And our schedule currently is: we come in at 6:00 in the morning, but we sometimes will not go on tape until the middle of the afternoon or later. There are shows that block and tape, you come in in the morning and you start. Your calls are staggered and you come in and work within two and a half hours of being in the studio, so everybody supposedly is fresh for their scene, up for their scene. We do it. We do the whole *enfin*, the whole enchilada, we do everything from dry block to full dress rehearsal. The weakness is you can be exhausted and you can have forgotten the blocking because it was hours ago the last time you rehearsed it. The weakness is, due to budget you can only have so many goes at it, only so many chances to tape it. The strength is, you are so desperate you are quite concentrated.[12]

Actor Quinn Redeker sees another advantage to the longs hours together in the studio: "Being together all day does build camaraderie."[13]

And Ed Mallory puts it all in perspective, "Getting a running part on daytime, or being involved in a show for 30 years, is about the same as winning the lottery. Mac once said to me, when I was screaming about this or that, 'Ed?' 'What, Mac?' 'Don't shoot the goose that's laying the golden egg.'"[14]

A Day on the Set[15]

A "typical" day on the *Days of Our Lives* set today seems barely controlled chaos. It all begins at 4:30 a.m. when the director arrives. Producer and director Steve Wyman explains, "In soap opera the name of the game is to try and do things extremely efficiently because we are doing an hour's worth of TV a day. So in order for that to happen, it has to start with [the director] coming in here and making sure the sets are perfectly prepared for the actors so that when they come in all the marks are laid down, all the furniture is in position. Because we have a two-hour period to give the actors their blocking for 45 minutes worth of material, that's a lot of material to get blocked out in just two hours. So I do everything I can to make it go smoothly, and that's what I do all day long with everything else."[16] The directors normally get their scripts approximately three days before shooting. Usually a day is spent preparing the script for shooting. An average script can have 400 camera shots, and all must be prepared by the director. There is no time for story boards on a soap opera set and directors mark their scripts in shorthand form.

After the director marks his script, he must meet with other members of the production team. As Assistant Director Roger Inman explains,

If the director is directing on Wednesday, then on Tuesday he has a meeting, that takes about 45 minutes or an hour, with the head carpenter, the head electrician, the property master, the lighting director, the art director, and the technical director and lays out everything that is going on. And then each Friday there is a weekly production meeting that somebody from all those departments as well as wardrobe, hair, and make-up attend. They do projections by the week and by the month, if there is something special they know is coming up. Hopefully, we don't get too many terrible surprises.[17]

Some days' tapings are more complicated than others. Disasters, ship wrecks, train wrecks, fires, and the like can be time-consuming and complicated, but other, less obvious scenes, can be just as difficult. Christmas, for example, can be one of the most complex times of year on a soap set, with large numbers of extras, usually children, and many intricate shots required. Viewers may think that those *Hortons* hanging those balls on that tree looks easy, but it is not. The ornaments have to be hanging in just such a way, then each has to be shot in isolation; then there are people singing; cut to a shot of the tree, then to a shot of people singing, cut to a shot of the tree, then the singing, always singing... As Wyman succinctly clarifies, "There are a lot of things in this business that we call 'gotchas.' Where the 'gotcha' is, it looks simple, but it is not."[18]

At 6:00 a.m the actors arrive; early is the director's hope, at least on time is his prayer. Not everyone is at their best and brightest at 6 o'clock in the morning. More than one actor has been known to quip that the true goal of "dry block" is to not wake up. Nonetheless, the actors begin work, script (and often coffee) in hand. Everything is set, nothing is left to chance. Strange and marvelous directions and commentary abound: "Drift downstage on that line." "Long ST beat." "Sit down sweepingly." "Hot, right-handed kiss." "Left-handed hug." "Perch prettily." "Hand up the arm, breathless break, the scene begins, hard slide, surge." "Pick up the pace or get cut!" "Quicker, faster, funnier." "Reality check!" "Do we really need that wall? It gets in the way of the camera." "I think we've discovered why Roman never solves any cases. He erases the blackboard every time he points at it." "Did you say 'clinic abuse director?' That's the person who dishes it out. It's abuse clinic director." "I think it would be best to strap her in." "Let the bed fascinate you." "How you fall on him is up to you." "Zoom in on the money." "You just did that whole scene with one hand tied behind your back." "Move the desk six inches." "Take a powder!" "Did you bring the powder?" "Is it day or night?" "Poor *Jennifer*? Nobody ever feels sorry for the people in the booth." "Remotely conceivable, not plausible or believable, it's a new standard." "It's not what we say, it's what we mean."

The actors annotate their scripts as the director walks them through their blocking, questioning, querying, and trying to make sense of the whole scene. Complicated blocking is bemoaned at 6:00 a.m. On the other hand, actors with simple blocking, like lying abed the whole scene, have been heard to say, "I *love* this blocking." As they work through a scene for the first time, everyone looks for the "gotcha." What do they need to do to make the scene work? "We need to make the pillow fight and the taking-off-the-shirt work." "Which way do you want the kiss?" "I'll be my most unctuous." "You shouldn't have your pants on since that's how I found you." "I am going to pull this lever and there will be a foot massager." "So this isn't a scene about the doorway, it's a scene about the sofa." "It's so long, so long..." "Is this sexual tension?" "Are we shooting the scene from the neck up again?" "Sorry, I got so excited there was a woman in my room." "Let me take off my shirt without knowing it." "I will try and keep it up, so to speak." "Are we dressed or undressed?" "Where's the robe?" "Where's the stunt kisser?" "Lipstick please!" "Goo goo goo joob."

The assistant director, stage manager, and prop master annotate their scripts as well during dry block. Props are commended, discarded, or discovered to be needed. "Move that plant." "Where is the chair that is usually there?" "We need espresso cups." "Does someone hear a clicking?" "You find the rhythm of the scene and we will click to it." "What about an heirloom fountain pen?" "We need one final confetti ball." "Where's the picnic? We need remnants of a picnic." "Everyone hates the scene, but loves the device." Endless discussions occur when there is physical action, how can we get that window to open, locker to stick or bed to break.

As each actor finishes her or his scene they head off stage, out the door to their dressing rooms. Many sleep. Some work on their scripts. Some head straight for the coffee and bagels (one can usually find the actors where the bagels reside). Still others work out. As the director and actors work, the crew begins to arrive: sound and lighting and camera. The noise level on the stage rises accordingly. Two to three hours after it has begun, dry block is over.

Now camera block starts. The set is a hub of activity. Camera operators, crew, and technicians abound. The director is no longer on stage but in the control booth. The stage manager is in charge of the stage, working from notes and directions given by the director during dry block and also constantly talking to the booth via headphones. There are numerous monitors on stage, both stage managers and actors refer to them frequently. There are normally three cameras on stage. The camera operators are initially prepared by the technical director, who has met the previous day with the director and received all the camera shots. The camera operators have the shots posted on their cameras, but make notes regarding cues or changes as needed. The extras also arrive for camera block. Salem can be a busy and densely populated town. The boom operators and sound technicians check sound levels, and ensure that no special equipment or microphone placement is needed.

The actors are still working from their scripts, although some have begun to hold them only for reference. Refinements are made as the director and actors can see exactly how a scene looks for the camera. For example, a part of a set, like a wall, cannot be moved, so marks must be changed. Blocking is altered as a scene is improved to look better, more impressive, or simply clearer. Cast and crew accommodate the changes accordingly. "Let's change that background, stick a tree there or something." "That's a high-rise, why are there trees outside the balcony?" "I tweaked this a bit." "Can we put the duck under contract?" "Let's try those pearl mist filters." "Give her a nice, English kiss." "Perch next to Hector, the ratings god."

The mood on the set is lighter as the crew ribs the actors and the actors joke with each other. Love scenes can often cause unmitigated laughter as actors who are good friends out in the real world are made to feign deep and abiding passion. Some couples attack each other in mock lust, causing outbreaks of guffaws, grins, and sniggers amongst the crew. Some call for the "stunt kisser" when the going seems to be too tough. Others, who cannot keep a straight face no matter how hard they try, promise to have "something worked out" and plead to be released from the torment of kissing each other, at least until dress rehearsal.

Meanwhile, up in the booth, the director sits in front of a huge console, constantly watching the action on stage on one of three monitors. The assistant director (A.D.) annotates the script and counts down to cue. The director will tell the A.D. whether shots are "cut tos" or "dissolves." The assistant director cues in music to monitor audio levels. The producers and music directors will come in later and confirm the musical choices. The audio console is in a connecting room, and the A.D. is in constant contact with the audio mixer. The assistant director has a stop watch and times the show to see that they are near to their allotted time. If the show is running long, lines or possibly an entire scene will be edited out. It is finally time for lunch, with everyone back in an hour and a quarter for dress rehearsal.

The actors use the time between camera block and dress rehearsal for a variety of things. This is the time when most have their hair and make-up done; some are already wearing the required wardrobe. Some go to the studio's "green room" to work out. Those with early calls and a possible long lunch head home for a lunch break. Many go to NBC's infamous commissary, dubbed "*Escoffier Concrete*" by some, for their midday meal. Salads and baked potatoes are popular choices for the always diet-conscious actors. And even in the commissary there is the ever-present TV monitor showing NBC's daytime line-up of shows.

Back in the studio, dress rehearsal has begun. By now, the actors should be in full make-up and wardrobe. They should also be "off" their scripts, although some are more prepared than others. Favorite hiding places for a script are under the covers (if it's a bedroom scene) or perhaps under a desk or behind a potted plant. If an actor has a very tight close-up, who knows where that script might be! Everyone is working to make the show look and sound the best that it can because this is the final rehearsal before taping. The actors are "getting into character" giving very much the same reading they will during tape. This is also the final chance to try out new lines and "ad-libs." "Ad-libs" are not encouraged, but many a writer has lamented the actors' penchant for ad-libbing. As Becky Greenlaw explains,

We do not encourage [ad libs] at all. There are some instances where, I would say for the most part, most actors will adjust a line to make it more in tune to their character. The intent we will not allow to be changed....The actors know if they have got a problem with the script, if they come to us the day before and they have got a serious problem, and a legitimate problem,

Rosie (Fran Ryan) and *Robert* (Robert Clary) celebrate the "Oceania Roll." Courtesy Bill Hayes.

something that we did not see, we can talk. They know their characters better than we do. We are dealing with 40 characters, they are dealing with their own and know them better than we do. We know where it [the story] is going and they do not. Basically it is taken on an individual basis and we will not let them change intent, we will allow them to adjust. If they have a major problem with a scene, we will rewrite scenes. And the writers are very involved in that. There is no yes or no or black and white to that.[19]

As Al Rabin bemoaned at the twenty-fifth anniversary dinner, "We have had hundreds of thousands of pages of dialogue in 25 years and maybe 100 pages of that have not been changed by the actors." Some actors are famous, or infamous, for their ad-libs. Some ad-libs never see nationally televised air time, but make the annual *Days'* bloopers reel. During Christmas 1990, when *Jack Deveraux* got his *Horton* Christmas ball, actor Matthew Ashford ad-libbed, "I've been balled by the *Hortons*." There was a moment of silence, as the cast waited to see if tape would roll or the scene would be stopped. Suddenly the director's voice boomed, "Matthew, you can't say *Hortons* on television."

Ashford also likes to create lines that skewer *Jack Deveraux*'s attempts at machismo or his lack thereof,

The line everyone liked so much, is, one day, Roman is saying, "This is the plan." And I said, "One question." "Wait, what is it?" I said, "You guys are going to go off and risk your lives to get Isabella out of this thing, right?" "Right." "Right." "And you expect me to stay behind here with the women?" "Right." "Sounds good to me." And I said it like that. And I did it at dress and so underplayed, Drake [Hogestyn] starts laughing, everyone, in the booth, all the cameramen, the guys on the booms, everybody starts laughing. Everyone was laughing so much the first take we could not do it. People love that stuff. It is funny, but he [*Jack*] did not intend it to be funny. And I said they laugh, not just because it is funny, but because it is true.[20]

Actor Wayne Heffley, who often seems to play "Sancho" to Matthew Ashford's "Don Quixote" admits:

We embellish the scripts. We don't change the scripts, we just embellish them. And Matt is very creative and wonderful to work with, and he injects everything with this madcap weirdness.... And there are times when you just cannot read certain lines. There was one script where *Jennifer* is trying to cajole *Vern* into fooling *Jack.* "Will you do it, will you do it?" "I don't know. He always catches me in a lie." The script said, "*Vern* looks deep into *Jennifer's* eyes and says, 'You know I can't resist you when you look at me like that." And I said to Stephen Wyman, who was directing, "Stephen, I am over 60 years old and this girl is 22, if she's a day. Give me a break. There is no way to read this line without being a dirty old man." And he said, "Well, what would you say to your daughters? Come up with something." I said, "OK, and if you don't like it, you can get the writers." And that is the beginning of changing some lines. And I changed it to, "You know I am putty in your hands when you give me that little Bambi look." Because she looks like Bambi. And I came up with that, and they liked it and went with it. *Vern* is foolish, but he is not a fool. Of course, he might look deep into *Jack's* eyes.[21]

The mood is light during dress, unless there are scenes of incredible tension or drama. During highly charged scenes, the set is quiet, and all involved are respectful of the actors and their sometimes raw emotions. During the simpler times, a favorite game of the crew is a form of clothespin tag. The object of the game is to pin a clothespin on unsuspecting victims and see how long they will walk around adorned with one or more wooden clothespins. Bonus points are given when the target walks off the stage, or better yet, off the lot. (The security guards can always spot a *Days* visitor leaving the lot; no one else ever departs NBC sporting an array of clothespins down the back.)

Many actors enjoy the light-hearted atmosphere often associated with dress rehearsal. Charles Shaughnessy fondly remembers a scene from 1990 in which *Shane* "tortures" *Johnny Corelli:*

That was so bizarre. We had such fun with that scene. It came out like a bolt out of the blue, so all the way through dress—I always have fun at dress—we did the whole thing as an extremely uptight *Hogan's Heroes* prison guard. [German accent] "*Johnny,* you have some information, and you are going to tell me, aren't you, like a good little boy? Or else we are going to have to drop you in this pit." And we did the whole thing like this, and I was stroking his cheek. It was this bizarre torture scene, so I thought fine, I will convince him that *Shane* has gone completely haywire and thinks he is the Marquis de Sade. As it is, in tape, the only way we could make any sense of it at all was to play that *Shane* was pretending to be a little bonkers, that *Johnny* had to believe he was a little unhinged. We had a lot of laughs that day. I got completely hysterical. *Shane* appears in a dress with a riding crop, it was that bizarre.[22]

Directors have also been known to make a joke or two. When *Jack Deveraux* made his dramatic 1991 reappearance to Salem and took off his ski mask for the first time, the director quipped, "Oh, it's you. I thought it was Stephen Nichols." Cast and crew alike roared as Ashford covered one eye with his hand to imitate *Steve's* famous eye patch.

Dress rehearsal may also be the time when practical jokes occur. Certain actors are a favorite target of the crew. The character of *Roman Brady* has found some unusual items in his police file: notes from his supposedly dead wife (before her resurrection), Playboy centerfolds, anything guaranteed to distract the actor. Characters with desks or paperwork are preferred prey. *Jack Deveraux* has received post cards from long-dead or missing relatives. And hospital charts can have photos or caricatures not normally associated with medicine. Actors involved in spy or action adventure plots are easy victims. An actor locked in chains or hoisted aloft in a prison cell could easily find himself left there as the stage managers call for a mock break.

Actors are not above entering into the fray. One might hit another with a break-away bottle when they misbehave; another might fake a karate chop or two to keep fellow actors in line. Some jokes are unintentional as an actor will add some physical shtick to a scene that surprises not only the audience, but a co-star as well. Jokes aside, actors are tweaking their lines for the final time, seeing if they can find a rhythm or words that better suit their character. If lines are to be changed, now is the time to do it, because audio, camera, and the cast take their cues from the script.

Up in the booth, the number of people increases dramatically for dress rehearsal. The costume designer watches dress rehearsal to ensure that the wardrobe and accessories chosen for the day look good on camera. The production designer monitors the appearance of the set. Is that photo on the mantelpiece flaring with the lights; are the flowers or lamps correctly placed? The production designer also works with the lighting to guarantee that a set is lighted correctly and that a prop, if too dark, can be moved or removed.

Dress rehearsal is the first time that a producer sits in the booth. While the actors and director arrive at 6:00 a.m., the producers normally arrive about 8:30 a.m. The producers, like the costume designer and set designer, have the ever-present monitor in their offices and can monitor camera block without going to the booth. Early in the morning they are looking for major glitches.

Dress rehearsal is over two to three hours after it has begun, maybe 2:00 p.m. on an "easy" day. The actors go to their dressing rooms to study their lines one more time, perhaps to run lines with a colleague. All go to the make-up room to guarantee that their hair and make-up are perfect for taping. Hair and make-up can range from the glamor look to shipwrecked, bedraggled, or bleeding. Make-up can even consist of transforming one of the show's leading men into a striking, albeit very tall, woman. Make-up artist Keith Crary created Matthew Ashford's glamorous metamorphoses from *Jack Deveraux* to *Wanda*. This make-over was so astonishing that it helped the make-up department garner an Emmy in 1991. The make-up room is the hub of the studio for the actors. The place where they can meet, talk, watch the monitor to study a colleague's work, or just gossip. The make-up room is also where the actors normally get their final notes from the producers. Notes can range from a discussion of intent or motivation to an actor's desire to modify lines to a problem with some physical action. All questions, misconceptions, and differences of opinion will be worked out during notes.

The final hour: taping has begun. The only people allowed on stage are the cast and crew. The mood is serious. Everyone works to finish as efficiently as possible. The goal is to get through a scene on the first take. This does not always happen. Sometimes an actor will stop himself as he thinks or knows he has misspoken a line. Names are often difficult: One actor calls another by their real name, rather than the character name, or, perhaps, an actor calls another by the wrong character's name. Physical action can often cause a problem. Baby food that should hit an actor squarely in the face flies over the shoulder or perhaps a romantic lift turns into a pratfall. Some actors break up more than others, and giggles and unrestrained laughter have destroyed more than one take. But somehow, they get through it all and another day is done.

The actors get their scripts, go home, and begin to prepare for another day. But the show is far from over. Crews come in to strike sets or put up sets for the next day. And what about the tape? The cast and crew are done with it, but is it ready for air? First it has to go to the editors.

Behind the Camera

The *Days of Our Lives* editors edit two shows a day, ten shows in ten days on their day-off/day-on schedule. According to the editors, *Days* normally shoots a very clean show so, unless it is a special event, it is usually an easy edit. However, "easy" still means there can be hundreds of edits per show and four to five hours of editing time.

Just what do the editors do? They add dissolves and make cuts. They can bring a voice level up or down, carry music into another scene, smooth the transitions. Add footsteps to cover cuts, or take away stray sounds, so that "pick ups" cannot be detected. They trim scenes to pick up the pace or to make them look smoother. Normally the A.D. who worked on the taping of the show sits with the editors and helps edit the show. If it is a special show, like a wedding, a grand ball, or a remote location, a producer is likely to be present. If a musical montage or flashback is called for, the video director looks through the old scenes for the appropriate footage and chooses what is needed, then the A.D. and video director edit the scenes, and the A.D. adds the "audio presence." Some directors ask for lyrics for the musical montages, so that they can shoot a character while the appropriate lyrics are playing. Depending on the nature of the show being edited, the A.D. and editors are allowed a certain creativity to enhance the show. The editors also ensure the show is at its required 43:43 time limit (43:46 with the Columbia logo); it cannot go over this time allotment. The editors also add the credits, full or partial, depending on the length of the show.[24] As with all of *Days*' technical crew, the editors work quickly and efficiently and, within several hours, the show is edited, "in the can," and the process begins all over again for the next episode.

Now what happens to that finished tape? Assistant Director Roger Inman explains,

> I give the paperwork to somebody in the production manager's area of NBC and the one-inch tape that I have is the master and that is the tape that will air in Canada. They will make another one-inch copy which will be Canada's protection copy. Then they will make three M2 copies: One is the New York master, one is the New York protection and one is the Burbank protection. They roll two copies in New York whenever the show airs in New York, and they have got master and protection. In Burbank they record that New York feed complete with commercials and news breaks and all that stuff, that becomes the Burbank master and then they have the protection copy in case the satellite does not transmit or whatever. On very short notice we can find the commercials here if we need to, but then at least we have a copy of the show in the house.[25]

This is the nature of the soap opera production; you finish with one day and immediately begin the next. The never-ending story, that "tune in tomorrow," is the quintessence of the serial. Even before editing is completed, the production designer and costume designer are already checking the script to see what will happen tomorrow and the outlines to see what will happen in the next two weeks' worth of tomorrows.

The Frosting on the Cake: Sets, Wardrobe, and Music

The production designer and costume designer give the show its look and feel. Longtime star Macdonald Carey has nothing but praise for the show's production values. "The production values have always been high. For years we had such a wonderful costume designer, Lee Smith. He was just wonderful. At the weddings he did—the women were all beautifully gowned, and all the ladies coiffured perfectly. The current designer [Richard Bloore] does a heck of a good job. Same thing is true of the sets. They are phenomenal. We have sets which have a degree of reality that is every bit as convincing as what you'd get in a movie studio. And believe me, a TV camera is much more exposing than a film camera."[26]

The production designer has a staff of four: a draftsman, two decorators, and an art director. What specifically does the production designer do? Says Chip Dox, the current production designer, "I design the scenery and the props and pick the props and wallpaper and floor covering and everything that is not being worn...I work with the lighting directors to get all of that done, but the visual stuff is mine."[27]

A typical day for the production designer and his team begins at 8:00 a.m., "[We] go down on the floor and finish dressing the sets that have been set up by the night crew [the night crew sets up from photographs of the sets] and fluff those sets until 11:30, all the way through camera blocking. Then they'll go into dress rehearsal, and I will sit down in the booth with the producers and get the notes there, and then we'll take a half-hour break, and we'll finish dressing them up. Then we'll come upstairs, and the set dressers will go out and prop more props, and I'll keep reading [future outlines]. It's never ending, really never ending."[28] While in the booth, the production designer looks for flaring props (props off of which the lights flare), set backings that are wrong, misplaced props, wilted flowers, dirty windows, anything that looks out of place or wrong (for example, trees visible from a high-rise balcony). The production designer and his team supply all the hand props: demitasse cups, ISA devices,[29] dressings inside of drawers, guns, badges, the *Horton* balls[30]—you name it, it has probably been purchased or invented by production design. The designers supply all the fresh flowers that decorate the sets, as well as the foliage, trees, and assorted greenery that adorns Salem's parks and mansion gardens.

The production designer and design staff develop all the floor plans. Daily floor plans are also needed because the scenery changes day to day. *Days'* two stages can accommodate ten standard-size sets. Studios 2 and 4 also have a "fly system," which means that the lights fly up out of the way and a two-story set can be rolled in with a minimum of effort. Most soap opera stages have "dead hung" lights, which means the lights have to be removed to bring in tall sets. *Days* has several two-story sets, including *Julie's* penthouse, the Fisherman's Village and *Lawrence's* mansion.

Although *Days* is shot in California, its look is more Victorian because Salem in supposed to be somewhere in the Midwest. This generally precludes avant garde designs in the sets and means that the *Horton* living room will always be mint green, because *Alice Horton* likes it that way. Sets are designed with input from the writers and producers and certainly with the characters in mind at all times. Thus when *Jennifer* moved into the loft, it was feminized to give it more style.

How the character is developing as well as budget constraints often figure into how or when a character gets a new set or an upgrade. For several years everyone seemed to enter *Jack Deveraux's* bedroom directly from his front door. As Dox explains, "Remember when he [*Jack*] lived with his father? When *Anjelica* and *Harper* were together and had a big living room? Then they had an upstairs bedroom and then *Jack* was sort of a peripheral character…That story line dissipated, then that big set was thrown away because we needed the room to store it. And we only had *Jack's* bedroom, and when *Jack* became popular then they didn't have enough money to build a new set."[31]

Sometimes bits of a set are changed for technical reasons. *Jack Deveraux's* office got a new door because the old glass door caused too much glare for the

Design sketch for *Neil*'s penthouse. Courtesy Chip Dox.

camera. And sometimes the production design team has some fun with the sets. There were features of *Nick Corelli*'s apartment that were never clearly seen by the viewers, but they were appropriate for an ex-pimps' apartment: prints that would have never made it past Standards and Practices [the censor], but surely provided inspiration to the actors using the set. And although sets match the character, sometimes the designers give it that extra special touch: "Sometimes we will give the character something that the character may not have, just because it is more fun to do it that way. A little trait or something to have. Like *Jack* with his golf clubs and swords and things like that. We sort of dressed that for fun and now the character has sort of picked up on it. The writers saw some of the stuff, and now they use it more and more."[32]

The production designer is also the one responsible for all those disasters, natural and otherwise: cave-ins, shipwrecks, and fires. The Cruise of Deception shipwreck in 1990 was a major disaster that required long weekend shoots, water tanks, and tilting scenery. The earthquake and cave-in in "*Lawrence's* country" (dubbed "Ubilam" by some) required loads of Fuller's earth, the better to shake, drop, and pour over the actors.[33] A disaster of epic proportions was the 1985 fire in which *Stefano DiMera* was "killed." That complicated scene was shot over a long weekend. As Dox remembers, "There is a special effects department here [at NBC], and they handle all the fire displays, but I sit and design it with them. I work out what is going to happen and when, and how it is supposed to happen and then we just do it...That was dramatic stuff with *Marlena* chasing around. That was real fire, so it was fun. And it is all controlled, gas jets and lots of sprinklers and actually fire hoses and all of that are ready to go in case there is a problem, but we have not had problems."[34]

Finally, the production designer is involved with location shoots. Normally *Days* hires a location scout who finds just the appropriate spot, like that house in Malibu that doubled as *Lawrence*'s villa or maybe just the perfect spot on some far-off shore. When *Days* shoots location remotes (Greece, England, Malibu, Mexico, or Universal Studios), the director (usually Al Rabin, who did double duty as producer and director prior to his retirement in 1992), another producer, the unit manager, and the set designer will go and survey the location first to ensure that everything is as it should be. Then they return to the location a month or so later with a full crew and shoot. Normally they shoot exteriors on location and interiors in the studio. Many photographs are taken so that the studio interiors can be made to match the location exteriors. Some are easier than others. *Lawrence*'s villa in Malibu ("Ubilam") allowed the production designer several visits, but locations in Greece or England were handled with lots of transatlantic phone calls and photographs.

The production designer and the costume designer often consult. If there is a new swing set[35] with a big ballroom scene they will consult; production will keep the colors neutral so the costume designer can use as many colors as desired. The current costume designer, Richard Bloore, explains his duties:

It is basically being in charge. Most of it is shopping rather than really designing—there is not enough time or money to really design anymore. So that is basically what the job title is. I have six people working with me. Two assistants, one who basically does the paperwork and the rentals and those kinds of things, and the other one does a lot of script reading and break down, so that I can get a quick overview rather than reading every single solitary word. And then there are people, one man and two women for the set, and they basically rotate and just make sure that clothing is pressed and in the rooms and oversee all the everyday stuff that keeps the show running. I go to the production meetings. I guess you would say I am the political head. Because you deal with talking to the producers when there are important things that need to be dealt with or talked about. We get the outlines a week ahead, so I scan over those and try to see where things are going. I have a weekly budget. So you can figure out if there is a party, if you are going to spend the money, you have to think about where it goes or the important story line of the week. How many days are there? Sometimes [each show] is a new day every day, sometimes it is three days in one [show] day. And you try and balance all of that out, any kind of strange fantasies or weddings, those kinds of things you pick out and you know that they are coming up.[36]

And Salem can have some very strange fantasies, indeed. Bloore has had to supply everything from a gorilla suit to "Jackbo" muscles for *Jack Deveraux* (courtesy of a suit borrowed from a neighboring studio) to a custom-designed firefighter's suit for a Ken doll. As Bloore describes, "We had this Christmas present, which was a Ken doll dressed as *Jack* as the fireman. So the props went out to get the Ken doll a fireman costume. You would think that would be easy enough. Mattel never made Ken as a fireman. So we had to make a little fireman's uniform."[37]

Although most of the clothes used in the show are purchased, many of the most spectacular creations have been designed by Richard Bloore. He designed the sensational red velvet dress worn by the character of *Julie* in 1992. He also designed the bewitching wedding gown *Jennifer* wore when she married *Jack*. The gown was a princess-line sheath made from imported Swiss cotton lace. The lace was hand-beaded with crystal bugle beads and seed pearls. The lace fabric was overlaid on off-pink silk satin. The shoulders were surrounded by off-pink satin fabric flowers, enhanced with aurora borealis lochrosen (crystals) and small butterflies made of net and pearls. The neckline was trimmed with pearls, and lochrosen were scattered over the bodice and sleeves. The five-yard Watteau train of silk satin was gathered in a fan-like shape at the shoulders with more fabric flowers and butterflies decorating the train where it dropped off the back. *Jennifer's* headpiece was a halo of gathered off-pink satin decorated with fabric flowers, lochrosen, and butterflies. The short veil was three layers of sparkle satin. (Three copies of the gown were made to accommodate the arduous wedding shoot.)

In Salem, USA, nothing is cutting edge or avant garde; no purple hair or chartreuse suits appear in Salem. The look is Midwestern, with seasonal fluctuations in clothing to match the changing weather. The costuming is also somewhat character driven. Many actors feel their character would or would not wear a certain style or color. Bloore says, "Mary Beth [Evans] is very conscious of that. She will say, "I would never wear this, but *Kayla* would."[38] Sometimes the actors themselves prefer a certain style or color. One actor might like to show off his chest; another might always wear a T-shirt. Some actresses like decollete gowns; others cannot abide strapless creations. As Bloore says, "I try to make everybody look good."[39]

But costumes can play a big part in the making of the scene, and the actors know it. Costumes can take weeks of planning (such as the designing of a wedding gown) or can be created at a moment's notice by the inventive costume designer. As Matthew Ashford tells the tale of *Jack* as Elvis,

The Elvis thing was totally put together at the last minute... It was thrown together. I was supposed to be like Tony Curtis-looking in this white tux and stuffed white evening dinner jacket. And I said I looked like *Jack* in a white dinner jacket. Billy [Hufsey] was being Brando in the fifties, I said, "Well, don't you have somebody in music in the fifties?" "What about Elvis?" "Well, Elvis wore black leather in the fifties, too." Or blue jeans or something that did not work. But then they came up, they said, "Well, we do have something else." But they had Elvis in the seventies. And I thought, "That would be like *Jack* to miss his decade." And we put it together in an hour. [The costume designer] sent out for it, they got it, they called in for these special glasses, the hairpiece, and it all came together.[40]

And the Cruise of Deception might have been just another shipwreck without the dress worn by Susan Hayes' *Julie*. As designer Bloore laments, "The infamous red dress. I think that is going to haunt us. And it is funny, I did not think about it at the time. I thought 'This really looks great on her.' But I have never had so much story or reference in magazines about that red dress."[41]

Soap Opera Digest's "Diva" wrote, "I did get quite a charge when most of the *Days of Our Lives* cast was forced to jump ship and went kerplunk! into that choppy water. I was especially intrigued by Julie and that spectacular red dress.

Susan Seaforth Hayes wearing Richard Bloore's creation for *Julie Williams*: an extravaganza in red (1992). Courtesy Susan Seaforth Hayes.

There she was, trying to climb into that rubber raft, obviously hindered by her evening wear, slip and panty hose. Of course, I loved Julie for leaving the dress exactly the way it was and not tying it into a knot at the knees to give her legs some room. The dress got wetter and wetter and tighter and tighter and Julie, her hair damp, looked positively bedraggled. But she was a champ throughout. Shipwrecked and stranded, Julie didn't need a life jacket. That red dress saved her—and the cruise."[42]

The costume designer is responsible for everything that is worn: earrings, dresses, suits, undergarments, rings, etc. This is the person who is responsible for making sure that those diaphanous peignoirs only look that way, but in fact are heavily layered. And that actresses are not suddenly caught in only their panty hose in those love scenes, but rather in some glamorous teddy. The costume designer must guarantee that the *Hortons'* clothing will not clash with their mint green living room.

Sometimes the costume designer plays with colors to obtain a whole look. "There are certain colors I think that also photograph better on screen and will enhance facial tones," Bloore said. "I don't think about color that much, but there was *Patch's* funeral. I was so tired of seeing black at funerals that it drove me crazy. I decided to do something different. So I did the whole thing in dark jewel tones. I tried to keep with the aubergine and the dark teal and the brown, just to break it up, just to make it look like something different. I don't know if anybody noticed."[43]

Some anomalies are peculiar to Salem and *Days'* wardrobe department. Years ago it became the standard to have men supply most of their own wardrobe. Designer Richard Bloore has tried to buy more men's clothes and fill in the stock, but some actors prefer to wear their own clothing. Those leather jackets worn by *Roman Brady/Forrest Alamain/John Black* all belong to actor Drake Hogestyn.

No discussion of *Days* would be complete without mention of the music. One of the men responsible for the past decade of original compositions is Ken Corday. As he tells the tale,

I came to Los Angeles in 1979 and was asked by the music coordinator on the show to write some cues. I wrote, I think, five cues. Nice enough to say, those five cues—out of 50 or 60 that were recorded—got played all the time. In late 1979 Ken Heller came in as the music coordinator, and a fine composer, and he and I wrote. For me it was the first complete music package of *Days of Our Lives*, in late 1979, 1980. And we went to London and recorded it. That is when it was a much more symphonic sound. In 1985 Shelley Curtis came in as producer. She was young and had a kind of "hip" musical sense and we started using more popular music in the show to score, actually to score a scene. Not so much people singing those songs, but you would lose dialogue, say, in the last act of a show, and we would have what we call musical montages. This was also the time *Miami Vice* was doing it at nighttime. That really set the pace. They would have a lot of scenes at the end of the show with just these songs...Marty Davich came in as the music coordinator in 1985, and he and I have been doing all the composing since then. And we still use a lot of popular music on the show and in night club scenes. But I really think that the most important music on the show is the background music.

It is the music you do not really pay attention to. If you are paying attention to it, we are missing the boat because it is nothing more than a frame for the picture. But a bad frame can make the picture look bad. When it is working, when it is a good frame, you are not aware of it, but you feel it.[44]

Music, song, and dance have always been important to *Days of Our Lives*, but the culmination of the show's musical moments was probably the popular "Variety Show" episodes. Bill Hayes talks about his intimate involvement with these classic episodes:

Ann Marcus was head writer, Wes Kenney was producer, and I said to them, "I have an idea that is not a plot, but it is something that your plots can work through and it would be unique and we can do it." And they said, "Well, write up your ideas." So I wrote musical ideas for the whole company. I had *Marlena* and *Samantha* doing a mirror dance, I had everybody in it. And I told them how they could go through a rehearsal period and then finally get to it. And they finally said, "OK, we will do it. We will give you two days for the variety show and we will give you 12 people to work with." And they gave me the list and I wrote numbers for all 12 and I said, "We have to have a director who can stage numbers." And they said, "We have directors." And I said, "Yes, but they don't stage numbers. You have to have a choreographer or somebody who is used to putting on musical numbers." They said, "Can he come in in the morning?" I said, "No, he has got to start weeks ahead." They said, "Well, we can't do that." I said, "Let's ask the cast members if they will rehearse." And I asked all the cast members that they were going to use, John Clarke and Suzanne [Rogers] and Susan [Seaforth Hayes] and Peter Brown and Jed Allan and Robert Clary, Fran Ryan. They said, "Fine, we will rehearse any time, just tell us when." We started and they finally said, "OK, we will give you $750 to get a choreographer to stage it." And I got my buddy Jack Bunch to come in, we started about five weeks ahead. And he would come in and we would stage and we wrote numbers and arranged them. And that was the first time Ken Corday was involved in the show. And it began to cost a little money because we had a few instruments. Marty [Davich] and about three others and we had a "big" orchestra, maybe four members. And there had to be some orchestrations for those people, and it was going to be a little bit more that $750. And Ken, bless him, came in and said, "Do it." So we rehearsed, we rehearsed, we got ready. The costumes were good, the numbers were wonderful. It was wonderful. We had an audience. They built a theater in the studio. We had a proscenium, we had an audience, and we had backstage places and Al Rabin directed and it was wonderful. It was an exciting time. That was just pure performing. Macdonald Carey did a soft shoe. Frances Reid played Groucho Marx. Jed Allen played Margaret Dumont. He was fabulous. Mark Tapscott played trumpet. The look on his face... Robert Clary played Shirley Temple in the Marx Brothers skit. And Fran Ryan sang "The Oceania Roll" just great. Oh my, she was good. Robert Clary, Jed Allan, John Clarke, Peter Brown and I did "Standing on the Corner." Suzanne Zenor was in it. Tracey Bregman was in it. We got everybody to do things that they don't normally do in the show. It was wonderful and I loved that.[45]

A Guest at the Wedding: On Location

The "Variety Show" was not part of the normal studio tapings and neither are the location shoots. It is only fitting that this chapter dealing with the show's production end with a description of a very special location shoot: *Jack* and *Jennifer*'s rodeo nuptials. The stated wedding location was Salem's Fairgrounds, but in reality the *Days'* cast, crew, and guests trekked to Universal

Jennifer Horton (Melissa Reeves) and *Jack Deveraux* (Matthew Ashford) were married on July 2, 1991, at "Salem Fairgrounds." The location shoot took place at Universal Studios, Hollywood, California. *Jack* and *Jennifer* share their first kiss as man and wife and the cameras get it all on tape. [Maureen Russell]

Studios, Hollywood, to stage a Wild West wedding at Universal's stunt show, "The Riot Act." The actors made their first appearance on Sunday, the day before the scheduled shoot. The nightmare wedding involved many stunts, and everyone wanted to be prepared.

Monday's wedding taping began bright and early. Scenes were shot in reverse order, with the "real" wedding being taped first so that everyone would look their best and brightest, and so the set with its flowers, greenery, and big white bows would look fresh. Rather than the normal schedule of dry block, camera block, dress rehearsal, and taping, the cast and crew blocked and taped. The wedding was shot over and over again, picking up the ceremony from different camera locations. The cast members acting as guests during the ceremony bravely suffered the heat and lack of shade, coping as best they could with umbrellas, sun glasses, and lots of liquids. But the minute tape rolled, out came the call for sun glasses and umbrellas to go down. The romantic "real" wedding came off without a hitch, and as *Jack* lifted *Jennifer's* veil to seal their vows with a kiss, the director exclaimed, "Sensational!" But then came the taping of the nightmare wedding.

The nightmare taping began with *Jack* falling headfirst into a well. Actor Ashford ran into the arena, straight to the edge of the well, then calmly hoisted himself head first over the edge, to be held in place by the stunt coordinator hidden at the bottom of the well. All present have vivid recollections of Ashford's legs sticking out of that well, pointed skyward, for what seemed an eternity. Once his shots were complete, the stunt double took over, running in and taking the headfirst fall all the way down the well. *Jack's* precipitous fall into the well caused an explosion of water, courtesy of the stunt show, to douse both *Jack* and *Jennifer*. Once the stunt double was out, it was back into the well for Ashford and time for the prop men to drench both him and Melissa Brennan Reeves *(Jennifer)* with water. The entire proceedings were viewed by fans who had come to witness the event and by Universal Studio guests who walked in to see what was going on. Director Al Rabin acted as coach for the day, inciting those attending to cheer, boo, and scream at the appropriate times.

Soon the ladies, including the bride's grandmother, *Alice Horton,* were involved in a heated brawl. Reeves won the hearts of the crowd and an accolade of "incredible" from the director, when she bravely performed her own stunt and went flying into the air, with one wrist attached to the end of a long fence pole. The only glitch was that in the previous day's rehearsal Reeves had worn jeans. However, she was now wearing the form-fitting wedding gown. Costume designer Bloore had designed a "stunt gown" with a looser fit, but that gown had been soaked in the well stunt, and after everyone came back from lunch, it was discovered to have shrunk. So up went Reeves in the real gown. Reeves held, the gown did not. But with lots of help from the wardrobe department, who basically sewed her back into the dress while she was wearing it, the actress braved on. More fights erupted among the ladies, a plunge from a collapsing balcony for *Jennifer* (Reeves' stunt double took the actual fall), a tumble off a horse for Ashford, and some ISA and "cop shop" macho fight scenes courtesy of *Shane Donovan* and *Roman Brady.* The evening wound down with Ashford and Reeves first cavorting on the roof, with Ashford's stunt double taking a two-story fall, and concluded with a building "collapsing" on the newlyweds. Not your average day at the studio, but a success for the cast, crew, producers, and writers.

CHAPTER 3

THE WRITERS

A soap opera begins with a "bible" of sorts: the show's creators' account of who is who in their fictional town, where that town is, and what those characters will be doing in that town their first 12 to 24 months of existence. This long-term story projection describes what happens to each character and each story within a designated time frame. The head writer details when each story will peak or come to a climax and when the secondary stories will move to the forefront. The complete bible is normally written once, at the show's creation, but long-term story must go on for the life of the show. In essence, the "bible," at least the long-term story projection, is written or rewritten every year. And that long-term story is the continuing responsibility of the head writer.

As former *Days* head writer, Pat Falken Smith, explains,

Writing the long-term story is rather like writing a novel. You take the various families or most of the people who are going to be involved in the story and you write their story for the next six to 18 months. Then you take another group of people and write their story. And in those stories there will be crossovers, which you will indicate from time to time.[1]

The head writer is also responsible for the short-term story, what will happen within the next month or two. As Falken Smith describes,

The head writer has to write the short-term story, too. And we usually, as some of us call it, beat it out. We do the beats for what will be Friday's shows for, say, six to eight weeks. In other words, we have got a story and on Friday so-and-so gets killed, and on the following Friday the wrong person is arrested, and on the following Friday and so on. We talk this out. The head writer can also write the thrust for the week. And that is all major stories and where they are going. There is the main story, there is the secondary story, and then there is a back-burner story that is bubbling up. There may be other tension-filled stories that are in conjunction with the main story, but there is one big story, a second big story, and then a third.[2]

There is a definite art of writing for daytime, as former *Days* head writer Elizabeth Harrower, explains,

43

It was a wonderful thing to have three stories going. One in full flower, one blooming, and one fading. It was a wonderful formula because you always had a balance. You also did not run a risk, because if people did not like the number one story, they would probably like number two or three, so you hooked them. That is really the art, since the stories are all basically similar. The content is not really all that different from one show to another. What is different is how it is squeezed out. It is like toothpaste. If you squeeze out too much it dries up on you. If you do not squeeze out enough, you do not get the effect. Squeezing it out every day, five days a week, 52 weeks a year in just the right place, that is the art.[3]

Ed Mallory would agree. "It takes talent and it takes courage to allow a story to unfold and not to force it and not to mallet you over the head with it and to cause someone to care about something."[4]

The head writer is responsible for much more than just the story. In many ways the head writer is responsible for the cost of the show. The head writer calls for specific sets and determines how long they will remain standing. The costs of moving and then lighting sets are high, so if a writer chooses to change sets often, that raises the cost of the show. The head writer is also responsible for actors' guarantees.[5] If the actor is not used up to her guarantee, she must still be paid. If she is used over her guarantee, she must also be paid.[6] And a large cast can mean that the head writer is responsible for keeping track of 40 or more actors and their guarantees. As Falken Smith explains,

The trick is to use the actors. It is like a giant jigsaw puzzle or chess game. You have got all your pieces. You have your kings and queens and your rooks, and you have to be sure that the kings and the queens get used to their guarantee. And then there are people that are expensive, you have to make sure that they get used, but you do not want to use them just to walk through the sets for a guarantee.[7]

The head writer must also be aware of a variety of emergency situations and preemptions. Falken Smith again:

You always have to be ready for preempts, the baseball play-offs, all emergencies, the war now [1990 Gulf War], being cut into at any time. You have to be especially careful when you are getting interruptions. You have to bring the audience up to date in a new and convincing way.[8]

Everyone involved in bringing a daytime drama to life knows the perils of "bringing the audience up to date" or "exposition." Actor Joe Gallison explains, "Writing an interesting exposition scene is difficult. In soaps there is not only a lot of exposition, but repeating stuff. Doing it well is the challenge and the trick. And not only writing it well, but having the actors make a commitment to making it work, how you play it, how you say it."[9]

When something interferes with that commitment, the show still must go on. As Pat Falken Smith says:

You have got such a control factor in telling a story on daytime because you have so many things to think about. Then, too, all the actors can have personal problems. So you have to be able to pre- and post-tape. That is how we handle a lot of situations. You will pull all the scenes that an actor is in, if it is an emergency, then pre-tape before the real taping, post-tape afterwards. But you have to wait for those sets to be up and for the cast to be within a free period. So it is really a challenge.[10]

In brief, this is what the head writer does. But there are other writers on a soap opera as well, such as the associate writers. The associate writers normally write what are called "breakdowns." Breakdowns are basically outlines for the week. In a narrative form the writer details what will happen each day in each scene, which characters will appear and where, and what they will do. Sometimes dialogue might be included to indicate the tone of the scene.

It is from these breakdowns that the scriptwriters work. The scriptwriter is essentially the dialogue writer. In a letter to Bill Bell, dialogue writer Bill Rega recounted Bell's advice, "I keep repeating the golden rules over and over to myself—find the moment, play the emotion, keep the dialogue back and forth and crisp."[11] The scriptwriter may find that moment, but he never deviates too far from the breakdown; otherwise, the entire story might be thrown off balance. That is an essential element in daytime writing: the team effort and being part of a whole.

This is the basic structure of a current soap opera writing staff. There can also be story consultants who feed story ideas to the head writer. And writers are not assured of complete autonomy. The producers, network, and, in some cases, sponsors all have a chance to look at the long- and short-term story and make corrections, suggestions, or amendments. At one time, censors also looked at the scripts. As producer Becky Greenlaw remembers,

There used to be Standards and Practices who read every script. And we would take their notes and cut the "damn," cut the "hell," add this, you can't say that. They would monitor feed, and they would come over for dress rehearsal. Not on the set, but in the control room or green room. But they would be at all dress rehearsals with their notes to make sure that their notes were taken care of. And if there were bed scenes, they would watch dress and say, "You can't have *Anna* soaping *Tony's* back in the shower." True story. So when the network did away with the Department of Broadcast Standards, it was basically left to the producers to uphold the standards. And when I edit scripts, I will take out the unnecessary "damns" and "hells." It is looser now than it was, but it would be looser, I do believe, with Broadcast Standards now than it was. The rule used to be, you could not have a "damn" or "hell" in the first three acts. They would let you have one in act 6 or 7, but not in the first three acts, even if it worked for a scene.[12]

The head writer, associates, and producers also meet on a weekly, if not daily, basis to discuss the story and where and how it is going. As Greenlaw explains,

We [the producers] work on the [story] outlines. There is a weekly meeting with the producers and the writers on the outlines. We give our notes, make any changes, whatever. Then they [the outlines] go to the dialogue writers. The dialoguers write them [scripts], then one of the [associate] writers edits. Then when she is done, I get it and then I make edits. My edits are kind of twofold. One is from a technical standpoint in that I also am a director and will do back-up directing and stuff like that. So, from a technical standpoint, will what they wrote work? Is it possible to do with the confines of the studio, the sets, the time, the place? And also, continuity, tracking, things will change. We will make, say, adjustments in tape, or through the day of doing the show, so I can adjust that. If something was not working we adjust it in the studio or whatever and then it will track through. So then I edit it, then it gets sent to mimeo to be typed up and brought out, so I do edit all the scripts. If something bothers me, if it [dialogue] is not in character, I will call and say, "Change this." Sometimes we do it right there on the phone, if it is just a matter of adjusting a few lines or cutting a few lines. Sometimes we will go to the point of rewriting a scene, but that is rare. It's usually adjustments—this doesn't work for me, it's too far out, it's a little too on the blue side. But I will call and discuss it because it is working in collaboration with the producer and the writer. And sometimes I give in, and sometimes they give in ... I will change and adjust dialogue to make it work. I will not change intent. If there is an intent change, I call them, and we work it out together.[13]

This situation is not necessarily the norm, however; some writers insist on more autonomy. Pat Falken Smith maintains, "A good head writer never lets a script go through with something wrong in it and will rewrite it if they have to. And that I have always done. I have always kept the final control, and I have always had somebody tell me that I can have final control. I get the notes from the executive producer, but then I make my choices about what I want to do. And that is the way the show goes out. Because in the final analysis, that's it. The head writer is responsible for it."[14]

Bill Bell gets little interference. "I do my shows. No one knows what I am doing until they get the scripts. And that only works as long as the numbers [ratings] are good and as long as we do not cross the line storywise. I am not here to offend an audience. We are here to bring fantasy and love and romance and adventure and all good things and some not-so-good things. And we want to reflect life."[15]

But soap opera life, like real life, has lulls—dreaded "dog days" when not a lot is happening. As Falken Smith says, "You should be able to keep the audience from guessing that every Tuesday will be a dog day on the show."[16]

Not everyone dreads those "dog days." As actor Matthew Ashford discloses, "I like to do something that the audience wants to watch every single day. Because I have worked enough Tuesday/Thursday shows to know that a lot of times people [producers, writers] will let you do whatever you want to do because it is Tuesday. There are a lot of people who watch now just to see what is going to happen, and I think that is the way it should be—there should be people watching on Tuesday and Thursday."[17]

Falken Smith agrees, "You have to have strong shows. You have to stop the audience getting used to the idea that there are going to be dogs on Tuesday. I used to switch them around. Sometimes I would barrel on Tuesday and Wednesday, and then I would keep them guessing. They would have to look every day because they never knew. Never let the audience go."[18]

One thing that can happen on daytime is that art begins to imitate life for both writers and actors. Obvious examples are pregnant actresses creating pregnant characters, but there are other cases as well. Falken Smith vividly remembers,

The strange thing that happens in daytime is that you are writing so many violently emotional stories that you tend to be writing stories about what is happening in your own life. I had to go through *Addie's* dying of cancer and her sudden remission right after my husband had died of a sarcoma. It was interesting because I got to write about combination chemotherapy, and that is what my husband had been on. He had been a guinea pig for it, so that kind of cancer is now curable. And we [at *Days*] got a nice citation from the AMA [American Medical Association] on our public service on giving hope to people…But you are always fighting your own identity, your own personal hang-ups, what you did—all the things that make you want to write about certain things.[19]

In the beginning was the word, but the word must be spoken. So a very special relationship exists between writer and actor. Actor Wally Kurth believes, "The development of character in daytime is such a collaborative effort with the writers and producers and the actors, unlike any other medium that I have ever experienced. Certainly in plays you have a script, and the actor's responsibility is to understand the writer's intention and portray that. But in a soap opera you are given basically a starting point, and the actor really has to make some decisions about the development of his character."[20] Fellow actor Wayne Heffley concurs: "Daytime is the closest thing to stage that I can think of on film. I like the leeway they give you. They give you a blueprint, and you bring that character to you."[21] Head writer Bill Bell agrees, "You can't write in a vacuum, you can't create story for any actor who does not give you something in return."[22]

The head writers create the characters, but the actors flesh them out and give them life. As writer Falken Smith believes,

There is a symbiotic relationship between you and the actors. You feed off of what they do, they feed off of what you give them and it goes back and forth, and you get your ideas of where to go with the characters. You also see which actors in real life are responding to each other sexually. That does not mean that they are going to have an affair, it just means that there is a chemistry there and you can use it and you can play with it.[23]

The actors know and appreciate this kind of symbiotic relationship. Joe Gallison remembers,

Pat Falken Smith, who was head writer when I began, really tunes into what the actors are bringing to a character, clearly she does. I started doing things and then found them in the scripts and said, "Whoa, why didn't I think of that? Oh yeah, maybe I did." But then she added two more levels that I had not even thought of. It was great. She started writing some fascinating, interesting stuff for the character [*Neil Curtis*]. It is exciting when that happens and you are on the same wavelength as the person who is writing. I feel like we have a special relationship because we both equally gave birth to this character.[24]

Falken Smith also has great respect for her actors.

The key is giving the actors space. Because by and large acting on daytime is far superior to almost all acting in every medium, including the stage. I think that is the excitement for the audience. They are seeing fine acting. And there are moments on daytime… I used to be teased a lot. If I didn't cry three times a week, I always said there was something wrong with the show. It can make you cry. That is what the best shows do.[25]

Longtime producer Jack Herzberg agrees and states succinctly, "Tears on daytime are like gold."[26]

Writer Elizabeth Harrower also acknowledges the importance of watching the actors.

You have to have a vision of somebody with their dramatic potential. Sometimes story comes out of the people with whom you have to work. You can make an actor better than he is if you give him a great story or you write to his weaknesses…You must be protective of your actors…Joe [Gallison] was one of the best actors on the show. We used to give him material and he would not only give you back what you wrote, which not everybody does, but he would give it back to you with a lovely something you did not even know was there.[27]

Falken Smith always allows the actors to give back that something extra.

Allow the actors time to act, use pauses. Pauses are very important. Allow the story to be told from an emotional point of view, without dialogue. You must give the actors the space. One of the things I always tell my writers, "Do not tell the actors how to read their lines. Do not say 'coldly,' do not say 'smugly,' do not say anything, just give them their lines." There are wonderful actors in daytime, just give them space.[28]

Actors fondly reminisce about those golden moments of silence. Suzanne Rogers says, "I remember when *Maggie* had to go into the funeral parlor to see *Mickey*'s coffin. Imagine walking into a funeral parlor alone, flowers all around, standing there, crying in silence…I miss those quiet moments."[29]

Actor George Jenesky remembers the so-called "Phantom" storyline in which he was involved and the often silent world it recalled.

I really loved that Phantom story. The thing I loved most about it was that in the very early going when he [*Nick*] was really non-verbal and it was almost like being a silent film actor. Because I had no dialogue to speak of, no pun intended, and so that was great. That was a wonderful experience to communicate what was going on without words. It was touching and romantic and pathetic.[30]

Jenesky also likes to remind people that not all story ideas originate with the writers.

The funny thing about that Phantom story is that it was Matthew Ashford's idea. He went to the producers with that concept for *Jack* and the producers thanked him very much and thought about it and they liked the idea, but they didn't like it happening to *Jack*. So they had it happen to *Nick*. Thank you, Matthew Ashford. Every time anybody mentions that story line I always trot out that story because I think it is important.[31]

The writers and actors do have a symbiotic relationship, and the writers must remember to give those actors involved in a hot, front-burner story a rest. Falken Smith, "One of the problems is wearing out the actors. I was on *Days of Our Lives* and poor Joe Gallison, I think he just freaked one day and did not show up because I had been working him five days a week, and we had gone to an hour and I did not realize it. This was during the time we were doing the *Amanda* story, and that was so great. The chemistry between the two of them was so great, and then there was his gambling and all that. And so I mean I practically wrecked the guy before I realized I had been working him five days a week."[32]

Most writers shy away from getting to know their actors personally. They prefer to watch them on the screen the same way an audience does. As Harrower explains,

You try to stay as far away from the actors as possible. If they have something wonderfully special that they do, to which they are devoted, if they have an odd talent, I will ask the casting director. Storywise, I shy away from them.[33]

Bill Bell lived in Chicago all the years he was head writer for *Days of Our Lives* and found the great distance between himself and the actors quite useful. "You have a much better objectivity when you are 2,000 miles away. You do not know the actors that well, you do not know the studio problems. And you should not know the studio problems. All you are interested in is what is on the tube. And that is called objectivity."[34]

Bell was legendary for his insistence that actors not stray from the written word. "When I was writing everything I was not too pleasant about it [ad-libs]. Certainly you do not let them ad-lib or get too far astray, too far from the dialogue. They can start putting in things that affect story and that affect character, and once they start using their own terminology, then we are getting the actor, we are not getting the character. But they still did it. I tried to pretend they never did, but I know they did. You can only control it so far when you are living 2,000 miles away."[35]

But the actors appreciate good storytelling. Bill Hayes knows,

That is where it is, in the words, the stories, the ideas, those first few years especially. We had Bill [Bell] planning the story, we had Pat Falken Smith and Bill Rega writing wonderful scripts…I could not wait to open the script, it was that much fun. I read every word of the script. Pat Falken Smith's lines read like a tennis match, back and forth. She is a wonderful dialogue writer, very talented and wonderful.[36]

Working with the actors is but one aspect of daytime writing. The telling of the tale is the writers' livelihood. And how they spin the story determines the life of the show. Bill Bell shares his excitement,

Writing is an addiction for a creative person. Every day is opening night. And the excitement of controlling characters, controlling their destinies, the challenge of finding new ways of continuing their stories, just as life has to continue. But making it more interesting and finding new stories. It is not all fun and games, there is the agony and the ecstasy.[37]

Bill Bell is the acknowledged master weaver of the yarn. Falken Smith said of Bell's intimacy with the creative process:

He described it, as Irna [Phillips] said once: there is always one more yank of the taffy. You get to a certain point and you think you are at a dead end and then there is a new door that will open. As long as you do not close doors, you keep opening doors.[38]

As Bell himself reveals,

Today writers seem to feel they need the revelation to move on with the story. But there is so much more power in not revealing it. Experience in storytelling tells you that you have something terribly significant here and that if you wait for the right moment it is going to be explosive. But too often people rush into something. But if you wait, sometimes you wait years. But if you wait long enough and keep playing it, then you will find that facets always open up. If you dig into the story and way inside your characters. I really like to motivate characters, and to motivate characters you have to know and understand them. You need time and depth. I often have something that I know will have a lot of impact today, but I also know that if we wait, I do not know how long, but someday that moment is going to be there, where it has so much more impact.[39]

Producer Jack Herzberg agrees.

In daytime you have to be careful not to develop the story too fast. We figured, this was before VCRs, that if a woman watched twice a week it was great and she had to know where we were because she had missed three days. If she watched three times a week, it was wonderful. And if she watched five times a week, that was gold. So we were telling a story in greater depth because we had a little more time to develop it without still trying to go too fast. One of the great dangers is going too fast. If you go too fast then you lose viewers because they don't know what is going on. Ted Corday used to tell the story about a soap in New York where the guy went through a revolving door and six months later he came out on the other side.[40]

What is it about soap opera writing that attracts so many talented people? As Falken Smith feels, "It is fun, and it is a challenge. You can do some wild and exciting things in daytime and I love it...You get a chance to do the kind of writing you seldom get to do. We did a split personality story with *Trish* three years before "Sybil" came out on nighttime. I would like to think that I did some things that were unusual and that I broke some new ground...Daytime is a forgotten golden nugget."[41]

As Falken Smith continues:

There are a hundred ways to tell a story, but of the hundred, there are perhaps ten ways that are better than those other 90. And then, of those ten, there are two or three that are the best. And you try as much as you can. And I suppose the fascination of daytime from a writer's point of view is the immediacy of it. And the horror of it is that it never ends. I mean you can never end a story. "Yes, that's fine, but what are you going to do next week?"[42]

Many things have changed about daytime in the past 30 years, including the pace of the shows and lack of secrecy regarding story line. Many of the changes in writing are attributed to *General Hospital* and the faster-paced action plot that it introduced in the 1980s with *Luke* and *Laura*. But Pat Falken Smith, who was *General Hospital*'s head writer during those glory years, feels that many have missed the point. "We sent a wrong signal in the *Luke* and *Laura* days. I knew it was a love story, we all knew it was a love story, but the world out there, the competitors thought it was because we did *Luke* and *Laura* on the run, the adventure. It was not. It was how they felt about one another. And so they missed the key element in it and then they started copying all the kookie things we did, which was a terrible mistake because *Luke* and *Laura* were about emotion, not adventure."[43]

Jack Herzberg remembers how Ted Corday stressed the significance of emotions and relationships.

Ted Corday used to say to me all the time—I remember this so well, he would say, "Women at home want to watch women in the wrong bed, doing the wrong thing, and getting caught at the wrong time. They want to see all the things that they would love to do, but can't." Today the shows have lost the knack of relating. It's all about cops and robbers, but it used to be about powerful, emotional insights into people.[44]

Bill Bell has always recognized the importance of those powerful emotional insights.

What we must all understand is that the truly powerful and richly identifiable stories involving the family are essentially very simple in their structure and substance. The key to the telling of this kind of story is in digging deep into the mind, body, heart, and soul of various members of a given family; in how they act and react to a given situation. In other words, it's the pulling apart of people and the putting them back together again. Life for all of us begins with the family. Life for all of us, if we're blessed and fortunate, ends with the family. But between birth and death are an infinite number of experiences and conflicts that tend to pull (or push) us away from the family—experiences and conflicts that can come from within or outside of the family—but still affect each member of that family. Affects them in terms of love or jealousy, fear or sadness, disgust or grief, anger or joy, hate—but above all—hope! We must again reach our audiences emotionally! We must portray the human equation in storytelling.[45]

Elizabeth Harrower agrees, "The great moments in drama, the great moments are always between two people. The glory of daytime is that you have the time to build to that. You have time to hook people. You do not have to do it in half an hour. You can take a year until you reach that moment when the tension is incredible. But that is where the story is worth telling."[46]

The human element is key to the telling of a dramatic story, but so is the element of surprise. Harrower laments the loss of surprise in daytime:

You want to give an audience something they did not expect. There is a talent for finding the unexpected, and it is not easy. And now we are dying of being over-publicized. Bill Bell and Betty Corday were wonderful about this. They said, "Do not tell the audience what is going to happen next week or next month." Stop publicizing who is sleeping with whom and when. Let some of it come...The story is told before it is even on the air. They pick the high moments and publicize them and here you have taken months to create a climax and the audience reads it. Who is going to tune in to find out? I agree we are highly competitive and that they are telling you this is a wonderful moment, but it is anti-climatic. It does not work. You have seen it in the preview.[47]

Days of Our Lives has had some of the best writers in the business, some more eccentric than others, and somehow they are all connected to Irna Phillips. Everyone has an Irna Phillips story. Many remember how she worked. Pat Falken Smith,

The first time I went to a meeting at the Corday home, they had a phone connection to Irna Phillips in Chicago. And we all had to sit there while she acted out the story. We were supposed to get the general thrust of the day to write a script, but what she did was dictate the whole thing. She would say, "And *Tom* comes down the stairs and he says, '*Alice*' and she says, '*Tom*' and everyone is sitting there writing it down. She dictated this whole half-hour script, and we were supposed to be writing during this phone session.[48]

Bill Bell also remembers Irna's writing habits. "She would dictate all her dialogue to her secretary, Rosie. And she would change her voice for the characters. And her secretary would know which character she was when she changed her voice."[49]

Bell recalls Phillips as a "talented and unique lady" who once told him he was too normal to be a writer. "One day she looked at me and she said, 'You know, you are never going to make it in this business.' And I said, 'Why?' I mean she was dead serious. She said, 'You are too well adjusted.' That really stuck with me."[50]

As Pat Falken Smith says, "One thing about daytime, there are colorful people in daytime. You are never bored."[51]

CHAPTER 4

THE ACTORS

"Always the locale of our story, and even the story itself will be secondary to our characters. For it isn't the plot that makes the characters, it's the characters that make the plot."[1] Creator Ted Corday wrote this for the *Days'* "bible" that appeared in 1964, and this philosophy has held constant through the years. Characters and the cast that create them remain first and foremost. Ken Corday, the current executive producer, says simply, "*Days'* [strong point] is casting...the cast on the show has seemed to have held on longer than any other cast in daytime."[2]

The First Family of *Days of Our Lives* is the *Hortons*; from the *Hortons* all other story lines and characters have evolved. Let us begin with the "story of the *Hortons*, and their search for happiness with its successes and failures, its joys and sorrows"[3] and introduce them as they were introduced in the "bible" in 1964. The patriarch of the *Horton* clan is *Tom Horton*, played until his death in 1994 by Macdonald Carey. *Tom Horton* was born in 1910 in Salem. His father was Salem's town doctor, and from youth *Tom* wanted to follow in his father's footsteps. *Tom* attended the local university and in 1929 married his high school sweetheart, *Alice Grayson*. *Tom* had been the star pitcher of his high school baseball team. Married and attending the university, *Tom* played baseball for a nearby minor league team to support his family and his schooling. The major league clubs made many enticing offers for *Tom's* services, but the day he earned his medical degree he gave up baseball forever.[4] *Tom* served for three years in the South Pacific in World War II at the rank of captain. *Tom* started his medical career as a staff internist at the University Hospital and professor of internal medicine at the university's medical school. The "bible" paints this picture of *Tom Horton*:

Good internists are rare. Great teachers, equally rare, are born, not made. *Tom* is both—a natural teacher and a true scientist. The fame and fortune that might have been his on the baseball diamond could not compare with the real reward of teaching younger men and in serving humanity as a physician.... *Tom* is neither saint nor superman, he has had to learn the hard way that mere words will never keep people...from making their own mistakes. Yet he always finds the time in his busy life to lend an understanding ear, a fast fifty bucks, and open mind and heart. To his own children and grand-children, his students and ex-students, his patients, or a poor soul in the charity ward, he gives the same loving kindness...This, then, is *Tom Horton*, great teacher, great doctor—perhaps; a great man—certainly; in some areas, a very weak man. In short, he is that ingeniously devised organism, a human being, living the days of his life in a precarious balance of strength and weakness, good and evil, wisdom and foolishness.[5]

As longtime viewers of the show will note, *Tom Horton* has changed little. For many years chief of staff at University Hospital, he gave up that position in 1991 and instead decided to head the Trauma Center. He still has an understanding ear and offers a helpful hand to all in need. Macdonald Carey says of *Dr. Horton*, "He's a professional man, a family man. He believes in basic family values."[6] Carey also adds the tidbit that *Tom Horton* never drinks coffee because Macdonald Carey does not drink coffee.

Salem's matriarch is *Tom*'s wife, *Alice*. The "bible" describes her as a "strikingly handsome woman," born in 1911. Her background differs greatly from *Tom*'s. Her father, *Sid Grayson*, originally a fine cabinetmaker, degenerated into an "odd-jobs man," a drifter.

[He] didn't beat his wife or abuse his children, he didn't steal and he was never in jail except for drunkenness. He was handsome and lovable and hopelessly irresponsible. The *Graysons* weren't 'common,' but they were dirt poor. *Alice* was an extremely intelligent and sensitive child. The insecurity and embarrassment of her family life caused her to shrink from reality and hide herself in a world of books and fantasy. In high-school, *Tom* became attracted to this strange, shy, and lovely girl. His first attempts to know her were rebuffed, and it wasn't until he followed her home one day that he understood her silences and evasions, her troubled eyes. Love was his only weapon. Without encouragement, he embarked on a campaign to bring this girl out into the world. And he succeeded.[7]

Longtime viewers know he succeeded. The *Alice Horton* we know today is not shy or silent. But today, just as 30 years ago, *Alice* wants comfort and security and love for her family. Ken Corday believes, "[*Tom* and *Alice*] are the ultimate super-couple. They were never billed as a super-couple. They were billed as a matriarch and patriarch, as almost the audience's voice, the truth sayers."[8] Bill Bell agrees: "*Tom* and *Alice* have functioned essentially as they have from the onset of *Days of Our Lives*. Their function was to represent a core of stability, to reflect rather than generate story."[9]

The *Hortons* had five children. The first two were the twins, *Dan* and *Adelaide*. (*Dan* later became *Tommy Horton*.) Then came *Michael (Mickey), William (Bill)*, and *Marie*. As the show opened, *Dan* had been killed in Korea in 1954, leaving behind a wife and son. In 1949, at age 18, *Adelaide (Addie)* married *Ben Olson*, the son of Salem's richest citizen and president of the First National Bank. The *Olsons* lived in Wycliffe Hills (or Wuthering Heights as *Tom* called it), Salem's exclusive suburb. *Addie* had two children, *Julie* and *Steven*. *Julie* was the first *Horton* grandchild, the first niece of many doting aunts and uncles. She

In Salem, you can always count on the traditional Horton Christmas. (l-r) (back) *Bill Horton* (Ed Mallory), *Jo Johnson* (Joy Garrett), *Jennifer Deveraux* (Melissa Reeves), *Jack Deveraux* (Matthew Ashford), *Julie Williams* (Susan Seaforth Hayes); (front) *Maggie Horton* (Suzanne Rogers), *Mickey Horton* (John Clarke), *Alice Horton* (Frances Reid), *Tom Horton* (Macdonald Carey) (1992). This portrait is especially poignant because it was the last time this group was ever together for a Christmas in the mint green Horton living room. Joy Garrett passed away the following February and Macdonald Carey was so ill the next Christmas (1993), that the Horton Christmas was celebrated in *Tom Horton's* hospital room. (Mac passed away three months later.) Courtesy Susan Seaforth Hayes.

"was such a beautiful baby that the family vied to see who could spoil her the most." *Steven*, two years younger, was an "A" student, popular, happy, and helpful. When *Steven* came along, the little queen, *Julie*, had to step down and become just an ordinary little girl. It was a shattering experience for *Julie* and marked her for life. In one way or another she has been trying to regain her position ever since."[10]

Actress Susan Seaforth Hayes remembers *Julie* in her early years. "When the show began, *Julie* had been knocked about and buffeted by life. Not ground under, but knocked about and buffeted. At best she survived it. She survived it, suffered through it, and survived."[11]

Michael (*Mickey*) *Horton*, the second eldest son, was born in 1932. When the story opened he was a bachelor with an apartment in the nice area of town, but managed to come home for dinner at least twice a week and still maintained his old room in the *Horton* house.

Alice chose the names of the first three children, *Tom* the names of the last two. Thus *Bill*, born in 1939, was named after Sir William Osler, and *Marie*, born in 1942, was named after Marie Curie. *Bill*, age 25, was in his last year at Harvard Medical School, soon to intern at Cambridge. *Marie*, age 22, was a graduate student at Salem University, specializing in biochemistry. Thus began life in Salem for the characters of the *Hortons*.

"You can't write in a vacuum, you can't create story for any actor who doesn't give you something in return," wrote *Days'* head writer, Bill Bell.[12] The writers conceive the characters, but the actors bring them to life. And some actors have brought their characters to vivid life, creating more than the writer ever hoped. One prime example is the character of *Doug Williams*, crafted by Bill Hayes. Bill Bell writes:

> There's no question but that Bill Hayes has not only made the character come to life, but has also become very popular with the audience. He's really quite a unique character among all of daytime largely because we've incorporated his singing talent into the show. However, as this character gestated over many months, what has emerged bears only slight resemblance to our original brainchild. This is in no way a criticism because due to the casting of Bill Hayes we now have a much more faceted character than originally planned. However, over the months I think we all became a little carried away with this character, your head writer being no exception. We had something very delightful, charming, and unique, and we played these qualities to full advantage. But in the process we tended to forget that *Doug* is essentially an opportunist, a very likable and lovable one to be sure, but nonetheless a man who is dedicated to feathering his own nest, a man who you can never be certain is completely sincere, that you want very much to believe and believe in. These are the qualities that make a *Doug Williams* so potentially devastating.[13]

Bill Hayes credits a collaboration with the writers for the creation of his character: "Bill Bell was wonderfully creative about *Doug*. I wrote him a letter describing *Doug* as I saw him, and he wrote back and commented and talked about *Doug* as he saw him. And I remember one thing that I wrote to him, which was so wonderful about *Doug*—you never knew if he was helping a lady across the street and being nice or unhooking her brassiere as they went across the street. You never really knew. And as long as he had that quality, he was wonderful to play."[14]

Doug's roguish charm was an essential part of his character, but so was something that only Bill Hayes could have brought to the part, *Doug's* singing ability. Bill Bell remembers, "I was there for that casting [*Doug's*], and Bill Hayes came in. I had adored him going back to *Your Show of Shows*, and I could not believe it was the same Bill Hayes. And the obvious took me six to nine months, to have him sing. People didn't sing much that way. But I thought that music, if used prudently, could have a lot of impact. And if you remember when he sang to *Julie*, 'The Most Beautiful Girl in the World,' that was electric."[15]

Everyone misses Bill Hayes' music. Fellow actor Frank Parker laments, "Bill Hayes is one of my favorite people. I miss him so much. I miss listening to him sing. In the original wedding of *Roman* and *Marlena*, when Wayne was playing *Roman*, Bill sang a great song. It was magic."[16]

Bill Hayes agrees that music was a part of the magic: "What they did was to write in the song, not just as entertainment ever, but as part of the show. And it always made a comment on either *Doug* or *Julie's* plot or somebody else's plot and it was great...The only songs that we repeated were those that Columbia owned, such as 'I'm a Believer,' 'The Look of Love,' 'The Last Train to Clarkesville.' But they owned those and it did not cost them as much money. And fortunately, 'The Look of Love' was a terrific song and we got to use that frequently. And it was a wonderful part of the show. People loved the singing."[17]

Bill Hayes' *Doug* was introduced into *Susan Martin's* story line, yet it was his on-screen pairing with actress Susan Seaforth Hayes' *Julie* that created the real fireworks. Susan Hayes was the third actress to play *Julie*, and as Bill Bell succinctly states, "Susan Seaforth came in, and suddenly we had a character."[18] Everyone agreed. "[*Julie* is] our most important actress...dear, precious *Julie*."[19]

As writer Bill Rega wrote to Bill Bell,

I was most impressed by your '*Julie*' [Susan Seaforth Hayes]. Not only because she's so lovely, and personable, but because she is so dedicated. At the line run-through and walk through, which is not deeply intent, she still kept her character all the way through, with pauses, shading, etc.—and this at a first reading. Small wonder she registers with the impact that she does."[20]

Bill Bell saw *Julie's* power, "And yet they must also find a hidden fascination to this young woman [*Julie*] who dares to say and do what so many women wish they had both the courage and opportunity to do. Suffice to say that the present—and more particularly the future design of this character—will be to bristle yet tantalize the libido of every homemaker."[21]

And tantalize she did. Susan Seaforth Hayes' sizzling portrayal of *Julie*, especially when paired with Bill Hayes' *Doug*, captured the imaginations of millions of daytime fans. Susan and Bill Hayes were the first and *only* daytime actors to make the cover of *Time* magazine, in the now famous, "Sex and Suffering in the Afternoon" cover story.[22] As actress Joan Blondell said of Susan Hayes in the article, "I don't know anyone but Sarah Bernhardt who could sustain all that suffering so long."[23]

But what was *Doug* and *Julie's* special chemistry? Bill Hayes has a theory:

There are, in my mind, two types of performer. One type you look at and you enjoy what they do, but you laugh at them, you don't feel things yourself. Then there are other kinds of performers and maybe all good soap people are this second kind. But I think both Susan and I are the kind of performer that you empathize with and through whom you live that experience. And you experience it yourself. And I think when we fell in love, Susan and Bill, they fell in love. They fell in love with us. They fell in love with each other. They experienced what we did. You know, Susan is as good an actress as you will find anywhere, but she cannot cover what she thinks. If she hates, it comes out. If she loves, it comes out. And from the first moment that we had little, glittery things going between us, the audience knew that, sensed it, felt it, experienced it.[24]

Viewers clamored for *Doug* and *Julie's* wedding. Head writer Bill Bell resisted, "I continue to be unalterably opposed to any marriage between *Doug* and *Julie*. All too soon the proverbial honeymoon would be over, inevitably the spark diminished, the love songs a little less exciting….It's still my conviction that the most effective love scenes are those in which love is so inherent that in seeing it, feeling it, we don't need to say it."[25]

Many agreed, Bill Hayes for one: "I felt the same way [not marrying *Doug* and *Julie*]. I think it was a mistake. It was an exciting time. We got mail ever since Susan and Bill got married. We got mail, tons of mail. 'You might as well marry them, they are already married in real life, we know that. Might as well get them married.' I think we should have held off and held off and held off as long as we could."[26] Jack Herzberg agreed: "Ted [Corday] always said, 'Keep people just out of reach, and there is the interest: when will they reach?' The sorriest day that ever happened on *Days of Our Lives* was when we let *Doug* and *Julie* get married. Because once we let them get married, we had to create phony situations….We lost the reality."[27]

Doug and *Julie* stayed apart as long as Bill Bell remained as head writer, but when he left *Days* to create *Young and the Restless* and remained with *Days* writing only long-term story, the decision was made to marry the two characters. The decision made, a dazzling wedding was planned. As Bill Hayes shares the story, "The first marriage of *Doug* and *Julie*, those were our [Bill and Susan's] wedding vows. They wanted to know what we wanted to use. The producers and the writers asked us, and we said, 'Why don't you use what we wrote, what we used to get married?' And, of course, they could not do the whole thing, that was too long. But do you think Susan was acting that day? When *Doug* and *Julie* got married? That was not acting. That was total involvement."[28]

And that total involvement mesmerized the fans. Bill Hayes has proof:

Do you know how many people came to our [*Doug* and *Julie's*] wedding? People sent us snapshots. They took off work the day we got married. And they got dressed up, and they would set up a card table with champagne and doilies. And the ladies wore hats, and they came all dressed up, and they came to our wedding. And when we got married, they announced that we would have a reception at NBC, and there were about 4,000 people out there that day. They had a big cake and champagne for everybody. They were out in the midway, like a driveway. That is where it was. And we finished shooting the show—it took us a long time—and they just waited out there, and they watched. They showed the wedding on monitors. And then we came out, and we were all dressed up, and they threw rice, and they came to our wedding. It was a national experience.[29]

Bill Bell offered immediate advice:

The status of *Doug* and *Julie* since their very spectacular wedding has been one of concern. No marriage ever—on this or any serial—was filled with more anticipation and expectation by an audience!…We should play this marriage and love affair as bigger than life.[30]…A postmarital situation cannot be laid out in long term. These are moments and scenes you've got to pull out of character and from the gut! We have this responsibility—if not to ourselves, then to our characters. And in reality, aren't our characters really an extension of ourselves as writers!…*Doug* and *Julie* offer us what a very few, if any, characters offer any other show on daytime. What they give us is the ultimate latitude in terms of material and performance. They can tear your heart out and/or put you on the highest of highs—and everything in between. What we need is more of *Julie's* sophistication! We have to see her mind work, the wheels turning! We need a provocative *Julie*, not in any sexual way, but in the way she handles people and situations. This is nothing you will find in long term. This is the character! I visualize scenes late at night, after closing hours, two sleepy people yet forever stimulated and invigorated by each other, these precious moments together where they talk about little inconsequential things—a man and a woman relating; a man and a woman in love without saying it! They don't have to! We see it and feel it! An occasional song together—but mooded for the time of night. Scenes like this at least once a week, scenes that an audience will look forward to. Scenes of everyday living. Like all of us.[31]

But every couple was created differently and Bell had different advice concerning the marriage of *Bill* and *Laura*.

If there is a marriage between *Bill* and *Laura*, it goes without saying that it would have to be a very tender, special and beautiful thing, the culmination of years of unrequited love. To consider even for a moment that there would ever be a serious breach in their relationship is to this writer unthinkable and dishonest. They would be bound together in love and devotion "till death us do part." Which means their stories would have to emerge from without rather than from within.[32]

Ed Mallory, who played *Bill Horton* for nearly 20 years, attributes much of *Bill* and *Laura*'s magic to the chemistry he and co-star Susan Flannery shared. "I had a great time with Susan Flannery. We respected each other. And we didn't have anything going on between us in a romantic way, as can often happen, which interestingly enough does not always transmit on camera. Flannery and I played the moments as acting moments, and that's what it is, it's acting. A lot of chemical stuff would happen in those moments. Then when they'd say, 'cut,' we would laugh about it and be buddies."[33]

And how would Mallory describe *Bill Horton*? "He was basically dedicated to medicine, and he was a good guy, loved his Dad, loved medicine and was misunderstood because he was impulsive. He suffered from impulsivity. Sometimes it led him into grand things, and sometimes it led him into the head. Impulsive in medicine in terms of being creative, being the defender of the faith. He'd be the one who'd go and scream, 'This is wrong. I don't care if it's against policy, I want it changed.' The audience was usually on his side."[34]

And in terms of the marriage of acting and writing, Mallory recalls a special scene. "It was a love scene Bill Bell had written. It was the moment where *Bill* tells *Laura* how much he loves her. He tells her how beautiful she was when they were first engaged. He tells her how her hair smelled like wildflowers. It was very romantic. It was very 'Heathcliffish.' And at that moment, *Laura* capitulates and says that she loves him, too. That moment touched me."[35]

Bill Bell knew how to "touch" both his actors and his audience. And he knew his characters. He said of *Maggie*:

I think it is important that we never characterize *Maggie* too far away from the loving, simple girl she has always been....For in a sense, *Maggie*'s character strength lies in her weakness, her sweetness and her love.[36]

Actress Suzanne Rogers, who has portrayed *Maggie* since the beginning, has her own ideas about the character.

I felt she had been a cheerleader. She was a farm girl, she was homespun. Her life was very idyllic, and then all of a sudden it was shattered. Her parents were killed, and there she was, left crippled, and it was all gone. The farm—the basis was there—but she had no one. That's when people said she was so weak, but they didn't see the strength it took to get through all of that.[37]

Suzanne Rogers' *Maggie* is also an example of art imitating life. After Rogers was diagnosed with myasthenia gravis, *Days'* producers asked if it could be written into the show and *Maggie* diagnosed the same.

They asked me. I immediately said, "Yes." I said, "Only if we do it, and that it's a positive effect. That it is informative, that it gets the word out." My mother was very against it. She felt it was not a good idea. Mother was afraid it might bring on more. People said, "Oh, you were so sick then, you looked so bad." And I felt I looked 100 percent better than I had. I had come leaps and bounds and yet still knew that I looked sick. It was a very interesting period of time. I felt they did enough, just enough. The show is supposed to be informative and happy and sexual and lovely, and it's an afternoon show. If we were going to do it, let's do it by what happened to me. It can affect different people differently. And that's what we tried to do. Now that I think back on it, it was pretty scary.[38]

Scary? Maybe. But Rogers did it anyway. And obviously shares something more with her character than myasthenia gravis. What the two share are strength and courage.

Then there are the characters who are the polar opposite of *Maggie*. Quinn Redeker, who played the often villainous *Alex Marshall*, says simply, "*Alex* was a self-serving pig. I don't know what else you could say about him."[39]

Redeker might not have much to say, but co-star Frank Parker, who portrays the rollicking Irish patriarch, *Shawn Brady*, has a lot to say about Redeker.

My old buddy Quinn Redeker, I loved working with him. We would have scenes when he was close to *Victor*, and you never knew what was going to come out of his mouth. I came walking in one day, and just as he leaves he says, "You didn't have to dress, *Shawn*" and keeps right on going. They are in suits, and I am in my Mackinaw. We are in the middle of tape. I bite my tongue and keep going. But when I got off, I was laughing so hard. That is the kind of actor he is. But when he says something, it is always right for the scene, so you just keep right on playing it with him. It is marvelous to have those things happen.[40]

Redeker admits that he did a lot of ad-libbing to make the character of *Alex Marshall* more entertaining.

When *Alex* first came on, he killed a couple of people. But then they [the producers] decided they kind of liked me, and they let me start doing the comedy. So I started joking it up a bit and they liked it, so they kept me around. I ad-libbed all that stuff, made it up as I went along. They didn't mind, it was fine, getting along, just get in the last word [for the cue], don't change the intent. Here was a guy [*Alex*] with a little flavor and color....But I think the big terminal problem was that they couldn't figure out what to do with *Alex Marshall*. So they put him in jail for trying to burn down the Salem Inn for the insurance money. Salem couldn't take a joke at all. I remember ad-libbing lines as they were carrying me off to the police station, "You can't take a joke."[41]

Redeker has a stock of humorous stories. He likes to tell a self-deprecating actor's yarn, what he calls a "Quinntessential" joke.

The kid is a box boy at Ralph's and wants to be a writer. Suddenly he realizes he is boxing the groceries of a William Morris literary agent. "Read my script, read my script, please." "All right, throw it in the back of the car." Six months go by, the agent calls up and says, "OK, kid, we are going to do your script." "Really?" "Yes, how do you feel about Mancini doing the music?" "Henry Mancini?" "No, Charlie Mancini, plays down at the church. He is going to be great. You are going to love it." "OK." "How do you feel about Coppola directing?" "Francis Ford Coppola?" "No, Harry Coppola. He works down at the shoe store. But he is going to be great. You are going to love it" "OK." "How do you feel about Streep doing the girl?" "Meryl Streep?" "No, Margie Streep. She is my secretary. She is going to be great. You are going to love it." "OK." "How do you feel about Redeker?" "Quinn Redeker?" "Yeah."[42]

On a more serious note, Redeker celebrates life as an actor on a daytime drama. "It is the best job in town. It is the intimacy of the camera, the longevity of a play, and it is different every day. You have the best of both worlds. Eclecticity at its best."[43]

It may be the best job in town, but how does an actor feel when he has fewer of those special moments and is off that so-called "front burner" for a while? Mac Carey explains:

There's a little jealousy of the actors involved [in more story]. There's no question that that's true. I remember when *Doug* and *Julie* were on the show and were very hot. He was having a make-up put on him of an old man or something, some disguise in relation to the plot, and I came into the make-up room, and he said, "Look at Mac's face. He's jealous." And I was, of course. You know you want to be on everything, you want to do everything, and you want to be on. That's the business of being there. And anything that makes it more interesting, you want to be a part of it.[44]

Joe Gallison also acknowledges the joy of creation for the actor.

As an actor, it is more enjoyable to have the character personally involved as deeply as possible. Whether he's having a gambling problem, a drinking problem or a woman problem, or whatever. It is more actable, it is more interesting, it is more challenging. I mean we all have to spend a certain amount of time doing exposition. Hopefully, we do it as well as we can, but the other is somehow more fun. In the good old days [when *Neil* was a gambler, womanizer and alcoholic] it was fun to play. The man contained his own conflict. He was a self-made success, to the extent that he was a success. And then he had all these problems—it was like a death wish, he was so self-destructive. They were operating constantly against each other in the same personality. I should have played scenes with myself.[45]

Making the character more interesting is the combined effort of the actor and the writer. But the actors have to know when to draw the line. Susan Seaforth Hayes clarifies:

The writing team always has the last word. The actors cannot have the last word. This is not a democracy. But if there is something in a scene with which you do not agree you can play against it, truly you can. Truly you can refuse to play the fool. Some actors often are angry with their story lines and play it with contempt. And, generally, that's towards the end of their time on a show. And I have been on soaps a long time. The problem, of course, is confusing who you are with who the character is and saying, 'I alone must defend this character's integrity. It's up to me. The producers know nothing. The writer just got here and hates me. The fans only have me to depend on, and I must protect them from the folly of—then the list—everybody else around me on the show. I am going to carry the flag!' Well, it is emotional suicide. It is career suicide and you will never be a success at it. It is a project that is doomed to failure. This is too much a committee effort. So when things are going bad, live through them, life is long. Life is longer than today's show. You have to rise above the chaos of 'I can't say this line, you have got to joking. Give me another line, give me a break, give me a close-up, put me in focus, if I could just get in the scene.' You must rise above that, and it is hard.[46]

And Hayes knows how difficult it can sometimes be to be an actor:

Most actors have egos that are self-nurturing because the world kicks actors around. If you take the risk of getting in the light, you really take the risk of looking unmade up or having a wrinkled dress or saying something stupid, these are silly comparisons to failing in public. The person who has the chutzpah to fail in public has to go into their closet every night and say, "No, I am going to be fine, I can do this. I did it before and I can do it again. I am all right, I am all right." And then the world comes out and says, "Thank you, we will let you know. You're off." And you have to separate that career non-connection with protecting yourself and say, "I am still all right. Even without the job, I am all right." But it is harder. It's like being happy if the person you love is happy, even though they don't want to see you. That's harder, as Charlie Brown would say.[47]

But acting in a daytime drama also holds great joy—and a responsibility. Joe Gallison contends:

One of the things that really disturbs me is the extent to which some actors, some performers, want to be heroes and heroines and stars, whatever, rather than making the material work. Which if they did it, might accomplish their goals more quickly than extra make-up or their lighting or standing further upstage, whatever those things are. I am an actor. I like to work. I have had enough years of looking for work and not working and going to acting classes, saying, "I have got to do a scene tonight." The fun of doing soaps, the wonderful part, the up part, the positive part, is that you work a lot. You work at your craft. And if you are a writer, you can write all the time. If you are a painter, a sculptor, a composer, you can work on your own. But for an actor to work at your art or craft you have to have other people around you, you have to have the words that somebody else wrote and people at lights and camera. The responsibility of the job is to make the script work. Especially in this medium where the scripts are written rather quickly and sometimes not polished. Your responsibility is to make it work, not complain about it. Not say, "Now this scene is going down the tubes and I am going to look good."[48]

Wally Kurth believes soap actors are amongst the best in a medium that is one of the most difficult:

I think soap operas prepare you. A soap actor can do anything. And the actors who make it have to be of a certain breed and a certain talent. When you start a soap, first there is survival. You must survive the first few weeks. I have seen actors come and go. They could not hack it. This is a tough job for an actor. Once you survive, then you can grow and blossom.[49]

Wally certainly survived and blossomed. But when he went into his first audition he was prepared for anything.

When I went in and auditioned I had this no-holds-barred attitude. Like Peter Noone. Remember Peter Noone from "Herman's Hermits?" He is a very, very delightful man. He and I did *Pirates of Penzance*. Every night before we would go out, we would be behind the screen, standing in the pirate ship, ready for the big entrance, swords in the air. And every night he would say, "Wally, take no prisoners, take no prisoners!" Just go out there and nail it. And I remember walking into the [NBC] studio saying, "Take no prisoners." Just go out there and nail it. I think they saw my enthusiasm.[50]

Enthusiasm for the character and the work is important. Charles Shaughnessy reveals, "I ended up here [at *Days*] as *Shane* the butler. And loving it. It's a great place to be, I love it. As a place to work it is a fantastic environment to work in."[51]

How would Shaughnessy describe his alter ego, *Shane*?

Shane is tricky. I have never really felt like I have got a bead on him. He is a good guy. He is full of integrity and ethics and is very upright. But he also tends to be very pompous. He has an enormous ego, can be very uptight about that. He has great pride. It's funny, he is not my favorite kind of guy. I mean, I don't think I like him. I think if I ever met *Shane* I would probably not like him very much. He used to have a sense of humor. He used to have a wonderful twinkle, but that is kind of gone a bit.[52]

And playing a super agent for the ISA can have its drawbacks:

Shane never solves a case. He is the world's worst spy. From the writing point of view it does not suit them for a crime to be solved easily, and it very often does not suit them to have *Shane* solve it. But also from the writing point of view, it is important that *Shane* is established as this incredibly brilliant, skillful agent, spy. So there is an irresolvable conflict. I mean, *Shane* will come out, and there will be a clue on the floor, and he will walk right over it, and then *Jennifer* will come over and say, "Hey, look at this." Oh yeah, *Shane* is amazing, Roboman, Robospy. But he is full of metal. *Shane* has so many bits of shrapnel and bullets in him that he stays well away from refrigerator magnets.[53]

Shaughnessy would like to see *Shane* be more than a super agent extraordinaire.

Shane has a very sexual side, and I think that is an interesting element that I would like to keep lurking there with the humor and the glint. Just that little, that maybe you haven't seen all of him. Maybe he would just get up and sing one day or something. You know, something so that he is not such a stick in the mud. It would be so much fun with *Shane*, who has all the potential. As far as I can see, there is so much we do not know about him. There is so much bottled up that I would love to see. I would love to see that he could be incredibly violent at times or he could be extremely vulnerable on a certain occasion or his whole thing with prostitutes. He married a prostitute. His daughter [*Eve*] was a prostitute. We did that at one time when *Kimberly* went undercover. We had a scene in someone's house, and she was going through all these clothes, and she was in her prostitute's outfit. And *Shane* is telling her, "How can you do this? You are taking too much of a risk." And she starts saying something back and *Shane* is throwing these clothes around. There is some big argument and finally he just grabs her and throws her on the bed and everyone was saying "Ooh, what are you doing? What's going on here?" And I said, "No this is it. This is the whole point. *Shane* fell in love with *Kim* looking at her through a telescope. So this is obviously what turns him on. That is just something we don't know." They [the producers] just said, "Oh no, I don't know if we can do that. *Shane* can't do that." I said, "No, show him some fishnet tights and leather boots, and he is gone [snap]." And I think that would be great. I think that makes so much sense, that this frightfully stiff upper lip *Shane* would say, "I care for you, and that is why I am doing this. But if you don't get out of those tights, I am going to do something very, very naughty." I think that would be terrific.[54]

A certain amount of air time is devoted to "love in the afternoon" and many actors have a theory about their character's sexuality. Matthew Ashford sees *Jack*:

His sexuality comes out in lots and lots of foreplay, mental foreplay. When it really comes down to it, *Jack* has gone beyond that point. He is a much older man in a younger man's body. And so he enjoys the maneuverings. It is like *Dangerous Liaisons*. I think there was so much more playing with people and that's where the whole sexual enjoyment came from, just as much as the doing. But to seduce someone to your way, to your way of thinking, to make people do what you want to do. Power was sex. So the enjoyment is there, too. But when it really gets down to it, when he [*Jack*] actually gets the thing there, he is actually very nervous. And that for me is the counterbalance. That he is not totally in control and to be out of control because he is in love. So it is either be in control or be out of control. *Jack* is definitely pent up in a lot of ways. But it comes down to a lot of control and power. I don't know. I don't think he is sexual in a normal way, but I think he is sexual. *Jack* is not a balanced person.[55]

When Ashford began on the show, *Jack* was a villain, and Ashford played the part well. Fellow actor Wayne Heffley describes exactly how well.

I did not like him when I came on the show. I thought, "I don't even want to get near that slimebag." I thought that was the way he was. I didn't know he was a nice, sweet young man. I thought he was a horse's ass. He was *Jack Deveraux*. And Genie [Francis] invited him to lunch one day—we were going out to lunch together—and I found him very charming. But still, I thought, "Well, *Vern* doesn't have anything to do with him, he is not on the paper." Little did I know he would soon be leading me by the nose, up the garden path from here to hell and breakfast. And that I would willingly follow. But by then I liked him.[56]

Jack might be a character with whom people would not like to spend a lot of time, but Ashford strives to make *Jack* stand for something, even if it is only the simple things.

The writers write the big headlines and underneath that I just try to say very simple things about people. What people like, what human beings are like. I just try to be honest about simple things, regular things. And especially if I don't feel well, I say, "why should *Jack*, why?" I think you have your down days and your not-so-great days, and I totally play into it. So when I have a good day, it's different. But that is just the way this character is. Sometimes they write it very hard for a lot of very good characters to have a down day. And just simply because they woke up and didn't feel well, they're not wearing their favorite outfit, they're not, they're not. Simple things. Things that we used to study in theater school. I used to think, "I could never think of all these things at once to create a character." And then I realized, you don't have to. But maybe one thing will key you into a whole world, a whole exploration. You realize you don't feel comfortable and say, "There's nothing wrong with that, go with that." Rather than trying to be something that you are not. I try to do those kinds of truths on a daily basis. It's not a big deal, but I think people respond to it. I get a lot of letters from people saying, "You are so real, you are like someone I really know." And to me, that's one of the things that I have strived for.[57]

If Ashford strives for truth with *Jack*, he also strives for humanity.

I think I understand what humanity is. It's just to be human. And it's to have a lot of faults. I think it takes a careful looking at people, looking at a tiny situation, finding just tiny moments and not just running through on the plot. All the human weaknesses that are exploited and self exploited and developed and fought against and standing up and falling down, and everybody has got them. I campaign to make my character really human. But I am the first one to laugh at him and poke fun and then, when he has his 20 seconds in the sun, it really makes a big difference. I don't want *Jack* to be a hero. Not a hero like Superman, but a normal, regular guy full of so many problems, but who has a moment. And when that moment comes, it makes you think everybody has that inside them. Everyone has that potential inside them. So that's the kind of humanism I strive for, much more understanding towards a person. A lot of people have written to me and said, "I've made a lot of mistakes in my life, and it was such a slow process." Then they could really see by watching it happen, day by day by day, falling down getting up and say, "Wow, I feel like I can change, too." I think we all need to be a little more human.[58]

Actor George Jenesky also believes that playing the less than heroic part is the most challenging.

It is much more interesting not to play Mr. Nice Guy. It's tough to come up with anything unexpected when you are the good guy. If you're the good guy then you know what he is going to do in a situation. You don't know what the bad guy is going to do, and there is a certain excitement in not knowing.[59]

But there was a time when *Days* turned *Nick* into a good guy. I used to kid about it on the set. I used to call myself Saint Nick and say that any day he was going to be walking on water. That there was a little glow around his head. But now *Nick* is going through a period [1990] where he's an angry, hurt, somewhat bitter, cynical man. And he's tried to fit into society and tried to play the game society's way, and he feels like there's no pay-off. Consequently, he's pretty much going back to his old way of looking at things. Which is that "Nobody gives a damn about me, so why should I give a damn about anybody else?"[60]

All of the above actors are or have been contract players with principal parts. But there are also actors on the show whom the fans might not notice or notice only briefly but without whom Salem would seem sparsely populated: the extras and "under fives" (U5).[61] Linda Poindexter, who does what is called "atmosphere casting" for *Days*, explains: "Atmosphere casting is atmosphere. It's the extras, it's the background. The people in the restaurants, in all the public places. We average about 40 to 90 extras a week."[62] The show's director is the one who calls for the extras on a given day.

Generally the extras are used in the background of the hospital or restaurants, an occasional grand ball or maybe a cruise. But sometimes extras are required for a very special purpose. Poindexter recalls:

They were looking for the role of *Marina* [in 1989], and they could not find anybody that they liked. So I had to cast a body double for *Marina* without knowing who it was, who it was going to be, because Doris [Sabbagh] was looking for the character, the principal, the contract role. They were interviewing all these people, so they said, "Find a double." And they were going to shoot all her angles, everything but her face, but we had no idea how tall *Marina* would be, what color her hair would be. It was weird.[63]

Sometimes only a portion of an extra's body is seen on screen. Poindexter has gotten some strange casting requests, "Once we had to cast just somebody's feet. They wanted a guy with big feet. He was supposed to be a stalker. We joked we were casting 'under five' feet."[64]

And sometimes extras must have a very special look:

I had to cast Dan and Marilyn Quayle look-alikes once. That was interesting. I called a lot of people and I finally got a guy who looked like Day Quayle, really. But it was funny, when I called around, you would be surprised how many people said, "Marilyn who?" I said, "Remember the Vice President?" That was fun.[65]

CHAPTER 5

THE FANS

It is a given in daytime television circles that *Days of Our Lives* has the most loyal fans in daytime. While this might be difficult to prove, *Days* fans have demonstrated an ardent 30-year devotion to the show. And their faithfulness and suggestions do make a difference. Ken Corday explains:

I read every drop of [fan] mail that I get, every drop, and so do the other producers and the writers ... "Why are you doing this? How can you do this?" Sometimes that is the desired response. But if we believe in something and we think it is going great and the fans write in and say, "We hate it, we hate it. This is never going to work." We take note and say, "Well, wait a minute, we may have made the wrong turn. Let's agree with what they are saying." They have a big, big impact.[1]

A prime example of the show's impact and the fans' involvement dates from the sixties: when *Susan Martin's* baby died, head writer Bill Bell received an avalanche of mail.

I did something in the early days with *Susan* and *David Martin* that I promised I would never do again, ever. And that was the baby on the swing, when *David* was looking the other way and the baby went down. Because it was at a time when I was getting all kinds of mail from people telling me how much they were praying for the child. Of course, by that time in the script I knew the child had died. And so many of those letters were so moving because these people were so caught into that relationship and into that mother's love for that baby that I decided I would never, ever, ever again kill another baby.[2]

Days fan lore is peppered with this kind of story. And the effects of fans' loyalty often extend far beyond soap opera circles. When the show that would have revealed whether or not *Mickey Horton* had died from a heart attack was preempted by the Watergate hearings, the NBC New York switchboard was flooded with phone calls. The next morning's *Daily News* carried a photo of *Mickey's* portrayer, John Clarke, under the headline "Will he live?" When the character of *Marlena* "died," thousands of her devoted fans marched on the

NBC studios, demanding that their heroine live. During the climactic moment when *Carly* was to tell *Bo* about the child she had had with *Lawrence*, a local news broadcast preempted the Chicago airing. Fans deluged station WMAQ with phone calls, and the station re-aired the show in its entirety later that night. When *Doug* and *Julie* were married, thousands of fans attended the wedding reception held at the studio, and millions more watched from their homes.

What inspires this kind of fervor? Everyone involved, of course, has an opinion. Ken Corday reveals,

If people were to say what is the one key word in *Days of Our Lives*, it is family. It is not the love stories, and that is a key in every soap. And it is not moral issues. It is not trying to do public service. And it is not bodies. It is just family. The family unit is the most important thing ... I think we have survived 30 years because we stand for, without sounding moralistic, what I believe the heartland of this country believes in. And we try, without being preachy, to put that forward. That love does conquer all, that right wins out over wrong, but it is not pie-in-the-sky. And I also think the fact that we still have not changed the core family that was there in the beginning. If anything, it is their sons and daughter that have repeopled the show.[3]

Tradition and family are words that appear again and again in relation to *Days*. Actor Charles Shaughnessy believes,

There is always the family. There is *Alice* and *Tom* to go back to. And there is always a feeling, even with everything that is going on, all these trials and tribulations, and these people doing these dreadful things, that sooner or later *Tom* or *Alice* is going to come in and say, "Now cut this nonsense out, come home. We are going to cook a nice, big dinner, and we are going to have hot chocolate and go to bed early." And I think, seriously, the audience responds to that. In a time when things are so unsure, that theme and that symbol is extremely reassuring. And then with that in the back of the mind, when you have got that anchor, then you can go and have fun with them. You can have them marry their own brother or have children by a father or turn into a mass killer, all these hideous things, because in the back of it is *Tom* and *Alice* and the donuts.[4]

Actor Don Frabotta, who has been with the show for many years as *Dave, the waiter*, is not sure he can explain the show's popularity, but knows it exists:

Days is a phenomenon. It is more than any other soap. In the popularity polls we are always number one. It has been that way as far back as I can remember. It has got to do with the characters we create, obviously. We are known for super couples now. There is something the fans relate to. But we are not number one in the ratings, yet the fans love us. In fact, they often love us and hate us at the same time. I go to the *Days* softball games and talk to the fans. They would complain about what we were doing, yet would watch us. It was like they had to have something to talk about.[5]

Linda Poindexter, *Days'* atmosphere casting director, believes it is the familiarity of old friends:

I think the reason a lot of people watch soaps is that it's a way to escape. And you can actually identify with these characters. So these characters become your friends, and you really do care about them. I mean, if the show is well written and acted you really care about what is happening to them. It is like visiting friends. And I think that is the bottom line as to why people watch. Because it makes you feel good. It is a familiar, comfortable place to be. And that is why people turn it on. You do not have to go, you do not have to drive to visit your

Mom or your cousin or whatever. You just turn it on, and there are these people and you know their lives.[6]

Frabotta makes numerous personal appearances and sees the fans in action:

Our fans are the most fanatic ... They love to touch, they love to talk, they like to be a part of it. They all want to be part of *Days*. If you look at our fan history, we have had some problems with the fans. They can get very possessive and they can feel that you owe them something. In a way they are responsible for us and for being alive and for working. That is what we are doing it for. But sometimes they get over-demanding. As an actor, you have to maintain, you can't give them every minute of your life. And sometimes, that is what they demand. Me, I am very accessible. I go everywhere, talk to everyone.[7]

Frabotta is right; sometimes, with the best intentions, the fans cross the line. After all, they see the actors in their living rooms five days a week, and that breeds a great deal of familiarity. Fans can walk up to actors and say things to them that they would never say to their own children, parents, or best friend. "My, don't you look old." "Don't hold your face that way, you should never hold your face that way, the wrinkles show." "Have you gained weight? You look heavy on TV." "Your hair is too long. Why don't you cut your hair?" "I hate that beard/moustache. Why don't you shave?" "Who did your makeup? You look like a vampire." "Did you know you have a hairy back? Have you tried waxing?" "The color of your eyes keeps changing. Are you wearing contacts?" "You don't know how to kiss. Why don't you take kissing lessons?" "How come you never take your shirt off?" "I hear you are dating so and so. Are you in love? Is he good in bed?"

Or the actors get blamed for things over which they have no control: the plot and the dialogue. "Why are you [your character] behaving like such an idiot?" "How can you [the character] not know such and such? Everyone knows!" "How can you blame him? You knew the truth!" "How can you blame them? They only slept together twice." "I can't believe you said something so stupid." "How could you [the character] do that! What a jerk!" "Can I have an autographed picture?" Most actors take such criticisms with a grain of salt and a smile. But strenuous fan attacks have been known to send an actor into a depression, if not tears.

Some fans identify the actor a bit too closely with the character the actor portrays. If the actor plays a villain, things can get rough. Actors have had their faces slapped, been verbally abused, and even been refused service in restaurants.

And fans can, and often do, disrupt the actors' lives off the set. Fans walk up to actors spotted eating in a restaurant and start talking; reach out and touch them or stroke their hair; follow them in department or grocery stores when they are out shopping; even follow them into the restroom!

But the upside is that, generally, this type of behavior is limited to a small number of fans. But *Days* fans are devout. Frabotta demonstrates:

Days fans are great fans. They are very, very loyal to us. Even though they hate us at moments, they are still there, they are still in our corner. People send me tons of pictures. A lot of the college students, their dorm rooms are plastered with photos, or anything they can get. When they go to the functions, they bring their albums. They take thousands of pictures and put them in their albums. Then they show them to other fans, and they either trade or sell off. ... Some people come out [to NBC Studios, Burbank] when actors leave the show. There is no special event. They just know it is the actor's last day, and somehow they find someone to get them onto the set or they wait in the parking lot for the actors to drive out.[8]

Actor George Jenesky also recognizes *Days* fan loyalty. "I think it has to do with *Days* being the soap that changes the least. The theme has always been the same. Frances and Mac have always been there. And there is a feeling to Salem that is old-fashioned. It seems like it is always the same, and there is a certain kind of person that likes that and really responds to that. And I think that is the loyal fan base."[9]

Susan Seaforth Hayes agrees:

[*Days*] has an enormous fan loyalty, more loyalty than any of the other soaps. We have been blessed with strong actors, strong personalities. And for certainly the first decade, we had some trail-blazing story. ... A lot of it is glamour, escape and glamour. Some of our viewers look at this as a proof and justification that the American Dream can come true. That there are lives untouched by money worries. That it is just a matter of juggling things around and you will have a handsome man in your life. It is a hopeful medium for people whose lives are perhaps without that kind of day-to-day glamour and hope. It is alive, as any ongoing story is, with people, with stories about people, with emotional explosions. ... You can talk to people, you can watch other lives go by, you can be a good neighbor, you can. You just turn on the set, and you are connected to the millions of people who turn on their set at the same time. And that can be a great thing.[10]

Ed Mallory credits talent and humanity for *Days'* ability to touch people. "We all did the best job that we could. And we were committed to making moments as real as we could. And, hopefully, the viewers would respond to the humanity of that. The show was family-oriented and romance-driven. It may have been melodramatic, but it dealt with family, and at its core, human emotion."[11]

Bill Hayes acknowledges the importance of the actors, writers, and the producers:

Days touched people. I attribute that to Betty [Corday], who was loving and dedicated and concerned. Jack Herzberg was the same. We had Bill Bell planning the story, we had Pat Falken Smith and Bill Rega writing wonderful scripts, and we had Wes Kenney as a producer and director. And when they cast people, and used them, they did a masterful job, masterful. You could not do a better choice for *Alice* than Frances Reid. I attribute a lot of it to casting. Macdonald Carey, Susan Flannery, Denise Alexander, Ed Mallory, Susan [Seaforth Hayes] were all incredibly talented. One after the other, they hired people that were wonderfully talented and exciting and to whom people could relate. You know it never goes away. The fans always remember.[12]

The fans do remember the actors and each usually has a favorite actor or two. Matthew Ashford, who portrays *Jack Deveraux*, has become a fan favorite. Ashford credits *Jack's* appeal to the character's emotional accessibility:

If *Jack* has any appeal, I hope that it is because he is kind of a regular guy. I try to show him good, bad or ugly. Then people pick up on that and write and say, "You're really having fun, aren't you?" ... A lot of guys write and say they are into *Jack* because he responds like a guy. He's not all "I love you dearest, sweet," and the male audience is picking up on that. And a lot of women who watch write and say, "You're just like my husband, boyfriend, father, little brother, whatever." Of course, I also have a lot of fans who are six years old. Mutant Turtles and me.[13]

Charles Shaughnessy, who plays the debonair *Shane Donovan*, says of *Shane's* appeal: "I think the accent has a lot to do with it. He [*Shane*] is English, continental. Americans get a great kick out of an English accent and the way English people say things. And he is Dudley Do-right. He comes along on a white horse, and he cares deeply."[14]

The upright, do-right characters are not the only fan favorites. George Jenesky's *Nick Corelli*, a gray character in the often black-and-white world of daytime, attracted his own share of attention.

I think the fan interest comes from the fact that *Nick* was just a real different sort of character. Maybe it was the combination of the pimp [*Nick*] and the prostitute [*Eve*] and their age differences and background differences—*Nick's* coming from the streets and her coming from that sort of wealthy background, with *Shane* as her father. It is just an interesting combination.[15]

Susan Seaforth Hayes has been a fan favorite for nearly 20 years. She says of *Julie's* magnetism: "The sexual brunette is often appealing. A feisty woman is appealing. The emphasis on the character now is that she is successful and caring at the same time. That she combines the mothering instinct with financial capability. That she can, in fact, do two and three things at once and do them all well. *Julie* has gotten a lot stronger. She had a strong streak for self-destruction in the past, which is interesting, which makes for drama, which makes for good story."[16]

Moyra Bligh, president of Susan Seaforth Hayes' fan club, "A Circle of Friends," describes what Susan and *Julie* mean to her. "So many layers of fantasy and reality. *Julie* isn't Susan, although they do look very much alike. *Julie* is an alter ego who has been with Susan for a very long time, push the right button and she can become *Julie* in an instant. *Julie* is a vehicle via which I get to watch Susan work and I love to watch her work, because she reaches me on a level that no other actress has ever been able to ... she has the ability to drag me into a particular moment or emotion and trap me there."[17]

The ability to pull an audience into a particular moment or emotion is the hallmark of a good actor, but of good soap opera actors in particular. Writer Pat Falken Smith contends that all daytime viewers are voyeurs. "We are always looking to see how these people handle problems in their life. We like to see chemistry between people. We love to see a relationship go. ... Soaps are an emotional reality with which we have empathy."[18]

Falken Smith adds that the time the show is aired may feed that empathy. "I think people get so passionate about it because daytime has a reality that nighttime does not have. And it comes into your home on a daily basis and it is all invasive. It takes over your life and becomes part of your family. Five times a week, especially when it is an hour show—that is something. It is a lot of your time. Your emotional investment goes into the show."[19]

Writer Elizabeth Harrower agrees,

You don't need a lot of words, you just need to build to a moment and then tear everybody's guts out with it. I always think it is a thing for the emotions. In watching yours, sometimes the audience relives it. I don't think that soap opera is any kind of necessary role model, but I don't know how close we get to each other. And this is a way to reach out and get closer to somebody. It is a form of community. And it is strange, but a great deal of the soap opera audience are people who travel or are on the road. People who tune in and watch it because it is a sense of family to them. There is somebody you know who was doing something yesterday that is doing the same thing today. If they were doing it in Detroit, they are now doing it in Chicago.[20]

Days is a community. On a daily basis the audience in New York or Los Angeles or Chicago or Kenosha (or Peoria or Des Moines or Toronto or Athens or Sydney or Wellington or Frankfurt or Paris!) sees the actors and their characters in Salem, USA. They watch them on televisions in their living rooms, in their bedrooms, in whatever strange and marvelous location they may have access to a set. Fans watch in groups in college dorms and cafeterias; they watch in the television department of their local department store; they watch on their miniature TVs during their lunch break; they watch in their own homes; and they watch in their cars!

Many fans have *Days of Our Lives* parties. When *Jack* and *Jennifer* were married in the summer of 1991, many fans made the pilgrimage to Universal Studios in Hollywood to watch the nuptials; many more hosted "wedding parties" in their homes. Fans reported elaborate wedding parties, complete with *Jack* and *Jennifer* story line–related party favors: a fire truck, Ken and Barbie as fireman and bride, miniature cruise ships, shell rings, and snow people. And when the *Days of Our Lives* cast, crew, and writers celebrated the show's silver anniversary party in Los Angeles, countless fans reveal that they had parties of their own, eating hourglass-shaped cakes, and showing and sharing *Days'* episodes that they had videotaped and preserved over the years.

A *Days* fan is never alone as long as there is another *Days* fan in the room. Linda Pidutti, president of the Lakeside Association (an organization of supporters of Mary Beth Evans, Stephen Nichols, and *Days of Our Lives*) explains, "One of the best results of my experience with the Association has been the number of truly terrific people I have met and become friends with. Our relationships began because of our interest in Mary Beth and Stephen and have then developed into lifelong friendships. My experience is very common among supporters."[21]

Making new and life-long friends through *Days* is common. Although fans might connect in a supermarket line reading the latest soap opera publication or in the dorm watching their favorite show or maybe via an electronic bulletin board, many more meet through the fan clubs and events that the clubs sponsor. *Days* fan clubs are numerous; many of the actors on the show have their own fan clubs.[22] And fan club members number in the thousands. Their ages range from nine to 90 and, although most are from the United States, many clubs boast members from Australia, Canada, New Zealand, and the West Indies![23]

Susan Seaforth Hayes' club vaunts a monk (who is the club's spiritual adviser) and a world-famous opera singer. Membership dues average about $15 per year. Membership kits vary, but most include a photo and a newsletter. Drake Hogestyn, Matthew Ashford, and Charles Shaughnessy send their fan club members audio tapes combined with, or instead of, a letter. Charles Shaughnessy and Susan Seaforth Hayes include personally autographed photos. Instead of a newsletter, Susan Seaforth Hayes' club publishes a journal featuring a variety of articles and illustrated with color prints. Every member of Hayes' fan club receives a birthday card from Susan on his birthday.

Besides distributing newsletters and merchandise ranging from "I brake for Drake" license plate frames to "I [heart] Drake" shoelaces to "I'm having a Jack Attack" T-shirts and pins, the fan clubs also sponsor fan club gatherings. Deidre Hall's "Lunch Breaks," which began in the seventies, seem to have started the trend. Now many clubs sponsor several gatherings a year. Events can range from a Halloween party to a family reunion to a Salem reunion to a night at *Wings*.

For example, in October 1991, Matthew Ashford's fan club organized a combination fan gathering/Ashford family reunion in Williamsburg, West Virginia. The fans were treated to what Matthew Ashford called "the Freudian pay-off": Matthew with his parents and siblings. The Ashford family delighted the crowd with their barbershop singing. In May 1992, Matthew's Memorial Day event spotlighted Matthew and his then-pregnant wife, singer Christina Saffran.[24] The party's theme was that of a baby shower, and fans surprised the couple with a baby book. At both events, fans came away feeling as if they had spent an evening with family and friends. They had. There are no strangers at any *Days* event.

While there are *Days* gatherings throughout the United States, probably the most well known are the Memorial Day *Days* events held in Southern California. A number of fan clubs host a series of gatherings that span the weekend. Fans come from across the United States and the world (there is always a large Australian contingent!) to spend an entire weekend celebrating *Days* with their favorite actors and fellow fans. In 1992 Susan Seaforth Hayes' club hosted "A Night at *Wings*"; Deidre Hall had her traditional lunch break; Drake Hogestyn's and Charles Shaughnessy's clubs sponsored a black and white themed luncheon, "Stepping Out at the Ritz"; and Matthew Ashford's club rounded out the weekend with "Bringing Up Baby."

Don Frabotta attends many of these events and paints a picture:

People come for the gatherings from all over. Sometimes they go to every event during Memorial Day. These are sane, normal people, yet this is their life. This is their vacation, they save for this. I know a few divorces have erupted from this because the wives got so into it, they forgot about their families. But the men come, too. And then there are those who come out with the whole family. I have talked to people with doctorates and to everyday people. How do they [the fans] afford it? It costs for these gatherings. You have got to pay for the hotel, you have got to pay for your trip, you have got to pay to attend, and other things. That amazes me, the amount of money they spend on things. Then there are the charity events. I have seen someone pay $1,000 for a visit to the set. I have seen them spend money on pictures, or if someone sneezed in this handkerchief or drank from this beer can, they want it.[25]

The clubs know how special these gatherings are to the fans and make a tremendous effort to create the perfect event. For example, when Susan Seaforth Hayes' and her fan club president decided in January 1992 to host a gathering, the choice of theme—"A Night at *Wings*" because Susan's character, *Julie*, owns Salem's hot spot, *Wings*—was the easiest part. Once the theme was chosen, the perfect location had to be found. The site needed to be in Southern California, near NBC Studios, Burbank, because the actors work Memorial Day.

Susan finally found the perfect room, complete with a stage to better create the illusion of a night club. The room chosen, colors for the table linens and flowers needed to be selected. In this case the colors were pink and salmon, two of Susan's favorites.

But planning was far from over. Actors had to be asked to attend, souvenirs of the evening ordered, and raffle items found. After much searching, the perfect memento was discovered: a brandy snifter inscribed with Susan's signature (in pink). Susan also acquired scripts for each and every fan attending. Raffle prizes started off in sumptuous style when Susan's husband, actor and singer, Bill Hayes donated a trip on a Caribbean cruise as the grand prize. Susan created her own gift baskets complete with photos, *Days* memorabilia, and souvenir clothing. Trips to the studio and breakfast with Susan were also added. Susan and some of her most devoted fan club members even did a photo spread for a soap opera publication, detailing their hard work planning the soiree.

Six months of preparation went into the event. Last-minute activities included: printing name tags and place cards, putting the finishing touches on the gift baskets, special ordering 600 cookies, and rehearsing with the actors and piano player for the planned show.

The day arrived: Friday, May 22, 1992. Susan and her fan club helpers were up bright and early to check the room to make sure everything was going according to plan. Floral centerpieces with long, white tapers were placed in the center of each table. Balloons festooned the walls. Last-minute preparations accomplished, Susan and her crew dashed home to put on their evening finery and quickly returned.

At 7:00 p.m. the doors opened, and the nearly 400 fans arrived. Don Frabotta (*Dave, the waiter*) chivalrously escorted the guests to their tables. Photos were taken with Susan as the fans entered. People purchased raffle tickets. Many took photos of the raffle table. Dinner was served at 8:00 p.m., and when it was over, the show began.

Cast, both current and past, appeared. Longtime favorites Deidre Hall (*Marlena*) and Jed Allan (*Don Craig*) started off the evening with just the right tone. Susan introduced Deidre by saying, "When Deidre said she would be here tonight, well, it was like John Wayne saying, 'Yes, I'll be in your rodeo.'" Susan and her longtime friend Suzanne Rogers (*Maggie*) sang "Friendship." Wesley Eure (*Mike Horton*), Patty Weaver (*Trish*), and Robert Clary (*Robert LeClere*) all sang. Michael Sabatino, who plays the villainous *Lawrence Alamain*, accompanied by Crystal Chappell (*Carly*), brought down the house with his accordion playing!

Roberta Leighton (*Ginger*) enchanted the crowd with a story and was joined by Shannon Sturges (*Molly*). Charles Shaughnessy delighted the fans as usual. Susan introduced Matthew Ashford as "apple pie, ice cream, and insanity." When Ashford came from backstage, he commented on Susan's five costume changes, quipping, "Five outfits. It has certainly been a great show from back here." James Reynolds (*Abe Carver*) and his wife read Christopher Marlowe's "The Passionate Shepherd to His Love." Robert Kelker-Kelly (*Bo Brady*), in his first Los Angeles *Days* fan event appearance, walked on stage to a chorus of screams. The show ended with everyone singing "Together."

The show over, Susan and Robert Kelker-Kelly stayed until almost 1:00 a.m. signing autographs and photos for the enraptured fans. Everyone finally went home. Susan celebrated the end of a successful evening by treating the friends who had worked for so long and hard on the event to a 3:00 a.m. champagne toast and pizza snack.

The Memorial Day events are famous, but actors make public appearances all over the United States and Canada. And sometimes their appearances are a little *too* successful. A personal appearance by Matthew Ashford in Edmonton, Alberta, Canada, ended after only 20 minutes when worried fire marshals decided that the mall in which he was appearing was not meant to handle 5,000 fans! And this number of people showing up for a personal appearance is not atypical. Mac Carey said that he and Judi Evans once did an autograph signing for a Detroit mall "and 3,000 people showed up. It was incredible."[26] And Susan and Bill Hayes drew a crowd of over 5,000 people at the airport in Adelaide, South Australia, when the couple was changing planes on the way to Alice Springs. Unbeknownst to them, word of their brief stopover had become public, and fans appeared for just a glimpse of their favorites. As Susan Hayes explained, "When we saw the crowd, we wondered why they were there. We thought that maybe there was a rock star arriving."[27]

To the fans a visit with a *Days* actor is an event to be cherished. Elizabeth Carpenter, Lisa Howard's (*April Ramirez*) fan club president, describes an event organized by Lisa's club.

Wes Kenney directs Susan Seaforth Hayes and Bill Hayes (c. 1974). Courtesy Susan Seaforth Hayes.

In November 1990 we had [a] luncheon in Connecticut. ... It was personal, friendly, and people got to spend time with Lisa. People traveled from all over the United States to attend the luncheon—New England, New York, Florida, Missouri, and even California. Lisa table-hopped, hugged fans, and showed her genuine appreciation for her fans and everything that they do for her. She was showered with birthday presents, the kind of gifts that you give to a friend, someone that you care for.[28]

That is, ultimately, the answer. The actor is someone about whom the fans care, someone to whom the fans will remain loyal. And the cast appreciates their good will. Actor Wally Kurth explains, "The *Days* fans are a phenomenon. There is nothing like it. And I will be forever grateful. These fans will follow me throughout my career. I know that. I have been very nice to them, and they have been very nice to me."[29]

Wally's fan club president, Marsha Seader, shares her thoughts on why the fans like Wally Kurth: "Wally is, I believe, the type of actor who appeals to a wide range of viewers — *Justin* was simply irresistible. Some [want] to give their total support to a very talented actor in the pursuit of his career goals, and some [like him] because of his dimples (just kidding!)."[30] And personally why Marsha likes Wally: "I'm the first one to admit that the reason I watched that very first scene was because I thought he was so adorable—but people who know me know that an actor has to be more than a 'pretty face' to capture my full attention. I immediately saw something beyond the big eyes and the great smile and the dimples, and it wasn't long before I was totally enraptured by Wally's heartfelt portrayal of *Justin.* ... It's been a thrill to see him blossom and grow over the past four years as he's fleshed out his character. He's given me (and a few other people!) so many hours of pleasure. ... Personally, he'll probably never be fully aware of how he's inspired me to reach for things that I thought were impossible."[31]

A minuscule percentage of fans have proven to be a problem. Ken Corday discloses,

You know, fan stands for fanatic. ... The thing that gets a little scary and it is only 1/100 of 1% of them, the fans that cannot divorce reality from fantasy. And they carry the fantasy of the daytime character into their own lives, will make a point of coming to Los Angeles and becoming consumed with the actor, following the actor home from work, knock on the actor's door, sit on their door step, threaten them if they don't get some kind of validation from the actor. And, of course, this gets turned over to the police. ... The classic story is that Andy Masset, who was playing *Larry Welch* on the show, had wrongfully married *Hope* in a black-mail situation. He [the actor] received a letter from a man that said, "When I get out of here, I've got my .45 loaded and I am going to blow your head off." Just that simple. "I've got two bullets for you, if you don't get your hands off *Hope*, I'm going to kill you." And the return address was cell block whatever, Folsom Prison. And we turned it over to the FBI and the FBI went straight to cell block whatever it was at Folsom Federal Prison and said, "Did you write this letter?" And the gentleman said, "Yes." And they said, "That will be seven more years" and slammed the door.[32]

Most fans are quite different, though, and seeing them can be heartwarming, Ken says. "The other side of it is that they really love the characters, and you see a 25-year fan come on stage and get their first look at Macdonald Carey. These are people who have shared an hour of your day with you in your living room for 25 years."[33]

This is finally what it means. The fans have shared their lives with the actors and characters on *Days* for years, and they are now part of the family, sometimes an astonishingly close and influential part. Fans write to the actors with the most intimate details of their lives, as one would write to a close friend or family member. At times, actors' letters or visits have significantly touched a fan's life.

A woman from New Zealand wrote to the show and reported that her daughter loved *Days*. The daughter had a chronic heart condition and was quite ill. When the family planned a trip to California, the production staff arranged a visit to the set. As it turned out, the mother had arranged the trip just so her daughter could see *Days*.[34] The girl arrived in a wheelchair. She was 20, but was so thin and frail she looked 12. She watched the dress rehearsal from her wheelchair, and all the cast came by to greet her and wish her well. Observers said they have never seen a happier person. The mother sent a thank-you note after the visit. Four months later a follow-up letter arrived. The girl had died watching *Days of Our Lives*. Everyone knew she was failing, but the episode she had

Doug (Bill Hayes) and *Julie Williams* (Susan Seaforth Hayes) were married September 16, 1976. Over 4000 fans watched the wedding on monitors at NBC Studios, Burbank. After the wedding was taped, Bill and Susan exited the studio to greet the assembled fans. Courtesy Susan Seaforth Hayes.

been watching was a Friday show that she had very much wanted to see. Her mother said her daughter had held on long enough to see the telecast.

There are many stories like this one. A young girl from British Columbia whose mother brought her to the Memorial Day fan events was very ill, suffering the side effects of chemotherapy. But again, she was thrilled and seemed to barely notice her pain. The cast treated her wonderfully and took her everywhere. Her visit to Los Angeles to meet the *Days* cast was her dying wish.

Some stories are less somber. One Boston teen-ager who came to the set was shy, a bit frumpy and lacked confidence. But actor Wesley Eure, whom she adored, was wonderful to her. Several months later her mother wrote to the producers to say that her sojourn on the set had turned the girl's life around. Because Wesley was so good to her, she had gained confidence. She made friends and even became a good student.

Sometimes an actor or a scene will touch someone in a very specific or special way. Bill Hayes recounts, "I got a letter one time that I sent to Bill Bell, a letter from a fan. When *Addie* was pregnant, *Doug* sang the 'Soliloquy' from *Carousel*, 'I wonder what he will think of me, my boy Bill...' I sang the whole thing. I got a letter from a lady who said, 'I want to thank you for singing that song and making me believe again. My husband and I talked, before we had any children, about whether we should bring them into this world because, as black kids, they were going to have troubled times. It is not easy being black.' She said, 'We have these three wonderful children, and the song that you sang about "my boy Bill," took us back and made us glad that we had children.'" Bill concludes, "It was a beautiful letter and a real tearjerker. I sent it to Bill [Bell] because he had done it."[35]

Some people turn to the friendship and familiarity of a soap in times of crisis. One young Marine sent a video of his daily life in the Persian Gulf during the Gulf War to the show. The group at *Days* responded with a video of their own to remind the young man of home. Further, an Army reservist, and 17-year fan of the show, stationed in Saudi began to write Susan Seaforth Hayes. Susan responded with her customary warmth, and the two became regular pen pals. When the reservist made it home safe and sound (except for a broken ankle), the yellow ribbon Susan had sewn and tied around a tree in her front yard came down. The two finally met and have been friends ever since.

Of course, an addiction to *Days* can complicate life. Some fans will go to any lengths to watch their favorite show. Fans have reported speeding tickets earned while racing home to catch the show. Some have turned entire department store TV departments into "teleplexes" for *Days*. Many carry their miniature TVs almost anywhere to avoid missing the broadcast of a special show. The most devout have at least two VCRs set up for taping as well as "back-up" provided by *Days* friends across the U.S. and Canada. That way, if your VCR goes on the blink or if you have a local preemption, you know that someone, somewhere will have a tape of the show. When *Days'* Christmas 1990 show was preempted in Los Angeles by a basketball game, local devotees had a tape supplied by a Canadian friend within 48 hours. No true *Days* fan could ever miss the traditional hanging of the *Horton* Christmas ornaments.

After 30 years of viewing, missing *Tom* and *Alice* and the familiar *Horton* Christmas would be like missing your own grandparents' holiday celebration. Returning full circle, we are back to *Days* providing a community of family and friends and warm donuts. Maybe now we understand why Susan Seaforth Hayes calls her fan club "A Circle of Friends."

CHAPTER 6

THE STORY LINE

What follows is a synopsis of 29 years' worth of *Days* story line (from November 8, 1965, through December 31, 1994). I have endeavored to introduce characters, explain their actions, and acknowledge their departure from Salem, but those tasks aren't always easy. Circumstances such as the arrival of a new head writer or an actor's abrupt departure often preclude any explanations of a character's exit. Thus resident quipsters explain that Tommy Horton* lives in the Horton attic and Don Craig went to mail a letter—in Santa Barbara. And as Susan Seaforth Hayes teased at the *Days* twenty-sixth anniversary party, "Many die, but few are buried."

Our story begins in Salem, U.S.A. No one is sure of its exact whereabouts, but the "bible" explains, "Salem was then [1910] a sleepy little mid-western community 40 miles from a large mid-western city. In the fifty-four years since Tom's [Horton] birth, both Salem and the nearby city have grown considerably, pushing their borders closer and closer together, until, today, they are barely twenty miles apart. Salem has grown large enough to support an excellent college and University. Being the County seat, Salem also has the County Medical Center, one of the most advanced and best equipped in the country. It is the fact that Salem, with its University and Medical Center, is such a good medical town that has kept Tom Horton rooted here all his life."[1] The Hortons live at the "rambling house at 280 Harris Avenue."[2]

The Hortons were the first family of *Days*: Tom and Alice Horton and their children: the twins, Tommy (originally called Dan in the "bible") and Addie, Mickey, Bill, and Marie. The story began with Tommy missing in Korea and presumed dead. Addie had moved to Europe with her wealthy husband,

---

Character names are not italicized in this chapter because the story line deals exclusively with the characters, not the actors.

Ben Olson, and their son, Steve, leaving their daughter, Julie, to be raised by Tom and Alice. Mickey was a successful lawyer, and Bill a brilliant surgeon. Marie was engaged to be married.

Julie felt abandoned by her parents and in the show's premier episode was caught shoplifting, an obvious bid for attention. Moreover, Julie searched for attention in all the wrong places. She fell in love with the older David Martin, and they became secretly engaged. However, Julie was soon devastated to discover that her best friend, Susan, was carrying his child. Susan married David with the understanding that they would divorce once the baby was born. Julie even agreed to act as maid of honor at the wedding. Susan never intended to keep her promise. However, Susan's happiness was short-lived as her infant son, Richard, died in an accident on a swing while David was watching him. A grief-stricken Susan, blaming David, shot and killed her husband!

Meanwhile, Bill Horton had fallen in love with a fellow intern, psychiatrist Dr. Laura Spencer. Their joy was cut short when Bill developed tuberculosis of the hand. Fearing he would be unable to remain a surgeon and feeling unworthy of Laura, Bill left Salem and moved to Pine Grove. While in Pine Grove, Bill met Mark Brooks, the town doctor. Mark recommended the surgery and therapy that eventually saved Bill's hand. Bill knew he was cured when his surgical skills saved a young boy from death. Bill's confidence was restored, and he and Mark returned to Salem.

When Susan Martin went on trial for David's murder she was defended by Mickey Horton. Mickey soon found himself falling in love with Susan's psychiatrist, Dr. Laura Spencer. Susan was acquitted on grounds of temporary insanity, and the bond that Mickey and Laura had formed in their common defense of Susan led to their marriage.

When Bill Horton returned to Salem, he was shocked to discover that his brother was married to the woman he loved. Working together at the hospital only increased the tension between Bill and Laura, and one night, in a drunken stupor, Bill raped Laura. Laura soon discovered she was pregnant, and a horrified Tom confronted her with the news that the child she was carrying could not be Mickey's. Unbeknownst to everyone save Tom, Mickey was sterile. Laura told Tom of the rape, and they vowed to keep their secret. Mickey was thrilled when "his" son, Michael, was born.

Marie's fiancé, Tony Merritt, had broken his engagement to Marie and left Salem. A heartbroken Marie turned to his father, Craig, for support. They eventually married, but the marriage did not last.

Dr. Mark Brooks was quickly accepted into the close-knit Horton family, especially by the newly divorced Marie. Mark returned her affections, and all seemed to be going well. But Bill and Tom were troubled by this seemingly mysterious young man. A variety of uncanny coincidences convinced Bill that there was more to Mark than met the eye. As it turned out, Dr. Mark Brooks was none other than his long-lost brother, Tommy Horton! It seemed Tommy had been a POW in Korea, tortured and so badly burned that he had had extensive reconstructive surgery on his face. The trauma of the war, the torture, and the surgery caused amnesia, and it was not until months after he returned to Salem that Mark (Tommy Horton) remembered the truth about his identity. While overjoyed to have her brother back alive, Marie was shocked and confused about having fallen in love with him. She turned to the church for comfort and eventually became a nun. Tommy, meanwhile, rediscovered his meddlesome wife Kitty, and their daughter, Sandy, both of whom had returned to Salem.

Kitty found a tape that had accidentally been made of Laura discussing her rape with Tom Horton. Kitty intended to use the tape against Bill and prove Michael's true parentage. Kitty and Bill struggled over the tape, and Kitty, who had a history of heart trouble, collapsed and died from a heart attack. Bill kept silent during the trial to protect Mickey from the truth of Michael's paternity. Bill was convicted of manslaughter and sent to prison.

Meanwhile, Julie Olson, distraught over David's death and pregnant with his child, went against her own feelings and gave up her son for adoption. Julie and David's child was adopted by Scott and Janet Banning and christened Brad. Joy soon turned to tragedy as the Bannings discovered Janet had a brain tumor and was dying. As chance would have it, their next-door neighbor was none other than Susan Martin, who was now Brad's regular, doting baby-sitter. Brad had become a substitute for the child she lost. Susan did not know that the boy was Julie and David's son. After Janet's death, Susan continued to care for Brad and soon found herself falling in love with Scott.

Tormented by the loss of her son and the thought that Susan, her hated rival, might become Brad's mother, Julie sued for his custody. The court took the baby from the widowed Scott and returned him to his birth mother, Julie, who renamed him David after his biological father. Meanwhile, Scott had grown so attached to the child that he agreed to marry Julie to remain the boy's father. Julie agreed to marry Scott to get even with Susan.

While in prison, Bill Horton met con man, adventurer, and singer Brent Douglas. Brent was enthralled by Bill's revelation that Salem's Susan Martin had inherited $250,000 after the death of her husband. When Brent was released from prison he raced to Salem, now calling himself Doug Williams, to woo Susan and her money. Susan was not interested in his obvious seduction, but instead had a counter plan. Susan offered money to Doug to romance Julie away from Scott Banning. The money was not needed, as Doug almost immediately fell in love with the beautiful Julie.

Julie's happiness was disrupted by her mother's reappearance. Addie Olson returned to Salem after the death of her husband in Paris. Her son, Steve, remained in France to finish his schooling. Julie could not hide her antagonism toward her mother. Julie felt twice rejected: first as a child when Addie left her in Salem, and second, when she, then pregnant, had gone to Paris seeking her mother's help and had been turned away. Therefore, Julie kept her private life a secret from Addie.

Addie, however, discovered Julie and Doug's liaison through a private investigator. Although she initially despised Doug for his seeming opportunism, Addie soon found herself attracted by Doug's charm and *joie de vivre*. Doug made Addie realize that her life with Ben had been nothing more than an empty shell. Desperate to discover true love and life, Addie asked Doug to marry her, on the same night he had quarreled bitterly with Julie. Both acted on impulse and eloped.

Doug and Addie's marriage became a love match, but Doug was still troubled. He knew Julie blamed herself for their breakup and his marriage to Addie, and was now willing to reunite with him at any cost. Despite Julie's ever-present threat, Addie strengthened her marriage to Doug by buying *Sergio's*, the club in which he sang, and renaming it *Doug's Place*. Their happiness increased when Addie became pregnant.

Julie realized that her life with Scott Banning was a sham and that Doug was her one true love. She began secret divorce proceedings. On the day she filed divorce papers, Scott died in a construction accident, killed on the site of a new structure he was building for architect and businessman Bob Anderson.

A guilt-ridden Julie turned to Bob Anderson and his wife, Phyllis, for support. However, Bob soon found his feelings for Julie more than paternal. Phyllis, unaware of Bob's feelings, turned to Julie for comfort when Bob informed her their 25-year marriage was over. Julie, however, still truly loved only one man: Doug, her mother's husband.

Julie resolved to make a new life for herself and agreed to marry her lawyer, Don Craig. What Julie did not know was that her mother, Addie, was dying of leukemia. The pregnant Addie refused chemotherapy for fear that it would harm her unborn child. She prayed for comfort and help and trusted in divine guidance. Addie vowed to keep her illness secret, but eventually everyone—except Julie—discovered the truth. Meanwhile, Addie's prayers were answered and she gave birth to a daughter, Hope. Julie finally learned of her mother's condition and rushed to the hospital. On her "death bed," Addie made Julie promise to take care of Doug and Hope. Julie and Don broke off their engagement. Miraculously, however, Addie went into remission. Poor Julie, while overjoyed at her mother's recovery, despaired of ever being with the man she loved. Deciding love would never be a part of her life, she cynically decided to marry wealthy Bob Anderson.

Phyllis Anderson was devastated to learn that her "best friend" had married Bob. Already disturbed by her divorce, Phyllis became even more emotionally distraught and tried to murder Julie. But in her troubled condition, Phyllis accidentally mistook her daughter, Mary, for Julie and shot Mary! Both Mary and Phyllis eventually recovered. Phyllis still harbored hopes of reconciling with Bob, especially when she noticed his marriage to Julie begin to crumble, but Bob encouraged Phyllis to be more independent, and he even helped her open her own boutique.

Julie's arch-rival, Susan Martin, was not faring any better. The night that Scott Banning left her for Julie, Susan had a sexual encounter in the park with a young stranger. Afterward she convinced herself she was raped. Using her inheritance, Susan bought a medical clinic offering free services, and she buried herself in her work to forget. When handsome Dr. Greg Peters began to help her run the clinic, Susan fell in love. However, to her horror, she discovered she was pregnant. She considered an abortion, but found she had uterine cancer. Dr. Tom Horton told her the child she was carrying would be her last, so she decided to keep the baby and tell Greg the truth—or what she believed to be the truth: that she had been raped and was now pregnant. A stunned Greg stood by her, and they eventually became engaged.

Everything seemed to be working out for Susan and Greg until she met his younger brother, novelist Eric Peters. Eric was the man in the park! Traumatized, Susan was finally made to realize, in therapy sessions with Laura, that she had willingly gone with Eric in the park and that her behavior was a result of losing both Scott and young David. Greg soon learned of the incident when he read a thinly veiled account of the episode in the park in Eric's novel, *In His Brother's Shadow*. Believing that Eric had raped Susan, a furious Greg assaulted his brother so badly that he needed hospitalization. A stunned Susan told Greg the truth of the encounter, he understood, and apologized to his brother. Greg and Susan were married, and little Anne was born. But Susan's memories of her night with Eric, plus the bond formed by their love for their daughter haunted Susan and begin to cause problems in her marriage. It also seemed Eric had fallen in love with Susan.

The lives of Bill, Laura, and Mickey continued to be unalterably entwined. After Bill returned from prison, Laura discovered the truth of his refusal to testify in court and of his struggle with Kitty Horton. Filled with compassion and love for Bill, Laura testified in a secret hearing before the medical board and got Bill's medical license reinstated.

Laura and Bill were in love, but did nothing about their feelings out of respect and love for Mickey and for each other. However, Mickey unjustly suspected them of having an affair and turned to his secretary, Linda Patterson, for comfort. Linda soon discovered she was pregnant, and both she and Mickey believed the child to be his. But Laura confronted her with the truth of Mickey's sterility. Linda eventually married the baby's real father, Jim Phillips, and left Salem.

Laura threatened to divorce Mickey, but decided against it when young Michael, overhearing his distraught mother and "Uncle" Bill declare their love for each other, ran into the street and got hit by a car. After the boy recovered, Laura decided to stay with Mickey, especially since Mickey's serious heart condition had been diagnosed.

Things might have worked out, but Michael discovered that Mickey had had an affair with Linda and that he had unjustly accused his mother and Bill. Mickey and Michael had a heated argument, which caused Mickey to have a near-fatal heart attack. His brother Bill, performing a brilliant emergency triple bypass, saved his life. However, Mickey, despondent about his health, Bill and Laura's love for each other, and his relationship with Michael, suffered a stroke, which resulted in amnesia. Alone in the hospital while everyone attended Greg and Susan's wedding, Mickey got up, got dressed, and disappeared.

He eventually found himself in Brookville on a farm owned by a beautiful redhead, Maggie Simmons. Maggie's parents, Elmer and Dorothy, had been killed in an automobile accident that left Maggie crippled. Mickey, remembering nothing of his past, called himself "Marty Hansen" because the initials "MH" were on his belt. Back in Salem, the Hortons and the Salem police department were frantically looking for Mickey. Although worried about Mickey, each day it became more and more difficult for Laura and Bill to deny their strong love for each other and live apart. Mickey also seemed to find peace and happiness with Maggie on the farm, and he married her. Maggie discovered the truth of Mickey's identity, but said nothing for fear of losing him. In Salem, Laura and Bill, having exhausted every effort to find Mickey, planned to marry.

Finally, Mickey's niece, Julie, saw a newspaper photo of a man who had just won a farming prize in a nearby town. The farmer looked exactly like Mickey, so Tom went to Brookville to see if, indeed, Marty was his missing son. The reunion was far from joyful because Mickey had no memory of his father or his life in Salem. When recent events were explained to him, he realized he had been a jealous and vindictive man and decided he would rather remain with Maggie on the farm than return to Salem for an operation that might restore his memory. Mickey and Laura agreed to a divorce, thus allowing Mickey and Maggie to remarry and Bill and Laura to marry.

Eventually, Maggie and Mickey returned to Salem for surgery that could enable Maggie to walk again. Being back in Salem was difficult for Mickey as bits and pieces of his forgotten past came back to haunt him. Linda Phillips came back to Salem to further complicate matters. She befriended Maggie to be near Mickey and did everything in her power to win back Mickey, including convince him that her daughter, Melissa, was his child. Jim Phillips, who had believed Linda wanted a reconciliation, discovered what was going on and intended to confront Mickey. But before he could reveal the truth of Melissa's paternity, Jim was killed in an automobile accident.

Mickey/Marty was soon to learn the truth himself. Michael had been spending time on the farm in hopes of becoming closer to his father. One day he had an accident and was rushed to the local hospital. He needed a transfusion. The doctors called Laura and told her to come to Brookville because her son needed a transfusion. Laura explained she was type O and the boy type A, so his father could be a donor. Not realizing that "Marty Hansen" thought he was Michael's father, the doctors told Mickey/Marty that he could not donate blood because his type B did not match Michael's. Mickey knew he could not be Michael's father!

Mickey spent the night checking medical records; Bill's blood type *did* match Michael's. His memory came flooding back as Mickey realized his beloved "son" Mike was really Bill's son. He went to Linda's apartment to find the truth about Melissa. Finally a distraught and desperate Mickey, gun in hand, went to Bill and Laura's home to wait for Bill. Bill, in surgery all day, was unaware of what had been happening. Mickey accused Bill of taking away everything that had ever been important in his life and shot him during a struggle. A confused Mickey then tried to strangle Laura and was finally taken to Bayview Sanitarium.

Laura, now pregnant, insisted she and Bill visit the sanitarium and, on the way back to Salem, got caught in a snowstorm. Laura went into labor, and their daughter, Jennifer Rose, was born in a nearby farmhouse with the assistance of its owner, Rosie Carlson. Rosie later became their housekeeper.

Bill rushed to Mickey's sanity hearing the next morning, bearing his own and Laura's written testimony, but to no avail; Mickey was committed. After the decision was read, Mickey's seeming calm evaporated, and all realized it was the right decision.

Michael (Mike), still hospitalized, was puzzled and hurt by his "father's" absence. Finally the family told him Mickey had regained his memory but was having problems adjusting. Mickey was brought in to see Mike. His visit helped Mike's recovery because Mike had no way of knowing that Mickey felt nothing for him. With Drs. Powell, Laura Horton, and Marlena Evans serving as his therapists, Mickey agreed not to reveal the reality of Mike's paternity to the boy, but in an irrational moment did so. Linda tried to cover, but failed. Mike later overheard Mickey tell another patient that Mike was not his son. Mike demanded the truth, and Bill gently explained that *he* was Mike's father, not Mickey. Mike was stunned and angry at his parents, and a distraught Laura went into a deep depression. Laura finally recovered because of Bill's constant devotion and therapy with Dr. Marlena Evans.

Maggie was terrified that she would lose Mickey forever following his hospitalization, and she had a secret to share. After several leg operations, she could now walk. Maggie had not previously told Mickey the truth because she feared he would return to Laura once he knew she could walk. But now the institutionalized Mickey could only brood about Laura and Bill; he did not even remember Maggie. Maggie decided that she had to show Mickey she could stand on her own two feet, both literally and figuratively, and that she deserved to be loved, not pitied. Maggie's patience, love, and understanding were rewarded when Mickey recovered and returned home to her.

In Salem, Julie's son, David, had become engaged to a young troublemaker,

Brooke Hamilton. Julie discovered she was pregnant with Bob Anderson's child. A stunned Julie decided to stay with Bob and keep the child. One day, overhearing Doug and Julie discussing the pregnancy, Brooke incorrectly assumed the baby was Doug's and spread the rumor. This false claim caused a rift between Julie and her grandmother, as Alice believed Julie had continued to have an affair with Doug after his marriage to Addie. The story also caused a fight between David and Julie.

Afterward, David rushed out of the house, got into his car, and had an accident. David was taken in by the Grants, a black family with whom he found the love and support he had missed his whole life. The Hortons, believing David dead, held a memorial service. When the Grants discovered who David really was, the father, Paul Grant, went to Julie with the truth. Julie, meanwhile, had fallen at the lake house and lost the baby.

Brooke soon discovered that she was pregnant with David's baby, but now David was living with the Grants and falling in love with their daughter, Valerie Grant. Brooke had other problems at home; her mother, Adele, was an alcoholic. In high school Adele had been involved with Bob Anderson, and Brooke soon discovered she was Bob's daughter. David finally decided to marry Brooke for the baby's sake, but Brooke realized how unhappy the decision made him and arranged for an abortion. Brooke, too, now turned to the Grants for solace, and the mother, Helen Grant, took Adele to a self-help alcoholics group. Adele, however, continued to drink, which complicated her medical problems. When Brooke discovered how serious her mother's condition was, she stole some blank checks from Anderson Manufacturing and planned a cruise for herself and her mother.

Paul Grant, Bob's bookkeeper, and David were the only two people with known access to the Anderson accounts, and both went under suspicion for embezzlement. Bob uncovered the truth before Brooke's cruise ship sailed, and he flew to New York to confront Brooke. There he found a dying Adele, who, on her deathbed, told Bob that he was Brooke's biological father. Bob decided not to prosecute Brooke, understanding why she had taken the money, and agreed to give her a job and let her pay back the money. Brooke, however, was injured in a car accident and did not survive.

David finally realized his love for Valerie and proposed. Her parents opposed the interracial marriage. But after much agonizing Valerie agreed to the engagement. Their happiness was short-lived. Valerie was offered a four-year medical scholarship at Howard University. David persuaded Valerie to accept the scholarship and move to Washington, D.C., but he vowed to continue their relationship.

Maggie and Mickey adopted a sweet little girl named Janice. One day, a mystery woman came to town and struck up a friendship with Janice, but the woman turned out to be Joanne Barnes, Janice's biological mother! It seemed that Joanne had given up Janice for adoption because Joanne believed herself to be terminally ill. When she discovered her daughter in Salem, Joanne wanted to see her one last time before she died. While in Salem, the Hortons discovered that Joanne could have an operation that would save her life. The Hortons agreed to pay for the operation (Joanne was poor) with the agreement that she leave Salem after her recovery and never tell Janice the truth.

Joanne's surgery was a complete success, but she did not leave Salem. Janice discovered the truth, and the confused child started to spend more and more time with Joanne. Maggie, unable to cope with the strain, began to drink. Joanne discovered Maggie's drinking problem and decided to sue for custody of Janice. Joanne had a strong legal case because of Maggie's drinking and Mickey's history of mental instability. Janice loved both Joanne and Maggie, and the strain took its toll on the little girl, who began to have nightmares. Maggie began to feel like an unfit mother, which caused her to drink even more. A bitter custody battle ensued and Joanne won, even though Maggie by then had sworn off drinking. Joanne took Janice to San Francisco. Maggie and Mickey were devastated, but found comfort in each other's arms.

Doug Williams was slowly recovering from the death of his wife. Addie had been killed in a car accident, sacrificing her own life to save her baby daughter, Hope. Doug had given Hope's care over to Tom and Alice while he grieved. But now he wanted Hope back, and he needed someone to care for her, so he hired Rebecca North as his housekeeper. Rebecca's husband and child had been killed in a car crash, and Rebecca desperately wanted another child. Doug, mourning for Addie, wanted a baby brother or sister for his little princess. Doug arranged for an artificial insemination with an unknown surrogate mother. He had no way of knowing that woman was Rebecca.

Rebecca used the money to send her boyfriend, Johnny Collins, to study art in Paris and told everyone that the baby was his and that she would give it up for adoption. Because the baby was Doug's, Rebecca knew she would end up raising the child herself. However, Robert LeClere, Doug's best friend, assistant manager, and singer at *Doug's Place*, knew none of this. He loved Rebecca and, thinking she would be forced to give up her child, contacted Johnny in Paris. Johnny returned to Salem and, believing the baby to be his, asked Rebecca to marry him. Rebecca was thrilled when her doctor, Neil Curtis, told her that Doug no longer wanted the child because of his increasing closeness to Julie and his hope that he and Julie would one day have their own children.

Neil also convinced Rebecca to tell Johnny the truth. She did, but Johnny could not handle it and left her at the altar, leaving behind a note of explanation in the apartment they planned to share. Robert stepped in and married Rebecca, hoping one day she would return his love. He even helped in the natural childbirth of little Dougie. Rebecca and Robert might have been happy, but Johnny returned. Torn between love and loyalty, Rebecca finally fled Salem with Johnny and the baby, leaving behind a heartbroken Robert.

Meanwhile, Greg and Susan's marriage had fallen apart. Greg blamed it on

Susan's frigidity, but she blamed it on Greg's growing involvement with the beautiful and wealthy Amanda Howard. Amanda had been having a passionate love affair with Dr. Neil Curtis while her older, wealthy husband was still alive. After her husband's death, a guilt-ridden Amanda broke off her relationship with Neil. However, she eventually realized she loved him and agreed to marry him. But, on the night before their wedding, she found him with another woman.

Neil was a compulsive gambler and, after losing Amanda, turned his charms on the well-to-do Phyllis Anderson because he needed money to pay his gambling debts. Neil and Phyllis married the night that Amanda realized she loved Neil unconditionally. Amanda called his service and left a message saying she would marry him any time, any place. Knowing that Amanda loved him, the newlywed Neil was unable to consummate his marriage to Phyllis.

Phyllis tried to buy the new chief of staff position at University Hospital for Neil, and he was furious at her bribe attempt. But the night of the hospital dinner, to the surprise of Phyllis and the entire Horton clan, Tom Horton was given a gold watch for 35 years meritorious, service and Dr. Greg Peters was named new chief of staff! Tom was crushed, but tried to hide his disappointment from his family. Alone in the living room, Tom suffered a stroke. Tommy found Tom, who was rushed to University Hospital. Fearing his father would not live, Tommy called Marie and asked her to leave the convent and return to Salem. Tom survived and eventually made a complete recovery due to the constant attention and devotion of his family, especially Marie.

Soon Amanda was diagnosed as having a brain tumor. She refused surgery because her mother had died following a similar operation. Neil and Greg joined forces to convince Amanda to have the surgery and want to live. Amanda finally had the operation and made a full recovery, despite some initial confusion and memory loss.

Susan gave Greg a divorce so he would be free to marry Amanda. She then moved to California with Eric, whom she loved, and their daughter, Anne. Unaware of Amanda's condition, Phyllis became increasingly jealous. Phyllis soon discovered she was pregnant and, afraid that Neil was not happy, went to Chicago for an abortion. Unable to get one, Phyllis considered an overdose, but Neil arrived, assured her he was happy about the baby, and they returned to Salem. Neil was stunned when he then discovered that Amanda had accepted Greg's proposal of marriage. He got drunk, was mean to Phyllis, propositioned her daughter, Mary, and passed out. Phyllis tried to move her drunken husband and went into premature labor. Despite all efforts, the premature infant, Nathan, died.

After Addie's death, the grieving Doug had been cheered by the friendship of the new singer at *Doug's Place*, Jeri Clayton. Jeri left town when her husband, Jack, told her daughter, Trish, that Jeri had once been a prostitute. When her mother left, Trish had Don Craig trace her father, James Stanhope. But

James wanted nothing to do with his daughter. Jeri returned to Salem in an effort to reunite Trish and her father, but she, too, failed. A frustrated Trish, feeling unloved, turned to her platonic roommate, Mike Horton. Their attempt at love-making was a disaster, and Mike fled the apartment in humiliation.

Linda Phillips, his "father's" former lover, discovered that Mike's failure with Trish had convinced him that he might be homosexual, so she took him to bed to "prove his manhood." Linda was unprepared for Mike's newborn obsession with her. Trish, upset by her encounter with Mike, found solace in David's arms. David, who believed his relationship with Valerie to be over, welcomed Trish's attentions.

Jack Clayton, Trish's stepfather, had been lurking outside the apartment the night Trish and David spent together and became obsessed with finding out whether she was still a virgin. He began writing anonymous threatening notes to her. One night he broke into the apartment and attempted to rape Trish. A hysterical Trish hit him with an iron. Mike returned home to find Trish wearing only a slip, shaking and incoherent. Jack lay dead on the floor. When the police arrived, Mike claimed he was the one who hit Jack. Unable to cope with the trauma, Trish developed a multiple-personality disorder. During the trial and through therapy sessions with Laura, Trish remembered what really happened and the truth finally came out. During the ordeal, Mike and Trish discovered how much they truly loved each other and vowed to spend the rest of their lives together.

Doug and Julie made yet another attempt at making a life together when their plans were destroyed by the return of Doug's first wife, Kim. Julie did not even know Doug had been previously married, and Kim's claim that their divorce had never been finalized was too much for Julie. All the complications threw Julie into the arms of lawyer Don Craig, a widower who had lost his first wife and their daughter, Betsy, in a tragic automobile accident. When Julie accepted Don's proposal, Doug retaliated by proposing to Kim.

The two mismatched couples constantly made clashing wedding plans. On the night before Julie's wedding, Doug took Addie's treasured clown pin to her; returning home, he had a car accident. Instead of going to her own wedding, Julie rushed to Doug's side. Don, realizing Julie's heart would always belong to Doug, told Julie to go to the man she truly loved. Doug and Julie were finally married in a beautiful ceremony. They recited their own vows, and Doug gave Addie's pearls to Julie as a wedding present, knowing Addie would want them to be together and happy.

Meanwhile, Don Craig found consolation in the arms of Dr. Marlena Evans. When Marlena's identical twin sister, Samantha, made a surprise visit to Salem, the sisters' old rivalry was renewed. Samantha was a medical school dropout who became a non-working actress. Samantha blamed Marlena for the ills of her life. By Machiavellian manipulations, the now mentally ill Samantha managed to get her sister, Marlena, committed to an institution as "Samantha," while Samantha passed herself off as Dr. Marlena Evans. Samantha fooled everyone for a while, but was eventually discovered, and Marlena was rescued.

Marlena's ordeal had repercussions for her close friends Bill and Laura Horton. Marlena was so shaken by her terrifying incarceration that she needed extensive help. Laura began devoting so much time to Marlena that she began to ignore her own husband. Bill turned to Dr. Kate Winograd, head of anesthesiology at University Hospital, for friendly companionship.

Neil and Phyllis Curtis' marriage crumbled after the death of their son, when Phyllis discovered Neil had had a brief affair with Mary. Phyllis divorced Neil and briefly left Salem on a world tour. Mary Anderson became involved with Chris Kositchek, the foreman in her father's construction firm. She was upset when her father, Bob Anderson, married the gold-digging Linda Phillips.

Meanwhile, Bob's illegitimate daughter, Brooke, presumed dead in a car crash, returned to Salem with a new face (thanks to reconstructive surgery) and a new name: Stephanie Woodruff. Linda and Stephanie tried to destroy Chris' career at Anderson Manufacturing. Linda further betrayed Bob by sleeping with Neil. When Chris bought Mary an engagement ring without consulting her, they fought and Chris found comfort in the arms of Amanda Peters, who was estranged from her husband, Greg. Their passionate affair finally ended, and Amanda returned to Greg.

Greg and Amanda left Salem, but not before Greg recommended that he be replaced as chief of staff by Tom Horton. The Hortons confronted new challenges as Alice was diagnosed as possibly having cancer. But exploratory surgery by Dr. Walter Griffen eventually proved that the Horton's prayers had been answered and that Alice was fine.

Doug and Julie Williams faced problems, as well, when the liquor license on *Doug's Place* was revoked. Business begin to suffer and a rival night club owner, Larry Atwood, lured away their best singers and the customers. Larry, a hoodlum, had gotten the liquor license revoked, but promised to get it back if Julie would sleep with him. When she refused, he raped her. Several days later, he was found dead and Julie was accused of his murder. Ultimately, Larry's henchman, Arlo, confessed to the crime.

Julie eventually recovered from the trauma of the rape and opened an antique shop, *Chez Julie*, with her brother, Steven, who had returned to Salem. Steven caused problems for a number of Salemites with his often nefarious dealings and finally left town.

Meanwhile, Valerie called off her engagement to Julie's son, David, and returned to D.C. to bury herself in her studies. David hastily married the pregnant Trish, but even the birth of their son, Timmy, could not resolve their differences. Trish realized she was really in love with Michael Horton. Unable to cope with all her problems, Trish again developed a multiple personality disorder. Trish finally left for Europe, hoping to find peace there.

She eventually returned to Salem and wanted to reunite with David and their son, now called Scotty. David was at first reticent, but eventually his love for Trish won out, and they began to live together as husband and wife. Mike, meanwhile, had fallen in love with and married Margo Anderman, a young woman in remission from leukemia.

Don Craig decided to run for the state Senate. During his campaign, a woman named Lorraine Farr Temple arrived in Salem, claiming Don was the father of her child, Donna. Don lost the election because of the scandal, but Lorraine fled Salem, leaving behind Donna. Don, meanwhile, had proposed to Marlena, and she accepted. But on their wedding day, the wedding had to be stopped when Donna threatened to commit suicide by jumping off a ledge at the Salem Inn. Don rushed to Donna and helped save her, but fell off the ledge himself as he hoisted Donna to safety. Bill Horton's brilliant surgical skill saved Don, who then took full responsibility for Donna as her legal father. Donna became pregnant from a one-night stand with Pete Curtis, but miscarried the baby after a motorcycle accident. Donna then mistakenly got involved in a pornographic photo ring and finally left town to go live with Don Craig's parents.

Bill and Laura's marriage was threatened when Laura began behaving strangely. Her mother, who had been in a mental institution for years, committed suicide, and Laura blamed herself. The guilt began to consume her, and she started to have visions of her mother, who told her what to do. Her behavior, both personal and professional, became erratic. She dangled Jennifer Rose from a window and told her to reach for the moon, but Rosie grabbed the child before Laura could drop her. Then Laura, on instructions from her mother, put Jennifer Rose alone on a bus headed to Dayton, Ohio. Luckily, Jennifer was found and returned unharmed. Laura was distraught over what she had done. This, coupled with the fact that she had become erroneously convinced that Bill was having an affair with Kate Winograd, persuaded Laura, again at her mother's instruction, to commit suicide. Laura took an overdose of pills and fashioned a noose to hang herself. Bill rushed in and saved her just in time, but now he knew that Laura was beyond his help and reluctantly agreed to send her to Lakewood Sanitarium.

Doug and Julie were also suffering. First Rebecca and Johnny died in a plane crash in Tokyo, Japan. Fortunately, little Dougie was not with them. In a letter she left in case of her demise, Rebecca told Doug that little Dougie was really his son. But, with Doug's consent, Robert gained custody of the boy. Dougie returned to Salem, where Robert renamed him Charles.

Meanwhile, one night at the farm while Maggie and Julie were preparing dinner, a grease fire erupted and Julie was badly burned on the throat, chest, and face. She required a tracheotomy due to smoke inhalation, as well as dialysis, hydrotherapy, and skin grafts for injuries sustained in the fire. Julie, feeling ugly and worthless, convinced herself that Doug remained married to her for pity's sake, and she flew to Mexico for a divorce. After much counseling from Dr.

Jordan Barr and several reconstructive surgeries, Julie's scars, both mental and physical, were finally lifted.

In the meantime, however, Doug married the scheming Lee Dumonde. Lee had come to town when she discovered Doug was the long-lost twin brother of her late husband, wealthy Byron Carmichael. When Byron died, Doug inherited all his money, and Lee wanted that money. Lee seduced Doug into marrying her. Doug believed he was helping his beloved Julie by letting her go. Lee soon realized that Doug would always love Julie and conspired to have them both murdered by hitman Brent Cavanaugh. Julie was shot, but survived the attack.

When her evil plan failed, Lee decided to kill Julie herself. Just as she was about to hit Julie from behind, Lee suffered a stroke and was paralyzed. Doug vowed never to leave her, believing he was the cause of her stroke, and told Julie he would never divorce Lee as long as she was paralyzed. Doug and Julie agreed they would not talk about divorce until Lee recovered. Lee continued to use her condition as an excuse to hold onto Doug, even though Julie realized it was deliberate subterfuge.

It seemed that Doug had lost all he held dear when Robert decided to move back to Paris and take little Dougie (Charles) with him. Doug closed *Doug's Place*, but eventually opened a new club. A casino built on the old Chisolm Mansion, it was called *Doug's Place on the Lake*.

Bill also left Salem. Laura had won her long, hard battle with her illness with Bill's constant love and support and finally recovered. Laura was released from the sanitarium, but decided she needed to make a fresh start, rather than return to Salem where her patients knew of her breakdown. Laura accepted a position at an out-of-town clinic, and Bill followed to be with his wife.

Julie grew tired of waiting for Doug and decided she had to move on with her life. She started dating Brad Connors, never knowing that he was really Brent Cavanaugh, Lee's hitman, with a new face after reconstructive surgery. Brent felt he had to complete the job he had begun for Lee. Besides, he was blackmailing Lee for $80,000, threatening to reveal her part in the murder scheme if she did not cooperate. Salem newcomer Liz Chandler, who had known Lee, finally revealed the truth: Lee had been a prostitute in Atlanta, and Brent, her pimp.

Lee, meanwhile, having undergone complete psychiatric and rehabilitative therapy, was horrified to realize what she had done. Eventually, Brent trapped Lee and Julie in the penthouse, and just as he was getting ready to kill Julie (and probably Doug, who had come to rescue Julie, and Lee, as well), Lee arose from her wheelchair and hit Brent over the head with a silver dumbbell! After that, Lee finally agreed to divorce Doug. She was then sent to an institution for her own good.

Doug proposed to his fair lady, Julie, and she accepted. But on Doug and Julie's wedding day, Lee was released from the institution and tried to stop the wedding. As Trish entertained the guests with song, Lee stole into Julie's room.

When Doug sang "Till There Was You," and Julie missed her cue to walk down the aisle, Doug knew something was wrong. He found the two women together. He told Lee she would never again hurt them, and he locked her in the room. Doug and Julie returned to their wedding and once again became husband and wife. The reunited pair then left on Doug's private jet for a honeymoon in Japan.

Meanwhile, Mike, trying to buy a house, overextended his credit and went into debt to loan shark Earl. When Mike could not pay his debts and tried to break off the deal and find evidence to put Earl in jail, Earl had Margo thrown down a flight of stairs as a warning. Margo recovered from the fall, but her health failed anyway. She came out of remission and finally died after a long and valiant struggle with leukemia.

Alex Marshall, a new arrival in Salem, pretended to be in love with Stephanie Woodruff in order to obtain information about Anderson Manufacturing. Marie Horton, who had known Alex in earlier days, suspected he was up to no good. When his plans with Stephanie failed, Alex wooed and won Mary Anderson. After Mary left him for Alex, Chris felt forsaken and betrayed. But he soon fell in love with attorney Leslie James.

On Alex and Mary's wedding day, Bob Anderson died of a heart attack. Alex tried to gain control of Bob's company. He was aided and abetted by David, who was so overcome with guilt at his own treachery that he began to drink heavily. Finally, David and Scotty left town and moved to Los Angeles. Mary eventually learned of her husband's true motives for marriage and divorced him.

Sister Marie was upset that Alex remained in Salem. Years earlier, in Manhattan, they had had a sadomasochistic relationship that had been laced with drug use. Marie had even witnessed the death of Alex's brother, Harley, after he plunged from a window following a fight with Alex. Even now Marie wondered if it was an accident or murder. Marie feared Alex would someday discover the truth: after their illicit affair, Marie had given birth to his daughter.

Don and Marlena were now happily married and celebrating the birth of their son, Don Jr., called D.J. But their happiness soon turned to despair as the infant died, a victim of Sudden Infant Death Syndrome (SIDS). Marlena and Don seemed to drift apart, and Don turned to Liz Chandler in his grief and confusion. Neil Curtis, Liz's former lover, was unhappy, for he was still in love with Liz. He took solace in gambling, running up higher and higher debts.

Marie did everything in her power to keep newcomer Jessica Blake from discovering that Marie was her mother and Alex Marshall her father. Alex and Marie took a trip to Montreal, to the orphanage where Jessica was placed for adoption. During their flight, their small plane crashed in the snowbound mountain wilderness. Forced to struggle for survival, Alex realized Marie was his true love and did everything he could to save her. Safely returned to Salem, they slowly rekindled their love for each other.

Chris Kositchek's romance with Leslie came to an abrupt halt, and she left Salem. Chris opened a health club, *The Body Connection,* with his new friend Joshua Fallon. Then Lee Dumonde's sister, Renee, who had recently arrived in Salem, tried to seduce Chris, thinking he was going to get rich from the sale of one of his inventions. Chris resisted. He was soon joined in Salem by his brother, Jake Kositchek.

As Don turned to Liz Chandler for comfort, Marlena turned to Liz's father, Kellam Chandler. Kellam was especially good to Marlena's newly adopted son, Johnny. Ultimately, Marlena realized she was not in love with Kellam and rejected his marriage proposal. An enraged Kellam raped Marlena. Afterward, Marlena phoned Don, but Liz answered the phone. Marlena then called her friend Joshua Fallon, who had been previously revealed to be the son of Kellam's murdered wife, Sunny. Joshua got a gun and went to the Chandler Mansion to confront Kellam with his rape of Marlena and murder of Sunny. But Joshua could not pull the trigger. Kellam got the gun and just as he was ready to shoot Joshua, Tod Chandler rushed in and grabbed his father's arm. They struggled, the gun went off, and Kellam fell dead to the floor.

Mary was a constant threat to Alex and Marie. Now divorced from Alex she could not stand to see him with another woman, especially a former nun. Mary discovered the truth of Jessica's parentage and made sure Jessica did as well. In response to the news, Jessica went to the convent to become a nun, but soon returned to Salem.

Eventually, unable to bear the truth about her parents, Jessica developed a split personality. During the day she was Jessica, but at night she was the bewitching Angelique, a "wanton woman" who was attracted to Jake Kositchek. Angelique secretly harassed Alex and Marie. Finally, Jake and Angelique went to Las Vegas to marry, but Marie stopped the ceremony just in time. Marie explained to Jake that Angelique was really Jessica, whom Jake had never met. Jessica was hospitalized, and a third personality, Sister Angelique, appeared. Jessica eventually recovered.

Meanwhile, Maggie, knowing Mickey would never be able to father a child, discussed the possibility of becoming a surrogate mother. Her doctor, Neil Curtis, warned her about the psychological problems involved, but Maggie insisted she could handle it and soon became pregnant. Mickey supported her decision. Meanwhile, Stuart Whyland arrived in Salem as the new hospital administrator. His son, Dr. Evan Whyland, also joined the staff at University Hospital.

Neil talked with Evan and was surprised to learn that Evan's wife, Ellen, died in a car accident, but not before she and Evan decided to participate in the surrogate-mother program. Evan determined that Maggie was carrying his child and told Neil that he wanted to fight for custody. Maggie did not know she was carrying Evan's baby. Neil told Maggie she was expecting twins and the Hortons thought to fight to keep one baby and give the other to the surrogate parents. Maggie eventually gave birth to a beautiful baby girl, Sarah (Neil had misdiagnosed twins).

Don and Marlena's marriage did not survive the death of their son and his affair with Liz. Liz and Don turned to each other for comfort and were married. Marlena took a job on a nighttime radio show and immersed herself in her work. One night she got a phone call from a man who said he was on the verge of murder and begged her to stop him! Marlena tried to keep him on the phone and stop the killing, but her efforts proved fruitless.

Trish wanted to see her son again and tracked down Scotty and David, who were living in San Diego. While watching David and Scotty play, Trish saw David wearing a gun and became convinced he was involved in some dirty dealings. Trish kidnapped Scotty and returned to Salem. David followed, still working for the man for whom he had worked in California, Stuart Whyland. Back in Salem, David apologized to Chris for hurting him during the plant takeover and asked that they all work together at Anderson's.

While David was in California, Trish grew closer to Mike. Now both men declared their love for Trish and vowed to fight for her. Trish decided to divorce David and accept Mike's marriage proposal.

Meanwhile, Alex Marshall was shot three times. Although there were many suspects (including Mary, for finally realizing Alex used her and never loved her and Tod Chandler for wanting to marry Jessica against Alex's will and for Alex's attempted hostile takeover of his plant), all evidence seemed to point to David Banning, whom Renee had seen at the scene of the crime, holding a gun while standing over Alex. It was soon discovered that Alex had been blackmailing David about his dealings in San Diego. Unknown to David, he had been making drug deliveries.

David was arrested for shooting Alex (who survived but retained no memory of the shooting). During the trial David said that he was an innocent victim in the drug deals. He had not known he was delivering drugs; he had thought he was delivering sealed packages. The judge promised leniency if David named names, but at the start of the trial, henchmen had threatened to harm Trish and Scotty if David talked. David was found guilty and sentenced to seven years in prison.

Renee overheard the threats made against David's life and on her radio show, she publicly apologized to David for testifying against him. On the way to the state prison, David, who was convinced he would be killed, escaped. The drug dealers panicked and tried to kidnap Trish and Scotty, but Mike foiled the attempt. Renee figured out where David was hiding. First she went to him because she thought she could make a fortune on his exclusive story, but later she came to care for him.

Mike followed Renee and, finding David's hideout, offered to help his cousin. However, a hitman discovered David and shot him. David, wounded, escaped and Nick removed the bullet. Soon most of Salem was on a quest to

Doug Williams (Bill Hayes) and *Bill Horton* (Ed Mallory) prepare a number (c. 1970). Courtesy Bill Hayes.

help David and discover the identity of the gunman who shot Alex. Julie, Doug, the recently returned Valerie Grant, Danny Grant, Mike, Trish, and policemen Roman Brady and Abe Carver all vowed to clear David. David was finally persuaded to give himself up, but Roman later allowed him to escape to catch the real killer. In a dramatic showdown, Abe Carver, now in love with Valerie, saved David's life by taking five bullets meant for David. Neil and Evan operated and saved Abe's life.

Stefano DiMera and his son, Count Anthony DiMera, became Salem's newest heroes when they turned over Stuart Whyland, the hospital administrator, as head of the organized crime syndicate. Stefano was really the head of the syndicate, and it was under his orders that Alex finally revealed that Stuart was the man behind the murder attempt. Stuart, held prisoner by Stefano in Rome, was made to "pay" for his misdeeds.

Alex, under further orders from DiMera, again began to romance Mary. This time he wanted to persuade her to sell Anderson Manufacturing to the DiMeras. Alex also took over as hospital administrator. Not everything was going well for Alex, however. When Marie discovered Alex's affair with Mary, she ended their relationship and began to date Neil Curtis.

Stefano controlled not only Alex, but Tony's wife, Liz, as well. It seemed Tony and Liz had been married in Europe, and their divorce never finalized. Now Stefano wanted an heir. When Liz refused to leave Neil and return to Tony, Stefano had a bomb sent to Neil. As Neil lay near death, Liz returned to her husband to save her beloved Neil. Liz soon discovered she was pregnant. Tony believed the baby to be his, but Liz knew Neil was the father. Neil vowed to destroy the DiMeras. Don, no longer married to the already married Liz, took Gwen Davies, Evan Whyland's attorney, as his lover.

Meanwhile, Marlena was tormented by strange phone calls and death threats. Detective Roman Brady was assigned to protect her and moved into her house, vowing to sleep in a sleeping bag on her living room floor until the strangler was caught. Although initially antagonistic toward one another, Marlena and Roman realized their growing attraction. But their relationship was complicated by the so-called Salem Strangler who was on a murderous rampage. Eugene Bradford, a former patient of Marlena's, was the prime suspect. Fearing the strangler might try to kill her, Marlena sent Johnny, for his own protection, to live with her parents in Colorado. Roman decided Marlena should leave town as well, for her protection.

However, the Salem Strangler, revealed to be Jake Kositchek, thought he saw Marlena in her home and made his move. He strangled "Marlena" and ran away. Roman returned to find her limp body and cried in anguish that he would find Jake. Much to his astonishment, it turned out that it was not Marlena who was strangled, but her twin sister, Samantha!

Jake attempted to kill Renee but was unsuccessful. However, Renee saw his face and could identify him. Shocked by the revelation, Renee blocked the memory from her mind. This bought Jake the time he needed. This time he found Marlena alone in the carriage house. He had the scarf wrapped around her neck when Roman burst in, saved Marlena and killed Jake. Chris was distraught that he had been unable to save his brother.

Jessica, in her grief, turned to Joshua Fallon for comfort. They were eventually wed, and Jessica's cousin, Sandy Horton, returned to Salem for the wedding. Joshua and Jessica finally left Salem to begin their new life away from memories of the past.

Julie Williams (Susan Seaforth Hayes) and *Dave, the waiter* (Don Frabotta), who was a fixture at Doug's Place (in all its incarnations) for nearly 20 years (c. 1974). Courtesy Susan Seaforth Hayes.

One of the strangler's many victims was Mary Anderson. In her will, Mary left half of her estate to her mother, Phyllis, and half to her "sister" Melissa Anderson (Linda Phillips' daughter, who became an Anderson when Linda married Bob). Alex now pursued Phyllis. Phyllis finally sold her half of Anderson to Stefano and left town. Chris returned to the plant as plant manager and vowed to protect Melissa's interests. At Marlena's suggestion, Chris hired Eugene Bradford, engineer and inventor, to work for him. Maggie and Mickey legally got custody of Melissa, and her natural mother, Linda, finally left town.

Mike and Trish broke their engagement. Mike began to date Kayla Brady, Roman's sister. Trish became involved with a singer named Woody and eventually left town. Mike finally decided to leave Salem to go to medical school, and Kayla started to date David.

Renee was shocked to discover that the man she now loved, Tony DiMera, was her half-brother. Lee revealed that she was, in fact, not Renee's sister, but her mother, and Stefano was Renee's father! Lee left town. Renee vowed to find another man and made a play for David Banning. David's current girlfriend, Kayla, was dismayed. Both women used Scotty to try to win his father's affections. Renee triumphed and became engaged to David. Kayla began to date Chris. When he flew to Los Angeles on business, she followed, and they became lovers.

On Renee and David's wedding day, Tony revealed to his mother, Daphne, that he was still in love with Renee. Daphne confessed that Renee and Tony were not related because Stefano was not really Tony's father. Tony rushed to the church to stop the ceremony, but it was too late. Renee and David were married.

Robert LeClere returned to Salem, on the run from the DiMeras. It seemed that he had agreed to do a job for a woman he loved, but, as it turned out, he was illegally transferring money from Italy to Switzerland. Both of his helpers were now dead, and Robert feared he was next. So Robert had fled Europe, leaving Dougie (Charles) safely behind in a Swiss boarding school.

Marlena was saddened to return Johnny to his biological mother, who now wanted him back. Roman proposed, and Marlena joyfully accepted. Their happiness was interrupted when Roman's "dead" wife Anna returned with their daughter Carrie (Caroline). Anna claimed that she had nearly drowned in a boating accident and, unbeknownst to Roman, had been saved by a nearby yacht. But her rescuers turned out to be evil people who, after Carrie's birth, forced her into white slavery and a life of prostitution on board the yacht. The undernourished and weakened Anna, with scars from whiplashes on her back, was further diagnosed as having multiple sclerosis. Roman stayed with Marlena, but he was plagued by guilt. However, it was ultimately revealed that the yacht story was a lie and that Anna worked for Stefano! A scorned Anna vowed revenge on Roman with the DiMeras' help.

Evan proposed to Sandy Horton, and she accepted. Unbeknownst to Sandy, Evan had all his late father's information on the DiMeras and was blackmailing Stefano for $1 million. Evan hid the key to the safe deposit box in which the information was stored in baby Sarah's rattle. But the baby's nanny, Delia, hired by Stefano, found the key and gave it to Stefano. With the information safely in his possession, Stefano had no reason to keep Evan alive and ordered him killed. Maggie finally discovered that Evan was Sarah's father, but Evan was killed shortly thereafter. His dying words were "Caracas" and "Stefano."

Mickey flew to Caracas hot on the trail of the DiMera secrets, vowing to discover the connection between Stefano and Evan. However, he was welcomed to Caracas by Stefano and his men and was captured. Stefano held Mickey prisoner, to be used as a bargaining chip if anything went wrong with DiMera's plans. Photos were sent to Maggie in Salem, telling of Mickey's "death." A funeral was held with an empty coffin, and a devastated Maggie turned to Don Craig for support.

Roman was discovered to be more than he appeared. He was, in fact, an agent for the ISA (International Security Alliance) investigating DiMera and his evil empire. Stefano feared that Roman could destroy his organized crime syndicate.

It seemed that most of Salem was now after Stefano. Doug and Julie discovered that there were coded maps of the lake area belonging to the late Stuart

Whyland. The couple faked a separation to try to discover what was hidden under *Doug's Place* and why Stefano wanted it so badly that he offered to buy the casino and the land beneath it. Stefano romanced Julie as she probed for information. Doug and Julie ultimately discovered that titanium was in the land beneath the club.

Julie, Doug, and Robert also searched for one of Stefano's ex-mistresses, hoping that she had information that could bring DiMera to justice. The search involved a madam named Foxy Humdinger, and Julie was mistakenly arrested for prostitution. When Julie's attorney, Don, arrived and demanded to know what was going on, the threesome revealed their plans. Don resigned as D.A. and joined Julie, Doug, and Robert to fight Stefano. The group uncovered a one-word clue, "Ridgecrest."

Roman was framed by DiMera as a drug dealer, and Eugene and Marlena united to prove his innocence. Stefano ordered Alex to arrange to choose someone to "pay" for Roman's pursuit. Roman's sister Kayla was poisoned, and Chris joined the fight against Stefano. The next intended victim was Alice Horton, but a programming error in Chris and Eugene's robot, Sico, reprogrammed to poison Alice, saved her. Alex and Anna began to worry and decided to join forces; they became lovers.

Roman and Marlena were to be married. On the wedding day, as Roman stood waiting for his bride at the altar, a DiMera hitman almost shot him. But Roman was saved by a warning delivered by his friend Eugene. It seemed Eugene was psychic, and his sixth sense saved Roman. The plan thwarted, Roman and Marlena were married. However, Don Craig, disguised as Roman, went on the honeymoon as Roman stayed in Salem to go undercover. Roman convinced the assassin from the church to confess everything he knew about Stefano and his organization. Evidence mounted as most of Salem worked against Stefano.

Fearing Roman and Abe were closing in on him, Stefano took Liz hostage. Chris tried to stop Stefano and was shot and wounded, but Neil performed surgery and saved Chris' life. DiMera and his hostage escaped through the tunnels that were found to connect the DiMera Mansion (formerly the Chandler Mansion) to the wine cellar at Doug's Place on the Lake. As Stefano and Liz emerged from the secret passage, they stumbled onto Marlena. Stefano nabbed Marlena as well, who left behind her scarf as a clue.

Stefano took Marlena and Liz to his secret hideout, Ridgecrest. The two women almost escaped, but Liz went into labor. Back in Salem, everyone compared notes and realized the mysterious "Ridgecrest" must be where Stefano had taken his prisoners. Alice Horton finally realized that Ridgecrest was the former name of Mountain View, a spot up in the hills outside Salem. Roman and Abe headed for Ridgecrest, closely followed by Neil.

At the hideout, Stefano decreed that Marlena would deliver Liz's baby. However, Neil, who had sneaked into the hideaway with Marlena's assistance, delivered his beloved Liz's baby girl, Noel, never realizing she was his daughter. Liz then slipped into a coma caused by kidney malfunction. Stefano fled, taking Marlena with him. Neil called the paramedics and rushed Liz to the hospital where he performed emergency surgery. Meanwhile, Stefano tried to escape in a helicopter with Marlena. Roman foiled the attempt, and Stefano was finally captured.

Roman had Stefano thrown in prison. While awaiting trial, Stefano was visited by his faithful daughter Renee, but during her visit he collapsed and died of a stroke. Tony comforted Renee. But now Anna planned to make a move on poor, lonely Tony. Roman and Marlena began their long-delayed honeymoon. And to start their married life, they bought a house, a "fixer-upper" next to Tom and Alice.

Mickey finally managed to escape from his South American prison and return home to Salem. His joy was short-lived, however, as he found his wife now in love with his best friend, Don. A confused Maggie was torn between the two men. When it appeared that she would choose Don, Mickey arranged for it to appear that Don and Gwen Davies were having an affair. Maggie returned to Mickey. The couple planned to renew their wedding vows, but Maggie could not go through with the ceremony and returned to Don. Mickey confessed his scheme to Maggie and Don and bowed out of the picture. But now Don was hurt by Maggie's lack of faith and was not eager to resume the relationship. But Don and Maggie eventually reunited and took a trip to Maui, where they made love.

Liz confessed to Tony that Noel was Neil's child, and Tony divorced Liz. He then tried to win back Renee, but she spurned his efforts, determined to remain loyal to David, by whom she was now pregnant. But she soon lost her baby in a riding accident. Tony, distraught and vulnerable, was easy prey for Anna Brady, Roman's ex-wife. Anna tricked a drunken and drugged Tony into marrying her.

Renee and David's marriage began to disintegrate, largely because of Stefano's will. According to the terms of the will, Renee and Tony were required to live together as siblings in the DiMera mansion for one year, but Renee was also required to stay married to David for that same year. Also, the first legitimate male heir born to Tony or Renee would inherit $5 million! Tony and David wanted nothing to do with this arrangement, but the two women squared off, willing to do whatever it took to get the money. Before long, Anna fell in love with Tony and became pregnant with his child. Anna miscarried the child in a boating accident arranged by the jealous Renee. Tony finally discovered Anna's deception and divorced her, even though she swore she loved him.

Neil saw what he believed to be the happy family of Tony, Liz, and Noel. Seemingly rejected by Liz, Neil married Marie Horton. But the next day he discovered that Liz's baby was his and that Liz had given him up in order to save him from Stefano. Liz and Neil were again drawn together. Liz did everything

Bill (Ed Mallory) and *Laura Horton* (Susan Flannery) share a quiet moment in front of the fire (c. 1973). Courtesy Corday Productions.

she could to win back Neil's affections. One night while Marie was out of town, Liz and Neil made love in his home. Afterward, Neil had to go to the hospital on an emergency call. Liz, hearing noises downstairs and fearing a burglar, fired a gun into the darkness. To her horror, she discovered she had shot Marie, who had returned home early!

Neil stood by Liz during the trial, realizing he would always love her. He vowed to wait for her, even after she was sentenced to five years in Rinehart Prison. He divorced Marie. On the day her appeal came through, Neil and Liz planned to remarry. Their vows were interrupted by a prison break, and Liz was injured. When she revived, she had no memory of the last two years and Neil! Liz believed herself to still be in love with Don and hearing him discuss wedding plans with Maggie broke Liz's heart. Neil could barely contain his emotions and longed for Liz and Noel to again be his family. Eventually, during the trauma of a robbery at *Doug's Place*, Liz's memory returned, and the couple reunited and married.

Meanwhile, Hope Williams fled from boarding school and returned to Salem, but all was not well. Hope had become a spoiled brat and continually clashed with Doug and Julie. Soon Hope became infatuated with Roman

Brady. But Roman's younger brother, Bo, returned to Salem, and Hope found herself falling in love with her childhood friend. Bo, with help from his friend, Howie Hofstedder, passed his private investigator's exam and became a P.I.

Eugene Bradford received a mysterious telegram from his grandfather and flew to Haiti. There his grandfather revealed that a curse was on the Bradford family: Family members attracted death to themselves and their loved ones. Eugene's grandfather gave him the key to a vault containing an object that was the defense against the curse, but the old man died before revealing the location of the vault. A perplexed Eugene returned to Salem. The mysterious object was eventually revealed as the so-called Baka.

Renee, divorced by David and rejected by Tony after he learned she had caused the boating accident that cost the life of Anna's baby, married Alex Marshall. Alex's only interest was in her money, for he had discovered a second will that left everything to Renee. Renee found out about the will and realized Alex's intentions. The night of the wedding announcement gala, Renee publicly denounced Alex and the rest of Salem, with the exception of her beloved Tony, who she had discovered was not really her half-brother. Admiring her spirit and realizing he still loved her, Tony went to Renee that evening. They made love and decided to marry. But the next morning, to everyone's horror, Renee was found murdered with a knife in her back and a raven's feather in her hand.

The night of Renee's murder, Eugene proposed to Trista Evans, Marlena's cousin, in the DiMera stables. Eugene and Trista had fallen in love when he helped her solve the mystery of the murder of her mother, Barbara Talmudge. Soon there was a second knifing. Another woman, Kelly, was found dead, a knife in her back, a raven's feather beside the body. Eugene began to wonder if the "Bradford Curse" was responsible. Eugene flew back to Haiti to try to learn more about voodoo and the mysterious Baka and end the curse. Trista followed him, and the two were wed in Haiti and had a short Haitian honeymoon.

Returning to Salem, they spent one blissful night together. Eugene went to the deli for pastrami, and when he returned, he discovered his bride's body, with a knife in her back and a black raven's feather in her hand! Eugene became the prime suspect in the murders and went into hiding He channeled all his energies into solving the case and the mystery of the Baka.

David, who had fought with Renee the night of her death, was a suspect as well. To protect her son, Julie confessed, but David was later cleared, and Julie admitted that she had lied to protect him. The police soon discovered that the murder weapons had been coated with a rare, exotic poison.

The plot thickened as Viper gang member Pete Jannings, a patient of Marlena's, became a suspect. However, soon Melissa Anderson found herself drawn to Pete. And Pete, with Chris' help, attempted to make a better life for himself.

As Renee's husband, Alex inherited the entire DiMera fortune and moved into the DiMera Mansion, now calling it Marshall Manor. Alex tricked Tony into selling his shares of Anderson, and with 53 percent of the stock, Alex finally reached his goal of controlling Anderson's. Alex then fired Chris.

Eugene's cousin Letitia, who had been hiding him, was murdered, a knife in her back, a raven's feather at her side. Roman was forced to arrest Eugene. But Marlena believed in Eugene's innocence and did everything she could to help, including decoding the secrets of the Baka. But the Baka was stolen by Tony on orders from a mystery man called Phoenix.

One day Marlena and Sandy went to see prostitute Daisy Hawkins. When they opened the door they saw a man who looked like Roman stab Daisy and place a feather in her hand. When the police found feathers and knives in Roman's house, they had no choice but to arrest him. Although Marlena was reluctantly convinced that her husband had had an emotional breakdown, both his brother Bo and longtime friend, Alice Horton, believed in his innocence.

Bo and Alice, with some help from drugged doughnuts, helped Roman escape. Roman faked his own death so that he could move freely in disguise through Salem. He revealed himself only to Marlena, Abe Carver, Eugene, Alice, and Bo, all of whom helped search for clues to the real killer's identity.

Meanwhile, Anna had been trying to frame Alex with a tape that proved his connection with Stefano. Alex ordered Anna's death, but the murder attempt failed, and Anna found herself on the run with her former husband, Roman.

The mystery of the Baka deepened and led Roman to a Trappist monastery. There Brother Andrew told him that the Baka was linked to the DiMeras and the Bradfords. There had been two crests on the Baka: the Bradford crest, which contained a raven and a leaf, and the DiMera crest, which held a leaf and a sword. These images were now worn off the Baka, but one faint image did remain, that of a phoenix.

Roman and Anna determined that the real killer must have worn a mask. It was soon revealed that indeed, Tony, while wearing a latex Roman mask, had been killing the women on orders from the Phoenix. He tried to kill Hope, but the attempt failed. The Phoenix was eventually unveiled and found to be none other than Stefano DiMera!

It was revealed that on the night of his "death," Stefano paid nurse Kelly Chase to switch his body with a corpse. Then he had her killed. The same night, Stefano ordered his personal physician poisoned, but made the death look like a car accident. When Trista, Eugene's wife, discovered discrepancies in the lab reports, Stefano had her killed.

The last remaining piece of the puzzle was uncovered by Anna DiMera. It seemed that Tony's cousin, Andre DiMera, was impersonating Tony, while the real count was chained in a secret room in his penthouse. Wearing a latex mask that made him look like Roman, Andre was the real murderer. Andre had been forced to make Renee his first victim when she realized he was not the real Tony, the night he came to her bed *after* Tony. Anna accidentally discovered the real Tony locked in the secret room and was thrown in with him, but they later escaped.

Alex sponsored a nationally televised charity concert to benefit University Hospital. Stefano planned to have Andre, wearing his Roman disguise, kill Marlena, then blow up the concert hall. But Roman, with help from Bo, Tony, Doug, and Neil, foiled the plan and went after Stefano in a high-speed pursuit. Stefano's car plunged into the icy waters of Salem Harbor, and Stefano was presumed dead. Tony and Andre dueled, and Andre was wounded. Andre escaped from the hospital and fled to London. Roman was acquitted of the murder charges, and he and Marlena soon found themselves the happy parents of twins, Eric Roman and Samantha Jean.

Megan Hathaway, Bo's ex-girlfriend, returned to Salem with her father, Maxwell Hathaway, a wealthy New Orleans banker. Playing the innocent, Megan tried to win back Bo by claiming that a young boy, Zachary, was their child. Bo was not fooled and soon discovered that Zachary belonged to his friend Diane, who was hiding in Europe from a crime syndicate led by Megan's father.

Meanwhile, on Hope's eighteenth birthday, Bo and Hope began to make love, but Doug found them together. Hope and Doug argued, and Doug suffered a massive heart attack. Further, as Bo worked with Roman to catch the killer, his romance with Hope began to interfere with the investigation. Bo also worried about the problems he was creating between Hope and her family. Bo, fearing for Hope's safety and well-being, pushed her away, making her believe he no longer loved her. Stung by Bo's rejection, Hope turned to district attorney Larry Welch for comfort.

Soon Hope and Larry planned to wed, but on the wedding day Bo rode to the church on his motorcycle, "kidnapped" Hope, and replaced the bride with Howie Hofstedder in a veil. Bo convinced Hope that he truly loved her, and the couple decided to run away together.

They fled to Maggie's deserted barn, where they almost made love. But Bo left the barn to investigate a noise, a planned diversion. While alone, Hope was kidnapped by two thugs of Maxwell Hathaway's and forced to write a "Dear Bo" letter and return to Salem. It seemed that Maxwell was a staunch supporter of Larry Welch's White House ambitions and wanted Hope with Larry. Further, Maxwell knew his daughter wanted Bo. Bo was crushed that Hope rejected him.

Bo eventually discovered that Hope had been forced to marry Larry because both Bo and her family had been threatened. It turned out that Larry was also ambivalent. A mystery man had threatened Larry's real love, Gwen Davies, if Larry did not marry Hope. With the help of Tom, Alice, Eugene, Abe, and Howie, Bo and Hope tried to find out who was trying to control Hope's life and why. Bo and Hope feigned indifference, and Hope avoided sleeping with Larry by lying to him and telling him she was pregnant with Bo's baby. Hope, however, was concerned about the presence of Larry's butler, Shane, a man who seemed more than a butler.

Maxwell convinced Bo to come and work for him. Almost immediately Bo learned about some mysterious prisms of power that interested Maxwell and Megan. Megan convinced her father to let Bo accompany them to the World's Fair in New Orleans. Hope followed Bo and finally, after months of separation, in a fantasy worthy of Rhett and Scarlett, the couple made love at a beautiful New Orleans plantation, Oak Alley.

Doug and Julie left Salem for an extended trip to Europe and sold *Doug's Place* to Neil, who renamed it *Blondie's* and gave the club to his wife. Neil, however, was forced to borrow money from Maxwell for this venture.

Maggie divorced Mickey so she could marry Don Craig, but her daughter Melissa disapproved. Eventually, Maggie broke off her engagement with Don and renewed her relationship with Mickey, after Mickey was wounded while trying to stop a gang "rumble."

Much to Mickey and Maggie's dismay, Melissa soon began to see gang member Pete Jannings. Ignoring her parents' wishes, Melissa continued to see Pete, and they decided to run away together. To make enough money to implement their plan, Pete began working as a male stripper at a club called *Beefcakes*, but he did not tell Melissa. Melissa's concerns about Pete's "secret" were soon compounded by the return of her biological mother, Linda Phillips Anderson.

Tess Jannings, Pete's sister, became involved with Chris Kositchek. But she could not decide between Chris and her abusive husband, Barry Reid, so she left town.

While in New Orleans, Bo stole one of the mysterious prisms, but while being pursued, threw it in the Mississippi River. Later, Eugene and Bo tried to find the prism, which was attached to a two-way radio watch of Eugene's devising, but an alligator ate it. Unable to locate the prism, Eugene and Bo returned to Salem.

Back in Salem, Anna, Tony, and Alex opened a dress business. Anna was the designer and her seamstress, Calliope Jones. Tony now found himself drawn to Kimberly (Kim) Brady, Roman's sister, recently returned to Salem. One night Kim borrowed a necklace from Tony's mother, Daphne. It was revealed that, unknown to Kim, the necklace contained the second prism. Calliope saw the necklace and asked to take it on a tropical fashion shoot in Haiti for Anna's new line of clothing.

The mystery man, Shane Donovan, spied on Kimberly because he thought she might know something about the crystal prisms and also because he found her beautiful. Kimberly, her career as a photographer failing, went back to what she did in Europe to make money: prostitution.

Andre DiMera returned to Salem, killed Maxwell Hathaway and took over his crime syndicate. But Megan soon began taking orders from her real father, Stefano DiMera! Stefano was still alive, but now dying. Megan vowed

Nick Corelli (George Jenesky), imagines a *Casablanca*-inspired daydream. *Nick* (seated) with *Scotty Banning* (Rick Hearst) (1989). Courtesy Corday Productions. [Chris Haston]

to help her father overcome his fatal illness and exact his revenge on Roman Brady. Stefano disclosed that the three prisms placed together under a laser light, revealed a coded pattern of a technological breakthrough which could change the world. Stefano also believed the prisms could cure his fatal illness.

The plane left for the fashion shoot in Haiti with Bo, Hope, Eugene, Calliope, Anna, Tony, Daphne, Liz, Carlo (an old friend of Neil's and Liz's business manager), and Nurse Honeycutt (a secret henchman of Stefano's) on board, with a disguised Andre as co-pilot. When the pilot had a heart attack, the plane crashed on a deserted island somewhere in the Bermuda Triangle. Daphne was seriously injured and died. Unbeknownst to everyone, save Anna, Andre was now masquerading as Tony. The real Tony was alive on the other side of the island, being tended by the island's sole inhabitant, the beautiful Jasmine.

Back in Salem, Larry's political aspirations seemed crushed when it was divulged that Larry's biological father was none other than Viktor Chovrat, an American who was found guilty of selling classified documents to the Soviets. However, Larry surprisingly won the election when he announced that his wife had miscarried their baby and was now lost and presumed dead in a plane crash.

Roman had been receiving mail threats, with all clues leading to Stefano. When news of the plane crash reached Salem, Roman feared that the crash was meant for him because he was supposed to have been on the plane. Roman asked to meet with his secret ISA contact and was stunned to meet none other than Shane Donovan. Shane admitted to spying on Kim and ransacking her apartment, looking for photos that she took of Stefano's island months before, while on a clandestine government job. Roman introduced Shane and Kim. Shane assured her that he would tell no one of her late-night business.

Roman left Salem for Haiti to search for Bo. Before he left, he declared his love for Marlena and their newborn twins. Shane, who finally found Kim's photos, went with him.

While on the island, Eugene and Calliope grew closer. Bo and Hope declared their love and vowed to tell the whole of Salem upon their safe return. Hope was stung by a stingray. She almost died, but Bo nursed her for two days, and she recovered. The real Tony was eventually discovered and he and Andre dueled (with bamboo spears). They fell into quicksand, and Jasmine saved Tony, but Andre died. Hope was kidnapped by Stefano's thugs, but Bo rushed to her aid and freed her.

When Roman went to the island to rescue his family and friends, he was caught off guard by Stefano and his henchmen. DiMera had resurrected like the phoenix to take his revenge on Roman. The two men struggled on a cliff, and as a horrified Bo watched from the offshore boat, Roman was shot and fell over the edge. With an evil laugh Stefano looked at the limp figure in the sand below, then boarded his helicopter.

Bo rushed to shore, found Roman and cradled him in his arms, declaring his love for his older brother. As Bo wept, Roman died in his arms. Finally, Bo left Roman in search of Stefano. When he returned to the beach, the body was gone! Bo had to tell Marlena that Roman was dead, and an agonized Marlena lashed out at Bo. She later apologized, but Bo was guilt-ridden and in turn alienated those around him.

The castaways were finally rescued. On their return to Salem, Hope announced that Larry was part of an evil cartel, denounced her husband, and told everyone her true love was Bo. Larry was forced to resign as lieutenant governor. But Bo had become obsessed with finding Stefano and agreed to work with Shane and the ISA to capture him.

Meanwhile, Stefano was back on his island, reveling in the fact that he had not only Roman's body, but one of the prisms. Stefano, suffering from a brain tumor, was convinced the prisms held the cure. He also had a plan to obtain the other two, one in the Soviet Union, the other, lost in the swamps of Cajun country. Shane had followed Stefano's minion, Honeycutt, to Louisiana and saw her retrieve the second prism, found by two alligator poachers in the belly of an alligator.

While Anna was on the island, Alex sold *Anna DiMera Designs* for much less than its worth. Anna demanded her fair share. Anna's life was further complicated by Tony's growing attraction to the beautiful Jasmine.

Neil Curtis had a cool reunion with wife Liz after her island ordeal, believing she had had an affair with Carlo. Liz denied it, but Neil would not believe her and stormed out to go drinking. Liz, too, headed for the liquor cabinet and when Carlo came to the house, he took advantage of her drunken state. They made passionate love just as Neil decided he had not been fair to Liz and returned home. Liz and Neil fought and planned for a divorce.

Carlo hoped to now make Liz his, but she hated him for taking advantage of her when she was drunk. Carlo tried another tactic: He brought up Neil's mysterious past. They investigated, and eventually Liz confronted Neil with what she had discovered. He confessed that his real name was Allen Jackson and that years ago he had amassed a huge gambling debt to the syndicate, which Carlo's father, Mario, helped him pay off. Mario and Neil were forced to work for a crime family until they no longer could face the atrocities and turned state's evidence; many criminals were indicted. Mario and Neil served time in prison. Mario was killed there; Neil was released and given a new identity. Now it seemed those people still wanted him dead.

Neil and Liz realized they loved each other and decided to leave town, but a jealous Carlo overheard their plan and tried to stop them. Carlo and Neil struggled in the barn and an anvil fell on Carlo. Neil saved Carlo, but Carlo eventually died after he discovered his grandfather, David Lebec, wanted him to head the crime syndicate. Lebec vowed revenge on Neil. On New Year's Eve Lebec sneaked into *Shenanigans*, and just as he was about to shoot Neil, he was shot.

Hope was distressed that Bo has put their wedding plans on hold and continued his quest to find Stefano. Although she sympathized with him, she could not understand why they could not move on, especially now that she had managed to extricate herself from her forced marriage to Larry Welch. While Hope was visiting Abe at the police station one day, she was mistakenly put on the Police Academy list. Abe and Bo laughed at the absurdity of Hope becoming a police officer, and she decided to call their bluff. She entered the academy determined to become a policewoman and prove them all wrong.

Bo's Uncle Eric was arrested for molesting a little girl. The Bradys rallied to his defense, with the exception of Kim. As a child, Kim was molested by her uncle, and her shame and guilt led her to a life of prostitution. When she told her father, Shawn, that his brother was guilty, Shawn had a heart attack. He eventually recovered.

Marlena befriended a man named Jim Potterfield, who began writing to her shortly after Roman's death. Jim's godmother, Mrs. Lafferty, an elderly recluse, was eager to meet Marlena. Marlena spent time with the "woman," unaware that beneath the gray hair and shawl sat Stefano DiMera! Stefano had found a new match in Roman's widow, Marlena. Marlena began to investigate the "Triad Experiment" and the three prisms. She used Eugene's help to break into the ISA computer and find crucial documents. Marlena eventually found Stefano's hideout in Caracas and sneaked in, horrified to discover Stefano was planning to kidnap her children!

Early on New Year's Eve, Linda told Alex that Anderson's was about to go bankrupt. Alex joked they should burn the place down. A devious Linda, however, made the plans for real. On the way to the New Year's party at *Blondie's*, Tom and Alice witnessed a huge explosion at Anderson's and a man in flames running from the building. Tom stopped to administer first aid, but when he injected the man with morphine, he died from an allergic reaction. The body was identified as Paul Selejko. His son, Speed, swore that his father never took off his medic alert bracelet and asked for Gwen's help in suing Tom for negligence in the death of his father. The suit was eventually dropped, and Tom cleared.

Meanwhile, a jealous Megan Hathaway was trying to kill Hope. Shane Donovan convinced Bo to work for the ISA and fool Megan into believing Bo loved her, the better to get information on her father, Stefano DiMera. Megan planned to electrocute Hope in a bathtub at the *Body Connection*. While rigging the hot tub, Megan overheard Larry discussing the possibility that the prism could blow up and destroy all of Salem. A furious Megan attacked Larry, who had withheld this information. They struggled, and Megan was accidentally killed. Hope was the prime suspect in the killing but was finally cleared. Gwen Davies eventually determined that her lover, Larry, killed Megan, but promised not to reveal that. She left Salem.

The prism plot thickened as Shane was forced to ask Kim to try and seduce information out of Russian agent Bronsky. Kim agreed to do so to help her brother, Bo, and pay back Shane, who had helped her destroy the incriminating tapes with which her former madam, Madame X, had been blackmailing her. Bo discovered Larry Welch was the son of Victor Chorvat, the creator of the prisms. Bronsky told Larry that his father altered the prism such that when it was thawed from its ice-sculpture camouflage, it would explode, destroying all of Salem. Bo discovered that Kim had been getting Bronsky drunk and telling him they had sex, thus obtaining information, and that she used to be a hooker.

His own daughter now dead, Stefano kidnapped Marlena and Roman's twins, Eric and Samantha, declaring he would raise them as his own with Marlena as his wife! Bo saved them, but Marlena vowed justice. She and Bo went to the ice arena where one of the three prisms was stored. Through a series of complicated events, the prism had ended up sewn to a costume that Hope was wearing, and it was ready to explode. Stefano and his henchman, Sonia, recovered the prism and were about to make their escape. But Marlena appeared, Roman's gun in her hand, "This is for Roman," she exclaimed as she shot Stefano in the stomach. Stefano dropped the prism, which started a fire on the stage below. Stefano grabbed Marlena and almost pulled her over the edge, but Bo reached her and grabbed her just as Stefano plunged to his death in the flames.

Shane braved the fires to retrieve the prism and plunged it into ice seconds before it was to explode. Stefano's henchmen, Honeycutt and Jimmy, went to Bo demanding the prism. Hope was shot in the struggle and lay near death. Bo stayed by her bed, night and day, declared his love for her and proposed. After two days, Hope awakened and happily agreed to marry Bo.

Hope was given a citation for her heroic behavior in helping stop Stefano DiMera. This encouraged her to pursue her career as a police officer. Bo protested, but later they agreed to open their own detective agency with Howie, the "Hofstedder/Brady Detective Agency." Marlena was arrested for Stefano's murder, but the charges were dropped.

Shane took the prism and dropped it into the middle of the Atlantic, lost to humanity forever. The ISA was furious and dismissed him. A disgusted Shane embraced the dismissal. He had lost too many friends and loved ones to a cause he no longer respected. Shane went to Kim and told her he was free. They grew closer, but Shane was reluctant to admit his love because his first wife, Emma, died as a result of his life as an ISA agent.

Melissa, meanwhile, got involved with Barry Reid. Barry initially convinced her he was a nice guy, but she soon discovered he was a drug dealer. Melissa called the police and reported the drug ring, but Barry caught her and threatened to kill her. She escaped and found a friend in Speed's sister, Ivy. Ivy was friends with Pete, whom she referred to as PJ. Melissa did not know that PJ and Pete were one and the same. Pete, thinking his relationship with Melissa was over, made love to Ivy. Melissa finally returned home and was reunited with Pete. However, Pete and Melissa were soon devastated to learn that Ivy was carrying Pete's child. Pete did the "right thing" and married Ivy, and she gave birth to a son, Charlie. But Pete and Melissa could not stay apart.

Liz and Neil, meanwhile had been enjoying months of peaceful existence with their daughter, Noel. But they were soon saddened to discover that Noel had juvenile diabetes. Further, Liz was shocked when the famous Lou Stanley Talent Agency made her an offer she could not refuse. Liz was unaware the crime syndicate, in an effort to get Neil, was behind the deal.

Calliope Jones was determined to become Eugene Bradford's bride. But his grandfather's will had declared that for his side of the family, not Stefano's, to inherit the vast estate, his aristocratic mother, Vanessa, must approve of the match. Calliope tried a number of schemes to woo both Eugene and his mother. Eugene finally decided to marry Calliope and informed his mother, who explained that if they married she would go to jail; she had already made investments with the estate money and had lost it. The attorneys insisted Eugene marry the "right" woman.

Calliope grew increasingly jealous of Eugene's relationship with Madeline, a young woman Eugene's mother wanted him to marry. Vanessa convinced a gullible Eugene to marry Madeline, get the money, get an annulment, and marry his real love, Calliope. Eugene finally divorced Madeline and renewed his relationship with Calliope.

Meanwhile, Anna was jealous of the tropical beauty Jasmine. Anna convinced Alex Marshall to back Jasmine as a high-fashion model, Anna figured with Jasmine out of the way, she could win back Tony. Tony was furious with Anna, but later had cause to be angry with Jasmine. Jasmine inadvertently helped Stefano in the ice arena, depriving Tony of his revenge. The innocent Jasmine did not understand Tony's need for revenge, but Tony talked to Anna, and she sympathized. Tony found himself drawn again to Anna.

But Anna met and fell in love with Prince Nicholas Arani. However, Prince Nicholas was killed by the Dragon, an anti-monarchist thought to be responsible for the death of Shane's first wife, Emma. The crime sent Bo, Hope, Shane, and Kimberly to England, for they had uncovered the Dragon's plan to kill British royalty. In England, Shane discovered Emma alive and trying to murder him under orders from the Dragon. Bo and Hope captured the Dragon and foiled his plans. In gratitude, the British threw them a lavish wedding.

Meanwhile, the Dragon escaped from prison, but he fell six stories to his death after an attempt to kill Shane. Shane returned to Salem with Emma, where he had the hypnotized Emma deprogrammed. Emma tried everything to win back Shane, but his heart belonged to Kim. Emma turned to her lawyer, Larry for support and they became lovers. But when her divorce from Shane was finalized, Emma vowed that if she could not have Shane, no one could.

Kim was suffering from temporary hysterical blindness as a result of all the trauma, especially Emma's return. Kim ended her relationship with Shane and turned to wealthy and powerful Victor Kiriakis for comfort, much to the dismay of her mother, Caroline. Caroline had had an affair with Victor some years before and revealed that one of the Brady children was, in fact, a Kiriakis.

The seductive Savannah Wilder arrived in Salem and immediately impressed Alex with her business sense. Savannah moved her so-called video business to Salem and asked Liz to star in a video with Liz's brother, Tod, as director. Tod, who had previously known Savannah, warned her not to involve Liz in her business.

Theo Carver, Abe's brother, convinced Bo to help him investigate Savannah and her video business. Theo's best friend, Danny Grant, Valerie's brother, had been murdered and Theo believed that the murder was somehow tied to Savannah. Savannah hired a one-eyed man, called Patch, to kill Bo and Theo. The one-eyed man seemed to relish the thought of killing Bo.

Theo and Bo discovered that the videos Savannah was shipping were pornographic and assumed that they had come across an illegal pornography ring. But they were soon to discover that the videos were cover for a heroin smuggling ring. Now a policewoman, Hope managed to make a drug bust, but the dealer, Patch, got away. Savannah then contacted her boss, Victor Kiriakis, with the news.

Bo and Patch almost killed each other in a brawl. Hope demanded to know what was behind the intense hatred the two men displayed, but Bo denied everything. However, he was soon haunted by memories of Stockholm, a tattoo parlor and three people who pricked their fingers and became blood family.

Meanwhile, Chris was attracted to the beautiful Savannah and, not knowing her criminal nature, became her lover. Alex and Linda joined forces to buy up Riverfront property and planned to terrorize the Riverfront area in order to lower property prices, but their plans were thwarted by Chris.

Meanwhile, Anna and Tony shared some outrageous adventures. On a trip to Bangkok, Anna was kidnapped by the "Baba" and forced to enter his harem. But with help from his friends Calliope and Eugene, Tony rescued Anna. Tony and Anna were married after their return to Salem.

Anna signed a prenuptial agreement to prove to Tony that she was marrying him for love, not money. But she was soon in desperate financial straits as she almost lost *Anna DiMera Designs (ADD)*. Anna even tried to sell a supposedly priceless statue from Bangkok, but the art dealer, Claus Van Zandt, deemed it worthless. Tony eventually discovered the truth and happily tore up the prenuptial agreement and helped Anna save *ADD*. However, Tony was soon shocked to learn that Claus had paid Anna only $100 for the statue. Tony knew the statue was not a fake and was covered with priceless emeralds.

Claus and Alex were soon revealed to be partners in the scheme to get the half-million-dollar statue away from Anna. But once they heard that Tony had uncovered the con, Claus agreed to pay Anna full market value. However, he tricked her into taking a Picasso instead, and it turned out to be a fake.

Anna went to Claus' office to demand the return of her money and was horrified to find him dead, a bullet through his chest. Anna, convinced she would be the chief suspect, took the gun and ran. Anna was arrested, and Tony bailed her out, vowing to prove her innocence.

Meanwhile, Pete accidentally picked up some photos at the photo lab that were intended for Patch. The photos were clues to some mysterious "Three P's" that were of interest to Victor Kiriakis, among others. Pete and Melissa fled Salem when their lives were threatened and went on the run. They were soon joined by Tod Chandler, who switched sides when he realized Savannah, on orders from Victor, was trying to kill Pete and Melissa. Tod took a bullet meant for Melissa, and the threesome, Tod wounded, now followed a series of clues they hoped would lead them to truth and safety.

Savannah planned to disburse heroin at a recording party held for Liz. But when a police raid was made, no heroin was found. Bo and Theo, who had tipped the police, realized someone tipped Savannah. During the bust, there was an exchange of gunfire, and Liz was shot by crooked cop McBride. The bullet lodged in her throat, and Dr. Mike Horton, who recently had returned to Salem, removed it, but said that damage to her vocal cords might prevent her from singing again.

Meanwhile, Emma made good on her threat and planted a time bomb in the Kiriakis stables. She phoned Kim and arranged a meeting at the stables. At the planned moment, the small bomb ignited fires in several locations, the doors were locked from the outside, and Kim was trapped. But Shane kicked down the doors and rushed into the burning building to save her. A flaming beam broke loose, and Kim warned Shane, just in time. The two escaped the blaze and, once outside, realized Kim could see! When Victor arrived on the scene, Kim faked blindness. Kim vowed to help Shane, who was on an ISA mission, with his partner, Livinia Peach (Peachy), to get Victor Kiriakis. Again working with Bo and Hope, Shane and Kim went after Victor.

Marlena had become romantically involved with Salem's newest police chief, Richard Cates. But Bo, Hope, Theo, and Alice Horton soon discovered that Cates was involved with the drug smuggling ring. The group told Abe Carver, who tried to arrest Cates. Bo and Theo then went looking for Hope, who had been in hiding since she found out Cates was a crook, but the pair was caught in an ambush. Theo was shot and died in the arms of his brother Abe. Cates realized everything was falling apart and, unable to live with the shame, forced Abe to shoot him. The drugs were found, and Savannah was warned by Kiriakis not to slip up again.

As Tony and Anna strove to find the real killer, their search was complicated by mystery woman Felicity York. Tony arranged to meet with Felicity on the docks. He discovered that Alex, Tracy Van Zandt, Claus' wife, and Robert, an art forger, had all received videos "proving" that they had killed Claus. Realizing that everyone was being blackmailed, Tony called Anna and asked her to meet him. Anna arrived at the docks, heard her husband call her name from the fog-shrouded pier, then nothing. Tony had disappeared into the mist.

With Tony gone, Anna was indicted for murder. But it was soon revealed that Felicity York was none other than Emma Donovan! She had blackmailed Tracy, Robert, and Alex for $3 million. With Eugene and Calliope's help, Anna found the three incriminating videos. Calliope correctly surmised that for the videos to have been made, Claus must really be alive. Claus and Emma planned to flee the country.

Anna's nightmare came to an end when the police arrested Tracy, Robert, and Claus. But they all swore they knew nothing of Tony's whereabouts. Emma escaped deportation by marrying Alex Marshall. Anna finally received a letter from Tony asking for a divorce, saying he could no longer give her the extravagant things she desired. But Eugene also received a letter from the count, explaining that something in his life made it impossible for him to be with Anna and that his leaving was for Anna's own good.

Eugene and Calliope went along with the ruse, knowing it was the only way Anna would let Tony go. Hoping to perk up Anna, they then announced their wedding. They were married in an unusual New Year's Eve wedding in the snow and honeymooned in Finland.

The investigation of Victor Kiriakis, the drug deals, and the mysterious Three P's continued, and soon all roads led to Miami. Bo, Hope, and Shane flew to Miami to investigate Kiriakis. Kim, who had accompanied Victor to protect her cover, was already there. Melissa, Pete, and Tod were there as well because the clues that they had uncovered on the road led them to Florida. Chris followed Savannah to Miami, now convinced that she was up to no good. The Three P's were soon found to be the "purse, the power, and the Pawn." Victor, Russian agent Petrov, and corrupt ISA chief Nickerson all attempted to possess them, while Bo, Hope, Shane, and Kim all tried to stop the deadly chess game.

In Florida, Hope was captured and tormented by Patch, who threatened to pour acid over her. But Bo and Shane saved her. Victor soon discovered Kim's ruse and threatened her by placing a deadly tarantula in her bed, his "calling card." Shane killed the spider, saving Kim's life, and returned it to Victor. The battle of wits between Shane and Victor continued.

Shane got trapped in the study of Victor's Miami estate while trying to decipher a secret-code book. Kim made love to Victor to keep him away from the study and save Shane's life. Shane escaped in time and, with help from Chris, rescued Bo and Hope from an exploding sunken treasure, a booby trap planted by Victor. Ultimately, Victor, Savannah, and Patch were arrested. But Larry Welch took the blame, fearing Victor would reveal the truth of Megan's death, and the three were set free.

Chris dumped Savannah when he discovered the truth about her, but the passion lingered. When Savannah realized she had no future with Chris, she gave up on her efforts to reform and returned to Victor's organization.

Meanwhile, back in Salem, the so-called Salem Rapist was stalking women. One of his victims was Maggie Horton. Maggie received counseling, and, with help from Mickey, she eventually recovered from the trauma of the rape. Mickey's constant support of Maggie during this crisis drew them closer together.

Shane continued to try and determine the players in the game. He finally deduced that Petrov was the second player and Nickerson the third. But Nickerson killed himself and destroyed his code book before Shane could learn more. Petrov soon arrived in Salem with the Pawn.

In his attempt to find the Pawn, Victor blackmailed Alex into working for him. Kiriakis finally found the Pawn, killing Petrov to get him. The Pawn, a mystery man swathed in bandages with no memory of his past, was counseled by Nurse Honeycutt, who was now working for Kiriakis.

When Kim discovered she was pregnant, she did not know who the father was, but feared it might be Victor, who could be her own biological father! To ease Kim's fears, Caroline finally revealed that Bo, not Kim, was the Brady who was Victor's child. Victor, learning the truth, offered Caroline a home with him, but she chose to stay with Shawn. Shawn and Caroline then took in two homeless street kids, teen-age Frankie and his little brother, Max, a troubled boy who could not speak.

Kim accepted Shane's marriage proposal and later told him about the baby, never revealing that it might be Victor's. One day Shane, in a plan concocted by Emma, overheard the truth, and the couple separated. Shane could forgive Kim's sleeping with Victor, but not her lying about the baby.

When Pete and Melissa returned to Salem, Ivy agreed to divorce Pete. At Liz's encouragement, Tod bought *JUMP!* and the *Body Connection* from Chris and brought in Pete as his partner. Pete and Melissa were married in a beautiful Valentine's Day double wedding, sharing the ceremony with the reunited Maggie and Mickey.

On their honeymoon, Melissa was attacked and Pete knocked unconscious by the Salem Rapist. Pete saved Melissa from rape, but neither saw the man's face. They cut short their honeymoon in a secluded mountain cabin and instead went to Bermuda. The rapist was eventually revealed to be Ian Griffith, Melissa's former parole officer. He had become obsessed with Melissa when she had ended their brief relationship after learning he was married. He was finally captured and put in jail.

The Pawn escaped from Victor and was taken in by Patch. But the Pawn soon escaped Patch as well. Victor, meanwhile, was having trouble with a local fisherman, who was reluctant to agree to his buy-out terms. Victor had Patch set a bomb at the Riverfront. It exploded, and Shawn Brady was almost killed.

Meanwhile, Mike Horton fell in love with Robin Jacobs, a fellow doctor and the new head of the surgery department. But their relationship was complicated by the fact that Robin was an orthodox Jew and that her father, Eli, objected to her relationship with Mike, who was not Jewish.

While in Salem, Eli reunited with his brother, Robert LeClere. Robert had recently returned to Salem and began singing at *Blondie's* (formerly *Doug's Place*). Now separated from Julie, for reasons unknown, Doug returned to Salem as well. Doug ran for mayor and bought Howie's detective agency for Bo and Hope. Doug eventually left Salem and returned to Europe.

Robert and Eli were soon shocked to discover that Dr. Fred Miller, a visiting Illinois physician, was really a Nazi war criminal, Dr. Fredrich Kluger. Kluger was responsible for their mother's death in a concentration camp. Robert, Eli, Robin, and Mike worked with the Justice Department to capture Kluger. They eventually succeeded, and the former Nazi was arrested.

Mike Horton also got his newly returned and runaway sister, Jennifer Rose, to settle down and move in with her grandparents, Tom and Alice. Jennifer hated high school, but summer vacation brought a romance with classmate Glenn Gallagher.

Liz eventually recovered from the shooting, but was in for more trouble. Her brother, Tod, an alcoholic, got drunk at Pete's club, *JUMP!*, and left with Savannah. A car crash killed Tod and injured Savannah. Liz vowed to sue Pete. However, Liz eventually got over her brother's death and, with the help of Neil's devotion, regained her voice. But career demands soon separated husband and wife and Liz moved to California, leaving Neil and Noel in Salem. Noel eventually went to her mother in California.

Chris grew closer to the widowed Marlena, but was still drawn to Savannah. On Alex's suggestion, Savannah hired someone to attack Marlena, so that Savannah could then rush to her rescue and play the heroine. But the plan backfired, and Savannah was stabbed. Robin and Mike operated and saved her life. Chris was moved to tell the wounded Savannah that he still loved her, but he soon discovered her deception, and they separated for good.

Meanwhile, the mysterious Pawn eluded all his pursuers. Unraveling his bandages, but with no memory of his past, the Pawn chose the name John Black. A number of incidents convinced him that he had been some sort of law officer in the past, and he opened his own security company. No one knew he was the Pawn, because no one had ever seen the Pawn without the bandages. John was soon accepted by the Salemites and even helped catch the Salem Rapist. He quickly found a friend in Dr. Marlena Evans Brady. He confided his memory loss to Marlena, and she vowed to help him recover his past.

Calliope, feeling sorry for the depressed and lonely Anna, tried to fix her up with John by suggesting she invest in his new security company. John, who remembered nothing of his past, had investigated and finally determined that he was the Pawn and somehow connected to Roman Brady and Stefano

DiMera. John worried when Anna told him about Stefano's affinity for phoenixes because there was a phoenix tattooed on his back.

Meantime, Shane was arrested in Stockholm on espionage charges, accused of having given the Soviets secrets that led to the invasion of Afghanistan. It was revealed that Bo and Britta Englund, an ex-Soviet spy, had once been lovers and that he had caught her in bed with his then-best friend Patch and, in a jealous rage, gouged out Patch's eye in a fight. Both Bo and Patch had believed Britta dead, but they now determined that she was alive. It was further disclosed that Roman had had some sort of connection with Stockholm, perhaps an ISA mission. Bo, Patch, and Hope went to Stockholm to clear Shane and find Britta. They found Britta on a train, being followed by the KGB. Hope helped her escape and was captured and taken to the Soviet Union. To clear Shane, Bo confessed to the crime, but Britta cleared both men by testifying that she had set up Shane. The KGB offered to trade Hope for Britta, but Bo, Shane, and Patch managed to rescue both Hope and Britta, and they all returned to Salem.

Britta's brother Lars was threatened with death when Britta came to the United States. Lars was a dancer with the Russian Ballet, and while the ballet was in Salem, Bo, Hope, Patch, and Britta helped Lars defect. Patch and Britta rekindled their relationship, but it was not to be. Britta fled Salem to save Patch from both Victor and the KGB, both of whom wanted something that Britta seemed to have.

Lars formed his own dance company. He was drawn to Melissa, who had discovered a newfound career as a dancer. Melissa's pursuit of the dance often separated her from her husband, Pete. Melissa soon found herself captivated by Lars and his dancing talents. Lars eventually made Melissa his partner both on and off the stage. Pete and Melissa divorced.

John and Marlena continued to investigate his past. They tracked down a plastic surgeon in West Virginia who purported to have a photo of John before the surgery. John and Marlena headed for West Virginia with Victor and the KGB in hot pursuit. The night they arrived, Marlena suggested that a nervous John take a shower to calm down. When he emerged from the bathroom wearing only a towel, Marlena was horrified to see the phoenix tattoo on his back. Fearing that John was Stefano DiMera, resurrected yet again, a terrified Marlena phoned Shane for help. Marlena almost killed John (by hitting him on the head with a rock) and tried to "escape," but was captured by the KGB. John rescued her, and they escaped in a stolen raft into whitewater rapids.

Bo, Shane, and Hope arrived just in time to see Marlena and John go down the river. They followed, but their raft capsized, and Hope almost drowned. Shane radioed Peach for help, but she suffered a stroke before she could tell anyone. Kim, who had been living with Peach since her break-up with Shane, finally found her and Peach revived enough to tell Kim that Shane needed help. Kim phoned the ISA, but Victor intercepted the call. Kim boarded an "ISA" helicopter, soon horrified to discover it was really Victor's. They flew to the river, but the pilot lost control in the heavy winds, and the helicopter crashed.

The KGB found the wreckage and the survivors and kidnapped Kim. Shane rescued her, but they were unable to go very far because Kim began having contractions. They found a cabin, and there Shane delivered, breech and premature, Kim's son, Andrew Shane.

Meanwhile, Marlena found herself still drawn to John and helped him elude both the KGB and Bo. But Bo, believing John was Stefano, finally tracked them down. Marlena discovered the KGB medical reports as Bo and "Stefano" struggled and "Stefano" fell over a cliff. Just as Bo was ready to step on "Stefano's" fingers and send him over the edge, Marlena rushed to Bo with the proof that John Black was not Stefano DiMera, but Roman Brady! Everyone returned to Salem, but John, now Roman, still had no memory of his past.

Still in Salem, the erstwhile engineer Eugene invented a time machine. He tried it, and its charred remains were found in the woods near Salem. Everyone believed Eugene to be dead. But, after hitting her head, Calliope saw Eugene from another age and believed him alive, even though no one else saw him. Eugene eventually returned.

On their return to Salem, Kim and Shane had a paternity test run to prove Andrew's parentage once and for all. Emma falsified hospital records to show that Victor Kiriakis was the boy's father, when, in fact, Andrew was Shane's son. But Shane stood by Kim, vowing to raise the boy as his own, and the couple reunited. Emma, trying to break up Shane and Kim, kidnapped the baby and gave him to a doctor in Cleveland for whom Kayla Brady had once worked.

Kayla had recently returned to Salem to help her family in this time of crisis. Victor ordered Patch to get close to Kayla, who had started to work at the Riverfront Emergency Center, so he could keep an eye on the Bradys. Kayla, not knowing his past, and Patch, to whom she now referred by his given name, Steve, grew closer. They were especially united in their efforts to help Frankie and Max.

Marlena, while trying to help a suicidal patient from a ledge, fell and went into a coma. But Roman stayed by her side, vowing his love, and she recovered. Roman and Marlena reunited and at last renewed their vows in a beautiful ceremony with Abe as best man and Maggie as matron of honor. Tamara Price, an old college friend of Marlena's, sang at the wedding.

Shane eventually discovered that Emma was responsible for Andrew's kidnapping, but she pleaded insanity and avoided jail. The strain of losing Andrew and their typical lack of communication caused Kim and Shane to split yet again, although, as always, they remained very much in love. Unknown to them, Shane and Kim's son arrived in Salem, as the newly adopted child of Paul and Barbara Stewart. When Shane's ISA partner, Peach, was reassigned, the beautiful but corrupt Gillian Forrester became his partner.

Britta returned to Salem and Roman tried to find out what she knew about his past, especially what happened in Stockholm. Roman got a clue from a dying man, Billings, who whispered, "three knives." Roman then received a letter mailed by Billings before his death, telling Roman to contact a man named Gregory in Sweden. Britta got to Gregory before Roman, and Gregory told her that the clue to the mystery lay in the three knife tattoos on Britta, Bo, and Steve. Gregory was killed before he could give this information to Roman.

Roman began to remember what happened in Stockholm. Britta gave him a box containing Treasury plates, which had been intended for Victor. Billings had helped him hide the plates, but now Roman could not recall where. Britta was found murdered, and Steve was the chief suspect. Kayla helped Steve escape, and they shared a brief time on the run, but Kayla convinced Steve to turn himself in.

Hope, Roman, and Steve went to Stockholm to find Gregory's ex-wife, Lana, in hopes of learning the meaning behind the three knives. But instead they found her dead body and the words "Roman Brady" written in blood. Roman was arrested, and Steve wounded in the scuffle. Hope phoned Kayla, and she flew to Stockholm. Hope got Roman released, and the group returned to Salem, where the ISA told Roman that he had been set up by a man called Orpheus, a killer.

Kayla and Steve grew closer, but Steve, because of his past, did not think that he was good enough for Kayla. Roman went to Shane with a plan to use Steve to catch Orpheus, but Gillian overheard and warned the man behind much of the mystery, ISA chief Vaughn! Kayla was then kidnapped by Orpheus, but Roman and Steve rescued her.

Meanwhile, in neighboring Brookville, a tornado struck, and many were injured, including Jennifer Rose. Jennifer's life was saved by Frankie, and a new and close bond formed between the two teen-agers.

Bo finally discovered that his natural father was Victor Kiriakis. Hurt and angry, Bo decided that he and Hope should move into the Kiriakis mansion so that Victor would leave the Bradys alone. Bo started to work for Victor's organization to find evidence that would destroy Victor. Hope did not know this and hated her new father-in-law and life at the Kiriakis Mansion. While Bo was away on a business trip the now-pregnant Hope miscarried their baby. Hope was upset with Bo, but he returned to "kidnap" her and take her on the romantic honeymoon they had never had. They reconciled, split, and ultimately resolved their differences when Bo revealed his true motives. They planned a feigned separation, which was complicated by Hope's new pregnancy and the fact that Bo had begun to care for his biological father.

Marlena was kidnapped by corrupt ISA Chief Vaughn, who wanted to coerce Roman into helping locate stolen treasury bonds. Marlena was eventually taken to Stockholm but escaped Vaughn and was recaptured by Orpheus. It was finally revealed that eight years previously, on the night he was hiding the bonds, Roman accidentally shot and killed Orpheus' wife. Now Orpheus wanted revenge. Roman, Steve, Hope, and Kayla saved Marlena and returned to Salem, but Orpheus escaped.

Steve and Kayla grew closer. Bo was not happy with the match and confided as much to Victor. Unknown to Bo, Victor sent a copy of the file that proved Steve had spied on Kayla for Victor. An angry and hurt Kayla broke up with Steve.

Justin Kiriakis, Victor's nephew, came to Salem to live at the mansion and found proof that Bo was working against Victor. Victor realized that Bo would never be truly happy as a Kiriakis and forged papers to "prove" that Shawn was really Bo's father. Only Caroline knew the truth: Victor was Bo's biological father. Hope gave birth to a son, Shawn-Douglas, and Bo and Hope left Salem, sailing off together into the sunset.

A bomb exploded in Marlena and Roman's house, and a skeleton identified as Marlena's was found in the ruins. A devastated Roman mourned his wife, but she was in fact alive, held prisoner by Orpheus on a deserted island. Roman was befriended by Orpheus' sister-in-law, Olivia. She initially wanted revenge, but soon fell in love with Roman. Orpheus tormented Roman with a video of Marlena in a garden. Roman realized Marlena was alive and began to search for her.

Roman finally located Orpheus' hideout. Olivia tried to help Roman and Marlena, but Orpheus was one step ahead of them and sent Marlena out the back way and to the airport. Roman frantically searched for Marlena, but instead found Orpheus. The two men struggled, and Roman's gun went off, killing Orpheus. Roman rushed to the airport, but Marlena's plane took off just as he arrived. Roman hurried to the control tower to radio the pilot, but before he could speak, he heard the pilot's "Mayday" and watched in horror as Marlena's plane plunged into the sea. Her body was never found.

Emma Marshall was murdered on New Year's Eve, and Kim was arrested and convicted. However, Shane was convinced of Kim's innocence and vowed to clear her. They again reunited, and Shane gave Kim back her engagement ring. Emma's husband, Alex, was eventually arrested for trying to burn down the Salem Inn, which he owned, for the insurance money and was hauled off to prison.

Meanwhile, Barbara Stewart learned that her adopted son, Teddy, was in fact Kim and Shane's missing son. When Barbara found out that Shane had finally discovered the truth, she panicked and tried to flee Salem with the baby. She had a car accident and was fatally injured. Andrew was fine. Barbara's deathbed confession, admitting that Teddy was Andrew and that she had gone to the Curtis Mansion with a gun to kill Emma, who knew the truth, cleared Kim. Kim and her son were finally reunited.

Shane's new ISA partner, Gillian, turned out to be Emma's killer. She had set up Kim because she loved Shane and wanted him for her own. Determined to have Shane, Gillian smuggled her twin sister, Grace, into town to help with the plan. Grace had no idea that Gillian was scheming to kill Kim. When Shane realized what Gillian was planning, he and Kim staged a mock break-up. Then Kim feigned a sham wedding to Paul Stewart. Paul agreed to help so that he could clear his late wife's name. Shane pretended to fall for Gillian and proposed. When Grace was told of her sister's plot, she joined Shane to help trap Gillian.

On the morning of her wedding, Gillian tried to murder Kim, but Peach and Grace outsmarted her. Gillian was arrested at the church. Shane surprised Kim with a stunning wedding gown, and the couple was married moments later. They honeymooned in Paris.

Upon their return, Victor publicly denounced Kim as a prostitute and got custody of "their" son, Andrew. Soon after, the baby was hit by a car and needed a transfusion. Victor's blood type did not match the baby's, and it was at last disclosed that Shane was Andrew's father.

Steve's family moved to Salem. It was revealed that his mother, Jo Johnson, had given up Steve and his baby brother, Billy, for adoption when they were young to keep them away from her abusive husband, Duke. But Jo had stayed with Duke. Steve convinced Jo to leave Duke, promising he would protect her. Duke came looking for Jo and demanded that Adrienne, Steve's younger sister, reveal Jo's whereabouts. Duke, enraged because Jo had finally left him and moved into a shelter for battered wives, raped the virginal Adrienne. Adrienne shot and killed her father, then blocked out the whole traumatic experience. Steve confessed to the crime, trying to protect his sister. But Adrienne regained her memory and cleared Steve of the murder charges. All charges against Adrienne were dropped because she had acted in self-defense. The family reunited and Steve forgave his mother for giving up her sons for adoption.

A leg injury ended Melissa's dance career. Her friend, Justin Kiriakis, tried to help, but to no avail. Without dance as a common bond, Lars and Melissa split. Melissa vowed to get on with her own life when Lars' dance company went on the road, leaving Melissa in Salem.

Justin, the former roué, was drawn to the shy and vulnerable Adrienne. Justin eventually gave up his wild ways, after having a liaison with Anjelica Deveraux, the wife of the rich and powerful Senator Harper Deveraux. Both the jealous Anjelica and Justin's Uncle Victor, who disapproved of the "lower-class" Adrienne, tried various schemes to break up the couple. But Justin and Adrienne eventually married in the Kiriakis family chapel in Greece and shared a blissful honeymoon.

Meanwhile, Harper and Anjelica's son, Jack Deveraux, came to Salem for treatment of Hodgkin's disease. Jo, Steve, and Adrienne were shocked to discover that Jack Deveraux was really Billy Johnson, the son Jo had long ago given up for adoption. But Jack had no idea that he was adopted; he believed Harper and the late Camille Deveraux to be his real parents.

Dr. Robin Jacobs still loved Mike Horton, and the couple made love one night while trapped on a deserted island in a storm. But Robin believed their religious differences were irreconcilable and married Mitch Kaufman. Robin's feelings for Mike would not die, and she was unable to consummate her marriage to Mitch. Their marriage was annulled, and Robin finally agreed to marry Mike, who decided to convert to Judaism.

Mike's old college friend, Diana Colville, came to town, determined to discover who murdered her fiancé, James. Mike first saw Diana when she was brought into University Hospital, the victim of a stabbing. While in the hospital she was poisoned, but Mike saved her. Diana warned Mike to keep his research on cancer quiet. Her fiancé had been doing similar research before he was killed.

However, a gala was soon given to honor his research. On the night of the event, Mike was summoned to the lab, but Kayla intercepted the message. As she entered the lab, the building exploded. Steve rushed in to save Kayla, but the two were trapped. On a hunch, Jack went to the wreckage, heard the couple and summoned help, saving their lives.

It soon appeared that the key to solving the case was a computer disc that accidentally fell into Robin's hands. Robin was shot when the disc was stolen from her office. Mike found Robin, and she was rushed to surgery. The surgery was successful. Meanwhile, Shane retrieved a copy of the disc, but, when he tried to decipher it, found only worthless formulas.

Mike went to the chapel to give a prayer of thanks for Robin's life. But as she was being wheeled to her room, Robin overheard him. She realized that Mike was converting only to please her, not for his own convictions. She sadly broke their engagement and eventually moved to Israel.

Dr. Simon Hopkins, an old flame of Alice Horton's, came to work at University Hospital. It was soon revealed that Hopkins and Ed Daniels, an unscrupulous FBI agent, were in league with Victor Kiriakis to find the disc, which was made of a special material they all coveted. The three concocted a scheme to assassinate Senator Harper Deveraux, who was running for president. Harper was seen as a threat to their plans. Daniels secured Steve's help by convincing him that Harper was in danger and needed to fake his own death. Steve thought he was working for the FBI when he agreed to be the assassin at a staged shooting. Steve did not know that the bullets in the gun were real. When he fired, Harper was wounded and went into a coma.

Realizing he had been double-crossed, Steve went on the run with Kayla, Adrienne, and Justin. The group ultimately discovered evidence that implicated Hopkins and cleared Steve. Simon was killed while trying to escape, using Alice Horton as a hostage. Harper recovered. Steve and Kayla declared their true feelings for one another and made love.

Diana's father, Philip, came to town. Diana suspected that he knew more than he revealed, especially since James used to work for Philip. But Philip would divulge nothing. Roman soon became involved in the investigation. Although initially antagonistic, Roman and Diana were drawn to each other.

Melissa Anderson, while working as Jack's assistant, became infatuated with him. But Jack had fallen for Kayla, who was now acting as his private nurse, but whom he had previously met in Hawaii. Jack's condition worsened, and Steve decided his brother needed a reason to live. Steve cruelly ended his relationship with Kayla and shoved her into Jack's arms. Hurt and confused, Kayla accepted Jack's proposal, and they were married. The newlywed couple moved into the Deveraux mansion. But the marriage was never consummated; Jack was too ill from his cancer treatments, and later, Kayla avoided him and then became ill.

Proud "father" Harper was thrilled when Jack announced he was running for State Assembly. Harper, determined to keep Jack's adoption a secret, fired his housekeeper, Jo Johnson, Jack's biological mother, and stole the adoption papers from her. When the adoption papers turned up missing, Harper feared that Kayla had taken them. To ensure Kayla's silence, Harper began to slowly poison her.

Meanwhile, Kim was again pregnant, but she contracted rubella and then pneumonia. Luckily, the unborn baby girl was unharmed. During this time, the Donovans befriended a teen-age runaway named Eve, who had fallen prey to pimp Nick Corelli. But Eve had a secret: She was Shane's daughter! Eve believed that Emma was her mother and vowed revenge on Kim for supposedly destroying her parents' marriage. Eve was eventually arrested for a car accident in which she hit Sarah Horton, Mickey and Maggie's young daughter. After the accident, Eve begged for Shane's help, and she was finally forced to tell him the truth. Using a letter from the midwife who delivered her as confirmation, Eve convinced Shane she was his daughter.

Meantime, Shane learned that Victor was plotting to kill him because of his ISA investigation of the missing computer disc. Shane staged a phony affair with his former partner and ex-lover Gabrielle Pascal to convince Victor he had been discharged from the ISA and was no longer a threat. But Shane continued his investigation with the help of both the ISA and Gabrielle.

Glenn Gallagher went undercover to expose his high school coach as a drug pusher. Young Max was shot in the sting operation when Frankie rushed in to save Glenn. Frankie and Jennifer grew closer, and the young artist, Frankie, painted a beautiful portrait of Jennifer. Jennifer and Glenn finally broke up when Jennifer, a virgin, would not make love to him. But Jennifer's friendship with Frankie blossomed into love. When their friend, Sasha, tried to break her ties to Nick, the pimp, Jennifer and Frankie helped her. Shawn and Caroline Brady officially adopted Frankie and Max. Max finally surmounted his emotional problems and spoke.

Bill Horton returned to Salem and became head of surgery at University Hospital. He and Jennifer clashed, and she rushed into an engagement with

Frankie. However, Jennifer soon learned that both her grandmother and mother were diagnosed schizophrenics. She broke up with Frankie, fearing the mental disorder might be hereditary.

Maggie became ill with myasthenia gravis and, with her family's support, struggled to overcome the disease. Janice Barnes, Maggie and Mickey's former foster child, returned to Salem as an intern at University Hospital. There she fell in love with Bill Horton, for whom she worked.

For months Calliope had professed that Eugene was working in the basement, but she finally confessed that he had left her. Calliope was wooed by Ethan Reilly, but she pursued Trevor Lodge.

Neil Curtis hired Jo Johnson as his housekeeper, and she fell in love with him. But Neil turned his attentions to the beautiful Grace Forrester. Neil soon proposed marriage, and Grace joyfully accepted.

After discovering that Victor had the missing disc, Shane and Roman enlisted Diana's help to spy on Victor. Diana feigned romantic feelings for Victor and accompanied him to Greece. Roman followed her and they finally admitted their feelings and made love. Victor learned of Diana's betrayal. Victor's arch-enemy, Serena, got the disc and warned Roman to take Diana and leave Greece. But Roman followed Serena, who was discovered to be secretly mining the element found in the computer disc. Roman was caught and almost killed by Serena's men, but he managed to escape, shooting Serena in the process. Diana was stunned to discover that Serena was her mother and that Roman had shot and captured her, turning the disc over to the government.

Victor told Diana that if she married him, he would have her mother released from prison. Diana loved Roman but agreed to marry Victor to save her mother. On her wedding day to Victor, Roman kidnapped Diana and freed her mother from Victor's manipulations. In the process, Philip Colville, Diana's father, was shot and killed by Ed Daniels.

After her father's death, Diana inherited her father's fortune and his newspaper, the *Spectator*. Diana wrote an exposé of Victor, revealing his mob connections. Roman feared that it would interfere with his investigation of Victor's mob connections with the Torres family.

Serena was abducted and taken to Peru. Diana, Adrienne, Justin, and Roman followed and ransomed Serena for $10 million. Roman finally discovered that the kidnapping was a fake and that Serena and Victor had schemed to gain Diana's inheritance through the ransom. Diana tried various schemes to get back her money from Victor, including stealing a Greek icon. She eventually devoted herself to running the *Spectator*.

Adrienne had trouble adjusting to life as Mrs. Kiriakis. Justin tried to renounce his uncle's tradition, but soon returned to the old ways. When Adrienne learned she was pregnant, she considered an abortion, but could not go through with it. Although she initially led Justin to believe that she had, the truth came out, and the couple reunited. However, Adrienne later miscarried.

Adrienne Johnson (Judi Evans) married *Justin Kiriakis* (Wally Kurth) on November 16, 1987, in Greece. Courtesy Corday Productions [Gary Null].

Justin and Adrienne's marriage further suffered because of the Kiriakis involvement with the Torres family. Justin went to Washington, D.C., and testified against the mob and the Torres family. Jose Torres attempted to kill Justin in retaliation, but Victor took the bullet meant for Justin. Victor survived. Justin was hailed as a hero for his part in destroying the Torres family. But Adrienne refused to live with her husband, who had moved back into the Kiriakis mansion.

Justin thought his marriage was over and, drunk and looking for comfort, had sex with Anjelica one night in the Kiriakis stables. When Anjelica discovered she was pregnant she assumed the baby was her husband's. But Harper angrily accused her of infidelity: He was sterile. Anjelica then knew the baby to be Justin's, but she did not tell him. Justin told Anjelica that he would always love Adrienne and that Adrienne had moved back into the mansion.

Steve rescued a dying Kayla from the Deveraux mansion. He obtained an antidote with Alice's help, and Kayla improved. Steve was aided by his childhood friend, Dr. Marcus Hunter, who had moved to Salem. Steve declared his love for Kayla, but she again vanished. Steve finally found her being nursed by the local eccentric, Professor Schenkel. The lovers reunited, and Kayla tried to persuade Steve to run away with her, convinced that someone was trying to kill her. Steve told Kayla the truth: that Jack was his brother Billy and that he had pushed her away in order to give Billy/Jack a reason to live and save his life. If they left now, Steve feared what would happen to Jack.

Kayla returned to Jack, intending to tell him the truth and ask for a divorce after the election. On election night, a tabloid reporter, Canby, gave Jack photos proving that Kayla had been sleeping with Steve when she was married to Jack. During the same time Kayla had refused to make love with her husband, Jack. Jack confronted Kayla with the evidence and, in a moment of rage, raped her.

Kayla fled with Steve to a mountain cabin, and there they exchanged vows. Jack discovered them and forced Kayla to return to Salem for his swearing-in ceremony, while his henchmen tried to dispose of Steve. They tossed Steve into a ravine, but he survived the fall and returned to Salem to confront Jack. The brothers battled on the roof, and Jack fell, damaging his kidney.

Jack had already lost one kidney to his Hodgkin's disease, so a donor was needed. Steve donated his kidney and saved Jack's life. Steve almost died, but while in a coma envisioned his future with Kayla and the rest of his family, including Jack, and resolved to live. Kayla pressed rape charges against Jack, but the case never went to trial. Instead, Jack agreed to divorce Kayla, and Kayla and Steve decided to wed.

Melissa discovered the adoption papers that proved Jack Deveraux was really William Earle "Billy" Johnson. Melissa decided to hide the truth from Jack because she loved him. But he eventually discovered the truth and was devastated by the confession that all he held dear was a lie. He was not the son of Senator Harper Deveraux, but rather the son of Duke Johnson, wife-beater and daughter-raper. Melissa, Steve, Adrienne, and Jo tried to convince him that they lied because they loved him, but Jack lamented that no one had loved him enough to tell him the truth.

Meanwhile, Harper framed Melissa for Kayla's poisoning. Melissa was arrested, but she convinced Kayla she was innocent, and Kayla dropped the charges. Jack turned to Melissa as the only person who still loved him, but he eventually came to use her to further his political career, and he proposed marriage. Melissa's father, Mickey, was nominated to fill Harper's vacant Senate seat, and Jack decided to run against him. Anjelica convinced both Jack and Melissa that Melissa would make a good politician's wife.

Another Salemite learned her parents were not who she had believed. Eve Donovan discovered that her natural mother was Gabrielle Pascal. Gabrielle had come to Salem to work on a case with Shane and had no idea that Eve was the daughter she had years before given up for adoption. Shane wanted Eve to move into the Donovan mansion with him, Kim, and Andrew. But Eve was determined to reunite her parents and destroy Kim and Shane's marriage. Gabrielle's presence in Salem combined with Eve's manipulations caused Kim, who was already under doctor's orders to remain calm after a near miscarriage, further stress.

Eve's problems overwhelmed Kim. And even though Shane accepted and acknowledged Eve as his daughter, the teen-ager returned to Nick and a life of prostitution. One night Eve was cornered by an enraged john and called Kim, who rushed to her rescue. Kim was beaten and thrown against a wall; she miscarried. Kim, distraught, left Salem to sort out her feelings.

In the meantime, Gabrielle tried to renew her love affair with Shane and make them, with Eve, a family. But troubles abounded. Eve found the body of her friend, Esther, a hooker. Later, Eve was attacked by a man with a knife who slashed her face, leaving her scarred. Eve's life as a hooker came to light, but Shane stood by her and legally adopted her to prove his love. When Eve came home from the hospital, Shane suggested Gabrielle move into the guest house to help Eve. Gabrielle was attacked by, but escaped, the Knifer.

Kim soon returned to Salem and went undercover as a hooker to help Shane, Gabrielle, and the Salem police catch the serial killer who had been terrorizing Salem. Working closely with Kim made Shane realize how much he loved her, and they again reunited. Finally admitting that Shane would never be hers, Gabrielle left Salem. Kim and Shane renewed their wedding vows and honeymooned in England. Eve went for counseling and tried to get along with Kim and Shane, but she had trouble with her high school peers.

While Shane and Kim were at Donovan Manor, Shane was shocked to have his identical twin brother, Drew, show up. Drew returned to Salem with the Donovans. Drew was also an ISA agent, but his past was clouded.

The series of brutal murders continued and even Jack Deveraux was a suspect, but the shocking revelation was that the respected Senator Harper Deveraux was the killer! After his initial attempt to kill Kayla with poison had failed, Harper tried again. He attacked her with a knife, but Kayla escaped. In the pursuit, Harper knocked over a can of gasoline which caused an explosion that caused Kayla to lose both her voice and her hearing. Harper made one final try to kill Kayla, the woman he blamed for destroying his life and that of his "son," Jack. Harper broke into the loft and took Kayla and her sister, Kim, hostage. He forced them to the roof and there confessed his crimes. Shane and

Steve captured Harper and rescued Kim and Kayla. Jack was again devastated, this time by the news that his beloved and revered "father" was a serial killer.

Kayla tried to cope with her deafness as both Steve and her family rallied around her. Steve wanted to marry her, and, after her initial refusal, she relented. She had an operation, but it seemed to fail. Kayla again turned away Steve. However, Kayla soon realized that she and Steve belonged together, no matter what, and accepted Steve's proposal. Steve gave Kayla her dream wedding aboard a yacht, and, during the ceremony, Kayla's hearing and voice miraculously returned as the lovers exchanged vows.

They honeymooned in the Orient, where they found a deaf child, Benjy, seemingly abandoned by his mother. They brought Benjy with them to Salem. Ellen, Benjy's mother, tried to see Benjy, to tell him that she loved him and wanted him back. But she decided it was too dangerous. She was right. Ellen was killed.

Benjy, his grandfather Orion, Roman's former Kung Fu master, and his mysterious and powerful father were at the heart of a mystery tied to Roman's past. After he fell from that cliff and was presumed dead, Roman had been programmed to become the Pawn, John Black. Although Roman had now regained his memory, he had "spells" during which he became susceptible to any command, including commands to kill. Diana eventually discovered the trances were induced by the image of a pagoda. Diana and Roman vowed to uncover the secrets of his past and found mysterious rings as the clue with which to begin their search.

Harper held a press conference from prison and announced he was giving all his money to a victims' rights organization. Anjelica panicked that she would have no money, but Jack promised to help her. With Harper in jail for murder, Jack went public with his true identity, announcing he was really Billy Johnson.

Neil had a brief relapse into drug dependency, but found solace and security in his new relationship with Grace Forrester. Neil was unaware of Jo's love for him, although he supported Jo during her battle with breast cancer. Neil planned to marry Grace, but she was killed by the Riverfront Knifer. Later, Neil married his friend, the pregnant Anjelica Deveraux, to protect her from Victor, who wanted to marry her and raise his grandnephew as his heir.

Not knowing that his father, Bill, was interested in Janice, Mike began to date her. The conflict between father and son escalated, but Janice decided she preferred Mike to his father. However, Janice was killed by the Riverfront Knifer. Bill left Salem to return to his wife, Laura, who had been re-institutionalized for her mental disorder.

Jennifer feared that she might inherit her mother's mental illness and broke up with Frankie. Frankie went to work on a Teen Emergency hotline and became involved with his counselor, Paula Carson. Frankie admitted to Paula that he was a virgin, and they made love. But Eve, who had wanted Frankie for herself, saw Frankie and Paula together and used that information to further

Kayla Brady (Mary Beth Evans) married *Steve Johnson* (Stephen Nichols) on July 25, 1988, on board ship. During the ceremony, the bride, who had been deafened, miraculously had her hearing restored. *Carrie Brady* (Christie Clark) looks on. Courtesy Corday Productions.

separate Frankie and Jennifer. Eve wrote a letter to the school paper accusing Paula of seducing her students. Paula resigned, and eventually Frankie and Jennifer were reunited.

The couple took summer jobs at the *Spectator*. But their happiness was short-lived as Trent returned to Salem. It seemed that Trent was Max's abusive father, and he wanted Max back. Frankie revealed that he and Max were not really related. Trent finally left Salem when he realized that Max and Frankie had found a true home with the Bradys. Jennifer and Frankie decided to make love, but Jennifer could not go through with it because Frankie was leaving Salem to attend Columbia University. Frankie left Salem, and Jennifer began to attend Salem University.

Steve agreed to work as a liaison between the Salem Police Department and the riverfront gangs when gang violence began to rise. While trying to stop a gang fight, Steve was held at gunpoint. Roman arrived and shot and killed Steve's captor, Raoul Ramirez. Feeling guilty about Raoul's death, Steve tried to help Raoul's brother, Emilio, by getting him a job as Justin and Adrienne's gardener. Adrienne befriended Emilio and tried to teach him to read. The youngest Ramirez brother, Julio, became an object of infatuation for young Carrie Brady. Emilio's sister, April, became involved with Mike Horton. Mike cared for Rosa Ramirez, the family's mother, who was dying of cancer. Rosa's husband

and the children's father, Monty, was an alcoholic, but with help from his family and Steve he stopped drinking.

Tom Horton began a second career as a beatnik poet, called Norm De Plume, at Calliope's club, the *Beat Bar*. Tom hid his newfound passion from his family, but they soon discovered his secret and gave him their blessing. To their horror, Tom and Alice learned that their 50-year marriage had not been legally performed, and they were really not married. Tom quickly remedied the situation by again proposing to his beloved Alice. The couple was married in front of their children and grandchildren.

The imprisoned Harper convinced Jack that he was being mistreated and asked Jack to get him transferred. Jack turned to his friends and family for help, but received none. Meanwhile, Anjelica turned down Victor's proposal again, hoping to get Harper's Swiss bank accounts. Victor offered to help Jack get Harper out of prison and into Switzerland, thus depriving Anjelica of any Swiss funds. The escape attempt went awry, and Harper was shot. Jack insisted that Victor's men get help, and, to his surprise, they returned with Kayla. Kayla saved Harper, and Jack demanded her release. But Steve and Marcus rescued Kayla, and Harper was returned to prison.

Jack and Melissa were to be married. But on their wedding day, Melissa found Jack kissing another woman. Melissa walked down the aisle, but denounced Jack at the altar, refusing to marry him. The press had a field day with Jack, and the next day Melissa left for Europe—alone.

Justin and Adrienne drifted apart as Justin became more and more like his Uncle Victor. Adrienne found herself drawn to the less complicated Emilio, and they became lovers. But Justin found out about their one-night stand and in a jealous rage arranged for Emilio to have an "accident" at the Kiriakis stables. However, the night of the accident, Justin discovered, to his horror, that Adrienne was in the barn. Justin rushed to save her and was the victim of a trap of his own making. His temporary paralysis drew Justin and Adrienne closer together, but his Uncle Victor again interfered in the life of the couple and secretly gave Justin medication that made him impotent. When the couple left town for a vacation and Justin was away from the drug, his problem was solved. Justin finally discovered the truth about his uncle, and Justin and Adrienne moved out of the Kiriakis mansion.

Victor plotted to ruin Neil and win Anjelica by enticing Neil back into gambling. Eventually Victor called in all of Neil's loans, and Neil was forced to put *Blondie's* up for sale. Anjelica and Neil Curtis finally divorced, and Anjelica pursued the man she really wanted: Justin, the father of her son, Alexander.

Justin was stunned to at last discover that he was Alexander's father. To force Justin's hand, Anjelica vowed to marry Victor, and it worked. Justin agreed to let Anjelica and the baby move into the penthouse with him and Adrienne. An insecure Adrienne, on Victor's advice, told Justin she was pregnant. When Justin discovered the lie, the couple divorced.

Rosa Ramirez died, and both Mike and April were suspected of turning off her life-support system. However, it was her husband, Monty, wanting to end her pain and suffering, who had pulled the plug. Mike and April's romance was destroyed by her dependency on alcohol. Jo Johnson finally got April to join AA, and Mike and April were briefly reunited. However, Robin Jacobs returned to Salem and revealed that she had had a son, Jeremy, by Mike. April loved Mike, but she decided he belonged with Robin and Jeremy.

Shane's twin brother, Drew, was finally revealed to be working for the mastermind behind the case involving Roman, Diana, Benjy, Orion, Steve, and Kayla. It was Stefano DiMera, arisen again like the phoenix to wreak havoc on the lives of those in Salem. Drew kidnapped Carrie and took her to Stefano's island to exchange her for Stefano's son, Benjy. Drew then lured Shane, Steve, Kayla, Roman, Kimberly, and Diana there as well. Roman finally broke free of Stefano's hypnotic powers and helped everyone to escape—everyone except Diana. Drew got shot saving Kim and Shane. Steve and Kayla escaped with Benjy. Roman went back to save Diana.

Stefano, who had been tantalizing Roman with the possibility that his beloved Marlena was still alive, demanded that Roman choose between the two women. Roman refused. Then Benjy, who had secretly stowed away in Roman's car, appeared and told his father, Stefano, that he was a bad man. Now knowing that he had lost his son, Stefano simply let Roman, Diana, and Benjy go and revealed that Marlena was not alive. Benjy finally left Salem with his grandfather, Orion. Drew recovered from his wounds and also left Salem.

Jack Deveraux became Diana's partner in her newspaper, the *Spectator*. Jack seemed to enjoy causing mischief. He tracked down the mysterious Cal Winters, who turned out to be Diana's MIA husband. Diana panicked and begged Roman to elope, but Cal found them and stopped the ceremony. Roman eventually proved that the marriage between Cal and Diana never happened. Roman and Diana again planned to marry, but had to postpone the ceremony when Roman's mother, Caroline, had a heart attack and emergency triple-bypass surgery. She recovered.

But Diana was still tormented with thoughts from her past and fears of Cal. During a struggle with Cal, Roman was shot. Cal confessed to the crime, but it was eventually revealed that Cal confessed to spare Diana. Diana, who had no memory of the shooting, remembered, under hypnosis, that she was the one who had accidentally shot Roman. Roman forgave her, but Diana, distraught, left town in secrecy, begging Roman not to follow and to move on with his life.

Justin wanted revenge on his Uncle Victor for destroying his marriage to Adrienne, so he hired prostitute Yvette Dupre to masquerade as a baroness and seduce Victor. Yvette met Roman, and sparks flew. Yvette tried to help Roman's daughter, Carrie, who had become involved with a "fast" crowd. Victor proposed to Yvette, but she was drawn to Roman. When she helped Roman spy on

Victor, Victor discovered the truth and vowed revenge. Roman helped Yvette leave town and start a new life.

Eve continued to be drawn to Nick Corelli, her ex-pimp. But she soon began to ignore her friend in favor of her obnoxious school chums. The group, led by Jake, challenged Nick to a drag race. During the race, Nick's car was cut off and plunged over a cliff and burst into flames. Eve told the police the truth about the race, but her "friends" lied and said she plotted Nick's death. Eve mourned for Nick and blamed herself for his death.

Nick was not dead, but he was badly disfigured from the burns he had suffered in the crash. Nick was taken in and cared for by Steve. Assuming Nick was dead and Eve would know the whereabouts of Nick's money, Eddie Reed kidnapped Eve and demanded the $2 million he and Nick had conned from Harper Deveraux. Eddie had been caught and sent to jail. Nick had promised Eddie the entire $2 million for not implicating Nick. Now Eddie wanted his money.

Nick came to Eve's rescue and hid her in a secret room of the mansion until Shane arrived to save his daughter and arrest Eddie. Eve never knew that Nick was her phantom savior, for he had worn a mask during the entire ordeal. Nick slipped away and left the deed to the mansion to Steve and Kayla in gratitude for their helping him. Nick eventually resurfaced, and he and Eve helped each other through the trauma of reconstructive surgery: Nick to repair the burns from the accident, Eve to correct the scar on her cheek left from the attack of the Riverfront Knifer. However, Eddie escaped and again took Eve hostage, as she awaited surgery. Eddie was killed in the ensuing gun battle, and Eve was rescued.

Jennifer began to work as an intern for Jack Deveraux at the *Spectator* (with Diana gone, Jack was now in charge). She soon championed the cause of Sally, a young unwed mother who could not keep her baby in prison. Jennifer moved into Steve and Kayla's old loft, for which Jack paid, and became Hannah's foster mother. Jack and Jennifer grew closer as Jack helped Jennifer take care of baby Hannah. When Sally's parents took baby Hannah to care for her until Sally was released, Jennifer was heartbroken, and Jack comforted her.

Working for the *Spectator*, Jennifer met Emilio Ramirez while researching a story on the gangs. Emilio was drawn to Jennifer. He named a horse he was training for Neil Curtis Jennifer's Beauty. When Jennifer was lost in a storm, Emilio saved her.

Meanwhile, Jack and Jennifer became closer friends. Anjelica realized Jack was falling for Jennifer, even if he would not admit it to himself, and suggested he see Jennifer away from Salem and the newspaper. Jack took Jennifer to a journalists' conference in Atlantic City, where a drunken Jack let slip that he thought he was not good enough for Jennifer. But the next morning Jack was back to his usual distant self and Jennifer, confused, returned to Salem. Her feelings for Jack grew, but he denied her growing affections as well as his own.

Jack devoted himself to the newspaper, pouring all his energies into making the *Spectator* a respected publication. In the process, he redeemed himself by becoming a top-notch journalist. His efforts were rewarded when he won the Ferraro journalism award. During the ceremony, Jack thanked his staff for their assistance and support, but his eyes were on Jennifer alone.

The Reverend Saul Taylor came to town and set up his revival tent. The tent collapsed, and the accident blinded his sweet daughter, Faith, and hurt Jennifer, who was knocked unconscious and suffered a concussion. Jack remained by Jennifer's side until she awakened but again pulled away. Faith, meanwhile, was tended by Dr. Marcus Hunter, Steve's oldest friend. Marcus and Steve had been raised together in the orphanage. Marcus operated to restore Faith's sight. He thought of her as a friend, but Faith was falling for the good doctor. Their growing friendship unnerved Saul. Faith thought it was because Marcus was black, but a far deeper mystery was involved.

As Jack continued to push her away, Jennifer found herself drawn to Emilio. Emilio wore his heart on his sleeve, unlike the reserved Jack. But Jennifer was torn. When Emilio was hurt in a gang fight, protecting Jennifer, Jennifer rushed to his side. But Jack was the one she thanked when he gave blood to save Emilio. Later, when Jack was badly beaten by the same gang, Jennifer nursed him back to health at her loft.

Dr. Gail Carson arrived in town and began to date Marcus. When Marcus went to Cleaver, South Carolina, to search for clues to his past, Gail accompanied him, fearing for his life. As a boy, Marcus had witnessed a church bombing in which three young black girls were killed. His parents were murdered protecting him, and the young Marcus was sent to the orphanage in an effort to save his life.

Meanwhile, Shane was abducted by Colonel Alfred Jericho, an old ISA buddy, now turned villain. Under threat of death, Shane was forced to call home and tell Kim he was away on a mission. When someone began to blackmail Kim about her past and later threaten her, she turned to Cal Winters for help. The man behind the threats was Adam, an employee at the radio station where Kim did her phone-in show. He was obsessed with Kim.

It turned out that Jericho was in cahoots with the Reverend Saul. Meantime, Gail was revealed to be an ISA agent out to get Saul and Jericho and to protect Marcus. Steve wanted to help his old friend and joined the ISA. Marcus performed plastic surgery on Steve's eye and, minus his trademark patch, Steve went undercover. Posing as drifter Daniel Lucas, Steve infiltrated Saul's group and its wilderness retreat. Kayla followed Steve to help him and secretly befriended Faith, who finally realized her father was up to no good. Steve found the kidnapped Shane and freed him, but Shane was shot as the two made their escape. Back in Salem, Marcus remembered that Saul and Jericho were the two who had set the explosion in Cleaver, killing those three girls.

Realizing they were about to get caught, Jericho killed Saul. Shane followed Jericho to his communications center, hidden in a cave. Jericho set off explosives to destroy all the evidence. As Shane and Jericho struggled on a cliff above the cave, the mountain exploded. Steve rushed to save Shane, but it was too late. All of Salem assumed Shane was dead. A devastated Kim turned to Cal for comfort. In her grief, Eve rejected Kim and their relationship returned to the bad old days of yore. When Marcus discovered Gail was an ISA agent, they split, and Gail left town.

Shane, as it turned out, was alive but had amnesia. He had been washed downstream after the explosion and was found by Rebecca Downey. Rebecca was on the run from her husband, Arthur, because she had discovered his illegal stock dealings. Rebecca and Shane joined forces. Shane, not knowing who he was, called himself Sam. Eventually Arthur tracked them down, and Shane killed him in self-defense.

Nick bought *Blondie's* from Neil, renamed it *Wings*, and hired Eve as a singer. Eve confessed her love for Nick. But knowing he was no good for her, Nick entered into a platonic marriage with his friend April Ramirez to discourage Eve. April agreed to marry Nick to discourage Mike, who she thought belonged with Robin and Jeremy. Eve schemed to win back Nick and get revenge on April, but Mike discouraged her plans.

Soon April and Nick found themselves drawn to each other as Nick discovered he had a brain tumor. Nick, believing he would die, decided to live his last days to the fullest with April. But April and Mike convinced Nick to have a dangerous operation. The brain surgery was a success, and Nick quickly recovered.

After her father's death, Faith was taken in by Tom and Alice Horton. Scott Banning, their great-great-grandson, returned to Salem and was drawn to Faith. A smooth operator, Scott managed Eve's singing career. Scott also became partners with Nick, informing Nick that although he owned *Wings*, Scott owned the land beneath it. Scott, Faith, and Eve soon became entangled with record producer Colin Dawson. After some dirty dealings, Colin left Salem.

Meanwhile, Eugene Bradford returned to Salem and hid in the Donovans' basement. He was working on a secret project: a robot that looked like his beloved Calliope. Eugene finally decided to let Calliope know he was back in Salem. But on the day of their rendezvous, Calliope was kidnapped by Eugene's competitor, Mr. Balboni, who thought Calliope was Eugene's robot. Eugene finally rescued Calliope with the help of his robot, and the couple reconciled. However, Eugene soon had to leave, although he promised Calliope it would be for only a little while.

Steve was shocked when his first wife, Marina Toscano, long thought dead, arrived in Salem. It seemed that she had not drowned the night she fell overboard a ship, but instead let Steve think she was dead. Now she was back to beg Steve's help in looking for the key to what her father, Ernesto, had called the family treasure. Steve was tormented with thoughts of Marina, and her appearance threatened his marriage with Kayla. Unknown to Steve, Kayla was pregnant.

Steve and Marina left for Italy to look for the key. Kayla did not tell Steve she was pregnant, wanting him to come back to her, not the baby. His brother, Jack, now determined to make up for the past and help Steve and Kayla, tried to get Steve to listen to reason, but failed. Jack then took Kayla to Italy, but Kayla found Marina and Steve in a compromising situation. Kayla left Italy without telling Steve the truth. While in Italy, Steve had a bloody battle with some thugs and again lost his eye. Steve returned to Salem, his eye too damaged for reconstructive surgery, and the patch returned. Unknown to Steve, Marina had found the key in Italy and brought it back with her to Salem.

Victor Kiriakis wanted the key for reasons of his own. Several attempts were made on Steve and Marina's lives. Soon, Marina was found murdered, and Kayla seemed the likely suspect. Then, falsely believing that Steve had the key, Victor had Kayla kidnapped and offered to trade Kayla for the key.

In his efforts to help Steve and Kayla, Jack had followed Marina to Bayview Sanitarium and there found her sister, Isabella. Jack eventually helped Isabella escape, and the two began to hunt for the key. To hide Isabella from Victor, Jack asked Jennifer for help. Jack and Jennifer grew closer, but Jack again pushed away for fear of putting Jennifer in danger. Jack and Jennifer finally found the key by accident. Marina had hidden the key in a piece of pottery at Steve's house. While Jack and Jennifer were searching the house, Steve returned, and the two intruders ended up hiding in a secret room. They shared their first kiss in the darkened room, and, while lost in Jack's embrace, Jennifer dropped the pottery. It broke, and the key was revealed. Now firmly convinced of the danger, Jack again pushed away Jennifer, telling her the kiss meant nothing.

Jack gave the key to Isabella, who in turn gave it to Steve to free Kayla. But the plan went awry, and Isabella was shot. Roman, who had come to help Steve free his sister, rushed Isabella to the hospital, and Steve freed Kayla. Meanwhile, Jack, who had made a duplicate key, flew to Italy and found the treasure, the diary of Loretta Toscano, Isabella's late mother. Jack surreptitiously ripped out several pages, then gave the diary to Isabella.

Shane was still wandering the countryside with Rebecca, who had fallen in love with him. But he was plagued by thoughts of another life. Kim, believing Shane dead, had sex with Cal Winters. Cal became obsessed with Kim.

Shane finally returned to Salem, but still had no memory of Kim, although under hypnosis he would remember bits and pieces of his past. Cal arranged an accident in which Kim shot Shane, believing him to be a prowler. Shane survived and began to suspect Cal. Cal coerced Rebecca into helping him keep the Donovans apart. But Rebecca finally rebelled, and Cal had her killed in a car crash.

Shane began to remember his passions for Kim, and one night the lovers gave in to their feelings. But Shane still could not remember his past. Eventually, in a flood of memory, Shane remembered everything, including the fact that Cal, working for Jericho, had tried to kill him in that mountain explosion. Cal panicked and kidnapped Kim, but Shane saved her. Cal was sent to prison, and the Donovans reunited.

However, their reunion was short-lived. Kim soon discovered she was pregnant. Her physician, Dr. Craig Norris, who was being blackmailed by Cal, lied about how far along she was, so that Kim would believe the baby was Cal's. Kim could not cope, and after the baby's "true" parentage was revealed, the Donovans split. Kim moved to California, where she gave birth to a baby girl, Jeannie. Shane eventually took his son, Andrew, to Los Angeles to live with Kim.

Julie returned to Salem, but without Doug. Julie was now a successful businesswoman and almost immediately had a confrontation with Victor Kiriakis. Julie strengthened her position in Salem by becoming a member of the hospital board. Julie also planned a surprise wedding anniversary party for Maggie and Mickey. The biggest surprise turned out to be Melissa's return to Salem.

Melissa quickly saw Jack and Jennifer's attraction to each other and warned Jennifer to stay away from Jack and Jack to stay away from Jennifer. But Jack ignored Melissa and secretly nominated Jennifer for the Ferraro Award. Jennifer won, never knowing that Jack had nominated her or that he had been there, hiding in the back of the room, to see her win. After winning the award, job offers poured in for Jennifer. Jennifer hoped Jack would ask her to stay at the *Spectator*. He would not, but Jennifer stayed anyway.

Melissa, now a singer, met Emilio, and the two decided to become a singing duo. The night of their big opening at *Wings*, Jack asked Jennifer to work late. The power went out, and the couple was trapped in the office. Jack almost succumbed to his feelings for Jennifer, but as his lips neared hers, the lights came back on, and Jack sent Jennifer off to *Wings* and Emilio.

Kayla and Steve were about to rewed. Steve had finally made peace with his brother, Jack, and asked him to be best man. But as the bride began to walk down the aisle, policeman Abe Carver stopped the wedding and arrested the bride for Marina's murder! The stress of the trial caused Kayla to go into labor, and she gave birth to a baby girl, Stephanie Kaye. After the birth, Kayla was convicted and sent to prison.

Steve hired a nanny who called herself Kelly. Her real name was Sheila. She had lost a baby, and her child's death had left her unbalanced. She kidnapped Stephanie in an effort to replace her own child. Kelly took the baby to Australia, but was closely followed by Steve and Kayla, who had escaped from prison. Steve and Kayla eventually rescued Stephanie with the help of Bo Brady, who unexpectedly came to their aid in Australia.

Meanwhile, Roman and Isabella were falling in love. Victor revealed to

Isabella that he had been her mother's lover. He told Isabella that it was he who had framed Kayla to protect Isabella for the sake of her mother's memory. Isabella, who did not remember the event, had shot Marina while struggling with her sister. Marina had been going to shoot Kayla, and Isabella stopped her. All charges against Kayla were dropped when Isabella confessed. Isabella never went to trial, as an impassioned plea from police commander Brady saved her. Roman and Isabella grew closer, and he accompanied her to Italy for the reading of her father's will. As his sole living heir, Isabella inherited his entire fortune.

Roman's partner, Abe, began to secretly date fellow police officer Lexie Brooks. Secrecy was necessary because Chief Samuels had decreed that police officers could not date each other. Roman warned his partner to be careful. Abe eventually was offered an out-of-town job as police commander and left Salem. Lexie went with him, and the two were married.

Meanwhile, Jack got a call from Harper. Harper was up for parole and wanted Jack to publicly support his release. Jack's old insecurities resurfaced. Jennifer kissed Jack and proclaimed her belief in him. Jack, torn between his feelings for the man who raised him and what was right, pushed away Jennifer. Jennifer, trying to protect Jack, went to see Harper and demanded that he stay away from Jack.

Meanwhile, Adrienne presented Jack with a gift, a watch inscribed "To Billy." Jack was torn: Was he Deveraux or Johnson? Jack had to find out and went to see Harper, who told him about Jennifer's visit. Jack was furious. He and Jennifer fought, and, in the heat of battle, he fired her. Jack went after Jennifer to apologize and arrived at *Wings* just in time to hear Emilio propose to her. Melissa stopped Jack from interrupting and a heartbroken Jack left. Jennifer got a new job at the local television station and interviewed Jack for her audition assignment. Jack gave a great interview, and the two realized how much they would miss each other.

A huge storm hit Salem, and Jack rescued Jennifer, who was stranded out on her first assignment. They almost kissed, but *Wings* collapsed nearby, and they rushed to help. Maggie was pinned under some rubble, but Emilio saved her, and Melissa was grateful. Faith nearly drowned in the nearby river. Jack and Julie rushed to aid Scott, and Faith was rescued but was left paralyzed.

Scott vowed to stand by Faith and help her walk again. Scott had gone to medical school for one year and still retained his dream to become a doctor. With Julie's encouragement, Scott decided to pursue his dream, and he moved to California to go to medical school. Faith accompanied him.

Jennifer went to Jack's house and confronted Jack with her love for him. Jack's feelings resurfaced, and the couple began to make love. But they were interrupted by a phone call from Melissa. Jennifer left Jack to go to *Wings* and do a story on Emilio and Melissa. Jennifer told Jack to meet her there to discuss their future or she would never come to him again. Jack started to follow but was haunted by the ghosts of Harper and Duke. Jack again decided he was not good enough for Jennifer and sent her a note saying he would not be coming.

At *Wings*, Emilio, at Melissa's instigation, proposed to Jennifer during their live television broadcast. Jack, horrified, rushed to *Wings* to stop Jennifer from marrying the wrong man. But he would not admit that he loved her. Jennifer begged Jack to reveal his feelings, but he refused. Emilio hit Jack, and Jack left *Wings*.

Jennifer accepted Emilio's proposal, but she gave Jack every opportunity to stop the wedding simply by admitting that he loved her. Jack simply told her Emilio was not the right man for her. Jennifer unhappily went ahead with her wedding plans, but on the day of the wedding, Jack, dressed as a firefighter, arrived at the church and kidnapped the bride, whisking her away on a fire truck to a secluded mountain cabin. But Jack still refused to acknowledge his feelings.

However, the next day Jennifer accidentally fell over a cliff, and when Jack feared she might be dead, he poured out his heart to her. Then in attempting to rescue her, Jack was trapped on the ledge as well. They braved snakes and a night together in the wilderness, and the next day, Jack kissed Jennifer. But just as Jack was on the verge of finally telling her how he felt, Emilio and Melissa arrived to "save" them. Emilio dropped Jennifer's engagement ring and fell off the cliff making a grab for it. Jennifer now pushed Jack away and vowed to marry Emilio, who she felt had been hurt trying to save her. What Jennifer failed to notice was that Melissa was falling for Emilio.

Nick Corelli annulled his platonic marriage to April, realizing April would never love him and would always love Mike. Mike and April made wedding plans, but the wedding was postponed when Mike was called to China to help in a medical crisis. Nick and April remained friends, and he comforted her when Mike's stay in China lengthened. In gratitude, April asked Shane to help find Nick's long lost-brother, Johnny Corelli.

Meanwhile, Bo confided to Steve that he was being followed. Victor was having Bo watched, but it was for his own protection. Bo left Australia and went to Paris to meet Hope. Julie flew to Paris to ask Bo and Hope to return to Salem. Hope longed to return home, but Bo wanted to stay away from Salem and Victor. Victor went to Paris and told Bo he wanted to reclaim him as his son.

Bo and Hope argued about going back to Salem. But Bo was soon kidnapped by none other than Ernesto Toscano, Isabella's father, who had been believed dead. Ernesto forced Bo to write Hope a note telling her he was leaving her. Then Ernesto revealed his evil plan: Ernesto would have a Bo look-alike replace Bo in Salem and get close to Victor. The man scheduled to have surgery and switch places with Bo turned out to be Johnny Corelli, Nick's long-lost brother. But Bo had a plan and convinced Johnny to switch places with him.

"The Cruise of Deception" Masked Ball. *Victor Kiriakis* (John Aniston) and *Julie Williams* (Susan Seaforth Hayes) are "Kate" and "Petrucchio," while *Jack Deveraux* (Matthew Ashford) and *Jennifer Horton* (Melissa Reeves) are "King Arthur" and "Guinevere" (1990). Courtesy Corday Productions [Joseph del Valle].

Bo returned to Salem, determined to protect his family and friends from Ernesto. Victor now publicly proclaimed Bo as his son and asked him to move into the mansion. Bo agreed. Hope hated Victor and wanted no part of him. Julie, Hope's half-sister and stepmother, counseled Hope not to give up on Bo.

Jack and Jennifer were soon embroiled in the adventure. Victor and a mystery man wanted the pages missing from Loretta's diary. Jack was beaten by thugs who were looking for the missing diary pages, and Jennifer saved him. While tending Jack's wounds, Jennifer snatched the pages from him, read them and discovered the secret Jack had been hiding. The couple vowed not to reveal the contents of the diary pages to anyone, and the secret bound them closer together. When Jennifer's life was threatened, she moved in with Jack for safety.

Meanwhile, Adrienne opened her own successful construction business.

Anjelica, jealous, paid Hank Tobin to sabotage a building that Adrienne's firm was constructing. The building collapsed with Hank and Adrienne inside. Hank was killed, and Justin became imprisoned trying to save Adrienne. Trapped together in the ruined building, the couple realized how much they loved each other, and Justin proposed. Jack and Jennifer covered the story, and Jennifer comforted Jack as he worried about his sister, Adrienne. Justin and Adrienne were finally rescued, with Jack's help, and all evidence began to point to Anjelica as saboteur.

Anjelica, realizing she was about to get caught, fled Salem with Alexander. The plane on which they were scheduled crashed, and everyone believed Anjelica and Alexander to be dead. However, in truth, they had missed their plane and were very much alive. Justin, mourning the loss of his son, was consoled by Adrienne. Jack, mourning the loss of the woman who had raised him and the baby he had thought of as a brother, was comforted by Jennifer.

Justin and Adrienne were remarried in a beautiful ceremony. Jack and Steve gave away the bride, with Jo looking on, and Adrienne rejoiced in her reunited family. The happy couple honeymooned in Tahiti, there they met Dr. Carly Manning, who decided to move to Salem after hearing tales of the city. Carly soon began work as an intern at University Hospital.

Mickey devoted himself to his work, and Maggie, feeling neglected, found herself drawn to Neil Curtis. The couple fought their growing feelings. But when Sarah was injured in a fire on a movie set, Maggie overheard Neil confess he was Sarah's father. When Maggie confronted him, Neil admitted the truth. Maggie had always believed Evan Whyland to be Sarah's biological father, but Neil revealed that the evil Stuart had really donated the sperm. Neil, not wanting Maggie to carry the villain's child, substituted his own sperm for the artificial insemination. Maggie was never to have known the truth, but now it drew the couple closer together, and they became lovers.

Soon Jennifer, Jack, Victor, Bo, Julie, Roman, and Isabella received invitations to a so-called romantic cruise on the ship *Loretta* in honor of Isabella's dead mother. Unknown to all save Bo, the cruise was the beginning of Ernesto's evil plan. Jack, Jennifer, Roman, Isabella, Victor, Julie, Bo and a stowaway Hope sailed on the *Loretta*. The mystery deepened as the lovers on board grew closer. During a masquerade ball, Hope, dressed as Scarlett O'Hara, surprised Bo. Bo finally revealed the truth behind his actions, and the couple joyfully reunited and made love. The Salemites were asked to perform a strange play, written by Ernesto, and all became suspicious. Jack and Jennifer began to investigate, and Ernesto had them locked in their cabin. Fearing the worst, Jack and Jennifer confessed their true feelings, but as they began to make love, they overheard a shocking revelation on the intercom. The man behind the cruise was none other than Ernesto Toscano, and he had set a bomb to go off!

Jack and Jennifer escaped from their cabin and rushed to the ballroom, but it was too late. Ernesto had kidnapped Isabella and disappeared. Fearing for

Isabella's safety, Jack and Jennifer finally revealed the mystery behind the diary pages. Ernesto had poisoned his wife, Loretta, for her infidelity. Isabella was not really Ernesto's daughter, but Victor's. Then the bomb exploded, and the ship capsized.

Meanwhile, back in Salem, Johnny Corelli was revealed to be a renegade ISA agent. Shane convinced Johnny to reveal Ernesto's plans. When news of the *Loretta*'s sinking reached Salem, Shane and Steve rushed to search for their family and friends.

But those on the sinking ship had found a life raft and managed to make it safely to an island. Jennifer had gouged her leg on a reef, and it became infected. Jack tenderly cared for Jennifer. When she recovered, they declared their love for one another and finally made love. Jennifer promised Jack it was more than she had ever hoped. Jack revealed he had known all along she was the one who would get past his defenses.

Meanwhile, Hope was dreaming portents of doom and feared for Bo's life. Roman rescued Isabella, but Ernesto took Hope hostage. A radio was found, and Jack and Jennifer radioed for help while Bo, Roman, Isabella, Julie, and Victor went into Ernesto's secret underground hideaway. Shane and Steve heard the radioed message and rushed to the island, but it was too late. The evil Ernesto had Hope suspended over a cauldron of boiling acid. Hope told Bo how much she loved him and their son. As a horrified Bo looked on, a huge explosion occurred, and Hope and Ernesto vanished without a trace. Bo searched everywhere, but was finally persuaded to leave when he found Hope's wedding ring among the ashes.

The group returned to Salem. At Hope's memorial service, her friends and loved ones shared their memories of Hope. Melissa sang. Bo initially refused to go to the service, but Alice Horton convinced him that his family and friends needed him. Bo searched for Hope but finally admitted that she was dead. Bo told Shawn-Douglas his mother would not be coming home.

Jennifer broke up with Emilio. He had fallen in love with his singing partner, Melissa, so he gladly ended the engagement. Emilio and Melissa concentrated on their singing careers.

Steve and Kayla joyfully planned their wedding with Jack as best man. On the wedding day, Harper escaped from prison and vowed to kill Steve, whom he blamed for destroying his life. Just as Harper was about to shoot Steve, Jack raced up into the bell tower and stopped Harper. The two men struggled and Harper accidentally plunged to his death. Steve thanked his brother for saving his life, and the wedding continued.

Despite support from Jennifer and his family, Jack was unable to cope with the guilt of "killing" his father and again became convinced he was not good enough for Jennifer and pushed her away. On Tom Horton's advice, Jack finally sought psychiatric help and began to see Dr. Whitney Baker.

Isabella inherited Ernesto's fortune and founded the Toscano Foundation, determined to do good works. She eventually opened her own private detective agency. Isabella was drawn to her father, Victor. Victor planned a surprise party for Isabella's birthday, but Roman spirited her away to a secluded cabin, and the two became lovers. But their happiness was short-lived as Roman and Isabella quarreled over her relationship with Victor, Roman's sworn enemy. Isabella moved in with Victor. Roman began to date Dr. Whitney Baker.

Julie hired Eve as her assistant. But when Julie tried to buy *Wings* from Nick, Eve helped Nick. Julie fired Eve, and Eve moved in with Nick. Nick and Eve finally became lovers. But Nick, convinced he would never be thought of as respectable, again became involved in some shady dealings.

Meanwhile, Johnny Corelli had been revealed as a fraud to his brother, Nick, who rejected him. So Johnny went to work for Victor. April was drawn to Johnny. She had given up on Mike when he moved to Israel to be near Jeremy and Robin. But Johnny moved into the Kiriakis mansion and began to court Isabella. Roman and Isabella continued to fight over Victor and Roman's continued investigations into Victor's criminal activities. One day, as Roman and Victor fought, Victor suffered a stroke. Both Justin and Isabella blamed Roman for Victor's condition. Isabella devoted herself to her father's care.

Now that they were again wed, Justin and Adrienne longed for a family. They tried to adopt, but there were long delays until Alexander's former nanny, J.J., returned to Salem pregnant with twins. J.J. wanted to give them a good home and arranged for Justin and Adrienne to privately adopt the two boys. After adopting babies Victor and Joseph (named for Victor Kiriakis and Jo (Josephine) Johnson), Adrienne became pregnant.

However, all was not well. Justin's company was failing, and he became involved with Jencon Oil. Many people in Salem protested the possible oil drilling, including Carly Manning and Bo Brady. When Bo's son, Shawn-Douglas, fell down a drilling shaft, it was Carly who went to his rescue. The boy was deafened by the accident, but his hearing was eventually restored. Bo and Carly were drawn together. Soon all roads seemed to lead to Jencon as the source of a variety of strange and nefarious activities.

Bo became the Riverfront Raider, a mystery man dedicated to sabotaging Jencon. He was aided by a waitress with whom he had slept soon after Hope died, Emmy Borden. Jencon's owner, Lawrence Alamain, ordered Nick, who now worked for him, to booby-trap Bo's boat. Steve, who had figured out that Bo was the Raider, learned of the bomb and raced to Bo's boat to warn him. But the bomb exploded, and Steve was gravely injured.

Kayla, Jack, Adrienne, and Jo all stayed by Steve's side and told him of their love for him and how much they needed him. It seemed as if Steve would recover. But Lawrence called a doctor in his employ and told him "to take care of" Steve. The doctor switched IVs and Steve died. His heartbroken family and friends eulogized Steve, and after Kayla privately wished her husband goodbye, some mystery men appeared and switched the coffin.

After Steve's death, Shane convinced Kayla to move in with him, in part to protect her and partly so she could assist him in his quest to prove that Jencon and Lawrence Alamain were somehow connected to Steve's death. April and Johnny began to investigate as well, convinced Nick was up to no good.

Further mayhem broke out in Salem when Nick was murdered on Halloween night. There were many suspects: Eve, for having overheard Nick say he would kill Shane, who was investigating Jencon; April and Emilio, for Nick's attempt on April's life when he believed she knew too much about Jencon; Bo, for Nick's part in Steve's death; and Johnny, because Nick disowned him in his will.

Back at University Hospital, Tom Horton resigned as chief of staff and opened up a new trauma center with himself as its head. Neil, after some difficulties with the hospital board because of his past indiscretions, became the new chief of staff, with Maggie as his assistant. Alice suffered a heart attack and got a pacemaker.

Meanwhile, Carly Manning was revealed to be heiress Katerina Von Leuschner. Years before, Katerina had been Jennifer's best friend at a Swiss boarding school. As a teen-ager Katerina ran away with Jennifer's help. Katerina was pledged to wed Lawrence Alamain on her twenty-fifth birthday and unite their two powerful families. Katerina's twenty-fifth birthday was fast approaching, and people were searching for her. In an effort to protect her friend, Jennifer impersonated Katerina, believing that none of the Alamains had ever seen the real Katerina. But the plan backfired, and Jennifer was taken against her will to Alamain's country.

Jack, now realizing his love for Jennifer would never die and that he was worthy of her love, followed and tried to save her. The evil Lawrence, who had known all along that Jennifer was not Katerina, forced Jennifer to marry him by threatening to harm Alice Horton (who, disguised as Katerina's nanny, had accompanied Jennifer) and Katerina's brother François, who turned out to be none other than Jennifer's old love, Frankie Brady! Jennifer wed Lawrence, then fled to his room, believing Jack would be waiting there, ready to escape through a secret passage. But Jack had been captured and imprisoned by Lawrence. Lawrence found Jennifer and raped her.

Jack managed to escape and teamed up with Shane, Kayla, and Julie, all of whom had come to Lawrence's country to look for Jack, Jennifer, and Alice and to find proof that Lawrence had had Steve killed. This group finally joined Bo and Carly. Carly had led Bo there, at Lawrence's behest, to be exchanged for François. A game of cat and mouse ensued. Jack finally got Jennifer, who had been protecting her friends and family, to admit that she did not love Lawrence, but loved Jack. Jack and Lawrence dueled, and Jack defeated him. The Salemites tried to escape, but Lawrence created an earthquake, and they were trapped. They were rescued by Leopold Alamain, Lawrence's kind father, who died for his efforts, and Roman, who had come from Salem to help.

It was further revealed that years before, Lawrence and Carly had been lovers, but Carly had not known his true identity and called him "James." When she discovered he was really Lawrence Alamain, she believed that he had feigned loving her to get her to agree to the arranged marriage. One night they fought and a merchant marine broke up the fight, allowing Katerina the time she needed to escape Lawrence. That sailor was none other than Bo Brady! Now Lawrence wanted revenge on Bo. But Bo and Carly wanted each other.

Back in Salem, Jennifer could not bring herself to tell Jack about the rape. Jack could not understand why Jennifer cringed every time he got near her. Jack began to fear that Jennifer still had feelings for Frankie, even though she vehemently denied it. Jack asked Jennifer to move in with him, but she refused. Instead, she asked Frankie, in whom she had no romantic or sexual interest, to be her roommate. Jack proposed to Jennifer, quoting "Romeo and Juliet" and declaring his love for her. But she turned him down. Jack then planned a romantic Christmas Eve tryst, reminding her of times past with his gifts, but again Jennifer rejected him. On Christmas Day, Jack, disguised as Santa, proposed again. This time Jennifer accepted, but she still did not tell Jack about the rape.

Jennifer's seeming aversion to a physical relationship with Jack finally came to a head when, in a moment of remembered terror, Jennifer slapped Jack and called him a rapist. Believing what he had always feared—that Jennifer would never forgive him his past—Jack broke off his relationship with Jennifer. Jennifer turned to Frankie for a friend.

Jennifer tried to divorce Lawrence, but he refused, threatening to tell Jack about the rape unless Jennifer convinced Frankie and Carly to sign over the Von Leuschner fortune to him. They gladly complied, and Jennifer was finally free of the marriage but not the pain or remembrance of the rape, because now Lawrence had moved to Salem.

Justin's business failed, and he accepted a lucrative job offer in Dallas. Johnny Corelli, trying to make points with Victor, tracked down Anjelica and Alexander and reunited the boy with his father. Anjelica remained in South America. Justin, Adrienne, Alexander, and the twins moved to Dallas, where Adrienne eventually gave birth to a son, Jackson (named for Adrienne's brother, Jack).

Emilio and Melissa broke their engagement. Melissa suspected that Emilio had killed Nick, and she helped police officer Brian Scofield investigate the case. During a New Year's Eve Murder Mystery Party hosted by Lawrence, Emilio was found dead. Had he fallen or was he pushed to his death from an upper-story window? Salem now had two unsolved murders: Nick's and Emilio's.

Emilio's sister, April, decided to leave the town where two of her brothers had been killed. She dumped her scheming boyfriend, Johnny, and moved to New York to be with her remaining brother, Julio, and her father, Monty.

Nick's will was read. He left April and Johnny each other, nothing more. He left ownership of *Wings* to Julie, as long as she allowed Eve to manage the club for as long as Eve desired. Nick left the rest of his estate to Eve, to be given to her on the day of her marriage for love. Julie was the one designated to ensure that Eve did marry for true love and not money.

Now that Frankie was back in town, Eve decided she could have both love and money. However, when Frankie discovered the contents of Nick's will, he believed Eve was interested in him because of Nick's inheritance, and the couple split. Eve decided if love was not for her, the money was.

Meanwhile, Lawrence, determined to destroy Jack, tried to take over the *Spectator*. Jack, convinced that Jennifer would never love him or forgive him his past, decided he would do anything to save his beloved newspaper, even if that meant marrying Eve. Jack and Eve agreed to a marriage of convenience. When Eve inherited Nick's money, she agreed to give Jack enough to save the *Spectator*. Julie knew the marriage was not a love match, but decided Eve should learn on her own. Besides, Lawrence would lose in his attempts to take over the newspaper if Jack received some of Nick's money. However, things did not go smoothly, and Eve was soon arrested for Nick's murder.

Neither Jack, Jennifer, Frankie, nor Brian believed Eve was guilty, and the search for the real killer continued. Brian's brother, Tanner Scofield, was revealed as someone who might be able to find the killer. Jack and Jennifer were drawn together in their attempts to catch Nick's killer and decided to work together. They soon discovered that Nick had possessed some sort of letter that he had been keeping as insurance to use against Lawrence and Jencon if needed. Jack and Jennifer began to search for both the letter and the murder weapon, convinced they would find evidence of Lawrence's evil doings and his connection to the murders. It also seemed as if someone wanted to prevent them from finding the letter. Their investigation eventually led them to a train and a cross-country train trip.

Soon Jack, Jennifer, Frankie, Eve, Brian, Tanner, and Melissa were all on board the train. The mismatched couples began to pair off with the correct partners. Eve was shot and slightly wounded, and Frankie vowed to stay with her. Jack and Jennifer then had to share a cabin, and Jennifer again grew accustomed to being close to Jack. Jennifer finally confessed to Jack that Lawrence had raped her. Although stunned, Jack quickly supported and comforted Jennifer. Jack eventually found the murder weapon, a gun, hidden on the train and hid it in his pants. When Jack, Jennifer, Frankie, Eve, Brian, Melissa, and Fluffy (Brian's police dog) all ended up in the baggage car, a hired thug, Nutty, released the car and the Salemites crashed in the wilderness.

Stranded in the snowbound wilderness, the group struggled for survival. Melissa and Brian drew closer and shared their first kiss. Jack and Jennifer made a bet that each would find the route to freedom before the other. But Jennifer got lost. She nearly froze, but Jack found her, took her to a nearby cave and warmed her, saving her life. Memories of another cave flooded back, and Jack and Jennifer were drawn to each other, but both pulled back, realizing it was too soon for a physical relationship.

Eve, meanwhile, had found a mountain girl, Molly Brinker, who drew her a map. The group found the road out of the valley to a clearing and were soon rescued. However, Eve fell in the rescue attempt and suffered a ruptured spleen. She survived, but her near brush with death prompted Frankie to confess his love. The two decided they needed to make a fresh start. Eve divorced Jack. When Frankie received a study grant to Africa, Eve accompanied him.

Meanwhile, Jack and Jennifer, with the help of Bo, discovered that Jack's mother, Jo, was the killer. She blamed Nick for Steve's death. When she went to confront Nick, who seemed likely to get away with the crime, they struggled, and Jo shot him. Jo pleaded insanity and was sent to Bayview Sanitarium.

Bo Brady was finally arrested as the Riverfront Raider. But an impassioned plea by the local community swayed the judge, and Bo was given a light sentence of community service. This sent Bo to work at University Hospital, where he came in constant contact with Carly. The two were drawn together, but Bo hesitated to make a commitment, fearing he might bring harm to Carly, as he had to Hope.

After Victor was felled by his stroke, Carly began to assist in his rehabilitation. Victor became infatuated with Carly and proposed. Carly really wanted Bo, but Bo rejected her yet again, and Carly agreed to marry Victor. Bo then changed his mind, but Victor and Emmy Borden conspired to keep Carly and Bo apart.

The police continued to investigate Emilio's death. As Detective Brian Scofield came closer to the truth, Melissa confessed. On the night of his death, Emilio threatened Brian, who he believed was about to arrest April for Nick's murder. Melissa and Emilio fought, and Emilio accidentally fell from the upper-story window to his death. Emilio's death was ruled an accident, but Brian could not forgive Melissa's deception, and the couple split.

Melissa's sister, Sarah, was faring no better. Sarah had discovered Maggie and Neil's affair and did everything in her power to break them up. When Sarah learned that Neil was her father, she could not cope. She told everything to Mickey, the man she considered her father. Maggie and Mickey separated, even though Maggie vowed she and Neil were through. Melissa decided it would be best if both she and her sister left town, so Sarah and Melissa departed Salem for Nashville, where Melissa could concentrate on her singing career. Maggie and Mickey reconciled, their marriage stronger than ever.

Kim sent divorce papers to Shane, which he reluctantly signed. Shane and Kayla were drawn to each other and soon fell in love. But their lives were complicated when Shane's ex–ISA partner, Peach, returned to Salem with a new case for Shane: Track down the creators of a horrible virus that was killing ISA agents. Shane was horrified to learn that Peach was already infected and dying.

Victor Kiriakis and Lawrence Alamain were somehow involved, the ISA was sure. Shane began to investigate the virus, as Carly became head of the research team charged with finding a cure.

Kim returned to Salem to work as the director of University Hospital's abuse clinic. Her dreams of reconciling with Shane were dashed when she discovered Shane's love for her sister, Kayla. Lawrence, playing on Kim's loneliness, insinuated himself into her life, trying to get information about Shane's ISA operations.

Meanwhile, Jennifer pressed charges against Lawrence for rape. Jack, Jennifer, Shane, and Kayla worked to find proof corroborating Jennifer's testimony. Jack and Jennifer even flew to Lawrence's country to find the maid, Lyla, who had heard Jennifer's screams for help on her wedding night. But it was to no avail. Lyla's testimony did not stand up under the attacks of the defense attorney, Marchand. Shane and Jack then searched for a security videotape that had been made of the rape, but Lawrence erased it. Finally, Jack and Jennifer found the letter for which they had been searching, but it turned out to help Lawrence. The couple hid the letter, but Kim stole it from them to give to Lawrence.

The letter revealed that Lawrence's mother had given him some magic pills that made him forget what he had done and commit evil deeds without remorse. With help from Kim, Lawrence stopped taking the pills and underwent hypnosis to unlock the painful memories of his past. As a young boy, Lawrence witnessed the death of his younger brother, Forrest. The two boys had been racing on their bicycles, and Forrest fell into a pool and drowned. Lawrence did nothing to save his brother and had been traumatized ever since.

Kim became convinced of Lawrence's innocence of Jennifer's rape. Lawrence and Kim became lovers. But Jack and Shane, with the aid of a former assistant of Lawrence's, Gregory, managed to get Lawrence's confession of the rape on tape. Kim was devastated to learn that Lawrence had played her for a fool. Lawrence was convicted and sent to prison to serve a short sentence for conjugal rape.

Now that the trial was over, Jack again proposed to Jennifer, and she joyfully accepted. As it turned out, Jack managed to propose in full view of a television crew from Jennifer's station and to invite all of Salem to the wedding. Soon most of Salem responded in the positive, and the lavish wedding was scheduled at the Salem Fair Grounds. Despite some last-minute hitches, Jack and Jennifer were married in a beautiful ceremony. Jennifer's father, Bill, even returned to Salem to give away the bride. And Marcus, standing in for Steve, acted as Jack's best man. The next day the couple left for a honeymoon in Hollywood.

Carly and Victor married. But at the wedding, Emmy, trying to forever keep Bo and Carly apart, spiked Carly's drink with the virus. But at the last minute, Bo drank from the glass, and he became infected. Once Kayla, Kim, and Carly discovered Bo was infected, they did everything to find a cure. Victor had Emmy kidnapped, fearing she would tell Bo about his role in keeping apart Bo and Carly. Emmy was killed, but not before she told Bo the truth. Carly annulled her marriage to Victor, and Bo and Carly declared their love for each other. Finally, Carly developed a cure for the virus with some help from a missing ingredient Victor had managed to get from Lawrence. Bo and the ISA agents were saved.

But a jealous Victor could not tolerate his son and his former wife together. Victor rigged an elevator to collapse, with Bo inside. But Carly entered the elevator instead. She was almost killed, but survived.

Violence continued throughout Salem, when the demented Cal Winters managed to escape from prison. He returned to Salem, bent on reuniting with Kim and "their" daughter, Jeannie. But Cal kidnapped Kayla by accident. While being held hostage, Kayla learned the truth. Shane was Jeannie's father, not Cal. Cal terrorized Kayla until Kim finally tried to rescue her. Eventually Shane managed to rescue both women.

Kayla and Shane finally declared their love and made love. But afterward, Kayla confessed the secret that Cal had revealed. Shane was Jeannie's biological father. Initially Shane rejected Kayla for the lie, but he soon came to forgive her as he accepted Jeannie as his daughter. Kim, realizing her life with Shane was over and still reeling from her affair with Lawrence, decided to leave Salem and moved to Los Angeles.

While honeymooning in Hollywood, Jack and Jennifer had been spotted by a group of con artists. The grifters, Howard Hawkins and his grandson, Hawk, lawyer Chauncey Powell, and fortune teller Desiree set up an elaborate plan to steal all of Jack's money. But Hawk soon came to desire more than the money and conspired to separate Jack and Jennifer. Hawk got Jack involved in a fake stock deal and stole all of Jack's money, including the collateral for the loan on the *Spectator*. Hawk then convinced Jack that he had shot and killed an FBI agent. Jack left Salem to protect Jennifer, but he vowed he would return. Jennifer, believing Jack had deserted her, used her trust-fund money to save the *Spectator* and grew closer to Hawk.

Meanwhile, Molly Brinker's grandfather had died, and she came to Salem. She was befriended by Julie, who gave her a job at *Wings* and let her move into the penthouse. Molly was drawn to Tanner, who was now working as a bartender at *Wings*. Tanner soon became involved in the mystery of finding Molly's supposedly dead mother, Genevieve.

Alice opened her own restaurant and called it *Alice's Restaurant*. Alice invited Maggie to help run the diner. Alice hired Ginger Dawson as a waitress. Ginger had moved to Salem in search of her daughter. Brian found a new love interest in Ginger.

But Tanner suspected there was more to Ginger than met the eye and finally uncovered the truth. Ginger was Molly's mother. Molly had been taken

Jack (Matthew Ashford) and *Jennifer Deveraux* (Melissa Reeves) take a romantic moment to stop and smell the flowers. [Maureen Russell]

from her as a baby, when Ginger's husband, Rusty, had died. It turned out that Molly's grandfather was none other than con man Howard. Ginger swore Tanner to secrecy, fearing for Molly's life if Howard and Hawk discovered her true identity.

Meanwhile, Roman and Isabella had finally reunited, and Roman proposed. His daughter, Carrie, decided to move to Europe to live with her mother, Anna DiMera. But all was not as it seemed. Somewhere on a tropical island, Marlena Evans Brady awakened from a five-year coma, smuggled herself on board a plane and returned to Salem.

Roman was stunned. He and Isabella called off their wedding. Marlena reacquainted herself with the twins, who were thrilled their mother was alive. When Roman and Marlena began to investigate her disappearance and five-year captivity, Roman began to have strange dreams. The real Roman was being held prisoner on an island. He escaped and returned to Salem, amazed to meet the impostor who had been living his life.

John Black, as he again called himself, Marlena, and Roman continued the investigation, determined to find the truth. Roman's former partner, Abe Carver, and his wife, Lexie, returned to Salem to help their friends. Victor and Lawrence were also interested in John Black's true identity. Soon, all roads led to Cancun, Mexico.

Meanwhile, Dr. Chip Laken arrived in Salem and was immediately drawn to Julie. But Julie was not sure she wanted a serious relationship, especially with a younger man. However, Chip pursued and romanced Julie, determined to prove his love for her. And Julie found herself liking the doctor.

Victor Kiriakis was shot and killed. Some wondered if his death tied into the investigation of Roman and Marlena's many years of confinement. Carly was arrested for Victor's murder, but she soon went on the lam, joining Bo, John, Isabella, Roman, and Marlena on their trip to Mexico in search of the truth. The group went to Chichen Itza because both Roman and John believed that the Castillo, or pyramid, held the answers to their questions.

While among the Mayan ruins, Isabella told a dazed John that she was pregnant. He vowed to stand by Isabella and the child. Bo and Carly also found love among the ruins and exchanged vows in a Mayan ceremony.

Searching for clues, Bo and Carly were stunned to find Victor alive but held captive in a dungeon. Victor revealed the name of the archenemy, and Bo ran to warn John and Roman. Now in the Castillo, John, Roman, and Marlena searched for the Mayan codices that could hold the secrets to the mysteries of their pasts. Lawrence appeared and got to the codices first. But Lawrence was not the mastermind; the true mastermind appeared and revealed himself. It was Stefano DiMera!

Stefano demanded the codices in exchange for a satchel that held papers that would reveal John's true identity. John agreed to exchange the codices for the satchel. But there was a struggle. Stefano was shot and killed. He fell into the flames, taking the satchel with him. John managed to retrieve the satchel, but now it contained only burnt fragments: a lump of gold, a broken locket, and part of a woman's photo.

In Salem, Jack was back. But he had not revealed himself to Jennifer. First he wrote her a note and left it in the penthouse, but Hawk intercepted it. Then he got a job at a meat-packing plant and arranged to deliver the Horton's Thanksgiving turkey. But he never got a chance to talk to Jennifer. Hawk conspired to keep apart the couple, but on Christmas Day, Jack crashed through the Horton's living room window and back into Jennifer's life.

Jack discovered that he had lost all his money and that Jennifer had saved the *Spectator* with her trust fund. Jennifer blamed Jack for leaving her and did not believe his tales of Hawk's con. Jennifer finally allowed Jack to move back into a divided penthouse and to sleep in the guest room.

Meanwhile, John agreed to undergo therapy with Marlena to uncover the secrets of his past. He had overpowering visions of water, but little else was revealed. But soon a mystery woman, Danielle Stevens, arrived in Salem, claiming to be John's wife. However, she knew him only as John Stevens and knew nothing of his earlier life. She did, however, lead him to a safety deposit box in Switzerland that contained a locket that he had told her belonged to his mother.

Danielle's story was untrue. She and John had been lovers, but were never married. Danielle was, in fact, an international jewel thief known as Romulus, and John was a private investigator who had been investigating Romulus. The couple had split when John uncovered her true identity. On the night of a masquerade ball, Danielle stole a locket from Katerina Von Leuschner. It was this locket that John found in the satchel. But the locket he discovered in the Swiss safety deposit box turned out to be a perfect match. John did not know what it meant, but Lawrence, who had given his own mother's locket to Katerina, suspected it meant a great deal.

Victor again became involved with the Torres family. The family, led by Rafi Torres, was dealing drugs. Roman, back in command at Police Headquarters, began to investigate Rafi and Victor. But Rafi vowed to stop Roman at any cost. Rafi kidnapped Bo and demanded Roman cease his investigation. Rafi also threatened Carly and Shawn-Douglas, but Lawrence came to their aid.

Shane began to work on the case as well. He convinced Julie to help with the investigation by hosting a party for Salem's movers and shakers. As the party neared its close, a bomb exploded. Among others, Shane and Julie were hurt. Julie suffered a ruptured spleen. Chip operated to save Julie's life. But while operating on Julie, another victim of the explosion, a young waiter named Dean Lombard, died.

Shane awakened to find himself in a hospital bed, paralyzed from the waist down. Kayla vowed to stand by him. But Shane grew more frustrated with his life in a wheelchair. When Shane and Kayla grew close, Shane, who was now impotent, had trouble dealing with her.

Roman, with help from Alice, eventually rescued Bo, and he returned to Salem. Rafi then threatened Marlena and the children. To protect his family, Roman feigned leaving Salem. In reality, he went undercover in a variety of disguises, determined to bring down the Torres family. Abe, Roman, and Bo captured Rafi, and he was sent to jail. Roman was demoted for faking his departure and going undercover without department approval. Abe became the new police commander.

Carly and Bo were now a couple, but Carly was haunted by memories of her past with Lawrence. And Lawrence continued to remind her of the great love they once had. Lawrence's Aunt Vivian came to town and was shown to be a friend to Carly. It seemed she had helped Carly in a time of trouble after her breakup with Lawrence. Carly had given birth to Lawrence's son, but the child had died. Or had he? It was soon disclosed that he had not. Carly's son was alive, somewhere. Carly and Bo began their quest to find her lost son. But their efforts failed, and they gave up the search, convinced the boy was dead.

Meanwhile, Jack and Jennifer continued to feud as Jack vowed to prove Hawk's con and win back his wife. On one stormy night, Jack and Jennifer got caught on the set of a game show, "Ask Dr. Love." Jack challenged Jennifer to a competition. He won both the game and his wife's love as his rendition of

"Wonderful, Wonderful" reminded Jennifer of their wedding day The couple passionately reunited and made love all night. But the reunion was short-lived, as the next day Jennifer again believed Jack was lying to her about his efforts to save the *Spectator*.

Hawk planned to convince Jennifer that Jack was having an affair. With some help from Desiree and some faked photos, Hawk "proved" Jack's infidelity. Jennifer swore their marriage was over. But Jack put himself on trial with Jennifer as judge. With a little help from his friends Ginger, Alice, and Marcus and a videotape showing Hawk in Hollywood on their honeymoon, Jack finally convinced Jennifer of his great love for her and of Hawk's deception. They blissfully reunited, vowing to never let anything come between them again and vowing to get Hawk.

Jack and Jennifer tricked Hawk into shooting and "killing" Jack. Jennifer then convinced the guilt-ridden Hawk to confess to the con and Jack's murder. Jennifer taped the entire confession. After Hawk's admission, Jack walked in, accompanied by the police. Jack and Jennifer had finally outsmarted the grifter, who was taken off to jail.

Carrie moved back to Salem to rediscover her real father and Marlena and to come to terms with John. But the rebellious teen had trouble coping and turned to Lawrence Alamain for comfort. Lawrence led on the infatuated girl so that he could obtain information about John.

John continued to search for his past. Danielle was almost arrested by the Swiss police as Romulus, but John helped her escape. When he returned to Salem, he confronted Lawrence with the two lockets, but Lawrence denied knowing what they meant. But Lawrence and Vivian suspected the worst. One night, Carrie tried to seduce Lawrence. An enraged John found Carrie in bed with Lawrence, rescued her and threatened to kill Lawrence.

Lawrence finally blurted out the truth. John was Forrest Alamain, Lawrence's brother. John did not believe it, but DNA tests confirmed the truth. Though John was entitled to half the Alamain empire, Vivian and Lawrence conspired to keep John away from the money.

John and Isabella finally got married. During the wedding, Isabella went into labor. She was rushed to the bride's room and, with the help of Marcus and Carly, Isabella delivered a boy. Mother and son then returned to the church to finish the ceremony. Isabella and John were married. The baby was named Brady Victor Black.

Meanwhile, the Lombards, the family of the waiter, Dean, who had been killed in the explosion at Julie's party, decided to sue the hospital for malpractice. Lawyer Lisanne Gardner arrived in Salem as the prosecuting attorney for the Lombards. The legal battle escalated, and the costs forced the hospital to make staff cutbacks. Kayla lost her job. The trial went badly for the Salemites until it was revealed that Dean Lombard had a pre-existing medical condition that caused his death. The suit was dropped, and the hospital cleared.

Chip, who had been suspended during the trial, decided to accept an out-of-town job and leave Salem. Although saddened by his departure, Julie could not give him a reason to stay.

Kayla decided that although she would always love Shane, they could never be together. She decided to get on with her life and accepted a job in Los Angeles. Kayla wished Shane and her family a tearful goodbye and left Salem with her daughter, Stephanie Kaye. Shane decided that although he could no longer work "in the field," he could be of service. He became an instructor at the Salem Police Academy.

Meanwhile, Molly discovered that Ginger was her mother, but Molly rejected Ginger. Molly then decided to move on with her life and enrolled in the nursing program at Salem University. Ginger, in an effort to improve herself, began to take classes as well, and the two grew closer. Molly met Professor Gavin Newirth, and he hired her as his research assistant. Gavin seemed attracted to Molly, but Molly failed to notice.

Tanner now began to suspect foul play in the death of his mother, who supposedly committed suicide when he was young. He discovered that his mother had taken classes at Salem University and had known Gavin. Gavin said he remembered Tanner's mother but could offer no real help.

Tanner's brother, Brian, continued to be drawn to Ginger, and the two became lovers. But they soon quarreled and split, Ginger believing Brian would never forgive her for her past.

The dysfunctional Lombard family became embroiled in the lives of those around them. The youngest son, Jesse, was a troubled youth. Marcus tried to help and became Jesse's big brother. Carrie befriended Jesse and tried to help as well. Marlena began to counsel Jesse's father, Roger. But his wife, Stella, was not sure she approved.

Meanwhile, Jack and Jennifer discovered they were broke. The bank took over the *Spectator*. They lost their penthouse and moved into a small apartment above *Alice's Restaurant*. Lawrence Alamain tried once again to take over the newspaper, with assistance from his new legal counsel, Lisanne. But Jack and Jennifer enlisted Julie's help to stop the takeover.

Jennifer did have wonderful news to share with Jack. It seemed more than a reconciliation had happened that stormy night on the set of "Ask Dr. Love." Jennifer was pregnant. Jack worried that he might not be a good father and soon developed sympathetic morning sickness. He went to Marcus and was given a clean bill of health. Jennifer convinced Jack to go on the "Ask Dr. Love" show so that they could win the grand prize, but Jack became too ill to go on. Jennifer attributed it to stage fright.

Jack and Jennifer were asked to co-host a debate segment called "Cross-fire" on Jennifer's TV station. But Jack continued to feel sick. Suspecting the doctors were not telling him something, Jack broke into Marcus' office and read his file, which stated he had only six months to live. However, unknown to Jack, his chart had been erroneously switched with that of a terminal patient. Jack was fine.

Convinced of his impending death, Jack took steps to ensure Jennifer and the baby's future well-being. First he sold the *Spectator* to Julie. Then he found a replacement husband for Jennifer: Brian Scofield. But Jack's plan backfired when Jennifer became convinced he was having an affair with Ginger. Jennifer left Jack. But Jo and Alice intervened and shortly thereafter the truth came out: Jack was not having an affair, and he was not dying. Jack and Jennifer passionately reunited.

But their reunion was short-lived. Jennifer was offered a co-host position on a network talk show hosted by Calliope Jones Bradford, who had moved to New York. Jennifer accepted the job to help earn money before her baby's arrival. Jennifer left for a six-week stay in New York, and Jack vowed to prove his worth to her upon her return. Jack took a job at television station WTGB as the reporter host of a reality-based, live-action cop show.

John Black, with Victor's help, succeeded in outsmarting Vivian and Lawrence Alamain. John became intent on gaining his rightful inheritance for himself and his son, Brady. Isabella began to worry that John was too consumed with the Alamain empire and that he was emulating Victor too closely. John took Isabella and Brady on a honeymoon in Italy to prove his devotion. Meanwhile, his brother Lawrence had become involved in a passionate liaison with Lisanne Gardner.

The Brady fish market was robbed, and Shawn was shot in the attack. He recovered, but the crime convinced Bo that the Salem Police Department needed him. Bo often clashed with his instructors, including Shane and his brother, police captain Roman Brady. Eventually Bo graduated from the academy and became a full-fledged police officer. His new partner on the force was the brash and outspoken Taylor McCall.

During the attack on the fish market, the robbers had destroyed the market. The Bradys were distraught—they did not have the money to rebuild. But the newly rich John, who had for years lived as their son, Roman, had a plan. He would make Shawn's life-long dreams of owning his own pub come true. After a major overhaul, the Brady Fish Market had its grand opening as the Brady Pub.

Meanwhile, Jack attempted to locate the "fake" police officers who had been robbing stores in Salem, so that he could claim the $10,000 reward. He succeeded, and the fake officers were arrested. However, Jack was soon fired from his job at WTGB and worried about how he would support Jennifer and the baby. Alice, seeing how much Jack missed Jennifer, gave Jack a plane ticket to New York. Jack and Jennifer had a brief, but passionate, reunion in New York. Jennifer and Calliope's talk show, "Talk To Me," was a ratings winner. The network praised Jennifer, offering her her own talk show, but she demurred, deciding she wanted to remain to Salem.

Jack returned to Salem and bemoaned the fact that his pregnant wife was in New York without him. One day, as Jack was watching the show, Jennifer went into false labor on the air. Jack flew to New York, got Jennifer and drove his wife back home to Salem. However, upon their return, they were evicted from their small apartment and forced to move into the Horton house with Tom and Alice.

Roman, meanwhile, continued to clash with his daughter, Carrie, who decided to declare her independence by moving into her own apartment. Carrie asked Jesse, who was also having problems at home, to be her roommate. The two got jobs at a clothing store, Ballistix, at Salem Place Mall. Carrie soon found herself drawn to her handsome neighbor, jazz pianist Austin Reed. However, Austin was not all that he seemed. He was running a gambling ring out of a restaurant, Johnny Angel's, at Salem Place. Austin was aided by a local, Tim Rollins.

Molly was accosted by Professor Gavin Newirth and decided to press charges. Tanner discovered that the professor had raped his mother many years previously and that she, feeling disgraced, abused, and alone, had killed herself. Ginger and Tanner kidnapped Gavin and tried to force him to confess to assaulting Molly. He maintained his innocence. However, shaken by their tactics, Gavin tried to flee town. The police took this as an admission of guilt and arrested him. He was never seen again. Molly and Tanner declared their love and left town.

Brian and Ginger reunited, and Brian resigned from the police force. Brian opened a dog-obedience school, but it was short-lived. Ginger, who had become a fashion columnist for the *Spectator*, got a job offer to write a syndicated column in Chicago. Molly encouraged her mother to take this new opportunity. Ginger left Salem, and Brian decided to accompany her.

Vivian Alamain's "son" Nicholas (Nikki) came to town. Unknown to Carly, he was the child to whom she had given birth eight years before. Vivian tried to keep Nikki hidden from Lawrence. But eventually Lawrence discovered his "cousin" Nikki, who Vivian claimed was her adopted son, born to an Alamain maid, Marie-Helene. Nikki and Vivian moved in with Lawrence.

Lisanne, who had decided she wanted to become the next Mrs. Lawrence Alamain, did not approve. Lisanne managed to trick Lawrence into asking her to move in with him. Lisanne and Vivian clashed. Lisanne suspected something was amiss regarding Nikki and began to investigate. She finally discovered that Carly had borne Lawrence a son and told Lawrence the truth. Lawrence, enraged, went to Carly and demanded the facts, but, with Vivian's help, Carly lied to Lawrence, claiming her now-dead child had been another man's. Eventually, however, Carly told Lawrence the truth. And ultimately they both discovered Nicholas was their long-lost son.

Lawrence and Lisanne also conspired to destroy John and get him out of Alamain Industries and the corporation, EcoSystems, they had given him.

Lawrence and Lisanne battled for control of the company against John and Isabella, who were aided by Victor. However, business soon became unimportant. Isabella began experiencing pain and nausea. Medical tests confirmed the worst: She was dying of inoperable pancreatic cancer and had only a few weeks to live. John devoted himself to Isabella. John and Lawrence declared a truce.

Isabella quickly succumbed to the devastating cancer. John took her back home to Italy, where she died in his arms.

John returned home and became involved with attorney Rebecca Morrison. They moved in together. Rebecca left town when she realized John still had feelings for Marlena.

Lawrence, meanwhile, in an effort to woo Carly away from Bo, began a campaign to destroy Bo's reputation. A Bo double, Mitch, was involved. Eventually, the truth came out, and Bo was cleared. But not before Bo's partner, Taylor, whom Lawrence had been blackmailing, was killed.

Lawrence's aunt Vivian became involved in a love affair with Victor Kiriakis. But Lawrence disapproved of the match and demanded that Vivian stop seeing Victor. Victor then became involved with Kate Roberts, who worked for him at Titan Publishing. Kate had recently arrived in Salem with her son, Lucas.

Kimberly Brady returned to Salem with a new fiancé, producer Philip Collier. Kimberly wanted to be the one to tell Shane about the new man in her life, and as she rushed to greet Shane at Salem Place, a drunken Roger Lombard ran her down. Shane tried to come to her aid but was able only to catapult himself out of his chair. Kim survived the accident but began to experience severe headaches. Shane decided that it was time to devote himself to his physical therapy and soon made miraculous progress.

Shane quickly make a complete recovery. Soon the ISA needed him for a dangerous mission that only he could risk. Shane followed his duty and left Salem.

Lisanne was accidentally killed by Nikki. Lisanne and Vivian had been fighting. Nikki, convinced his aunt was in danger, pushed Lisanne. Lisanne fell and hit her head on a stone cat. Lawrence covered up the truth of Lisanne's death to protect his son, but eventually all was discovered. Nikki, who never knew he had killed Lisanne, was not tried, and the death was ruled accidental.

Marlena and Roman continued to disagree about her involvement with the Lombard family. Marlena devoted much of her time to Roger, and he recovered from his drinking problem. Marlena also discovered that Roger was a frustrated artist. With Marlena's encouragement, Roger began to paint again. Marlena failed to notice that Roger was falling in love with her. However, Roger's wife, Stella, did notice and became insanely jealous of Marlena.

Stella hatched a plot to destroy Marlena by trapping her in a pit in an abandoned warehouse. Marlena spent weeks trapped in the hole in the ground. Finally Marlena was saved by John and Roman. Stella was killed by a hit-and-run driver as she made a phone call. Roger and Jesse left town.

Kimberly's headaches intensified, and it was soon revealed that Kimberly had developed a multiple personality disorder, seemingly triggered by childhood abuse at the hands of her Uncle Eric. One of Kim's personalities, the wild and wanton Lacey James, was involved in the killing of a biker, Randy Huston. Kimberly remembered that "Lacey" had killed Randy when he tried to rape her. The killing was ruled self-defense. Kimberly sought psychiatric help and eventually moved to Los Angeles with her fiancé, Philip.

Meanwhile, Carrie had decided Austin was not interested in her and became involved with Tim, the co-leader of the gambling ring. Austin's motivation for heading the gambling ring was the need for money to keep his sister, Billie, in rehabilitation. Billie, however, escaped and came to Salem. Almost immediately she got in trouble. Billie and Tim went to a "rave" party, and Billie was arrested by Bo for trying to buy the drug XTC or "ecstasy."

Billie soon fell in love with Bo, but she didn't think she was good enough for him. Bo was drawn to her, but he was still engaged to Carly. Carly, however, had now discovered she was infertile. This made her feel even more compelled to get close to the only child she would ever have: Nicholas.

Meanwhile, Jack and Jennifer were joyfully preparing for the birth of their first child. However, as was typical of Jack and Jennifer, not everything went according to plan. Jack ended up delivering his own daughter when Jennifer went into labor as the couple was stranded in the mountains. Jack and Jennifer rejoiced in the birth of their firstborn: Abigail Johanna Deveraux (named after Jennifer's great-grandmother, Alice's mother).

Julie got a frantic call from a friend of Doug's in Switzerland, Doug had been hurt in an accident. Julie left Salem and rushed to Doug's side, where, she discovered, the call was a ruse of Doug's to win back his fair lady. It worked. Julie reunited with her beloved Doug, and they remarried in Switzerland. Doug and Julie returned to Salem at Christmas to visit Tom Horton, who was ailing. The Horton Christmas 1993 was spent in Tom's room at University Hospital.

Life for Jack and Jennifer grew difficult after the birth of Abigail. Jack lost all but 10 percent of the *Spectator*, which was sold to Kate Roberts. Kate tried to seduce Jack, but she ended up firing him.

Then Abigail, became ill. She had aplastic anemia and needed a bone marrow transplant. Jack could not be a donor because of his Hodgkin's disease. No one else in the family matched. Finally, a donor was found: none other than Jennifer's talk show co-host, Austin! Abigail was saved.

But there was more heartache for the Deverauxes. Abigail's illness was caused by industrial pollution and the source was tracked down to something called Tract Five. Victor appeared to own the land, but when Jack confronted Victor, he discovered that Victor had left Tract Five in protest of the toxic dumping. Victor turned it all over to his partner, Harper Deveraux. Worse, there was one young man's signature on all the paperwork: a 16-year-old Jack had approved all the illegal waste dumping. Jack was responsible for his own daughter's illness! Jack decided his family was better off without him. Kissing his sleeping wife and child goodbye, Jack left Salem. A few months later, Jack sends divorce papers, via his attorney, to Jennifer.

Meanwhile, Vivian, discovering she had an inoperable heart condition and not long to live, devised a plan to kill herself and frame Carly for her death. Vivian murdered two hospital patients as part of her efforts. But, ultimately, her plan failed. Vivian jumped off a building and tried to make it look as though Carly had pushed her, but Carly ended up performing life-saving surgery on Vivian. (The surgery also miraculously repaired Vivian's inoperable condition.) So Vivian hatched a new scheme: Fake Carly's death, and bury her alive!

Ivan, Vivian's accomplice, began to realize that Vivian might be driven to these bizarre acts by the Chinese herbs she was taking. Ivan stopped giving Vivian the herbs, and she came to her senses. She told Lawrence about Carly. Lawrence and Vivian dug up Carly and took her back to the Alamain Mansion. Carly was alive but had one problem, she thought that the year was 1983, not 1993, that she was Katerina, and that Lawrence was her lover, James.

Eventually, Carly regained her memory, but she decided she truly loved Lawrence and not Bo. Bo and Carly broke up. Carly and Lawrence, accompanied by their son, Nicholas, flew off to Paris to live happily ever after. Bo found comfort in the arms of Billie Reed.

Meanwhile, on the night of Marlena and Roman's anniversary, John decided to leave town because he could not be with Marlena. Marlena followed John to the corporate jet and persuaded him to stay in Salem. They made love. Later, John and Marlena shared a night of passion in the conference room at the Titan Publishing party. Unknown to them, Marlena's daughter, Sami, saw them. Soon, Marlena discovered she was pregnant and was unsure who the father was—Roman or John. When Sami learned of her mother's pregnancy, she became bulimic, unable to cope with the pressures of keeping her mother's secret and worrying how the truth would affect her beloved father, Roman. Frightened, Sami faked the blood-test results, so Marlena thought her baby's father was Roman.

John was now in love with the mysterious Kristen Blake, but he was soon stunned to learn that Kristen was Stefano DiMera's adopted daughter. To further complicate matters, his lover was engaged: to Tony DiMera!

Stefano returned to Salem, suffering from an inoperable brain tumor. Marlena saw him at the hospital and was so distraught at the sight of her old arch enemy, she fled to the Horton's island cabin to think. Alas, there was a huge storm; she was trapped and went into labor. Luckily, Kristen had followed Marlena, hoping Marlena could give her some insight into her adopted father's past. Kristen arrived at the island and found Marlena in labor. John, meanwhile, had followed Kristen to the cabin. Kristen and John delivered Marlena's baby. The baby stopped breathing, and John resuscitated the infant. A grateful Roman and Marlena named the baby Isabella (Belle), after John's late wife.

Sami, fearing the truth of her baby half-sister's paternity would tear apart her family, kidnapped Belle and attempted to give her up for adoption. John eventually tracked down Belle, and the baby was reunited with Marlena.

However, the truth eventually came out: that John and Marlena had an affair and that baby Belle was John's daughter. Roman and Marlena divorced. Roman left Salem.

Meanwhile, the Salem Pacifier hit town. He was a vigilante who left a baby's pacifier around the criminals' necks when he caught them and turned them over to the police. Eventually, Jonah Carver was identified as the Pacifier.

Abe and Lexie tried to decide whether to have a child. But Lexie found herself sexually attracted to Abe's brother, Jonah. And vice versa.

John, meanwhile, grew more involved with Kristen. He tried to win her away from Tony, but Kristen decided to marry her fiancé. However, Kristen and John could not stay apart, and despite her marriage to Tony, they continued as lovers. Matters were further complicated when Tony was blinded in an accident, and Kristen felt compelled to stay with her husband out of guilt. Tony, however, soon regained his sight but hid the fact from Kristen, in the hope of finding out if his suspicions about an affair between his wife and John were true.

All the while, John was still trying to discover his long-lost past. It was finally revealed that John was a priest! Kristen was devastated, torn between her love for John and her concern over his breaking his priestly vows.

Meanwhile, Austin and Carrie finally became lovers, but the course of true love did not run smooth, as Sami and Lucas schemed to break up the young couple. Sami wanted Austin, and Lucas wanted Carrie. Further, Sami had been raped by Alan Harris and blamed her sister, Carrie, for the rapist's not being convicted.

July 1994 marked the end of an era for the Horton family. The family's patriarch, Tom Horton, passed away. Family and old friends flew in from all over the world to say goodbye to Tom. Doug, Julie, Melissa, Kimberly, Bill and Marie returned to Salem. Doug sang "Danny Boy" to wish his old friend farewell. There was not a dry eye in the chapel.

Vivian, meanwhile, plotted to win Victor Kiriakis away from his wife, Kate. To do this, Vivian strove to find the connection between Kate and Laura Horton, who has been institutionalized for the past 18 years. Ultimately, Vivian discovered that Kate had had an affair with Laura's husband, Bill, and given birth to his son, Lucas Roberts!

Laura was now returned to her home, when it was revealed that Laura had been drugged all those years. Laura was joyfully reunited with her daughter, Jennifer, but her marriage to Bill was over.

Jennifer, now involved with Stefano's adopted son, Peter Blake, was happy to have her mother home. But Laura did not trust Peter. And with good reason. Unknown to Jennifer, Peter had been working with Stefano, aiding and abetting his nefarious deeds at every turn. Peter began a plot to "gaslight"

Laura. He succeeded, and Laura was reinstitutionalized. While at the sanitarium, Laura met a new man, "Clark."

Peter, however, had a change of heart and vowed to turn over a new leaf so that he could be worthy of Jennifer. He divested himself of all his questionable financial holdings.

Kate had never divorced her first husband, Curtis Reed, who was now in Salem blackmailing Kate. Familial connections were revealed: Kate was Billie and Austin's long-lost mother. Curtis molested Billie, his daughter. When Curtis was killed, Billie was the chief suspect. The very night of his death, Curtis shot up Billie with heroin and raped her. But Stefano killed Curtis, who was harassing Stefano's adopted daughter Kristen. Stefano and Curtis struggled, the gun went off, and Curtis was killed. Billie, on trial for her father's murder, went free.

Stefano, meanwhile, faked his own death and implicated John as the killer. But the phoenix rose again and was soon back to his old tricks. Luring a group of Salemites to New Orleans, he attempted to imprison John and Marlena. John discovered a mystery woman there, who turned out to be none other than the resurrected Hope. Alas, no one could prove whether she really was Hope because she had no memory of her past and called herself Gina.

Hope's (or was it Gina's?) return put a crimp in the romance of Billie and Bo. Both women wanted Bo, but he couldn't decide which woman he wanted. Finally, concluding that Gina was not Hope, Bo chose Billie and the couple made love. Alice, however, remained convinced that "Gina" really was her granddaughter, Hope, and that it would simply be a matter of time before "Hope" remembered the truth about her past.

Mike Horton returned to Salem from Israel. He began to receive mysterious phone calls. In order to stop the killing of innocent people, he had agreed to "sell his soul" and follow the bidding of arms dealers. Mike soon learned his orders: Get close to Marlena. Not knowing the reason why, Mike did so. Unknown to Mike, the phone calls were coming from Stefano's henchwoman, Celeste.

Stefano, meantime, orchestrated a twisted stratagem to win (or is it drive insane?) Marlena, as he haunted her dreams (and her closet!). Could demonic possession be involved?

Meanwhile, Jack had returned to Salem vowing to win back Jennifer. Overhearing Jennifer and Peter discussing Peter's ability to express his feelings, Jack decided to go to a sanitarium, the Meadows, to seek therapy to learn how to be open and honest about his own feelings. By doing this, Jack hoped he could prove to Jennifer how much he had changed. At the Meadows, Jack found himself drawn to a woman named "Monica." Unknown to Jack, "Monica" was Jennifer's mother, Laura! And, unknown to Laura, "Clark" was none other than Jack! "Clark" and "Monica" became lovers.

Vivian, in the interim, continued her efforts to destroy Kate and Victor and win Victor for herself. Victor wanted a son. But it turned out Kate could not conceive. The couple decided to try in vitro fertilization. But Vivian stole Victor and Kate's embryo and had it implanted in her womb. Now Vivian was carrying Victor's (and Kate's) baby!

As the old year ended and the new year began, the plot continued to thicken in Salem.

Jack told Jennifer he was back and vowed to woo her. Jennifer countered that she could not get past the anger she felt at his earlier desertion. Jennifer declared Peter to be the man for her. Peter pushed Jennifer to accept his marriage proposal.

Laura, still unaware that her lover, "Clark," was really Jack, started dating, but had a hard time forgetting her feelings for "Clark."

Vivian tricked Victor into marrying her. Meanwhile, Ivan hoped against hope that he could be the man in his "Madame's" life.

John searched for the "Salem Desecrator." Marlena levitated, and her eyes glowed green, while Stefano realized he had lost control of Marlena's psyche. Celeste warned Stefano that an evil force had come to Salem. Kristen was kidnapped, stripped naked and painted red by the possessed Marlena. Kristen remained married to Tony but loved John. Tony continued to fake blindness and pushed Kristen to bear his child. Kristen secretly began to take birth control pills.

Bo and Billie were determined to wed, but their only chance seemed to be having Hope declared legally dead. Alice, however, continued in her conviction that Gina was really her granddaughter, Hope. Gina became nanny to Brady and Belle.

Jonah decided that he wanted a relationship with Wendy, but was he fooling himself into thinking he had gotten over his feelings for his brother's wife, Lexie?

Sami's plot to break up Carrie and Austin seemed to be working. Carrie suspected Sami of lying, while Austin believed Sami. Meanwhile, Alan tried to attack Sami again, but she fought him off and shot him in the groin.

Tune in tomorrow...

CHAPTER NOTES

Introduction

1. The longest running soap opera, combining both radio and television broadcasts, is *Guiding Light*.

2. I interviewed Jack Herzberg in September 1991. Sadly, he passed away in April 1992.

3. For a discussion of the origin of soap opera, see: Robert C. Allen, *Speaking of Soap Operas* (Chapel Hill and London: University of North Carolina Press, 1985), Peter Buckman, *All for Love* (London: Secker & Warburg, 1984), Muriel Cantor and Suzanne Pingree, *The Soap Opera* (Beverly Hills, Ca.: Sage Press, 1983) and Robert LaGuardia, *Ma Perkins to Mary Hartman: The Illustrated History of Soap Operas* (New York: Ballantine Press, 1977).

4. For a discussion of the Hummerts, see: Raymond William Stedman, *The Serials: Suspense and Drama by Installment* (Norman: University of Oklahoma Press, 1971, 1977).

5. For a discussion of Irna Phillips, see: Raymond William Stedman, "A History of the Broadcasting of Daytime Serial Dramas in the United States." Ph.D. Diss., University of Southern California, 1959.

Beginnings

1. Interview with Ken Corday, Burbank, California, 9 July 1990.

2. Ibid.

3. For Macdonald Carey's complete filmography, see his autobiography *The Days of My Life*, New York: St. Martin's Press, 1991.

4. Interview with Macdonald Carey, Beverly Hills, California, 10 October 1990.

5. Ibid.

6. Allan Chase worked with Ted Corday on a number of projects in New York. He was credited in the early years of the show because he had been in on the initial planning. His input was minimal, and he is no longer credited with the show's creation.

7. Ted Corday, pilot presentation, 1965?, p. 1.

8. Ted Corday, "Days of Our Lives," 1965?, p. 3.

9. Ted Corday, pilot presentation, 1965?, p. 1.

10. *Morning Star* premiered in 1965 as well, but lasted only nine months. It concerned the lives and loves of four working women in New York. Its epigraph was, "No matter how dark the night, there is always a new dawn to come, the sun is but a *Morning Star*."

11. *Days of Our Lives*, pilot script, 1965, p. 1.

12. Interview with Joe Behar, Santa Monica, California, 20 September 1990.

13. Jackie Cooper to Ted Corday, telegram, 8 July 1965.

14. The hourglass was not always the same, as Jack Herzberg attests: "We put the hourglass on tape, but they kept stealing the damned hourglass from NBC. When the last one was stolen, I think the prop man had to put it under lock and key. We had about four of them stolen, and they are hard to find."

15. *Days of Our Lives*, Script, episode 2, 11. [1]

16. Interview with Jack Herzberg, Temecula, California, 19 September 1991.

17. Interview with Ed Mallory, Encino, California, 10 December 1994.

18. Jack Herzberg, Temecula, California, letter to the author, 28 January 1991.

19. *Variety*, 10 November 1965.

20. Interview with Bill Bell, Malibu, California, 21 September 1990.

21. Ibid.

22. Ibid and Behar interview.

23. Interview with Bill Bell, Malibu, California, 21 September 1990.

24. William J. Bell, "Days of Our Lives, 1966." TMs, p. 2, Theater Arts Library, University of California, Los Angeles.

25. Irna Phillips continued to collaborate with Bill Bell and *Days* until she left the show for her own creation, *Love Is a Many Splendored Thing*, in 1967.

26. William J. Bell, "Days of Our Lives, Summer-Fall-Winter, 1967-68." TMs, p. 29, Theater Arts Library, University of California, Los Angeles.

27. Interview with Wes Kenney, Los Angeles, California, 7 February 1991.

28. Interview with Bill Hayes, North Hollywood, California, 22 September 1991.

29. Interview with Frank Parker, Los Angeles, California, 4 October 1990.

30. Interview with Ed Mallory, Encino, California, 10 December 1994.

31. Interview with Pat Falken Smith, Woodland Hills, California, 5 October 1990.

32. Interview with Ken Corday, Burbank, California, 9 July 1990.

33. Interview with Ken Corday, Burbank, California, 6 August 1990.

34. Becky Greenlaw left *Days* in May 1993.

35. Interview with Becky Greenlaw, Burbank, California, 23 January 1991.

36. Interview with Ed Mallory, Encino, California, 10 December 1994.

37. Interview with Macdonald Carey, Beverly Hills, California, 10 October 1990.

38. Speech by William J. Bell at the Eighth Annual Soap Opera Awards, Beverly Hills, California, 10 January 1992.

39. Speech by Ken Corday at the Eighth Annual Soap Opera Awards, Beverly Hills, California, 10 January 1992.

40. *Days of Our Lives*, unpublished promotional mss., 7 December 1964, p. 2.

On the Set

1. Interview with Ken Corday, Burbank, California, 9 July 1990.

2. Interview with Ed Mallory, Encino, California, 10 December 1994.

3. Interview with Charles Shaughnessy, Burbank, California, 8 January 1991.

4. Blocking: directing the actors' movements; dry blocking: run-through rehearsal with director and cast only, no crew; camera blocking: run-through rehearsal with cast and crew.

5. Interview with Jack Herzberg, Temecula, California, 19 September 1991.

6. Interview with Joe Behar, Santa Monica, California, 20 September 1990.

7. Interview with Wes Kenney, Los Angeles, California, 7 February 1991.

8. Interview with Bill Hayes, North Hollywood, California, 22 September 1991.

9. Ibid.

10. Interview with Joe Gallison, Burbank, California, 23 October 1990.

11. Interview with Wes Kenney, Los Angeles, California, 7 February 1991.

12. Interview with Susan Seaforth Hayes, Burbank, California, 3 August 1990.

13. Interview with Quinn Redeker, Hollywood, California, 9 January 1991.

14. Interview with Ed Mallory, Encino, California, 10 December 1994.

15. In May 1993, *Days* also began to block and tape.

16. Interview with Steve Wyman, Burbank, California, 30 November 1990.

17. Interview with Roger Inman, Burbank, California, 8 January 1991.

18. Interview with Steve Wyman, Burbank, California, 30 November 1990.

19. Interview with Becky Greenlaw, Burbank, California, 23 January 1991.

20. Interview with Matthew Ashford, Burbank, California, 27 November 1990.

21. Interview with Wayne Heffley, Burbank, California, 11 September 1990.

22. Interview with Charles Shaughnessy, Burbank, California, 8 January 1991.

23. Interview with Matthew Ashford, Burbank, California, 27 November 1990.

24. Full credits must be run once a week to meet a variety of union and contractual obligations. The actors' names are run in order of seniority under contract.

25. Interview with Roger Inman, Burbank, California, 8 January 1991.

26. Interview with Macdonald Carey, Beverly Hills, California, 10 October 1990.

27. Interview with Chip Dox, Burbank, California, 14 December 1990.

28. Ibid.

29. The ISA is the International Security Alliance, Salem's answer to the CIA, FBI and Interpol.

30. The *Horton* balls, or *Horton* Christmas ornaments, are the same ones that have been used since 1965. They used to be painted by a scenic artist and cost about $150 each to hand paint. Now they are machine made by the graphics department, so it is cheaper and faster.

31. Interview with Chip Dox, Burbank, California, 14 December 1990.

32. Ibid.

33. Fuller's earth was also the staple that blackened *Jack's* Santa suit for his slide down *Jennifer's* chimney and a Christmas Day 1990 proposal of marriage.

34. Interview with Chip Dox, Burbank, California, 14 December 1990.

35. A swing set is one that is brought in for short-term, not permanent, use. For example, *Lawrence's* villa was a swing set, as was *Justin* and *Adrienne's* Texas apartment.

36. Interview with Richard Bloore, Burbank, California, 6 November 1990.

37. Ibid.

38. Ibid.

39. Ibid.

40. Interview with Matthew Ashford, Burbank, California, 6 February 1991.

41. Interview with Richard Bloore, Burbank, California, 6 November 1990.

42. Diva von Dish, "It Takes All Kinds: Diva Names Her Favorite, Most Outrageous Moments of 1990 (or Thereabouts)," *Soap Opera Digest*, 13 November 1990: 135.

43. Interview with Richard Bloore, Burbank, California, 6 November 1990.

44. Interview with Ken Corday, Burbank, California, 18 July 1990.

45. Interview with Bill Hayes, North Hollywood, California, 22 September 1991.

The Writers

1. Interview with Pat Falken Smith, Woodland Hills, California, 11 October 1990.

2. Ibid.

3. Interview with Elizabeth Harrower, North Hollywood, California, 8 August 1990.

4. Interview with Ed Mallory, Encino, California, 10 December 1994.

5. Actors' contracts give them a guarantee of appearing in a certain number of shows at a given salary. Guarantees generally range from one to three shows or a fraction thereof. For example, an actor could have a guarantee of one and a quarter. That means that every fourth week the actor does an extra show.

6. The actors normally work in cycles of 13 or 26 weeks or occasionally 52 weeks. Their contracts usually run for two or three years, but their option comes up in those 13-, 26- or 52-week cycles.

7. Interview with Pat Falken Smith, Woodland Hills, California, 11 October 1990.

8. Ibid.

9. Interview with Joe Gallison, Burbank, California, 23 October 1990.

10. Interview with Pat Falken Smith, Woodland Hills, California, 11 October 1990.

11. Bill Rega, letter to Bill Bell, undated [197?]. William J. Bell Collection, Theater Arts Library, University of California, Los Angeles.

12. Interview with Becky Greenlaw, Burbank, California, 23 January 1991.
13. Ibid.
14. Interview with Pat Falken Smith, Woodland Hills, California, 5 October 1990.
15. Interview with Bill Bell, Malibu, California, 21 September 1990.
16. Interview with Pat Falken Smith, Woodland Hills, California, 19 July 1990.
17. Interview with Matthew Ashford, Burbank, California, 27 November 1990.
18. Interview with Pat Falken Smith, Woodland Hills, California, 5 October 1990.
19. Interview with Pat Falken Smith, Woodland Hills, California, 19 July 1990.
20. Interview with Wally Kurth, Los Angeles, California, 31 October 1990.
21. Interview with Wayne Heffley, Burbank, California, 11 September 1990.
22. William J. Bell, "Days of Our Lives, February 29, 1968." TMs, p. 1, Theater Arts Library, University of California, Los Angeles.
23. Interview with Pat Falken Smith, Woodland Hills, California, 19 July 1990.
24. Interview with Joe Gallison, Burbank, California, 23 October 1990.
25. Interview with Pat Falken Smith, Woodland Hills, California, 19 July 1990.
26. Interview with Jack Herzberg, Temecula, California, 19 September 1991.
27. Interview with Elizabeth Harrower, North Hollywood, California, 8 August 1990.
28. Interview with Pat Falken Smith, Woodland Hills, California, 11 October 1990.
29. Interview with Suzanne Rogers, Burbank, California, 30 November 1990.
30. Interview with George Jenesky, Burbank, California, 11 September 1990.
31. Ibid.
32. Interview with Pat Falken Smith, Woodland Hills, California, 19 July 1990.
33. Interview with Elizabeth Harrower, North Hollywood, California, 8 August 1990.
34. Interview with Bill Bell, Malibu, California, 21 September 1990.
35. Ibid.
36. Interview with Bill Hayes, North Hollywood, California, 22 September 1991.
37. Interview with Bill Bell, Malibu, California, 21 September 1990.
38. Interview with Pat Falken Smith, Woodland Hills, California, 19 July 1990.
39. Interview with Bill Bell, Malibu, California, 21 September 1990.
40. Interview with Jack Herzberg, Temecula, California, 19 September 1991.
41. Interview with Pat Falken Smith, Woodland Hills, California, 19 July 1990.
42. Ibid.
43. Ibid.
44. Interview with Jack Herzberg, Temecula, California, 19 September 1991.
45. William J. Bell, "Days of Our Lives, February 14, 1977." TMs, pp. 2-3, Theater Arts Library, University of California, Los Angeles.
46. Interview with Elizabeth Harrower, North Hollywood, California, 8 August 1990.
47. Ibid.
48. Interview with Pat Falken Smith, Woodland Hills, California, 19 July 1990.
49. Interview with Bill Bell, Malibu, California, 21 September 1990.
50. Ibid.
51. Interview with Pat Falken Smith, Woodland Hills, California, 19 July 1990.

The Actors

1. *Days of Our Lives*, unpublished promotional mss., 7 December 1964, p. 5.
2. Interview with Ken Corday, Burbank, California, 9 July 1990.
3. *Days of Our Lives*, unpublished promotional mss., 7 December 1964, p. 5.
4. It must be noted that *Tom Horton*'s love for baseball was acquired from Ted Corday. Ted's love of baseball is legendary and his son Ken has inherited the passion.
5. *Days of Our Lives*, unpublished promotional mss, 7 December 1964, pp. 8-9.
6. Interview with Macdonald Carey, Beverly Hills, California, 10 October 1990.
7. *Days of Our Lives*, unpublished promotional mss., 7 December 1964, pp. 10-11.
8. Interview with Ken Corday, Burbank, California, 9 July 1990.
9. William J. Bell, "Days of Our Lives, February 14, 1977." TMs, p. 2, Theater Arts Library, University of California, Los Angeles.

10. *Days of Our Lives*, unpublished promotional mss., 7 December 1964, p. 15.

11. Interview with Susan Seaforth Hayes, Burbank, California, 3 August 1990.

12. William J. Bell, "Days of Our Lives, February 29, 1968." TMs, p. 1, Theater Arts Library, University of California, Los Angeles.

13. William J. Bell, Chicago, to Betty Corday, Burbank, 12 November 1970. TMs, p. 24-25, Theater Arts Library, University of California, Los Angeles.

14. Interview with Bill Hayes, North Hollywood, California, 22 September 1991.

15. Interview with Bill Bell, Malibu, California, 21 September 1990.

16. Interview with Frank Parker, Los Angeles, California, 4 October 1990.

17. Interview with Bill Hayes, North Hollywood, California, 22 September 1991.

18. Interview with Bill Bell, Malibu, California, 21 September 1990.

19. William J. Bell, "Days of Our Lives, 16 November 1975." TMs, p. 77, Theater Arts Library, University of California, Los Angeles.

20. Bill Rega, letter to Bill Bell, Chicago, 20 August 1970. Theater Arts Library, University of California, Los Angeles.

21. William J. Bell, Chicago, to Betty Corday, Burbank, 12 November 1970. TMs, p. 36, Theater Arts Library, University of California, Los Angeles.

22. *Time*, January 12, 1976, pp. 46-53.

23. Ibid, p. 51.

24. Interview with Bill Hayes, North Hollywood, California, 22 September 1991.

25. William J. Bell, "Days of Our Lives, 16 November 1975." TMs, pp. 1-2, Theater Arts Library, University of California, Los Angeles.

26. Interview with Bill Hayes, North Hollywood, California, 22 September 1991.

27. Interview with Jack Herzberg, Temecula, California, 19 September 1991.

28. Interview with Bill Hayes, North Hollywood, California, 22 September 1991.

29. Ibid.

30. William J. Bell, "Days of Our Lives, 14 February 1977." TMs, p. 1, Theater Arts Library, University of California, Los Angeles.

31. William J. Bell, "Days of Our Lives, 14 February 1977." TMs, pp. 50-51, Theater Arts Library, University of California, Los Angeles.

32. William J. Bell, "Days of Our Lives, 11 December 1970." TMs, p. 38, Theater Arts Library, University of California, Los Angeles.

33. Interview with Ed Mallory, Encino, California, 10 December 1994.

34. Ibid.

35. Ibid.

36. William J. Bell, "Days of Our Lives, 16 November 1975." TMs, p. 68, Theater Arts Library, University of California, Los Angeles.

37. Interview with Suzanne Rogers, Burbank, California, 30 November 1990.

38. Ibid.

39. Interview with Quinn Redeker, Hollywood, California, 9 January 1991.

40. Interview with Frank Parker, Los Angeles, California, 4 October 1990.

41. Interview with Quinn Redeker, Hollywood, California, 9 January 1991.

42. Ibid.

43. Ibid.

44. Interview with Macdonald Carey, Beverly Hills, California, 10 October 1990.

45. Interview with Joe Gallison, Burbank, California, 23 October 1990.

46. Interview with Susan Seaforth Hayes, Burbank, California, 3 August 1990.

47. Ibid.

48. Interview with Joe Gallison, Burbank, California, 23 October 1990.

49. Interview with Wally Kurth, Los Angeles, California, 31 October 1990.

50. Ibid.

51. Interview with Charles Shaughnessy, Burbank, California, 8 January 1991.

52. Ibid.

53. Ibid.

54. Ibid.

55. Interview with Matthew Ashford, Burbank, California, 6 February 1991.

56. Interview with Wayne Heffley, Burbank, California, 11 September 1990.

57. Interview with Matthew Ashford, Burbank, California, 6 February 1991.
58. Ibid.
59. Interview with George Jenesky, Burbank, California, 11 September 1990.
60. Ibid.
61. Under fives are "special business" extras. That means they have interaction with a principal character, or they are singled out of a group. They are called "under fives" because they have under five lines of dialogue. All actors on the show are AFTRA members and are paid at least the minimum according to union scale: $156 for extras, $269 for under fives, $580 for principals [1994].
62. Interview with Linda Poindexter, Burbank, California, 24 August 1990.
63. Ibid.
64. Ibid.
65. Ibid.

The Fans

1. Interview with Ken Corday, Burbank, California, 18 July 1990.
2. Interview with Bill Bell, Malibu, California, 21 September 1990.
3. Interview with Ken Corday, Burbank, California, 9 July 1990.
4. Interview with Charles Shaughnessy, Burbank, California, 8 January 1991.
5. Interview with Don Frabotta, Burbank, California, 11 September 1990.
6. Interview with Linda Poindexter, Burbank, California, 24 August 1990.
7. Interview with Don Frabotta, Burbank, California, 11 September 1990.
8. Ibid.
9. Interview with George Jenesky, Burbank, California, 11 September 1990.
10. Interview with Susan Seaforth Hayes, Burbank, California, 3 August 1990.
11. Interview with Ed Mallory, Encino, California, 10 December 1994.
12. Interview with Bill Hayes, North Hollywood, California, 22 September 1991.
13. Interview with Matthew Ashford, Burbank, California, 27 November 1990.
14. Interview with Charles Shaughnessy, Burbank, California, 8 January 1991.
15. Interview with George Jenesky, Burbank, California, 11 September 1990.
16. Interview with Susan Seaforth Hayes, Burbank, California, 3 August 1990.
17. Moyra Bligh, Toronto, Ontario, letter to the author, 24 November 1990.
18. Interview with Pat Falken Smith, Woodland Hills, California, 19 July 1990.
19. Ibid.
20. Interview with Elizabeth Harrower, North Hollywood, California, 8 August 1990.
21. Linda Pidutti, Mt. Clemens, Michigan, letter to the author, 29 September 1990.
22. The best way to obtain fan club information is to write the actors at the studio: *Days of Our Lives*, c/o NBC-TV, 3000 West Alameda Avenue, Burbank, California 91523.
23. *Days of Our Lives* is shown in a number of foreign markets, including Australia, Canada, New Zealand, Germany, Greece, France, Spain, English-speaking Asia and the British Virgin Islands. *Days* is the number one show in Australia.
24. Grace Saffran Ashford was born June 15, 1992.
25. Interview with Don Frabotta, Burbank, California, 11 September 1990.
26. Interview with Macdonald Carey, Beverly Hills, California, 10 October 1990.
27. Interview with Susan Seaforth Hayes, Burbank, California, 3 August 1990.
28. Elizabeth Carpenter, Oakville, Conn., letter to the author, 16 December 1990.
29. Interview with Wally Kurth, Los Angeles, California, 31 October 1990.
30. Marsha Seader, Merrick, New York, letter to the author, 4 March 1991.
31. Ibid.
32. Interview with Ken Corday, Burbank, California, 6 August 1990.
33. Ibid.
34. The *Days* set is normally a closed set and was never included on the NBC Studio Tours.
35. Interview with Bill Hayes, North Hollywood, California, 22 September 1991.

The Story Line

1. *Days of Our Lives*, unpublished promotional mss., 7 December 1964, p. 6.
2. Ibid., p. 20.

APPENDIX A

GENEALOGIES*

Descendants of Alice Horton

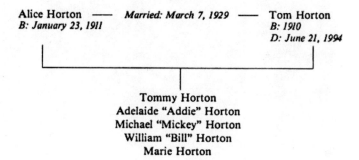

Alice Horton —— *Married: March 7, 1929* —— Tom Horton
B: *January 23, 1911*   B: *1910*
                                                                                   D: *June 21, 1994*

Tommy Horton
Adelaide "Addie" Horton
Michael "Mickey" Horton
William "Bill" Horton
Marie Horton

Descendants of Caroline Brady

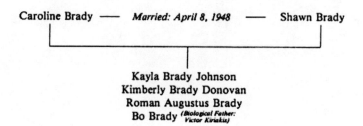

Caroline Brady —— *Married: April 8, 1948* —— Shawn Brady

Kayla Brady Johnson
Kimberly Brady Donovan
Roman Augustus Brady
Bo Brady *(Biological Father: Victor Kiriakis)*

The dates are from "the bible" or the actual air date of the event.

Ancestry of Scotty Banning

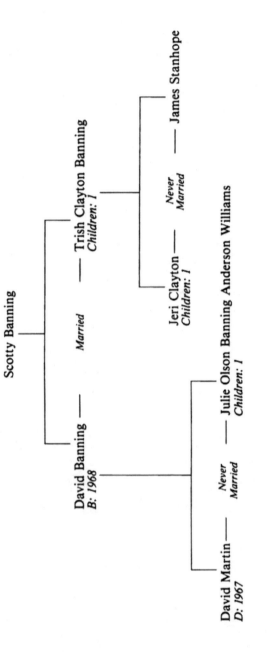

Ancestry of Abigail Johanna Deveraux

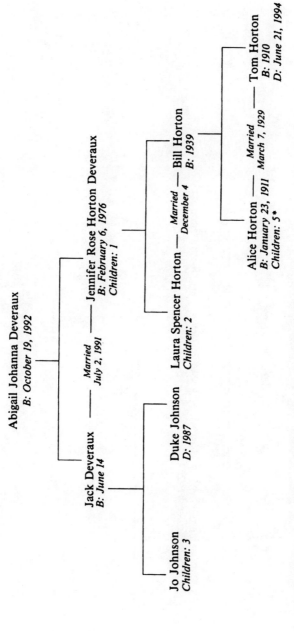

Abigail Johanna Deveraux
B: October 19, 1992

Jack Deveraux
B: June 14

Married
July 2, 1991

Jennifer Rose Horton Deveraux
B: February 6, 1976
Children: 1

Jo Johnson
Children: 3

Duke Johnson
D: 1987

Laura Spencer Horton
Children: 2

Married
December 4

Bill Horton
B: 1939

Alice Horton
B: January 23, 1911
Children: 5*

Married
March 7, 1929

Tom Horton
B: 1910
D: June 21, 1994

*Other Horton Children: Tommy Horton 1931– ; Adelaide "Addie" 1931–1974; Michael "Mickey" Horton 1932– ; Marie Horton 1942–1994

Ancestry of Jeremy Jacobs

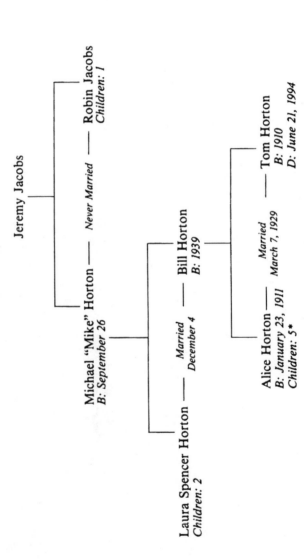

Jeremy Jacobs

Michael "Mike" Horton ——— *Never Married* ——— Robin Jacobs
B: September 26   *Children: 1*

Laura Spencer Horton ——— *Married* ——— Bill Horton
Children: 2   *December 4*   B: 1939

Tom Horton
B: 1910
D: June 21, 1994

Alice Horton ——— *Married* ———
B: January 23, 1911   *March 7, 1929*
Children: 5*

**Other Horton Children*: Tommy Horton *1931– *; Adelaide "Addie" *1931–1974*; Michael "Mickey" Horton *1932– *; Marie Horton *1942–*

Ancestry of Lucas Roberts

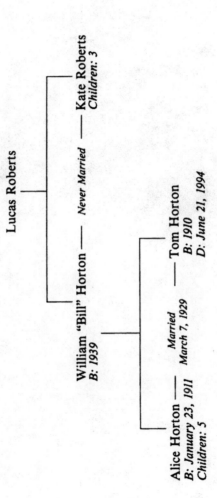

Lucas Roberts

William "Bill" Horton —— *Never Married* —— Kate Roberts
B: 1939   *Children: 3*

Alice Horton —— *Married* —— Tom Horton
B: January 23, 1911   *March 7, 1929*   B: 1910
Children: 5   D: June 21, 1994

Other Horton Children: Tommy Horton 1931– ; Adelaide "Addie" 1931–1974; Michael "Mickey" Horton 1932– ; Marie Horton 1942–

Ancestry of Carrie Brady

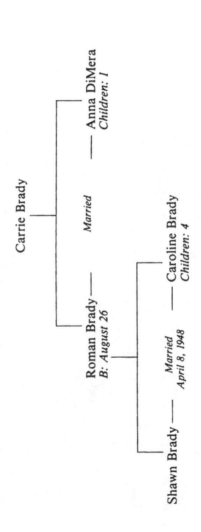

Carrie Brady

Married

Anna DiMera
Children: 1

Roman Brady——
B: August 26

——Caroline Brady
Children: 4

Married
April 8, 1948

Shawn Brady ——

Ancestry of Eric Roman and Samantha Jean Brady

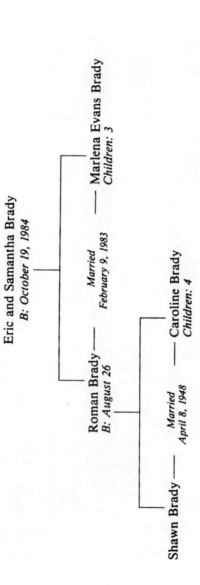

Eric and Samantha Brady
B: October 19, 1984

Marlena Evans Brady
Children: 3

Married
February 9, 1983

Roman Brady
B: August 26

Caroline Brady
Children: 4

Married
April 8, 1948

Shawn Brady

Ancestry of Shawn-Douglas Brady

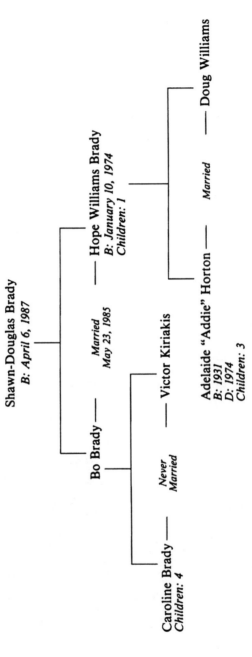

Shawn-Douglas Brady
B: April 6, 1987

Married
May 23, 1985

Bo Brady —

— Victor Kiriakis

Hope Williams Brady
B: January 10, 1974
Children: 1

Adelaide "Addie" Horton —
B: 1931
D: 1974
Children: 3

Married

— Doug Williams

Caroline Brady —
Children: 4

Never
Married

*Other Horton Children: Tommy Horton *1931–* ; Michael "Mickey" Horton *1932–* ; William "Bill" Horton *1939–* ; Marie Horton *1942–*

CAST LIST

(in alphabetical order)

Michele Abrams (*Teresa*) 1994
James Acheson (*Jack Deveraux*) 1987
Sharon Acker (*Pamela*) 1987
Peter Ackerman (*Photographer*) 1993
Deborah Adair (*Kate Roberts*) 1993–95
Arthur Adams (*Officer Hicks*) 1971–72
Hank Adams (*Lane Hollister*) 1990
Hank Adams (*Jordan*) 1991
Joseph Adams (*Jack Deveraux*) 1987
Laurel Adams (*Mrs. Campbell*) 1981
Mike Adams (*Driver*) 1993
Susan Adams (*Meredith*) 1971
Wesley Addy (*Dr. Cooper*) 1966–67
Marc Alaimo (*Alex's Henchman*) 1982
Bob Alberti (*Piano Player*) 1978
Beth Albright (*Mandy*) 1992
Andrea Alcantar (*Baby Linda*) 1980
Antony Alda (*Johnny Corelli*) 1990–91
Robert Alda (*Stuart Whyland*) 1981
Rhonda Aldrick (*Kayla Brady Johnson*) 1989
Michael Aldridge (*Steve*) 1977
Marilyn Alex (*Nurse*) 1971
Marilyn Alex (*Saleswoman*) 1973
Denise Alexander (*Susan Hunter Martin*) 1966–73
Newell Alexander (*Dr. Hopkins*) 1990
Hope Alexander-Willis (*Myra Cox*) 1988
Hope Alexander-Willis (*Roz Fuller*) 1989

Kristian Alfonso (*Hope Williams Brady*) 1983–87; 1990; 1994–
Isaac Allan (*Tim*) 1988–89
Isaac Allan (*Bellboy*) 1991
Jed Allan (*Don Craig*) 1971–85
Darrell Allen (*Mr. Link*) 1967
Dominick Allen (*Simon*) 1989–90
Jeremy Allen (*Jeremy*) 1989
Michael Allen (*Ponce*) 1972
Ralph Allen (*Ted Lambert*) 1980
Sheldon Allman (*Howard Emory*) 1970
Sheldon Allman (*Ben*) 1972
Diane Almeida (*Stacy*) 1993
Matthew Alloway (*Baby Gideon*) 1989
Chris Allport (*Clark*) 1986
John Alton (*Laundryman*) 1971
John Alvin (*Mr. Stipson*) 1965
Brian Amber (*Andrew Donovan*) 1988–89
Lee Amber (*Dr. Knight*) 1970; 1972–73
Richard Amend (*Quinn*) 1992
Paul Amendt (*Geoff*) 1994
John Amour (*Michael Horton*) 1971–73
Karen Anders (*Betty Ray*) 1983
Richard Anders (*Flood*) 1968
Richard Anders (*Florist*) 1968
Arline Anderson (*Mav Jaroslavski*) 1980
Carl Anderson (*as himself*) 1985; 1986; 1988
Daryl Anderson (*Fisher Andrews*) 1993–94

*Information is taken from the Days of Our Lives' *cast charts. Note: the dates are* tape *dates and not U.S. air dates.*

Deke Anderson (*Eddie*) 1989
Ernest Anderson (*Mr. Russell*) 1968
Larry Anderson (*Andrew Hosmine*) 1978
Larry Anderson (*Dr. Edward Parks*) 1990
Larry Anderson (*Emissary*) 1993
Lora Anderson (*Chelsea*) 1989
McKee Anderson (*Nurse Carson*) 1978
Pamela Anderson (*Cindy*) 1992
Sam Anderson (*Hotel Manager*) 1982
Valerie Anderson (*Patron*) 1977
Valerie Anderson (*Nancy Trotter*) 1978
Bill Andes (*Harley Marshall*) 1979–80
Ben Andrews (*Detective Perry*) 1973
Brian Andrews (*Baby Michael Horton*) 1970
Christian Andrews (*Bud*) 1987–90
David Andrews (*Ronnie Marley*) 1983
Tina Andrews (*Valerie Grant*) 1975–77
Kelly Andrus (*Bridget*) 1992
Susan Angelo (*Amy Roberts*) 1992
John Aniston (*Eric Richards*) 1970
John Aniston (*Victor Kiriakis*) 1985–
David Ankrum (*Dr. Randall*) 1984; 1992
Frank Annesse (*Barry Reid*) 1984–85
Michael Ansara (*David Lebec*) 1984
Lee Anthony (*Dr. Herman*) 1977
Lee Anthony (*Dr. George Hillary*) 1982
Christina Applegate (*Baby Burt Grizzell*) 1972
Robert Arcaro (*Alex's Man*) 1983
Ben Archibek (*Neil Curtis*) 1973
Alex Ardenti (*Whitney's Guard*) 1991
John Armour (*Michael Horton*) 1971–73
Herb Armstrong (*Carl Sawyer*) 1965
Vaughn Armstrong (*David Caldwell*) 1994
Adrian Arnold (*Max*) 1987
James Arone (*Viper Slick*) 1985
Ronit Aronoff (*Baby Samantha Brady*) 1984
Rod Arrants (*Chief Richard Cates*) 1985–86
Armand Arrelin (*Sheriff Hodges*) 1994
Martin Ashe (*Milt Culver*) 1965
Matthew Ashford (*Jack Deveraux*) 1987–93
Frank Ashmore (*Brent Cavanaugh*) 1981
Armand Asselin (*Mr. Doyle*) 1987
Wendy Augustus (*Nurse Jacob*) 1970
Jeff Austin (*Danny Novak*) 1980
Michael Austin-Petron (*Barry*) 1992
William Austyn (*Drew's Double*) 1988
Brian Autenreith (*Zachary*) 1984–85
Conrad Bachman (*Member of the Parole Board*) 1970
Margaret Bacon (*Miss Perkins*) 1978
Dennis Bailey (*Fred*) 1994
Joel Bailey (*Cameron Davis*) 1985–86
Joel Bailey (*Hartman*) 1988
Alretha Baker (*Clancy*) 1991
Terri Baker (*Waitress*) 1966
Elizabeth Baldwin (*Barbara Hackett*) 1993

Richard Balin (*Vasco*) 1992
George Ball (*Minister*) 1977
Sandy Balson (*Miss Jenkins*) 1969
Sandy Balson (*Sandy Stanhope*) 1976
Arlene Banas (*Dr. Marisa Alvarez*) 1992
Jack Bannon (*Walter Larkin*) 1967
Jack Bannon (*Assistant State Attorney*) 1967
Rosa Barbatos (*Italian Woman*) 1968
Andrea Barber (*Carrie Brady*) 1982–86
Ann Barber (*Sister Theresa*) 1969
Steve Barbro (*Fred*) 1992
Steve Barbro (*Volunteer*) 1992
Ron Barker (*Tarrington*) 1988–92
Beege Barkette (*Susie Pocentalik*) 1978
Jennifer Barlow (*Brooke*) 1989
Joe Barnaba (*Ben Caldwell*) 1980
Julian Barnes (*Shane's Father*) 1988
Julian Barnes (*Dr. Goddard*) 1992
Eileen Barnett (*Brooke Hamilton/Stephanie Woodruff*) 1978–80
David Baron (*Lennie*) 1983
Sharon Barr (*Inmate Billie*) 1983–84
June Barrett (*Nurse Pam*) 1982
Mace Barrett (*Judge Davies*) 1994
Mercer Barrows III (*Baby Charlie*) 1986
Samantha Barrows (*Noel Curtis*) 1984–86; 1988
Guerin Barry (*Mystery Caller*) 1981–82
Guerin Barry (*Jeweler*) 1992
Ivor Barry (*Grandfather*) 1983
Patricia Barry (*Addie Horton Olson Williams*) 1971–74
Chad Barstad ("*Brad*"/*David Banning*) 1968–70
Dan Barton (*Earl Carnes*) 1979–80
Larry Barton (*Cab Driver*) 1967
Lisa Barton (*Miss Douglas*) 1967
Anastasia Barzee (*Valerie*) 1994
Janice Barzilla (*Marsha Robbins*) 1977
Larry Basham (*Craig*) 1980
Patrick Basile (*Thug #1*) 1990
Bill Bassett (*Scott Blake*) 1968
Bill Bassett (*Jerry Barnes*) 1968–69
Laura Bassett (*Nadine*) 1983–84
William H. Bassett (*Dr. Walter Griffin*) 1977–78
William H. Bassett (*Government Official*) 1988
Charles Bateman (*Maxwell Jarvis*) 1980–81
Jeanne Bates (*Jean Perkins*) 1966–68
Jeanne Bates (*Mrs. Anne Peters*) 1972–75
Katherine Bates (*Loretta Toscano*) 1990
Jamie Lynn Bauer (*Dr. Laura Horton*) 1993–
Nina Bauer (*Sister Marguerite*) 1992
Melissa Baum (*Cassie Scofield*) 1990–91
Susan Bay (*Rose Douglas*) 1966
Michael Bays (*Julio Ramirez*) 1988–89

Brigid Bazlen (*Mary Anderson*) 1972
Cheryl Beach (*Adele*) 1992
Terrance Beasor (*Jonathan Rutherford*) 1985
Terrance Beasor (*Ernesto*) 1989
Terrance Beasor (*Newscaster*) 1990
Dianne Beatty (*Mrs. Jonathan Carlton*) 1984
Rory Beauregard (*Baby Eric Brady*) 1984
John Beck (*Sam Wilson*) 1966
Barbara Beckley (*Caroline Brady*) 1984–85
Denisa Beckman (*Harem Wife*) 1985
Micah Bedrosian (*Little Bo*) 1990
Micah Bedrosian (*Josh*) 1992
Fred Beir (*Larry Atwood*) 1977–78
John Belche (*Bartender*) 1992
Thomas Belgrey (*Honor Guard Chief*) 1990
Thomas Belgrey (*Mr. West*) 1992
Charles Alvin Bell (*Harold Trask*) 1978–80
Felecia Bell (*Glynnis O'Connor*) 1990–91
Vanessa Bell (*Denise Preston*) 1985
Vanessa Bell (*Charlene*) 1988
Scott Bellomo (*Richie Hackett*) 1993
Abby Bemiller (*Little Isabella Toscano*) 1990
Nick Benedict (*Curtis Reed*) 1993
Brenda Benet (*Lee Dumonde*) 1979–82
Jim Bentley (*Law Clerk*) 1982
Oscar Beregi (*Colonel Dubovic*) 1968
Oscar Beregi (*Sergio*) 1970; 1972
Judith Marie Bergan (*Elizabeth Harley*) 1987
Alan Bergman (*Dr. Strother*) 1974
Richard Bergman (*Brett Fredricks*) 1983
Elliot Berk (*Vegas Informant*) 1991
Jason Bernard (*Preston Wade*) 1982
Walter Berns (*Mr. Ross*) 1977
Collette Bertrand (*Amazon Yolanda*) 1984
John Beshara (*Drug Dealer*) 1993
Martine Bestwick (*Abigail*) 1984
Ivy Bethune (*Letty*) 1974
Ivy Bethune (*Nurse Blake*) 1975
Val Bettin (*Clyde Franklin*) 1980
Victor Bevine (*Mr. Ogins*) 1992
Rich Bichner (*Jim Weston*) 1977
Fred Bier (*Larry Atwood*) 1977–78
Richard Biggs (*Dr. Marcus Hunter*) 1987–92
Billie and the Beaters (*as themselves*) 1984
Eric & Brandon Billings (*Brady*) 1994–
Dick Billingsley (*Scotty Banning*) 1981–83
Len Birman (*Judge Milton Bartlett*) 1992
Matthew Paul Bischof (*Baby Don "D.J."*) 1980
Whit Bissell (*Dr. Miller*) 1971
Stephen Black (*Rob Stemkowski*) 1992
David Blackwood (*Harry*) 1985–86
Martin Blaine (*Judge Bridges*) 1965
Martin Blaine (*Dr. Joe Hendricks*) 1966–67
Megan Blake (*Hilary*) 1993
Barry Blakely (*TV Clerk*) 1970
Barry Blakely (*John McGuire*) 1972

Barry Blakely (*Dr. Sherman*) 1973
Barry Blakely (*Charlie*) 1973
Barry Blakely (*Jerry Rinehart*) 1978–79
John Blouin (*Bailiff*) 1985
Robert Bock (*Minister*) 1980
Steven Boergadine (*Chauffeur*) 1994
Vasili Bogazianos (*Ozzie*) 1993
Stan Bohrman (*Moderator*) 1978
Gary Bolen (*Clayton Fraser*) 1990
Gary Bolen (*Mr. Peterson*) 1992
Ivar Bonar (*Justice of the Peace*) 1975
Ivar Bonar (*Judge Gelson*) 1976; 1977
Ivar Bonar (*Judge Clarence Foster*) 1985
Craig Bond (*Baby Michael Horton*) 1969
Raleigh Bond (*Priest*) 1988
Fritz Bonner (*James Miller*) 1993
Carla Borelli (*Mary Anderson*) 1975
Joseph Bottoms (*Cal Winters*) 1991
Steven Bourne (*Officer Casey*) 1982
Pamela Bowen (*Leslie Landman*) 1986–87
Carla Bower (*Woman Patient*) 1992
Charles Boyd (*Dr. Schiller*) 1977
Mike Boyd (*Roland*) 1991
Tanya Boyd (*Celeste*) 1994–
Andrew Boyer (*Dr. Moffett*) 1993
Teresa Bowman (*Mother*) 1992
Gary Bradford (*Police Officer*) 1993
Stewart Bradley (*Lieutenant Danton*) 1967–71; 1973; 1977–79; 1981
Janet Brady (*Adrienne's Stunt Double*) 1988
Tony Brafa (*Dr. Eisenstadt*) 1987
Tony Brafa (*Swiss Maitre d' Antonio*) 1992
Richard Branda (*Assistant D.A.*) 1977
Gregory Brandell (*Dr. Shepard*) 1983
Jane Brandon (*Hitchhiker*) 1977
John Brandon (*Ken Mahoney*) 1978
Peter Brandon (*Dr. Lloyd*) 1971
Peter Brandon (*Bruce Jamison*) 1977
Eddie Braun (*Student*) 1991
Tracey E. Bregman (*Donna Temple Craig*) 1978–80
Ryan Brennan (*Max Brady*) 1986–88; 1990–92
Katie Brenner (*Katerina, 10 years old*) 1990
Daniel Bright (*Brian*) 1987
Lisa Brinegar (*Sarah Horton*) 1985–89
Lisa Brinegar (*Little Isabella*) 1989
Danielle Brisebois (*Sasha*) 1987
Don Briscoe (*Tony Merritt*) 1966
Bill Brochturp (*Hank*) 1992
Stanley Brock (*Howie Hoffstedder*) 1983–86
Timothy Brocker (*Baby*) 1967; 1968
Gerald Brodin (*Police Officer*) 1993
Elaine Bromka (*Stella Lombard*) 1992
Sheila Bromley (*Mrs. Riley*) 1967
Fritz Bronner (*Rusty*) 1989
Blance Bronte (*Arlene Harris*) 1978

Walter Brooke (*Wayne Charles*) 1967
Aimee Brooks (*Jamie*) 1989
Aimee Brooks (*Sarah Horton*) 1990
Alan Brooks (*Security Guard*) 1992
Dean Brooks (*Thug*) 1981
Dean Brooks (*Bart Devereaux*) 1981
Dina Brooks (*Amy*) 1991
Elizabeth Brooks (*Theresa Harper*) 1978–79
J. Cynthia Brooks (*Taylor McCall*) 1992–93
Jason Brooks (*Peter Blake*) 1993–
Matthew Brooks (*Young Boy*) 1987
Randy Brooks (*Desmond*) 1988
Stephen Brooks (*Joshua Fallon*) 1980–81
Shellye Broughton (*Lexie Carver*) 1993
Alli Brown (*Sarah Horton*) 1991
Ernie Brown (*Pawnbroker*) 1970
Graham Brown (*Jeffrey Jones*) 1970
Lew Brown (*Shawn Brady*) 1984–85
Pat Crawford Brown (*Minnie*) 1993
Peter Brown (*Dr. Greg Peters*) 1972–79
Phil Brown (*Jeff*) 1972
Richard Brown (*Delivery Boy*) 1969
Roger Aaron Brown (*Danny Grant*) 1981–85
Tom Brown (*Nathan Curtis*) 1975–76
Vivan Brown (*Martha Halstbad*) 1977
Vivian Brown (*Sister Veronica*) 1979
W. Ernest Brown (*Clerk*) 1967
Michael Brownlie (*Paramedic Barnes*) 1980
Robert Brubaker (*John Martin*) 1966–71
Robert Bruce (*Basil*) 1990
Shelly Bruce (*Juror*) 1965
Shelly Bruce (*Nurse*) 1966; 1967
Shelly Bruce (*Juror Hanson*) 1967
Shelly Bruce (*Scrub Nurse*) 1967
Shelly Bruce (*Nurse*) 1970
Pamela Brull (*Ellen*) 1988
Don Brummer (*Reporter*) 1993
Kathleen Buchanan (*Nurse*) 1977
Phil Buckman (*Larry*) 1990
Tara Buckman (*Norma Kirkland*) 1984–85
Michele Buffone (*Nanny*) 1994
Kryshanna Buford (*Timothy*) 1977
Tami Bula (*Sally Kirk*) 1980
Perry Bullington (*Brent Cavanaugh*) 1980–81
Brooke Bundy (*Rebecca North LeClere*)
 1975–77
Lauren Ann Bundy (*Baby Samantha Brady*)
 1985
Rosalyn Burbage (*Nurse*) 1966
Burt Burger (*Man's Voice*) 1966
Richard Burgi (*Philip Collier*) 1992
John Burke (*Mitch*) 1993
Amy Burkhard (*Amy*) 1989–90
Stephen Burleigh (*D.A. Moore*) 1990
Joe Burns (*Young Man*) 1990
Joe Burns (*Jimmy*) 1993
Robert Burns (*Ambulance Driver*) 1968

Robert Burns (*Bartender*) 1977
Terry Burns (*Dr. Miceli*) 1989
Terry Burns (*Doctor*) 1992
Wally Burns (*Mr. Nelson*) 1978
Betsy Burr (*Barbara Stewart*) 1986–87
Fritzi Burr (*Beulah Boden*) 1985
Bonnie Burroughs (*Gretchen Lindquist*) 1991
Jean Burton (*Technician*) 1966
Jeff Burton (*Guard*) 1970
Norman Burton (*Cab Driver*) 1967
Steve Burton (*Harris*) 1988
Steve Butts (*Billy*) 1974
Ruth Buzzi (*Letitia Bradford*) 1983
Brian Byers (*Dr. Ralph Smith*) 1991
Carl Byrd (*Waiter*) 1967
Carl Byrd (*Detective Perry*) 1969–70
Lorenzo Caccialanza (*Nico*) 1988–91
Robert Caffey (*Maitre d'*) 1966
Bill Cakmis (*KGB Agent Yuri*) 1986
John Callahan (*Tyler Malone*) 1983
John Callahan (*Doyle*) 1989
Gloria Calomee (*Annie Mae*) 1968–69
John Calvin (*Arthur Downey*) 1989–90
Casey Jack Campbell (*Baby Billy*) 1987
Joseph Campanella (*Harper Deveraux*)
 1987–88; 1990–92
Rafael Campos (*Jose*) 1982
Bobbie Candler (*Trixie*) 1989
Sandra Canning (*Grace Jeffries*) 1989–90
Harold Cannon (*Eddie*) 1984
Cate Caplin (*Nurse Cate*) 1987–90
Bill Capizzi (*Cab Driver*) 1993
Joe Lee Carey (*Police Officer Gates*) 1978
MacDonald Carey (*Dr. Tom Horton*) 1965–94
Adam Carl (*Jerry*) 1993
Catherine Carlen (*Tallulah*) 1990
Steve Carlisle (*Judge Stuart Perkins*) 1991
Karen Carlsen (*Sheila Hammond*) 1971
Linda Carlson (*Dr. Shaeffer*) 1989
Steve Carlson (*Paul Webber*) 1991
Steve Carlson (*Jeffrey Taylor*) 1990
Carl Carlsson (*Polka Dancer*) 1991
Ruth Carlsson (*Polka Dancer*) 1991
Cliff Carnell (*Leo*) 1980
Bill Carr (*Dr. Bill Horton*) 1965–66
Karen Carr (*Miss Carter*) 1976
Larry Carr (*Patron*) 1977
Larry Carr (*Dr. Blandford*) 1977
Paul Carr (*Dr. Forbes*) 1968
Robert Carraway (*Scott Banning*) 1968
Corinne Carroll (*Mrs. Lewis*) 1990
Dee Carroll (*Adele Winston Hamilton*)
 1975–76
Frank Carroll (*P.A. Voice*) 1968
Victoria Carroll (*Mrs. Roberta Neely*) 1984
Jody Carter (*Caroline Brady*) 1984
Mike Caruso (*TV Camera Operator*) 1992

Michelle Casey (*Zoe*) 1983
Dan Cashman (*Father O' Toole*) 1992
Michael Cassatt (*Dr. Fred Kingsley*) 1983
Candy Castillo (*Guard*) 1983
Noel Bennett Castle (*Baby Shawn-Douglas*) 1987
Bob Caudana (*Accordion Player*) 1980
Lane Caudell (*Woody King*) 1982–83
Robert Elliot Cauko (*Baby Andrew Donovan*) 1986–88
Michael Cavanaugh (*Palmer Reinhold*) 1984
Julio Cedillo (*Firefighter"Bradley"*) 1990
Carlos Cervantes (*Police Officer*) 1990
George Cervera (*Bus Driver*) 1973
Rudy Challenger (*Dr. Montgomery*) 1980
Patrice Chanel (*Gail Carson*) 1989
Karen Chandler (*Molly*) 1978
Judith Chapman (*Anjelica Deveraux Curtis*) 1989–90
Mark Lindsay Chapman (*Trevor*) 1987
Crystal Chappell (*Dr. Carly Manning/Katerina Von Leuschner*) 1990–93
Ariana Chase (*Kimberly Brady*) 1992–93
Courtney & Erica Chasen (*Baby Billie*) 1994
Elizabeth Chauvet (*Rita*) 1977
Lilyan Chauvin (*Suzanne*) 1979–80
Maree Cheatham (*Marie Horton*) 1965–68; 1970–73; 1994
Al Checco (*Motel Manager*) 1973
Al Checco (*Ed Rausch*) 1978
Mickey Cherney (*Mel Copley*) 1980
Colby Chester (*Kurt Randall*) 1980
Eric Chiff (*Kevin Cates*) 1986
Zachary Childs (*Bailiff*) 1970
Alise Christensen (*Spectator Secretary*) 1993
Sonia Christensen (*Girl in Park*) 1971
Frank Christi (*Edgar Pippin*) 1980
Panos Christi (*Cliff Masterson*) 1987
Leigh Christian (*Phyllis Casey*) 1971
Natt Christian (*Arlo*) 1977–78
Dick Christie (*Stanley Krakowski*) 1990
David Chow (*Dr. Wong*) 1971
David Chow (*Dr. Smith*) 1972
Andreana Marie Chutuk (*Baby Anne*) 1972–73
Carl Ciarfalio (*Thug*) 1992
David Ciminello (*Rafi Torres*) 1991–92
Charles Cioffi (*Ernesto Toscano*) 1990
Joe Clae (*Attacker*) 1988
Janis Claire (*Nurse*) 1966
Christie Claridge (*Susie*) 1984
Brett Baxter Clark (*Fantasy Howard*) 1991
Christie Clark (*Carrie Brady*) 1986–90; 1992–
Cynthia Lea Clark (*Nurse*) 1991
Cynthia Lea Clark (*Nurse*) 1992

David Carlisle Clark (*Casey*) 1992–93
Jeffrey Clark (*Jeremy*) 1989
Kendall Clark (*Police Officer*) 1968
Lynn Clark (*Madeline Armstrong*) 1990–92
Phillip Clark (*Dr. Todd Russell*) 1979
John Clarke (*Mickey Horton*) 1965–
Mindy Clarke (*Faith Taylor*) 1989–90
Robert Clarke (*Senator George Alden*) 1980
Robert Clary (*Robert LeClere*) 1972–73; 1975–80; 1981–83; 1986
Stanley Clay (*Young Man*) 1977
Clive Clerk (*David Martin*) 1966–67
Clive Clerk (*Man*) 1968
Ralph Clift (*Dr. Simone*) 1990
George Clifton (*Dr. Bruce Blake*) 1971
George Clifton (*Police Officer*) 1977
George Clifton (*Andre*) 1984
George Clifton (*Dr. Greer*) 1990
Pat Clifton (*Sandy Waters*) 1977
Pat Clifton (*Denise*) 1981
Robert Coburn (*Trucker*) 1993
Rhodie Cogan (*Mrs. Ivy Lowell*) 1974
Sarah Cohen (*Sarah*) 1980
Catero Colbert (*Corey*) 1993
Betty Cole (*Mrs. Boatwright*) 1973
Brian Cole (*Derek*) 1986–87
Elisa Cole (*Juana*) 1985
Jack Coleman (*Jake Kositchek*) 1981–82
Richard Colla (*Tony Merritt*) 1965–66
Barbara Collentine (*Lois Parker*) 1980
Joe Colligan (*Ethan Reilly*) 1987–88
Greg Collins (*Burly Dude*) 1990
Jolina Collins (*Jasmine*) 1984–85
Robert Evan Collins (*Molly's Grandfather*) 1991
Tony Colitti (*Stingray*) 1988
Tony Colitti (*Pickpocket*) 1993
Booth Colman (*Dr. Sands*) 1967
Scott Colomby (*Jose Torres*) 1988
Alex Colon (*Luis*) 1991
Mark Colson (*Gabe*) 1994–
Peter Colt (*Police Officer*) 1975
Dawn Comer (*Jodi*) 1990
Paul Comi (*Rick Brenner*) 1967
Jeffrey Concklin (*Ben*) 1991
Gino Conforti (*S. S. Mangino*) 1992
Corinne Conley (*Phyllis Anderson*) 1973–82
Darlene Conley (*Warden Baker*) 1983
Carole Conn (*Miss Jackson*) 1967
Carole Conn (*Nurse Bergin*) 1968
Carole Conn (*Mrs. Maltby*) 1977
Kathy Connell (*Barbara Newirth*) 1992
Sid Conrad (*Dr. Macdonald*) 1968
Sid Conrad (*Carter*) 1968
Sid Conrad (*Ribiwitz*) 1970
Sid Conrad (*Justice of the Peace*) 1972
Sid Conrad (*Mr. Salton*) 1973

Sid Conrad (*Reverend Jennings*) 1974–75
Sid Conrad (*Nick*) 1976–77
Sid Conrad (*Ed Gordon*) 1978
Sid Conrad (*Judge Albert Kabanis*) 1981
Dick Contino (*Gondolier*) 1976
Dick Contino (*Accordion Player*) 1978
Peggy Converse (*Mother Superior*) 1981
Steven Douglas Cook (*Tim Rollins*) 1992
Lawrence Cook (*Paul Grant*) 1975–76
James Cooper (*Alfonse Le Beque*) 1992
Rich Cooper (*Richie*) 1989–90
Ken Corday (*Ken*) 1978
Regis Cordic (*Langford*) 1977–78
Anthony Cordova (*Member of the Parole Board*) 1970
Mike Corgile (*Party Bartender*) 1993
Aneta Corsaut (*Blanche Dailey*) 1984
Robert Cornthwaite (*Dr. Bronson*) 1979
Mark Costello (*Hotel Manager*) 1991
Paul Coufos (*Michael Horton*) 1981–82
Jean Coulter (*Julie's Stunt Double*) 1979; 1981
Sean Coulter (*Martin*) 1989
Mimi Couzzens (*Sally*) 1977
Con Covert (*Phoenix*) 1984
Barry Cox (*Billy*) 1972
Doug Cox (*Bob Rush*) 1990
Walter Cox (*Shadowy Figure*) 1986
Walter Cox (*Stage Manager*) 1992
Don Craig (*Dr. Crispin*) 1992
Tony Craig (*Marvin Vale*) 1982
Barbara Crampton (*Trista Evans Bradford*) 1983
Brian Cranston (*Darryl*) 1982
Cindy Crawford (*Teen-ager*) 1978
Karen Criswell (*Amazon Simone*) 1984
Roark Critchlow (*Dr. Mike Horton*) 1994–
Jim Crofwell (*Beckwith*) 1978
Jim Crofwell (*Dr. Walker*) 1990
Patrick Cronin (*Dr. Monroe*) 1989
Patrick Cronin (*Dr. Baines*) 1990
Denise Crosby (*Lisa Davis*) 1980
Joan Crosby (*Country Inn Proprietor*) 1986
Chris Cruz (*Bailiff*) 1994
David Cryer (*Dr. Walters*) 1976
Kernie Cullen (*Lee's Stunt Double*) 1981
Zara Cully (*Mrs. Davis*) 1971
Jason Culp (*Jerry Pulaski*) 1989
Ron Cummins (*Ron*) 1980
Rusty Cundieff (*Theo Carver*) 1985
William Brian Curran (*Victor*) 1983
Sondra Currie (*Interior Decorator*) 1991
Christy Curtis (*Choreographer*) 1992
David Curtis (*Luke*) 1986
Dick Curtis (*Wilbur*) 1987
Donald Curtis (*Minister*) 1966
Ken Curtis (*Phil Winfrey*) 1992
Robb Curtis-Brown (*Dr. Craig Norris*) 1990

Sonia Curtis (*Nancy*) 1986
Janet Daily (*Janet Davis*) 1986
Deborah Dalton (*Cassie Burns*) 1980
Cindy Daly (*Cathy Breton*) 1979–80
Vito d'Ambrosio (*Kurt*) 1991
Dante D'Andre (*Waiter*) 1976
Brett Daniels (*Magician's Assistant*) 1990
Michael Dante (*Barney Jannings*) 1984
Oliver Darrow (*Flint*) 1989
Bryan Dattilo (*Lucas Roberts*) 1993–
Lew Dauber (*Frank*) 1993
Marty Davich (*Marty, the piano player*) 1977–93
Lolita Davidovich (*Mona*) 1985
Eileen Davidson (*Kristen Blake*) 1993–
Blair Davie (*Judge Weedman*) 1966
Lane Davies (*Dr. Evan Whyland*) 1981–82
Brian Davila (*Andrew Donovan*) 1991–92
Annette Davis (*Polly Walters*) 1975
Annette Davis (*Mrs. Hauser*) 1977
Jesse Davis (*Baby Eric Brady*) 1985–86
Jessica Davis (*Baby Samantha Brady*) 1985–86
Lindy Davis (*Engineer Frank*) 1985
Susan Davis (*Nurse*) 1992
Greg Dawson (*Piano Player*) 1992
Peter Dawson (*Mover*) 1966
Richard Davies (*Butler Cranshaw*) 1984
Davey Davison (*Miss Marston*) 1972
Davey Davison (*Virginia Lewis*) 1973
Davey Davison (*Mr. Emerson*) 1988
June Dayton (*Ruth Evans*) 1967
June Dayton (*Miss Williams*) 1969
June Dayton (*Mrs. Franklin*) 1980
Vince Deadrick, Sr. (*Hit Man*) 1985
Floy Dean (*Dr. Laura Spencer Horton*) 1966
Jenny De Basso (*Ingrid*) 1986
Denis Deboisblanc (*Masseur*) 1991
Shirley DeBurgh (*Delia Abernathy*) 1982–84
Rosemary De Camp (*Mother Superior*) 1979–80
Alan Decker (*Michael Horton*) 1970–71
Dick DeCoit (*Michael Horton*) 1973
Dick DeCoit (*Announcer*) 1991
Mary Jane Deegan (*Mrs. Martin*) 1978
Ed Deemer (*Lieutenant Bradley*) 1980
Louis De Farra (*Eduard Alesi*) 1992
Ashley Deguichi (*Sherelle*) 1985
Roger De Koven (*Dr. James Spencer*) 1968–69
John DeLancie (*Eugene Bradford*) 1982–86; 1989
Bill DeLand (*George*) 1981
Larry Delaney (*Jay Livingston*) 1973–74; 1976; 1979
Diane Delano (*Olga*) 1994
Marcia del Mar (*Marguerite Salazar*) 1992

Marcia del Mar (*Maria Diaz*) 1993

Anthony De Longis (*Claus Van Zandt*) 1985

Anthony De Longis (*Hans*) 1990

Sandy Dell (*Nurse Kelly*) 1993

George Deloy (*Orpheus*) 1986–87

Janet Demay (*Kate Halperin*) 1983

John Demita (*Father Pat*) 1993

Jack Denbo (*Jack Clayton*) 1974–77

John Dennis (*Cab Driver*) 1968

John Dennis (*Courtroom Door Guard*) 1970

John Dennis (*Jason Eggers*) 1971

John Dennis (*Waiter*) 1972

John Dennis (*Investigator*) 1976

Mark Derwin (*Mr. Brown*) 1988

Francis De Sales (*Dr. Rusty Lincoln*) 1965–66; 68

Francis De Sales (*Dr. Jim Spencer*) 1971

Nico De Silva (*Doorman Marvin*) 1969

Robert Deslonde (*Waiter*) 1966

Tom Dever (*Warden Rogers*) 1985

Sheila De Windt (*Sergeant Joan Hopkins*) 1983–84

Angelique de Windt (*Charlene*) 1988

Angelique de Windt (*Lexie Brooks*) 1989–90

John Dewnis (*Larry Hunter*) 1975

Alan Dexter (*Frank Ferguson*) 1965–66

Bud Diamond (*Wayne*) 1978

Don Diamond (*Nikos*) 1987

Don Diamond (*Judge*) 1990

Don Diamont (*Carlo Forenza*) 1984–85

George Dickerson (*Rev. Campbell*) 1981

Charles Dierkop (*Rocko*) 1984

Richard Dillard (*Sheriff Dan Cox*) 1989

Dan Dillon (*Bodyguard*) 1990

Susan Diol (*Emmy*) 1990–91

Ben DiTosti (*Ben, the piano player*) 1974–77; 1980

Glenn Dixon (*Judge Lind*) 1969

Charla Doherty (*Julie Olson*) 1965–66

Trent Dolan (*Allen Hamlin*) 1980

Trent Dolan (*Detective Steel*) 1988

Trent Dolan (*Commissioner Samuels*) 1992

Elinor Donahue (*Kate Honeycutt, R.N.*) 1984–86

Kate Donohue (*Marion Cook*) 1992

Chad Doreck (*Little Shane*) 1988

Stephen Doreck (*Kevin Tursi*) 1993

Michael Dorn (*Jimmy*) 1986–87

Steve Doubet (*David Banning*) 1975

Steve Dougherty (*Paramedic Steve*) 1983–84

James Doughton (*Henry Carpenter*) 1976

Burt Douglas (*Jim Fisk*) 1965

Burt Douglas (*Sam Monroe*) 1974–75

D.C. Douglas (*Bellman*) 1991

D.C. Douglas (*Brad Camp*) 1992

Diana Douglas (*Martha Evans*) 1977–79

Harrison Douglas (*Ian Griffith*) 1985

Garrick Dowhen (*French Actor*) 1993

J. Downing (*Malcolm Donnelly*) 1992

Roger Downing (*Randy Huston*) 1992

Aleana Downs (*Waitress*) 1982

Frederic Downs (*Hank*) 1973–80

Ken Drake (*Walter P. Bennett*) 1966

Ken Drake (*Ward Tilson*) 1966

Lieux Dressler (*Mabel*) 1989

Allison Drew (*Judy*) 1985

Mark Drexler (*Roger Lombard*) 1992

Denise BuBarry (*Twyla*) 1993

Don Dubbins (*Prospective Juror McGraw*) 1978

Marty Dudek (*Dr. Irvine*) 1984

Doug Dudley (*Ted McMannes*) 1978

Geoffrey Duell (*Voice*) 1966

Laura Duff (*LaToya*) 1985

Thomas Duffy (*Frank*) 1992

Bruce Dukov (*Tyler Lee*) 1993

Robert Dulaine (*Mr. Powers*) 1967

Robert Dulaine (*Technician*) 1968

Mary-Ellen Dunbar (*Lorraine*) 1991

Olive Dunbar (*Mary Ellen Donahue*) 1984

Angus Duncan (*Dr. Tony Romano*) 1968–69

Robert M. Duncan (*Rob Stemkowski*) 1992

Catherine Dunn (*Julie Olson*) 1967

Steve Dunne (*Mr. Draper*) 1968

John Durant (*TV Announcer*) 1992

Kim Durso (*Melissa Anderson*) 1975–76

Marj Dusay (*Vivian Alamain*) 1992–93

Michael Dwight–Smith (*Danny Grant*) 1975–78

Gene Dynarski (*Lieutenant Hastings*) 1982

Jeff Eagle (*Will*) 1984

Jeff Eagle (*Lester*) 1991

Steve Eastin (*Ralph*) 1986

Steve Eastin (*Colonel Jericho*) 1989–90

Mary Eastman (*Nurse*) 1966

Peter Eastman (*Lieutenant Governor*) 1978

Peter Eastman (*Judge Tamberg*) 1980

Joyce Easton (*Mrs. Blake, R.N.*) 1968

Joyce Easton (*Janet Banning*) 1968–69

Michael Easton (*Tanner Scofield*) 1990–92

Dian Eaton (*Mrs. Lewis*) 1977

Bonnie Ebsen (*Dagmar*) 1983

James Edson (*Rapist*) 1985–86

James Edson (*Marc*) 1992

Jack Edwards (*Lloyd Burton*) 1970

Sam Edwards (*Mr. O'Keefe*) 1978

Susan Edwards (*Andrea Levin*) 1988–89

Bobby Eilbacher (*Michael Horton*) 1970

Robin Eisenman (*Nurse Kelly Chase*) 1982–84

Ike Eisenmann (*Arthur Hall*) 1979

David Eisenstein (*Charles*) 1991

Chris Elia (*Amazon Tarina*) 1984
Gary Elliott (*Doug's Campaign Manager*) 1986
Jane Elliot (*Anjelica Deveraux Curtis*)
   1987–89
Sandy Elliott (*Sunny Chandler*) 1980
Larry Ellis (*Detective Jean Laclasse*) 1981
Lemoria English (*Court Stenographer*) 1991
George Englund (*Sax Man*) 1989
Darrin Erickson (*Ricardo*) 1990
Darrin Erickson (*Jacob*) 1990
Karen Ericson (*Nora Bassett*) 1979
Nicole Ericson (*Nurse Debbie*) 1985
Rob Estes (*Glenn Gallagher*) 1986–87
Roger Etienne (*Dr. Jouvet*) 1979
Bob Eubanks (*as himself*) 1986
Wesley Eure (*Michael Horton*) 1974–81
Tricia Evangeline (*Patrice*) 1990–91
Ellen Evans (*Phyllis*) 1978
Judi Evans (*Nurse Becki*) 1983
Judi Evans (*Adrienne Johnson Kiriakis*)
   1986–91
Lena Evans (*Jody*) 1985
Mary Beth Evans (*Kayla Brady Johnson*)
   1986–92
Terrance Evans (*Irwin*) 1989
Dana Dru Evenson (*Vivian's Stunt Double*)
   1994
Roger Everaert (*Dr. Jouvet*) 1980
Joseph Trent Everett (*Baby Melissa*) 1971
Tom Everett (*Speed Selejko*) 1985
Denise Ezell (*Reporter*) 1993
Michael Fairman (*Mr. Schroeder*) 1977
Tom Falk (*Bruce Wallace*) 1970
Brian Farrell (*Philip Briggs*) 1981
Mike Farrell (*Scott Banning*) 1968–70
Frank Fata (*Stefano DiMera*) 1991
John Fatooh (*Lawrence's Prison Guard*) 1991
Joe Faust (*Ferry Captain*) 1993
Farrah Fawcett (*Blonde*) 1970
Melinda Fee (*Mary Anderson*) 1981–82
Tim Felix (*Orderly*) 1966
Frances Ferguson (*Mrs. Forman*) 1977
Gregory Fernandez (*Guard #2*) 1990
Cathy Ferrar (*Julie Olson*) 1967–68
Daniel Ferrone (*Lou*) 1968
Chip Fields (*Toni Johnson*) 1977–78
Bruce Fischer (*J.T. Crenna*) 1991
Ruthie Fischer (*Nurse Paull*) 1972
Brianna & Chalice Fischette (*Baby Isabella
   "Belle"*) 1993–
Cindy Fisher (*Patti Griffin*) 1977–78
Cindy Fisher (*Diane Parker*) 1984
George Fisher (*Cherenkov*) 1985
Robert Fisher (*Foreman Bauer*) 1978
Patrick Flanagan (*Claude Conway*) 1979
Susan Flannery (*Dr. Laura Spencer Horton*)
   1966–75

Eric Fleeks (*Bailiff*)
Mary Fletcher (*Miss Johnson, R.N.*) 1967
Gertrude Flynn (*Mrs. Sawyer*) 1965–66
J. Michael Flynn (*Dan*) 1988
Cindy Folkerson (*Kayla's Stunt Double*) 1988
Rose Fonseca (*Valerie Grant*) 1977–78
Michael Forest (*Corely Maxwell*) 1979
Michael Forest (*Dr. Remy*) 1990
Misty Forest (*April*) 1985
Fil Formicola (*Dr. Lucero*) 1979
William Forrest (*Dr. Roberts*) 1967
Rosemary Forsyth (*Dr. Laura Spencer Horton*)
   1976–80
Ronald L. Foster (*Orderly*) 1966
Jacques Foti (*French Captain*) 1970
John J. Fox (*Mac*) 1971
Marilyn Fox (*Miss Roberts*) 1966
Myeva Fox (*Ladonna*) 1993
Sandra Fox (*Customer*) 1977
Viveca Fox (*Carmen*) 1988
Don Frabotta (*Dave, the waiter*) 1973–93
Jonathan Frakes (*Jared McCallister*) 1986
Angelique Francis (*Lexie Carver*) 1992
Genie Francis (*Diana Colville*) 1987–89
Ivor Francis (*Harry Larson*) 1969
William Frankfather (*Dr. Arthur Nole*) 1979
Doug Franklin (*Robber*) 1990
Mary Frann (*Amanda Howard*) 1974–79
Tony Fraser (*Small Boy*) 1967
Treva Frazee (*Woman Patient*) 1977
Treva Frazee (*Mrs. Porter*) 1978
Treva Frazee (*Mrs. Tate*) 1980
Iris Friedman (*Nurse*) 1977
James Friedman (*Hitchhiker*) 1977
Paul Friedman (*Intern*) 1968
Larry Friel (*Stanley*) 1987
Denise Friend (*Nurse Denise*) 1986
Erwin Fuller (*Fred*) 1990
Erwin Fuller (*Pawnbroker*) 1993
Katherine Fuller (*Mabel*) 1980–81; 1985–86
Helen Funai (*Kim Williams*) 1971–72;
   1976–77
John Forey (*Joe Cook*) 1979
George Furlong (*Richard Wells*) 1976
Loretta Fury (*Amelia Craig*) 1978–79
Holly Gagnier (*Ivy Selejko*) 1985–86
Steven Gagnon (*Airport Police Chief*) 1992
M.C. Gainey (*Gunman*) 1983
M.C. Gainey (*Arthur Warren*) 1988
Paul Gale (*Police Officer*) 1977
John Galeteo (*Greg*) 1989
Denise Galik (*Kim McDavid*) 1980
Silvana Gallardo (*Rosa Ramirez*) 1988
Joe Gallison (*Dr. Neil Curtis*) 1974–91
Duncan Gamble (*Roy*) 1981
Duncan Gamble (*Ed Daniels*) 1987
Julian Gamble (*Galluzzo*) 1987

Julian Gamble (*Peter*) 1991
Paul Ganus (*Matt Rhodes*) 1992
Brooks Gardner (*Tony Becker*) 1993
Winnie Gardner (*Daisy*) 1983
Joy Garrett (*Jo Johnson*) 1987–92
Andy Garrison (*Limousine Driver*) 1993
Richard Garst (*Mr. Devaney*) 1978
Bennye Gatteys (*Susan Hunter Martin*) 1973–76
Gregorio Gaviati (*Mario*) 1991
Monica Gayle (*Sharon*) 1973
Ted Gehring (*Sydney Forbes*) 1980
Kirk Geiger (*Chad Webster*) 1990
Ray Genedry (*Jasper*) 1987
Livia Genise (*Mitzi Matuso*) 1982
Robert Gentry (*Dr. Hunt*) 1994–
Babetta George (*Nurse Joanna*) 1986
Haile Gerima (*Western Union Messenger*) 1971
Amanda Getty (*Nurse*) 1967
Leeza Gibbons (*Woman Passerby*) 1994
Gerry Gibson (*Simmons*) 1986–92
Jody Gibson (*Sunny Chandler*) 1984
Mary Ann Gibson (*Anna Brennan*) 1970
Mary Ann Gibson (*Mrs. Price*) 1978
Robert Gibson (*Officer Murray*) 1980
Stacy Gibson (*Diane Almeida*) 1993
Amber Gilbert (*Claudia*) 1986
Linda Gilbert (*Woman with Baby*) 1973
Jan Gillen (*Nurse*) 1969
Antonia Gilman (*Miss Adams, R.N.*) 1971
Antonia Gilman (*Mrs. Walters*) 1971
Antonia Gilman (*Mrs. Cooper*) 1973
Joe Gironda (*Thug #2*) 1990
Dick Gittings (*Waiter*) 1970
Dick Gittings (*Dr. Foster*) 1971
Dick Gittings (*Bob Anderson*) 1978
Kate Gladfelter (*Lauri*) 1992
Regina Gleason (*Kitty Horton*) 1967–69
Leslie Glick (*Nurse Liza*) 1979
William Glover (*Emissary*) 1985
Harvey J. Goldenberg (*Harvey Keating*) 1992
Marcy Goldman (*Saleswoman*) 1972
Eric Goldner (*KGB Agent*) 1986
Eric Goldner (*Dr. Anderson*) 1993
Jonathan Goldsmith (*Dr. Jergens*) 1987
Terence Goodman (*Sergeant McBride*) 1984–85
Gerald Gordan (*Man*) 1967
Paul Gordon (*Guitar Player*) 1985
Cindy James Gossett (*Lexie Brooks*) 1988–89
Dov Gottesfeld (*Yakov*) 1985
Andre Gower (*Derek*) 1980
Sam Gowland (*Man's Voice*) 1967
John Graham (*Walter Edison*) 1965
Alan Graf (*Thug #1*) 1990
Toni Grant (*Dr. Toni Stone*) 1982

Bruce Gray (*Police Commissioner*) 1984
Coleen Gray (*Diane Hunter*) 1966–67
Esther Gray (*Lyla Peterson*) 1990
Staci Greason (*Isabella Beatrice Toscano Black*) 1989–92
Brian Green (*Alan*) 1987–89
Bud Greene (*Lieutenant Russo*) 1977
Bud Greene (*Mr. Kroener*) 1979
James Greene (*Ferry Captain*) 1994
Kim Morgan Greene (*Sheila Salsbury/Kelly Parker*) 1990
Otis Greene (*Bailiff*) 1965–66
Adam Gregor (*Giuseppe Vitello*) 1990
Michael Gregory (*Captain Cyril Edwards*) 1982
Ed Griffith (*Johnny Beacon*) 1970
Helen Griffiths (*Australian Nurse*) 1990
Maria Grimms (*Wendy*) 1977
Michael Griswold (*Judge Collins*) 1987
Michael Griswold (*Kramer*) 1988
Michael Griswold (*Minister*) 1991
Michael Griswold (*Dr. Wethers*) 1993
Scott Groff (*Shawn Douglas Brady*) 1990–95
Loretta Gross (*Nurse*) 1977
Jay Gruska (*Bandleader Jay*) 1985
Gino Guadio (*Bo's Guard*) 1985
Vincent Guastaferro (*Agent Herb*) 1986
Evelyn Guerro (*Soledad*) 1991
Bennet Guillory (*Tilson*) 1983
Amanda and Jessica Gunnarson (*Stephanie Kay Johnson*) 1990–92
Brandi Lynn Gunnarson (*Brandi*) 1991
Richard Guthrie (*David Banning*) 1975–81
Michael C. Gwynne (*Dr. Le Blanc*) 1993
Ivan G'Vera (*Henri Von Leuschner*) 1990
Ivan G'Vera (*Ivan Marais*) 1991–
Joe Hacker (*Jared MacAllister*) 1986
Chris Hager (*Hank*) 1994
Diana Hale (*Nurse*) 1966
Diana Hale (*Miss Jameson*) 1968
Diana Hale (*Jerry's Mother*) 1989
Deidre Hall (*Dr. Marlena Evans Brady*) 1976–87; 1991–
Margie Hall (*Nurse*) 1969; 1970; 1971; 1972; 1973
Michael Hall (*Dr. Moore*) 1994
Rachel Hall (*Wendy's baby*) 1993
Roger Hall (*Skip*) 1992
Andrea Hall–Lovell (*Samantha Evans*) 1977–80; 1982
Tom Hallick (*Maxwell Hathaway*) 1984
Lori Hallier (*Yvette Dupres*) 1989
Bradley Hallock (*Eric Brady*) 1986–92
Michael Halsey (*Karras*) 1984
Brian Hamilton (*Guard*) 1990
Gene Hamilton (*Mr. Morrison*) 1978

Hal Hamilton (*Dr. Sydney Fell*) 1965–66
Kim Hamilton (*Miss West, R.N.*) 1968
Kim Hamilton (*Nurse Leona*) 1979
Lynn Hamilton (*Rita*) 1987
Randy Hamilton (*Ron*) 1986–88
Ben Hammer (*Mr. Farris*) 1968
John Hammil (*Brainwasher*) 1988
John Hammil (*Dr. Burke*) 1989
John Hammil (*Clayton Roberts*) 1993
James Hampton (*Rev. Saul Taylor*) 1989
Shirley Handley (*Mrs. Stark*) 1967
Shirley Handley (*Female Court Reporter*)
   1970
Robert Hanley (*Mystery Man*) 1984
Robert Hanley (*Cecil*) 1990
Robert Hanley (*Brent Maller*) 1991
Robert Hanley (*Uncle Eric*) 1992
Arthur Hanson (*Coroner Andy Harper*) 1967
Bob Harcum (*Young Man*) 1977
James Hardie (*Hitman*) 1993
Eloise Hardt (*Rita Beacon*) 1970
Leslie Hardy (*Maid Rhonda*) 1989
Sarah Hardy (*Jean Sawyer*) 1965–66
Armand Hargett (*Dr. Ralph Smith*) 1991
Magda Harout (*Madame Blavastsky*) 1990
Dianne Harper (*Leslie James*) 1980–81
John Harper (*Mr. Compton*) 1970
Samantha Harper (*Silver*) 1985
Terry Harrington (*Oscar*) 1989
Terry Harrington (*Robbie*) 1993
Rossie Harris (*Kelly*) 1978
Stacy S. Harris (*Drake*) 1967
Elizabeth Harrower (*Mrs. Calder*) 1966
Kathryn Harrow (*Miss Adams*) 1967
Mary Hart (*Newscaster Betty Howard*) 1980
Butch Hartman (*Harvey*) 1988
Butch Hartman (*Jake*) 1989
Kathy Hauber (*Miss Kegley*) 1986
Alan Haufrecht (*Dr. Matt Dorman*) 1993
Thomas Havens (*Stan Kositchek*) 1979
Jerry Hawkins (*Fred*) 1993–94
Larry Hayden (*Mitch; Voice Only*) 1993
Bill Hayes (*Doug Williams*) 1970–84;
   1986–87; 1993; 1994
Bill Hayes (*Byron Carmichael*) 1979
Susan Seaforth Hayes (*Julie Olson Williams*)
   1968–84; 1990–93; 1994
Johnny Haymer (*Manager Sam*) 1984
Myron Healey (*Wayne Charles*) 1969–70
Patti Healy (*Rhonda*) 1991
David Hearst (*Scotty Banning*) 1989–90
Dominique Heffley (*Candy Striper*) 1990
Wayne Heffley (*Vern Scofield*) 1988–93
Robert Hegyes (*Viper*) 1985
Brian Heidik (*Tim Rollins*) 1992–93
Heidi Helmer (*Lindsay Callahan*) 1986
James Hendo (*Bluejay*) 1983

James Hendo (*Blake Johnson*) 1983
Elaine Hendrix (*Brandee*) 1993
Stephen Anthony Henry (*Luke*) 1986–88
Richard Herlan (*Paul Jamison*) 1993–94
Alfred Hernandez (*Small Boy*) 1976
Lynn Herring (*Lisanne Gardner*) 1992
Peter Heuchling (*Exterminator*) 1991
James Higdon (*Mr. Dunne*) 1989
James Higdon (*Guy #2*) 1990
Phyllis Hill (*Mrs. Williams*) 1968
Richard Hill (*Kyle McCollough*) 1980
Connie Hilliard (*Desk Nurse*) 1992
William Hillman (*Dr. Lewis*) 1966–67
William Hillman (*Dr. Richards*) 1967
Richard Hilton (*Arnie Leonard*) 1990; 1992
Del Hinkley (*Man*) 1976
John Hines (*Minister*) 1973
Darby Hinton (*Ian Griffith*) 1985–86
Deborah Hobart (*Molly Chase*) 1984
Deborah Hobart (*Dr. Ashley*) 1988
Deborah Hobart (*Jill Bailey*) 1990–91
Peter Hobbs (*Dr. Lawrence Andrews*) 1968
Peter Hobbs (*Dr. Clements*) 1968
Peter Hobbs (*Dr. Andrews*) 1969
Peter Hobbs (*Judge Riley*) 1983
Kane Hoder (*Roman's Stunt Double*) 1984
Robert Hogan (*Scott Banning*) 1970–71
Drake Hogestyn (*John Black/Roman
   Brady/Forrest Alamain*) 1986–
Victor Holchak (*Jim Phillips*) 1971; 1974–75
Harry Holcombe (*Clergyman*) 1966–70;
   1973; 1976; 1978; 1979; 1981
Harry Holcombe (*Mr. Sommers*) 1966
Kevin Holczner (*Bayview Attendant*) 1989
Ashaneese & Nasharin Holderness
   (*Benjamin*) 1994–
Wade Holdsworth (*Baby Michael Horton*)
   1969
Fred Holliday (*Ron Wyche*) 1988–91
Fred Holliday (*Randy Freeman*) 1991
James Hong (*Colonel Chengsu*) 1967–68
James Hong (*Dr. Haramkai*) 1977
James Hong (*Baba Soo Lan*) 1985
Ed Hooks (*Balboni*) 1989
Stephen Hopkins (*Peter's Ski Double*) 1994
James Horan (*Gary*) 1986
Olive Horan (*Woman Patient*) 1967
Olive Horan (*Flower Vendor*) 1967
Suzie Horne (*Cleopatra*) 1983
Pat Hornung (*Janene*) 1969–70
Tommy House (*Baby Charlie Jannings*) 1985
Paula Houston (*Mrs. Dorrell*) 1980
Anne Howard (*Kimberly Brady Donovan*)
   1990; 1991
John Howard (*Clifford Patterson*) 1970–71
Lisa Howard (*April Ramirez*) 1988–91
Rance Howard (*Henry Clovis*) 1985

Rebecca Howard (*Nurse*) 1977
Dean Howell (*Rick Paige*) 1984
Jean Howell (*Mary McCall*) 1967
Stephanie Howell (*Tiffany*) 1989
Charles Howerton (*Tony Viola*) 1978
Elizabeth Hoy (*Little Anne*) 1975–76
John Huffman (*Dr. Collins*) 1993
Billy Hufsey (*Emilio Ramirez*) 1988–90
John Hugo (*Crockett*) 1991
Craig Hundley (*Dan McCall*) 1967
Drew Hundley (*Member of the Parole Board*) 1970
Leann Hunley (*Anna Brady DiMera*) 1982–86
Patricia Hunt (*Mrs. Melnick*) 1978
Will Hunt (*Frank Tucker*) 1978
Henry Hunter (*Mr. Abbott*) 1967
Sherry Hursey (*Paula Carson*) 1987–88
Hettie Lynn Hurtes (*Tracy North*) 1979
Ron Husmann (*Tony Merritt*) 1966–67
Patricia Huston (*Addie Horton Olson*) 1965–66
Patricia Huston (*Helga*) 1986
Patricia Huston (*Gladys*) 1989
Rif Hutton (*False Newscaster*) 1990
Bob Hyman (*Mr. Larson*) 1979
Jennifer Ide (*Contest Finalist*) 1993
Gary Imhoff (*Byron Randall*) 1993
James Ingersoll (*Dr. Shriner*) 1983
Barry Ingham (*Leopold Bronsky*) 1985
Sam Ingraffia (*Mario Vitello*) 1990–91
Jay Ingram (*Daniel*) 1986
Julie Inouye (*Nurse Becky*) 1986
Geoffrey Inseld (*Kevin*) 1991
Benjamin Iorio (*Baby Joey*) 1990
Jacob Iorio (*Baby Victor*) 1990
Michael Irving (*Dr. Darnley*) 1979
Jimmy Ishida (*Dr. Wu*) 1993
Al Israel (*Captain Lacamara*) 1988
Paul Henry Itkins (*Johnny Collins*) 1975–77
Stan Ivar (*Clay Heffron*) 1985
Stan Ivar (*Daniel Scott*) 1994
Anna Ivara (*Virginia McGuire*) 1978
Curt Ivey (*Juror*) 1965
Curt Ivey (*Waiter*) 1966
Marjorie Jackson (*Helen Trask*) 1978
Marjorie Jackson (*Daphne's Double*) 1983
Mollie Jackson (*Cassie*) 1979
Sylvia Jackson (*Nurse Jackson*) 1976
Jesse Jacobs (*Lab Technician*) 1967
Jon Jacobs (*Clerk*) 1985
Marc Jacobs (*Artie Bergen*) 1977–79
Billy Jacoby (*Vito*) 1987
Dorothy James (*Esther Kensington*) 1982
Richard Jamison (*Walter Henry*) 1985
Richard Jamison (*Bo's Guard*) 1985
Toni Janotta (*Nurse Swanson*) 1968

Toni Janotta (*Nurse*) 1969
Toni Janotta (*Miss Phillips*) 1973
Al Jarreau (*as himself*) 1984
Robert Lee Jarvis (*Diver*) 1975
Frank Javorsek (*Guitar Player*) 1983
Ben Jeffrey (*Mr. Monroe*) 1980
George Jenesky (*Nick Corelli*) 1981; 1984; 1986–90
Barry Jenner (*Mr. MacKenzie*) 1985
Julie Jeter (*Sasha Roberts*) 1986
Ken Jezek (*Lars Englund*) 1986–87
Betty Jinette (*Seamstress*) 1982
Betty Jinette (*Mrs. Polk*) 1989
Anita Jodelson (*Sonia*) 1985
Bonnie Johns (*Officer Reid*) 1978
Bonnie Johns (*Mrs. Longley*) 1980
Patti Johns (*J.J. Bagwood*) 1989–90
Chip Johnson (*Dylan O'Grady*) 1980
Chris Johnson (*Paramedic Lewis*) 1980
Christina Johnson (*Francine*) 1985
Gail Johnson (*Mimi*) 1978–80
Russell Johnson (*Harold Rankin*) 1980
Sara Rose Johnson (*Little Hope*) 1990
Sherry Johnson (*Latoya Preston*) 1985
Audrey Johnston (*Warden*) 1990
Peter Jolly (*Kiriakis Bodyguard*) 1989; 1990
Amanda Jones (*Dora*) 1977–78
Amber Jones (*Baby Isabella*) 1990
Betsy Jones-Moreland (*Mrs. Collins*) 1972
Betsy Jones-Moreland (*Mrs. Chambers*) 1975
Betsy Jones-Moreland (*Mrs. Abbott*) 1977
Morgan Jones (*Dr. Manley*) 1976
Renee Jones (*Nikki Wade*) 1982–83
Renee Jones (*Lexie Carver*) 1993–
Bobbie Jordan (*Jeanette Levin*) 1993
James Carroll Jordan (*Steve Olson*) 1972
Jan Jorden (*Helen Cantrell*) 1975
S. Marc Jordan (*Eli Jacobs*) 1986–87; 1989
Elaine Joyce (*Paula Hammond*) 1993
William Joyce (*Kellam Chandler*) 1980–81
Jack Jozefson (*Mr. Hancock*) 1977
Jacee Jule (*Waitress*) 1983–
Alexander G. Jump (*Juror Hanson*) 1967
Gordon Jump (*Waiter*) 1966
Katherine Justice (*Eleanor Smith*) 1989
Katherine Justice (*Jane*) 1993
Arielle Kain (*Carol*) 1977
Virginia Kaiser (*Mrs. Whiting*) 1983
Stanley Kamel (*Eric Peters*) 1972–76
Milt Kamen (*Plato*) 1973
Andrew Kane (*Paramedic*) 1992
Valerie Karasek (*Serena*) 1987–88
Lenore Kasdorf (*Dr. Veronica Kimball*) 1983–84
Allan Katz (*Alien*) 1987–88
Jonathan Kaufman (*Nicholas Fortier*) 1992
Leslie Kawai (*May*) 1984

Jacqueline Kaye (*Heather*) 1977
Zitto Kazann (*Tailor*) 1983
Jane Kean (*Dianne Hunter*) 1965–66
Jean Kean (*Grace Hutton*) 1985
Noah Keen (*Jim Fleming*) 1967
Noah Keen (*Wayne Charles*) 1969
Noah Keen (*Ralph Foster*) 1971
Noah Keen (*Ray Stone*) 1979
Paul Keenan (*Tod Chandler*) 1980–81
William Keene (*Dr. Bronson*) 1966
William Keene (*Bartender*) 1968
William Keene (*Mr. Bellows*) 1969
William Keene (*Reverend Foley*) 1971
William Keene (*George Ambrose*) 1973
William Keene (*Dr. Lubick*) 1973–76
Liz Keifer (*Amy*) 1985
Bonnie Keith (*Nurse*) 1977
Bonnie Keith (*Sally Richards*) 1984
Robert Kelker–Kelly (*Bo Brady*) 1992–95
Susan Keller (*Mary Anderson*) 1980
Barry Kelly (*Dwight Lowell*) 1977
Dennis Kelly (*James DeGrogh*) 1993
Leonard Kelly–Young (*Gus Bartoli*) 1992–93
Tony Kelvin (*Lionel Jones*) 1970
Warren Kemmerling (*Dr. Hendricks*) 1966
Sally Kemp (*Landlord*) 1981
Sally Kemp (*Nora*) 1983
Sally Kemp (*Vanessa*) 1984–85
Harris Kendall (*Marie*) 1993–
John Kendall (*Mahoney*) 1991
Paul Kennan (*Tod Chandler*) 1980–81
Don Kennedy (*Juror Webster*) 1967
Ed Kenney (*George Parker*) 1980
Enid Kent (*Ms. Collins*) 1980
Janice Kent (*Dr. Perkins*) 1994
Caro Kenyatta (*Patient*) 1972
Sandy Kenyon (*Junior*) 1992
Gary Kernick (*Gary*) 1987
Gary Kernick (*Bret Carlysle*) 1990
Gary Kernick (*Jack's Caller*) 1991
Herb Kerns (*Manager, Salem Hotel*) 1978
Hubie Kerns (*Jack's Stunt Double*) 1988
Hubie Kerns (*Driver*) 1993
Michael Kerns (*Hank*) 1985
Elizabeth Kerr (*Flower Vendor*) 1967
Anne Kerry (*Tracy Van Zandt*) 1985
Paul Kersey (*Alan Harris*) 1993–95
Lee Kessler (*Anne Goldberg*) 1993–
Paige & Ryanne Kettner (*Abigail Johanna Deveraux*) 1994–
Miki Kim (*Willie Yamoto*) 1992
Dana Kimmel (*Diane Parker*) 1983–84
Andrea King (*Jane MacAllister*) 1974–75; 1977
Kathleen King (*Gretchen*) 1981–83
Kevin King (*Randy*) 1979
Meegan King (*Pete Curtis*) 1978–79

Lenore Kingston (*Ethel*) 1969
Charles Klausmeyer (*Canby*) 1987–88
Ray Klein (*Accordion Player*) 1991
David Knapp (*Frank Walker*) 1976
Don Knight (*Geoffrey*) 1987
Ed Knight (*Detective Locke*) 1967
Ron Knight (*Lieutenant Baker*) 1981
Ted C. Knight (*George Becker*) 1965
Bill Knopf (*Banjo Player*) 1983
Tom Knutson (*Orderly Nick*) 1970
Jean Koba (*DiMera Housekeeper*) 1982
Alex Kobe (*Mr. Baker*) 1978
Alex Kobe (*Dr. Weston*) 1978
Tracy Kolis (*Rebecca Downey*) 1989–90
Shirlee Kong (*Mrs. Naguchi*) 1975
Pamela Kosh (*Lavinia Peach*) 1986–91
George Kotanides (*Stavros*) 1987
Robert Knapp (*Ben Olson*) 1965
Ross Kramer (*Stage Hand*) 1992
Katie Krell (*Baby Sarah*) 1982
Wortham Krimmer (*Cal Winters*) 1989–90
Dale Kristien (*Maid Janet*) 1985–86
Kurt Kross (*Thug*) 1990
Kurt Kross (*Security Guard*) 1993
Alex Kubik (*Panama Jack*) 1985
Bernie Kuby (*Jake*) 1975
Ron Kuhlman (*Jimmy Potterfield*) 1984–85
Ron Kuhlman (*Hank Tobin*) 1989
Aaron Kuri (*Lance*) 1986
Linda Kurimoto (*Nurse*) 1992
Wally Kurth (*Justin Kiriakis*) 1987–91
Ken Kurtis (*Racetrack Announcer*) 1991
Dylan Kussman (*Christopher*) 1988
Jeremy Kutner (*Young Lawrence*) 1991
Kimberly La Belle (*Lacey*) 1986
Hilary Labow (*Felicity York*) 1985
Steve La Chance (*Toby*) 1983
Katherine Lader (*Joan Barrow*) 1978
Florence Lake (*Mrs. Ivy Lowell*) 1974
René Lamart (*Jake Kositchek*) 1981
Steven Lambert (*Andre*) 1984
Steven Lambert (*Steve's Stunt Double*) 1988
Steven Lambert (*Class Instructor*) 1991
Lisa Lamont (*Bonnie*) 1986–87
Terry Lamont (*Antique Dealer*) 1980
Stacy Lande (*Cindy*) 1977
Renee Landers (*Sheryl*) 1986
Renee Landers (*Ms. Densmore*) 1993
Monte Landis (*Gaston Chamier*) 1990
Monte Landis (*Gerard*) 1992
Stephen Landis (*Sheriff Stokes*) 1985
Stephen Landis (*Lee Wilson*) 1991
Laurene Landon (*Denise Murphy*) 1991
Clayton Landey (*Gregory*) 1990–92
Shauna Lane-Block (*Sarah Horton*) 1989
Charley Lang (*Rob Stemkowski*) 1991–92
Michael Lang (*Bad Viper*) 1984

Jeanne Lange (*Lola Jasper*) 1982
Mary Lansing (*Mrs. Sommers*) 1966
Doug Larson (*Philip Collier*) 1992
Linwza Larson (*Myrna P. Lambert*) 1975
Adrienne LaRussa (*Brooke Hamilton/*
  Stephanie Woodruff) 1975–77
Michael Laskin (*Chet Lambert*) 1984
Robert Lasky (*Dr. Wilson*) 1967
S. John Launer (*Justice of the Peace*) 1976
Mitchell Laurance (*Colin*) 1989
Harry Lauter (*Craig Merritt*) 1966
John Lavachielli (*Hank Tobin*) 1989
Kwa Lawrence (*Rachel*) 1977
Toni Lawrence (*Wanda Owens*) 1983
Eric Lawson (*Sergeant Ferraro*) 1978
Susan Leahy (*Lana Montrose*) 1984
Cynthia Leake (*Lori Masters*) 1981
Ron Leath (*Henderson*) 1987–
Donna Lynn Leavy (*Judge*) 1993
Jean Le Bouvier (*Eleanor Anderson*) 1965
Jean Le Bouvier (*Mrs. Ballard*) 1967
Jean Le Bouvier (*Nurse*) 1969
Jean Le Bouvier (*Elaine Paschall*) 1970
Jean Le Bouvier (*Frances Bellamy*) 1971
Jean Le Bouvier (*Mrs. Brooks*) 1972
Jean Le Bouvier (*Mrs. Warner*) 1975
Joe Le Due (*Detective Harry Frost*) 1983
Bob Lee (*Judge Murdoch*) 1987
Gracia Lee (*Mrs. Sims*) 1989
Michael Patrick Lee (*Waiter*) 1993
Robin Lee (*Tammy*) 1980–81
Stuart Lee (*Michael Horton*) 1973
Beverly Leech (*Bianca*) 1988
Linda Leighton (*Nurse Harper*) 1971
Roberta Leighton (*Ginger Dawson*) 1991–92
Mark Lenard (*Richard Ludwig*) 1977
Alex Lende (*Milo*) 1988
Alex Lende (*Ricardo*) 1990
Michael Leon (*Pete Jannings*) 1983–86
Fred Lerner (*Intruder*) 1980
Michael Lerner (*Barnes*) 1992
Gloria Leroy (*Queenie*) 1989
Lori Ann Lesmeister (*Susie*) 1992
Ketty Lester (*Helen Grant*) 1975–77
Edward Le Veque (*Pawnbroker*) 1973
Philip Levien (*Mitch Kaufman*) 1986
Floyd Levine (*Lou Stanley*) 1985
Christopher Lewis (*Christopher*) 1988
Colin Lewis (*Maggie's Baby*) 1981
Craig Lewis (*Janitor*) 1990
David Lewis (*Minister*) 1976
Greg Lewis (*Walter Van Damm*) 1992
Helena Lewis (*Elaine*) 1994
Nicholas Lewis (*Dave Hardy*) 1977
Thyme Lewis (*Jonah Carver*) 1993–
Linda Lightfoot (*Jennifer's Stunt Double*)
  1991

Marie Lillo (*Matron*) 1978
Nancy Linari (*Nurse Sarnoff*) 1993
Cec Linder (*Dr. Turner*) 1975
Richard Lindroos (*Rapist*) 1985
Richard Lineback (*Charleston Detective*) 1989
Daniel Lishner (*Italian Guardsman*) 1990
Joyce Little (*Amazon Ayla*) 1984
Joyce Little (*Vanessa Walker*) 1988
Craig Littler (*Henchman Geoffrey*) 1984
Craig Littler (*Colonel Brand*) 1992
Doug Llewelyn (*Winston Taylor*) 1978
Julie Lloyd (*Lynn Evans*) 1991
Julie Lloyd (*Sister Jean*) 1992
Robert Lloyd (*Salem Inn Waiter*) 1982
Bill Lockwood (*Marcel*) 1974
Kathryn Loder (*Miss Tilson*) 1978
Roger Lodge (*James Dixon*) 1987
Cary Loftin (*Stephanie's Crash Stuntman*)
  1980
Christopher Lofton (*Dr. Jack Cushing*) 1982
Christopher Lofton (*Dr. Marshall*) 1987
John Lombardo (*Man in Park/Eric Peters*)
  1971
John Lombardo (*Fred Barton*) 1977–78
Tamara Long (*Helen Cameron*) 1978
Suzanne Longo (*Contest Finalist*) 1993
Ann Loos (*Mrs. Anderson*) 1966
Rosemary Lord (*Shane's Mother*) 1988
Rosemary Lord (*Phoebe*) 1990
Rosemary Lord (*Maid Mary*) 1994
Christopher Lore (*Man at Party*) 1993
Gloria Loring (*Liz Chandler Curtis*) 1980–86
Tanya Louise (*Emily*) 1991
Heather Lowe (*Michelle*) 1991
Heather Lowe (*Suzanna Cooper*) 1992
Lawrence Lowe (*Bailiff*) 1991
Curt Lowens (*Brother Andrew*) 1984
Curt Lowens (*Herr Markel*) 1992
Max & Alex Lucero (*Brady Black*) 1992–94
Charles Lucia (*Dr. Phelps*) 1993
Chip Lucia (*Joe*) 1977
Chip Lucia (*Hart Bennett*) 1985–86
Bill Lucking (*Harry Chaney*) 1981
Barbara Luddy (*Mrs. Davis*) 1966
Barbara Luddy (*Juror Ryan*) 1967
Barbara Luddy (*Telephone Operator*) 1967–68
James Luisi (*Duke Johnson*) 1987; 1990–92
James Luisi (*Earl Johnson*) 1989
Christine Lunde (*Sada*) 1987
John Lupton (*Dr. Tommy Horton*) 1967–72;
  1975–79
Kathryn Lust (*Janet Granger*) 1992
Charles Lyles (*Process Server*) 1969
Lisa Lynch (*Baby Anne*) 1974
Amy Lynne (*Phyllis Cook*) 1992
Debbie Lytton (*Melissa Anderson*) 1977–80;
  1982

Jay McAdams (*Jody McKay*) 1992
Patrick McArdle (*Rick*) 1992
Diane McBain (*Foxy Humdinger*) 1982–84
Mark McBride (*Lumpy*) 1992
John McCafferty (*Dr. Berger*) 1987
John McCafferty (*Magazine Man*) 1993
Siobhan MacCafferty (*Bitsy*) 1991
Jade McCall (*Newscaster*) 1980
John David McCall (*Radio Announcer*) 1977
Macon McCalman (*Freddie*) 1976
John McCann (*Tony Klingman*) 1980
Charles MacCauley (*Dr. Eliot Kincaid*) 1967–68
Peggy McCay (*Caroline Brady*) 1983; 1985–
Judith McConnell (*Miss Douglas*) 1967
Judith McConnell (*Miss Evans*) 1968
Marilyn McCoo (*Tamara Price*) 1986–87
George McDaniel (*Dr. Jordan Barr*) 1979–80
Charles McDaniels (*Scrub Nurse*) 1967
Ryan MacDonald (*Scott Banning*) 1971–73
Ryan MacDonald (*Priest*) 1985
Ryan MacDonald (*Chauncey Powell*) 1991–92
Tommy McDonough (*Little Austin*) 1994
Howard McGilin (*Minister*) 1984
Richard McGonagle (*Bishop Andrews*) 1994
Bennie Lee McGowan (*Darlene*) 1989
Oliver McGowan (*Floyd Peterson*) 1966
Joseph McGuinn (*Dr. Evans*) 1970
Gary McGurrin (*Hazeltine*) 1977–78
James McIntyre (*Viper*) 1988
Marilyn McIntyre (*Jo Johnson*) 1993
Andrew McKaige (*Aussie Doctor*) 1990
Deck McKenzie (*Dragon*) 1985
Patch MacKenzie (*Victoria Wallis*) 1980
Jim McLarty (*Court Reporter*) 1970
David McLean (*Craig Merritt*) 1965–67
Frank MacLean (*Dr. Curry*) 1985
Frank MacLean (*Shawn Brady*) 1989–90
Peter McLean (*Paul Whitman*) 1977
Vicki McLean (*Jane*) 1979
Catherine McLeod (*Claire*) 1969
Duncan McLeod (*Dr. Croner*) 1965
Duncan McLeod (*Elderly Priest*) 1974
Duncan McLeod (*Auctioneer*) 1980
Richard McMurray (*Dr. Mel Bailey*) 1968; 1971; 1973–77
Heather McNair (*Lydia Rockwell*) 1985
Catherine MacNeal (*Shirley*) 1988
Catherine MacNeal (*Biological mother*) 1992
Catherine MacNeal (*Pat Hamilton*) 1993–
Billy McNichols (*3-year-old boy*) 1967
George McPeak (*Orion*) 1988
Marnie McPhail (*Harley Monaghan*) 1992
Hugh McPhillips (*Mr. Pearson*) 1979
Elizabeth MacRae (*Barbara Randolph*) 1976
Elizabeth MacRae (*Phyllis Anderson*) 1977
Eve McVeagh (*Mrs. Kositchek*) 1980

Courtenay McWhinney (*Cora*) 1983
William Madden (*Tony's Stunt Double*) 1984
Robert Madrid (*Charles*) 1991
Sharon Mahoney (*Tiffany*) 1993
Robert Mailhouse (*Brian Scofield*) 1990–92
Christina Maisano (*Baby Noel*) 1983
Arthur Mallet (*Nigel Peabody*) 1990
Edward Mallory (*Dr. Bill Horton*) 1966–80; 1991; 1992
Maggie Malooley (*Miss Draper*) 1968
Biff Manard (*Dr. Dieter Von Leyden*) 1992
Ned Manderino (*Waiter*) 1967
Ned Manderino (*Real Estate Agent*) 1968
Ned Manderino (*Russ*) 1968
Jim Manin (*Bell Boy*) 1966
Stephen Manly (*Billy Barton*) 1977–78
Gloria Manners (*Carrie Spencer*) 1971; 1975; 1979
Gloria Manners (*Autograph-Seeking Woman*) 1973
Gloria Manners (*Mrs. Jennings*) 1974–75
Jack Manning (*Mr. Harmon*) 1971
John Mansfield (*Jonathan Carlton*) 1984
Paul Mantee (*Lieutenant Spalding*) 1975
Bruno Marcotulli (*Security Guard*) 1991
Bruno Marcotulli (*Commander Rizzo*) 1992
Ellen Marcus (*Ellen Greer*) 1978
Flip Mark (*Steve Olson*) 1965
Craig Marks (*Mr. Carney*) 1993–94
John Marlo (*Cash Bowman*) 1992–93
Curtiss Marlowe (*Man as Britta*) 1986
Scott Marlowe (*Uncle Eric Brady*) 1984
Mae Marmy (*Mrs. Lyons*) 1987
Gary Marshall (*Burt Atwater*) 1972–74
Melora Marshall (*Thistle Gentleheart*) 1975
Scott Marshall (*Nick*) 1985
Lynne Marta (*Inmate Charlene*) 1983
Fred Martell (*Intern*) 1967
Ann–Marie Martin (*Gwen Davies*) 1982–85
Jesse Martin (*George*) 1973
John Martin (*Robert Brennan*) 1985
Lori Martin (*Sally Reed*) 1974
Marta Martin (*Amy Madison*) 1993
Mikey Martin (*Dougie Le Clere*) 1979–80
Jean Martinez (*Dorothy Mason*) 1974
John Martinuzzi (*Louis Coureville*) 1984
Gregg Marx (*David Banning*) 1981–83
Joseph Mascolo (*Dr. Tutano*) 1968
Joseph Mascolo (*Stefano DiMera*) 1982–85; 1988; 1993–
Gabriella Maselli (*Cherish*) 1993
Eric Mason (*Ernesto Toscano*) 1990
Lola Mason (*Albertina Kogan*) 1980
Margaret Mason (*Linda Anderson*) 1970–72; 1975–80; 1982
Gabriella Massari (*Jeannie Donovan*) 1992
Andrew Masset (*Larry Welch*) 1983–85

Sean Masterson (*Alan*) 1983
John Mathews (*Kincaid*) 1968
Brian Matthews (*Brother Francis*) 1985–86
Hedley Mattingly (*Smitty*) 1975–76
Maurishka (*Secretary*) 1971
Maurishka (*Sarah*) 1972
Douglas May (*Guy*) 1993
Melonie Mazman (*Tess Jannings*) 1984
Monet Mazure (*Brandee*) 1993
Candace Mead (*Baby Victor*) 1990
Loren Mead (*Baby Joseph*) 1990
Joyce Meadows (*Customer*) 1992
Judy Meadows (*Waitress*) 1966
Ken Medlock (*Wally*) 1983
Trisha Melynkov (*Stewardess*) 1991
Trisha Melynkov (*Nora*) 1992
Tina Menard (*Mrs. Velez*) 1975
Steven Mendel (*Reporter Randy*) 1982
Ronald Meszaros (*Dockworker Vinnie*) 1985
Dorothy Meyer (*Mrs. Anderson*) 1971
Dorothy Meyer (*Mrs. Grant*) 1973
Dorothy Meyer (*Mrs. Matlin*) 1978
Michael Meyer (*Bartender Eric*) 1983
Paul Micale (*Dr. Enrico Martinelli*) 1968
Corinne Michaels (*Joanne Barnes*) 1978
Gregory Michaels (*Rick Stevens*) 1977–78
Kerry Michaels (*Mrs. Swenson*) 1985–86
Lori Michaels (*Nurse Jodi*) 1986; 1988; 1992
Tony Michaels (*Train Conductor*) 1967
Tracy Middendorf (*Carrie Brady*) 1991–92
Tom Middleton (*Reverend Woods*) 1981
Mark Mikita (*Gambina*) 1990
Kelly Miles (*Dana*) 1982
Doris Miller (*Mrs. Curtis*) 1967
Doris Miller (*Charwoman*) 1968
Evan Miller (*Little Lawrence*) 1990
Gary Miller (*Hogan*) 1987–88
Mark Miller (*J.R.*) 1975–76
Eric Mills (*Matt*) 1985–86
Candi Milo (*Janey Richardson*) 1985
Richard Minchenberg (*Anson Tobias*) 1994
Stephen Mines (*David Martin*) 1966
Dani Minnick (*Rebecca Morrison*) 1992–93
Muriel Minot (*Marjorie Rutherford*) 1985
Muriel Minot (*Newscaster*) 1992
Donald Mirault (*Lyle Davis*) 1991
Rose Mitchell (*Fitzie*) 1968
Robert Moberly (*Mr. Rudolph*) 1983
Bill Molloy (*Jeff Michaels*) 1972
Eugene Molnar (*Mr. Rice*) 1967
Eugene Molnar (*Rick*) 1968
Eugene Molnar (*Intern Casey*) 1969
Gene Molnar (*Boy in Park*) 1971
Victor Mohica (*El Hombre*) 1994
Karen Moncrieff (*Gabrielle Pascal*) 1987–88
Bill Moneymaker (*Larry*) 1965

Terence Monk (*Hopkins*) 1978
Del Monroe (*State Trooper*) 1977
Belinda Montgomery (*Silvie Gallagher*) 1986
Ralph Montgomery (*Security Chief, Gus*) 1977
Adrienne Moore (*Anna Bowers*) 1971
Adrienne Moore (*Saleswoman*) 1974
Adrienne Moore (*Libby Randolph*) 1975
Adrienne Moore (*Doris Gibson*) 1975
Adrienne Moore (*Mrs. Reeves*) 1978
Alvy Moore (*John Purcell*) 1981
Deborah Moore (*Danielle Stevens*) 1991–92
Tony Moran (*Ted*) 1984
Camilla More (*Janice Kennedy*) 1985
Camilla More (*Gillian Forrester/Grace Forrester*) 1986–87
Carey More (*Grace Forrester*) 1987
Lupe Moreno (*Jeronimo's Mother*) 1975
Nicky Moreno (*Jeronimo*) 1975
Bill Morey (*Judge*) 1977
Bill Morey (*Reverend Hollingsworth*) 1983
Bill Morey (*Dr. Merriwether*) 1994
David Morgan (*Milos*) 1985–86
Molly Morgan (*Patty*) 1989
Shelley Taylor Morgan (*Anjelica Deveraux Curtis*) 1989
Paul Morin (*Bass Player*) 1993
Tom Morgan (*Attacker*) 1990
Louisa Moritz (*Esther*) 1987–88
Beans Morocco (*Marty Silver*) 1991
Paula Morris (*Sergeant Ford*) 1978
Ann Morrison (*Jenny Blake*) 1971
Anne Morrison (*Miss Munson, R.N.*) 1968
Anne Morrison (*Miss Norris, R.N.*) 1968
Byron Morrow (*Judge*) 1965–70
Gregory Mortensen (*Paul Stewart*) 1986
Howard Morton (*Richard White*) 1978
Harry Moses (*Intern Wayne*) 1985–86
Harry Moses (*Rusty*) 1989
Ken Mosesian (*Dr. Mitch Roftom*) 1991
Ron Moss (*Las Vegas Waiter*) 1984
John Mueller (*Reporter*) 1992
Patrick Muldoon (*Austin Reed*) 1992–95
Scott Mulhern (*Baxter Reese*) 1989
Pat Murouse (*Miss Davis*) 1973
Christopher Murray (*Art*) 1989
Christopher Murray (*Ben*) 1989
Clayton Murray (*Dr. Dwyer*) 1993
Tyler Murray (*Carol Wells*) 1980
Carroll Myers (*Nurse Kristie Lynn*) 1985–86
Paulene Myers (*Mrs. Ward*) 1967
Paulene Myers (*Mrs. Jackson*) 1969–71
Paulene Myers (*Mrs. Goldman*) 1978
Andrea Nand (*B.J.*) 1983
Hugo Napier (*ISA Agent*) 1986
John Napier (*Jerry Barnes*) 1968
Paul Napier (*Mr. Weber*) 1968

Bob Nash (*Dr. Jenkins*) 1970; 1972; 1973
John Nation (*Camera Operator*) 1993
Myron Natwick (*Rick*) 1972
Myron Natwick (*Joe's Friend*) 1977
Myron Natwick (*Minister*) 1987
Paul Navarra (*Thug*) 1988
Deborah Neal (*Bass Player*) 1985
Marr Nealon (*Debbie*) 1990
Marr Nealon (*Stephanie*) 1993
Christopher Neame (*Dr. Vertigo/ISA Director Ogden Vaughn*) 1986
Bruce Neckels (*Attorney*) 1982
Roger Nehls (*Stage Manager*) 1992
George Nejame (*Bobby*) 1989
George NeJame (*Singing Telegram Man*) 1990
Meghan & Michael Nelson (*Abigail Johanna Deveraux*) 1992–94
Herb Nelson (*Phil Peters*) 1972
Desiree Neriz (*Hannah*) 1989
Stuart Nesbitt (*Henry*) 1975
Ed Ness (*Judge Robinson*) 1978
Arthel Neville (*Sondra Stevens*) 1993
Janet Newberry (*Marlena's Body Double*) 1986
Tom Nibley (*Dr. Harvey*) 1989
Michelle Nicastro (*Sasha*) 1987
Aaron Nichols (*Young Steve*) 1986–88; 1990
Robert Nichols (*Buddy Rose*) 1992
Stephen Nichols (*Steve "Patch" Johnson*) 1985–90
Vanessa Nichols (*Kelly*) 1986–87
Vanessa Nichols (*Teen-age Stephanie*) 1990
Katherine Nicholson (*Candice*) 1992
Michael Niederman (*Jamie De Bono*) 1978
Eric Nies (*Disc Jockey*) 1993
Yvette Nitar (*Sasha*) 1987
Martha Nix (*Janice*) 1975–76; 1978
Chelsea Noble (*Christina*) 1988
Sharon Noble (*Dr. Parker*) 1988
Claire Nono (*Connie Soo*) 1984
Kerry Noonan (*Jane*) 1993
Ted Noose (*Wilkens*) 1983
Maidie Norman (*Gracie Jones*) 1970
Heather North (*Sandy Horton*) 1967–71
Wayne Northrop (*Roman Brady*) 1981–84; 1991–94
Danny Nucci (*Marv*) 1987
Tarah Nutter (*Karen*) 1985
Christina Nyberg (*Maid Janet*) 1985
Wanakee Oatts (*Dorothy Jones*) 1970
Philip O'Brien (*Chancey Powell*) 1991
John O'Connell (*Al Betrand*) 1977
Michael O'Connor (*Dimitri*) 1991–92
Connor O'Farrell (*Dr. Chase*) 1994
Lani O'Grady (*Mrs. Kramer*) 1990
Tom Ohmer (*Agent Thomas*) 1987
Valerie Ojala (*Nurse Lisa*) 1986

Jim O'Keefe (*Phone Man*) 1978
Jeff Olan (*Reporter*) 1993
Susan Oliver (*Dr. Laura Spencer Horton*) 1975–76
Nelson Olmstead (*Dr. Harkins*) 1967
Kathleen O'Malley (*Flora*) 1984
Kathleen O'Malley (*Mildred*) 1985
Grey O'Neill (*Prince Nicholas Arani II*) 1985
Michael O'Neill (*Father Jansen*) 1994–
James Ong (*Dr. Wu*) 1993
David Orange (*Brent Matthews*) 1988
Rin O'Reilly (*Miss Masters*) 1969
Ray Oriel (*Santos*) 1989
Tom Ormeny (*Lloyd Garrison*) 1990
April Ortiz (*Jodi*) 1990
Joe Ortiz (*Fire Truck Driver*) 1990
Kristina Osterhaut (*Baby Hope*) 1974
Terry O'Sullivan (*Richard*) 1966–67
Virginia Otto (*Hessian Inn Maid*) 1980
Grant Owens (*Martin*) 1980
Judy Pace (*Miss Kenneth*) 1967
Gordon Paddison (*Father Kyle*) 1993–
Justin Page (*Andrew Donovan*) 1989–90
Joe Palese (*Werner*) 1986
Joe Palese (*Ray*) 1992
Tom Paliferro (*District Attorney*) 1993
Eddie Palma (*Baby Eric Brady*) 1986
Tiffany Nicole Palma (*Baby Samantha Brady*) 1986
Scott Palmer (*Joshua Fallon*) 1981–82
Alan Palo (*Drug Dealer*) 1993
Lew Palter (*Mr. Mackowitz*) 1968
Vincent Pandoliano (*Antoine*) 1983
Norm Panto (*Accordion Player*) 1975
John Pappas (*Greek Head Waiter*) 1987
John Pappas (*Leo*) 1994
Barbara Pariot (*Paula*) 1984
Donald Parker (*Extra*) 1966
Donald Parker (*Orderly*) 1967
Frank Parker (*Car Salesman*) 1977
Frank Parker (*Dr. Patrick Hennesy*) 1982
Frank Parker (*Shawn Brady*) 1983–84; 1985–89; 1990–
Warren Parker (*Hotel Desk Clerk, Carver*) 1969
Wes Parker (*Mr. Hawkins*) 1988
Patrick Parkhurst (*Photographer*) 1993
Catherine Parks (*Mitzi Matuso*) 1982
Larry Parks (*Psychiatrist*) 1984
Julie Parrish (*Sister Theresa*) 1980
Miriam Parrish (*Jamie Caldwell*) 1993–
Nancy Parsons (*Nurse Jackson*) 1994
David J. Partington (*Oscar*) 1993
Robert Parucha (*Eddie*) 1988–89
Rocco Pascale (*Gonzales*) 1972
Mary Patton (*Matron*) 1974
Mary Patton (*Mrs. Nowlin*) 1975–76

George Paulsin (*Delivery Boy*) 1968
Edith Pavelec (*Nurse*) 1968
David Paymer (*Chino*) 1985
Robert Peacock (*Dr. Perry Collins*) 1990
Barry Pearl (*Dr. Abbott*) 1989
Nancy Pearlburg (*Mrs. Cross*) 1978
Robert Pearsoll (*Tony*) 1991
Patsy Pease (*Kimberly Brady Donovan*)
 1984–90; 1990–91; 1991–92; 1994
Anthony Peck (*Porter Rollins*) 1990
Austin Peck (*Austin Reed*) 1995–
J. Eddie Peck (*Howard "Hawk" Alston
 Hawkins III*) 1991–92
Thaao Penghlis (*Count Antony DiMera*)
 1981–86; 1993–
Chris Pennock (*Joe Taylor*) 1978
David Perceval (*Lady Joanna's Husband*) 1985
Raul Perez (*Jerry*) 1977
Raul Perez (*Bailiff*) 1978
Dan Perrett (*Lionel*) 1985
S.E. Perry (*Loan Shark*) 1992
Saverio Persico (*Rosie*) 1993
John Petlock (*Dr. Karlin*) 1977
John Petlock (*Briggs Lamar*) 1982
John Petlock (*Mr. Armstrong*) 1992
John Petlock (*Judge*) 1994
Kay Peters (*Sarah Fredericks*) 1970
Erick Petersen (*"Timmy"/Scotty Banning*)
 1978–80
Jennifer Petersen (*Jennifer Rose Horton*)
 1977–78
Gene Peterson (*Mr. Draper*) 1968
Gene Peterson (*Peter Larkin*) 1969–70
Steve Peterson (*Snake Rogers*) 1992
Sue Peterson (*Amazon Drew*) 1984
Brent Pfaff (*Stalker*) 1993
Donald Phelps (*Waiter*) 1971
Gary Houston Phillips (*Drew*) 1984
Mark Piatella (*Mr. Webb*) 1992
Matt Piatelli (*Public Defender*) 1992
Lisa Piazza (*Madam Justice Brooks*) 1970
Lisa Piazza (*Eric's Mom*) 1971
Lisa Piazza (*Mrs. Jackson*) 1972
Lisa Piazza (*Miss Perkins*) 1973
Robert Pickering (*Dr. Goddard*) 1979
Jay Pickett (*Dr. Chip Lakin*) 1991–92
Lisa Picotte (*Tracy*) 1992
Bradley Pierce (*Andrew Donovan*) 1990–91
Stack Pierce (*Kenny*) 1977
Geoff Pierson (*Barney*) 1989
Emily Luann & Alicia Nichole Pillatzke
 (*Jeannie Donovan*) 1991–92
Drew Pillsbury (*Martin*) 1992
Daniel Pilon (*Waiter*) 1984
Daniel Pilon (*Gavin Newirth*) 1992
Phillip Pine (*Dr. Kincaid*) 1967
Robert Pine (*Walker Coleman*) 1987

John Pinero (*Luis*) 1991
Mark Pint (*Desk Clerk*) 1977
Judy Piolo (*Guinevere Rutherford*) 1985
Cary Pitts (*Police Officer*) 1977
Patricia Place (*Dr. Lindsey Allison*) 1992
Patricia Place (*Meredith Hampton Hyde*) 1993
Robin Pohle (*Amy Kositchek*) 1978–79
Larry Poindexter (*Ben Welch*) 1984
David M. Polak (*Pilot*) 1993
Carmelita Pope (*Mrs. Woods*) 1981
Herman Poppe (*Henchman Kurt*) 1985
Mark Porro (*Carl Fisher*) 1992
Hale Porter (*Bailiff*) 1981
Rick Porter (*Hank Tobin*) 1989–90
Keisha Powell (*Mary Jane Jones*) 1970
Randolph Powell (*Tyler Malone*) 1983
Susan Powell (*Trish*) 1993
Melissa Power (*Nurse*) 1972
Robert Poynton (*Pawn*) 1985
Debra Pratt (*Lacey*) 1984
Judson Pratt (*Vince Jaroslavski*) 1980
Ed Prentiss (*John Martin*) 1966
Ed Prentiss (*Mr. Peterson*) 1966
Ed Prentiss (*Dr. Ralph Dunbar*) 1967
Ed Prentiss (*Chairman of the Parole Board*)
 1970
Ed Prentiss (*Alex Marshall*) 1971
Lindsay Price (*Mary*) 1994
Samantha Price (*Gertrude Willoughby*) 1975
Sari Price (*Wife of the Justice of the Peace*)
 1975
Nancy Priddie (*Mrs. Grizzell*) 1972
Dan Priest (*Earle Roscoe*) 1978
Michael Prince (*Ted Cooper*) 1980
Elaine Princi (*Kate Winnegrad*) 1977–79
Elaine Princi (*Linda Anderson*) 1984–85
Babette Props (*Veronica*) 1985–86
Stephen Prutting (*Mr. Price*) 1990
Kyle Puerner (*Baby Michael Horton*) 1968–69
Karen Purcill (*Dale Griffith*) 1985
Mara Purl (*Nurse Darla*) 1986
Jessica Puscas (*Young Girl*) 1987
Lillyan Quarin (*Mrs. St. John*) 1975
May Quigley (*Maid Lily*) 1989
Ed Quinlan (*Rich*) 1977
Ed Quinlan (*Hendricks*) 1978
Bill Quinn (*Dr. Atwater*) 1969
Patrick Neil Quinn (*Renfro*) 1989
Ron Quint (*Process Server*) 1965
Karen Racicot (*Gaby*) 1992
Bettina Rae (*Little Marina Toscano*) 1990
Cassidy Rae (*Karen*) 1993
John Ragin (*Joe Donald*) 1971
Ford Rainey (*Frank Evans*) 1977–78
Jessica Rains (*Ruthie*) 1972
David Ralphe (*Salem Inn Desk Clerk*) 1980
Jeff Ramsey (*Attacker*) 1990

Marian Ramsey (*Sarah*) 1977
Anne Randall (*Sheila Hammond*) 1971–72
Lillian Randolph (*Mrs. Hausing*) 1971
Fred Rapport (*Juror*) 1965; 1966
Fred Rapport (*Mr. Rice*) 1967
Marguerite Ray (*Sara Blandish*) 1971
Marguerite Ray (*Floor Nurse*) 1973
Marguerite Ray (*Merrill*) 1977
Eddie Rayden (*Michael Horton*) 1970
Paula Raymond (*Nancy*) 1977
Gina Ravarra (*Vanessa Mitchell*) 1993
Elsa Raven (*Olga's Mother*) 1994
Alex Rebar (*Andre*) 1981–82
Marie Alise Recasner (*Lynn*) 1994
Peter Reckell (*Bo Brady*) 1983–87; 1990–91; 1995–
Quinn Redeker (*Alex Marshall*) 1979–87
Jeff Redford (*Dr. Etienne*) 1988
Cyndi James Reese (*Sally Johnson*) 1981–82
Cyndi James Reese (*Lexie*) 1987
Melissa Brennan Reeves (*Jennifer Rose Horton Deveraux*) 1985–
Scott Reeves (*Jake*) 1988
Mick Regan (*Bodyguard*) 1986
Frances Reid (*Alice Horton*) 1965–
Scott Reiniger (*Frank Weston*) 1984
Randy Reinholz (*Adam Scott*) 1989
Deborah Rennard (*Dr. Whitney Baker*) 1991
Alejandro Rey (*Karl Duval*) 1976–77
Peggy Reyna (*Peggy*) 1989–90
James Reynolds (*Abe Carver*) 1981–90; 1991–
Ron Reynolds (*Baggage Handler*) 1993
Tony Rhodes (*Jesse Lombard*) 1992
Michael Rhoton (*Max*) 1986–87
Madlyn Rhue (*Daphne DiMera*) 1982–84
Adrian Ricard (*Lizzie*) 1989
Merl Rice (*Harem Wife*) 1985
Regina Richardson (*Lacey*) 1984
Hal Riddle (*Chief Justice*) 1970
Hal Riddle (*Max, the waiter*) 1971–75
Devin Rider (*Baby Billy*) 1989
Sue Rihr (*Madelaine Rutherford*) 1985
Lisa Rinna (*Billie Holiday Reed*) 1992–
Mark Charles Ritter (*Dr. Craig Norris*) 1990
Richard Roat (*Conrad Hutton*) 1985
Richard Roat (*Professor Henry Moore*) 1991
Brenda Robbin (*Nurse*) 1967
DeAnna Robbins (*Diane Parker*) 1984
Mark Roberts (*Paul Dixon*) 1966
Randolph Roberts (*Reverend Keene*) 1978
Sandy Roberts (*Waitress*) 1966
Dennis Robertson (*Brother Martin*) 1985
Carol Robins (*Harp Player*) 1990
Ann Robinson (*Bobbie Jeannine*) 1978
Bumper Robinson (*Jonah Carver*) 1987–88
Donald Robinson (*Paramedic*) 1992

Jay Robinson (*Monty Dolan*) 1988–89
Kim Robinson (*Nurse Roxanne*) 1985
Valentin Robles (*Farmer*) 1983
Robert Rockwell (*Dr. Simon Wilkinson*) 1987
Al Rodrigo (*Connor Dennison*) 1991
Marco Rodriguez (*Sergeant Hernandez*) 1988
Maurice Roeves (*David Halpern*) 1985–86
Maurice Roeves (*The Professor*) 1989
Ed Rogers (*Ed Simpson*) 1979
Suzanne Rogers (*Maggie Simmons Horton*) 1973–84; 1985–
Gyl Roland (*Sheila Hammond*) 1972
J. P. Romano (*Sword Fight Coordinator*) 1991
John Romano (*Andre's Stunt Double*) 1984
Robert Romanus (*Speed Selejko*) 1983–85
Jane Romney (*Miss Lee*) 1993
Buck Rooney (*Bo's Guard*) 1985
Gary Rooney (*Harry Hill*) 1991
Toma Rosa (*Erik*) 1988
Jeff Rosenberg (*Sam Jeeves*) 1983
Clive Rosengren (*Professor Smiley*) 1991
Clive Rosengren (*Judge Carrington*) 1993
Tom Rosqui (*Mr. Ralph Jannings*) 1984
Charlotte Ross (*Eve Donovan*) 1987–91
Frank Rossi (*Lurker*) 1990
Jennifer Roven (*Laura*) 1982
Pamela Roylance (*Sandy Horton*) 1983–84
Lantz Rubin (*Marcus, age 5*) 1988
Derya Ruggles (*Dr. Robin Jacobs*) 1985–87; 1989
Skye Rumph (*Andrew Donovan*) 1989
Skye Rumph (*Injured Little Boy*) 1992
David Ruprecht (*Dan Ryan*) 1990–92
Al Ruscio (*Lieutenant Kendall*) 1981
Al Ruscio (*Miguel Torres*) 1988
Tony Russel (*Dr. Wayne*) 1978
Tony Russel (*Dr. Glen Seymour*) 1979
Arland Russell (*Ambassador Pajar*) 1990
Sharon Rushton (*Francie*) 1982
Ian Ruskin (*Gunter Hoffman*) 1990
Michael Russo (*Andre*) 1992
Michael Russo (*Chauffeur Charles*) 1994
John Russon (*Baby Dougie*) 1977
Edmond Ryan (*Judge Alexander*) 1967
Fran Ryan (*Olive Newton*) 1975
Fran Ryan (*Rosie Carlson*) 1976–79
Matthew Ryan (*Paul*) 1994
Natasha Ryan (*Hope Williams*) 1975–80
Christopher Saavedra (*Young François*) 1990
Michael Sabatino (*Lawrence Alamain*) 1990–93
Daniel Sabia (*Agent Alexi*) 1986
Marcella Saint-Amant (*Danielle Forenza*) 1984
David St. James (*Hotel Manager*) 1991
David St. James (*Dr. Love*) 1992
Diane Sainte Marie (*Lawrence's Mother*) 1991

Jim Saito (*Kameha*) 1989
Pat Sajak (*Kevin Hathaway*) 1983
Susan Saldivar (*Kristina*) 1988
Philece Sampler (*Renee Dumonde*) 1980–84
Ed Sancho-Bonet (*Detective Gary Klein*) 1983
Casey Sander (*Billings*) 1986
Linda Sanders (*Mrs. Ogins*) 1992
Richard Sanders (*Mrs. Slater*) 1986
Vanessa Sandin (*Leslie*) 1994
Ken Sansone (*Dr. Powell*) 1976
Bert Santos (*Farmer*) 1983
Olan Sauly (*Reverend Goodhue*) 1977
Lanna Saunders (*Marie Horton Curtis*) 1979–85
Pamela Saunders (*Dr. Whitney Baker*) 1990
Eunice Saurez (*Mrs. Rose Ruiz*) 1972
Brad Savage (*Joseph*) 1983
Paul Savior (*Sam Reynolds*) 1975
Jeff Schafrath (*Ari*) 1991–92
Marion Scherer (*Prom Trustee Gail*) 1983
Eric Schiff (*Kevin*) 1985
Georgia Schmidt (*Woman Patient*) 1975
Mark Schneider (*Harry*) 1989
Mark Schneider (*Maurice Marchand*) 1991
Stephen Schnetzer (*Steve Olson*) 1978–80
Jeremy Schoenberg (*Johnny*) 1980
Frank Schofield (*Ralph Newton*) 1977
Frank Schofield (*Frank Evans*) 1979
Avery Schreiber (*Leopold Alamain*) 1990
Catherine Schreiber (*Denise*) 1979
Joshua Schreiber (*Stage Hand*) 1992
David Schroeder (*Homer*) 1990
Arland Schubert (*Wilbur Austin*) 1969
Don Sciarrino (*Italian Guardsman*) 1990
Anna Scott (*Marie-Helene Fortier*) 1992
Anna Scott (*French Actress*) 1993
Avis Scott (*Mother Marie*) 1969
Camilla Scott (*Melissa Anderson*) 1990–91
Jean Bruce Scott (*Jessica Blake*) 1980–82
Joseph Scott (*Rafi's Bodyguard*) 1991–92
Simon Scott (*Mr. Armstrong*) 1968
Tom Scott (*Jim Bradley*) 1977–78
Jocelyn Seagrave (*Tanya*) 1994
Anthony Seaward (*Baby Sarah Horton*) 1981–82
Manuel Sebastian (*Dr. Garcia*) 1979
Judith Searle (*Dr. Madelaine Fairchild*) 1978
Kimberly Sedgewick (*Ashley*) 1988–89
David Selkirk (*Professor*) 1989
Carolyn Seymier (*Saleswoman*) 1993
Edmund Shaff (*Judge Greenville*) 1992–93
Hassan Shaheed (*Danny Grant*) 1976
Diane Shalet (*Judge Reynolds*) 1978–81
Jerry Shane (*Mr. Valentine*) 1970
Tressa Sharbough (*Laura*) 1988

Howard Shangraw (*Ray LeGrand*) 1991
Charles Shaughnessy (*Shane Donovan*) 1984–92
Scott Shaughnessy (*Albert*) 1990
Dorothy Shay (*Miss Frazier*) 1971
Dorothy Shay (*Miss Rogers*) 1972
Nancy Sheebar (*Nidia*) 1991
Todd Sheeler (*Paul*) 1992
Regina Sheil (*Amazon Paris*) 1984
Tom Shell (*Piano Player*) 1978; 1983
Brian Sheehan (*Karl*) 1983
Laurie Shepard (*Harriet Cameron*) 1993
Jenny Sherman (*Betty*) 1977–79
Jessica Sherrel (*Baby Vanessa*) 1988
Peg Shirley (*Dr. Morgan*) 1993
Robert Shook (*Jack's Stunt Double*) 1991
Jim Shorup (*Lab Technician Jarvis*) 1978
Patricia Sides (*Matron*) 1967
Patricia Sides (*Nurse Carter*) 1968
Edythe Sills (*Woman Patient*) 1965
Gino Silva (*Domingo Salazar*) 1991
Hannah Taylor Simmons (*Jeannie Donovan*) 1991
Hank Simms (*Announcer*) 1967
Lincoln Simonds (*Thug # 2*) 1990
Annette Sinclair (*Amy*) 1984
Eric Sinclair (*Durand*) 1979
John Sinclair (*London*) 1984
Joey Singer (*Piano Player*) 1993
E. A. Sirianni (*Court Clerk*) 1967; 1969
E. A. Sirianni (*Judge*) 1978
Woody Skaggs (*Mr. Berle*) 1978
Suzee Slater (*Kayla's Body Double*) 1987
Chuck Sloan (*Lane Thomas*) 1991
Chuck Sloan (*Leonard Crestwell*) 1992
Nancy Sloan (*Sally*) 1989
Nancy Sloan (*Young Woman*) 1990
Nancy Sloan (*Lyla*) 1991
Burr Smidt (*Drunk Man*) 1970
Anthony Smith (*Benjamin*) 1993
Donegan Smith (*Harold Dailey*) 1984
Holly Smith (*Nurse Pamela*) 1987
Holly Smith (*Morgan Collier*) 1991
Jason Grant Smith (*Jeff*) 1994
Mark W. Smith (*Joel*) 1994
Martha Smith (*Sandy Horton*) 1982
Merritt Smith (*Dr. Arthur Baron*) 1970; 1972–73
Michael O. Smith (*Commissioner Samuels*) 1990
Patricia Smith (*Alma Clovis*) 1985
Steve Smith (*Piano Player*) 1979
Jeff Smolek (*Bartender*) 1992
Jocelyn Somers (*Marion Barton*) 1973
Jocelyn Somers (*Jean Barton*) 1977–78
Diane Sommerfield (*Valerie Grant*) 1981–82
Eleanor Sommers (*Sister Teresa*) 1968

Louise Sorel (*Vivian Alamain*) 1992–
Jon Soresi (*Rafael Abruzzo*) 1990
Arleen Sorkin (*Calliope Jones Bradford*) 1984–90; 1992
Spike Sorrentino (*Woody*) 1985–86
Olan Soulé (*Mr. Jerome*) 1975
Frances Spanier (*Lil*) 1965–66
Carole Speed (*Elaine Jones*) 1970
Kim Spiess (*Patty*) 1984
Sandra Spriggs (*Darci Banks*) 1992
Eric Stabenau (*Young Punk*) 1990
Timothy Stack (*Mark Garrett*) 1981
Richard Stahl (*Attorney Marks*) 1985
Richard Stahl (*Louie Markson*) 1985
Sumer Stamper (*Mandy*) 1991
Suzanne Stanford (*Penny Larkin*) 1980
Barbara Stanger (*Mary Anderson*) 1975–81
Harry Stanton (*John Spencer*) 1967
Sally Stark (*Sharon Duval*) 1976–77
David Starwalt (*Stage Manager*) 1984
David Starwalt (*Greg Pierson*) 1985
Jack Stauffer (*Leo Rogers*) 1976
Anthony Steedman (*Werner Bayer*) 1990
Antoinette Stella (*Joan*) 1987–89
Al Stellone (*Stash Winowski*) 1978
Nancy Stephens (*Mary Anderson*) 1975
John Stephenson (*Terry Gilbert*) 1979–80
Maren Stephenson (*Jennifer Rose Horton*) 1976–77
Ashleigh Sterling (*Samantha Brady*) 1986–90
Carrie Stevens (*Heather*) 1992
Gary Stevens (*Officer Peterson*) 1983
Kaye Stevens (*Jeri Clayton*) 1974–79
K. T. Stevens (*Helen Martin*) 1966–67; 1969
Shawn Stevens (*Oliver Martin*) 1982–83
Benjamin Stewart (*Eames*) 1981
Budd Stewart (*Baby Dickie*) 1967
Catherine Mary Stewart (*Kayla Brady*) 1982–83
Ray Stewart (*Mr. Lyons*) 1989
Peg Stewart (*Joretta Hicksby*) 1982
Peg Stewart (*Dr. Rhonda Haines*) 1982
Peg Stewart (*Sweetheart*) 1983
Amy Stock (*Britta Englund*) 1986
Walter Stocker (*Sergeant Wicker*) 1974
Morgan Stoddard (*Piano Player*) 1980; 1981
Hank Stohl (*Major Hawkins*) 1980
Jodi Stolove (*Jodi*) 1990
Christopher Stone (*Dr. Bill Horton*) 1987–88; 1994
Eric Stone (*Conway*) 1992
Eric Stone (*Photographer*) 1993
Leonard Stone (*Judge*) 1990
Elizabeth Storm (*Dancer Charlene*) 1986
Elizabeth Storm (*Janice Barnes*) 1987–88
Marte Boyle Stout (*Judge*) 1991
Darryl Strauss (*Nadine*) 1988–89

Joanne Strauss (*Nurse*) 1966; 1968; 1969; 1972
Angie Strickland (*Mother Mary Joseph*) 1980
Paul Strickland (*Chuck*) 1990–
Ray Stricklyn (*Howard Alston Hawkins*) 1991–92
Randy Stumpf (*Ron*) 1977–78
Shannon Sturges (*Molly Brinker*) 1991–92
Maggie Sullivan (*Astrid Langstrum*) 1982
Richard Lee Sung (*Chinese Soldier*) 1967–68
Steve Susskind (*Warden Rand*) 1990
Don Swayze (*"Warrior" Rip*) 1984
Alison Sweeney (*Samantha Brady*) 1992–
Harold Sylvester (*Warren Heywood*) 1980
Cynthia Szzgetti (*Hester Pitkins*) 1975
Ron Taft (*Mr. Tobias*) 1992
Charles Tamburro (*Justin's Stunt Double*) 1988
Mark Tapscott (*Bob Anderson*) 1972–80
Glenn Taranto (*Marty*) 1994
Milt Tarver (*Dr. Olsen*) 1993
Milt Tarver (*Dr. Layton*) 1994
Joe E. Tata (*Warren*) 1981
Charles Taylor (*Kai*) 1987
Curtis Taylor (*Jennifer's Bodyguard*) 1990
Josh Taylor (*Chris Kositchek*) 1977–86; 1987
Tammy Taylor (*Hope Williams*) 1981
Marshall Teague (*Leonard Stacy*) 1984
Marshall Teague (*Colin*) 1989
Frank Telfer (*Mr. Donnell*) 1988
Frank Telfer (*Josh Mills*) 1990
Carlos Tentino (*Stingray*) 1988
Walter Teper (*Dr. Kramer*) 1992
Allen Terry (*Radio Engineer*) 1981
Jonathan Terry (*Dr. George Korman*) 1991
Christopher Thomas (*Dr. Mantash*) 1979
Dale Thomas (*KGB Agent Leonid*) 1986
Emanuel Thomas (*Bailiff*) 1977
Paul Thomas (*Bailiff*) 1970
Ryan Thomas (*Bob*) 1985
Sharon Thomas (*Blonde*) 1974
Kathy Thornston (*Mrs. Maltby*) 1977
Jonathan Thornton (*Alexander Kiriakis*) 1989–91
Russell Thorson (*Dr. White*) 1965–66
Russell Thorson (*Judge Wolf*) 1969–70
Russell Thorson (*Dr. Jim Bennett*) 1970
Russell Thorson (*Dr. Emory*) 1972–73
Paul Tinder (*Paul*) 1986–87
Paul Tinder (*Father Pat*) 1993
Ken Tobey (*Dr. Parker*) 1976
Matthew Tobin (*Milt Stanley*) 1980
Lisa Marie Todd (*Chelsea*) 1992
Tricia Tomey (*Edna May*) 1992
Shaquille Toney (*Benjamin*) 1993–94
Melinda Toporoff (*Patty*) 1986
Janice Tori (*Harem Dumpling*) 1985

Liz Torres (*Gail*) 1987
Dierk Torsek (*Artist*) 1990
Dierk Torsek (*Mr. Bailey*) 1993
Robert Torti (*Charles Van Dieter*) 1993
Patty Tossq (*Miss Adams*) 1972
Tammy Townsend (*Wendy Reardon*) 1994–
William Traylor (*Officer Jennings*) 1971
William Traylor (*James Stanhope*) 1976
Lawrence Trimble (*The Dragon*) 1985
Derek Triplett (*George Blandish*) 1971
Jan Triska (*Nicolai*) 1984
Thomas Trujillo (*Boy*) 1975
Lisa Trusel (*Melissa Anderson Jannings*)
    1983–88; 1994
Laura Tubelle (*Marthy Lewis*) 1977
Tinan Turner (*Rita*) 1977
Tinan Turner (*Stenographer*) 1978
William Turner (*Voice*) 1978
Nadyne Turney (*Linda*) 1970
Michael Twain (*Mr. Beltzer*) 1980
Shannon Tweed (*Savannah Wilder*) 1985–86
Hunter Tylo (*Marina Toscano Johnson*)
    1989–90
Corazon Ugalde (*Harem Wife*) 1985
Vallie Ullman (*Mrs. Goodman*) 1979
David Underwood (*Mark Palmer*) 1980
Diana Uribe (*Backup singer*) 1993
Julie Urive (*Nidia*) 1992
Darrell Utley (*Benjy*) 1988–89, 1990
Mikki Val (*Backup Singer*) 1993
Raquel Valdez (*Inmate Andry*) 1983
Donna Vale (*Jennifer's Ski Double*) 1994
Paul Valentine (*Conductor Anatole*) 1984
Hugo Valentino (*Man in Dungeon*) 1984
Louis Valenzi (*Waiter*) 1985
Mark Valley (*Jack Devereaux*) 1994–
Joan Van Ark (*Janene*) 1970
Mark Vance (*Dr. Reynolds*) 1967
Gwen Van Dam (*Jeanie*) 1983
Gwen Van Dam (*Imelda*) 1987
Nadine Van Der Velde (*Jane*) 1983
John Van Dreelen (*Dr. Berger*) 1977
Charles Van Eman (*Officer Greg*) 1984
Charles Van Eman (*Bartender Phil*) 1984–85
Charles Van Eman (*Trent*) 1988
James Van Harper (*Guy #1*) 1990
Linda Van Ness (*Helen Parker*) 1975
Jeannie Vargas (*Penny*) 1984
Renata Vasselle (*Mrs. Whitehead*) 1977
Tony Vatsula (*Ralph*) 1989
Ondine Vaughn (*Ruthie*) 1968
Etienne Veazie (*Messenger Boy*) 1970
Eddie Velez (*Malko*) 1993
Glen Vernon (*Harold Wade*) 1965
Michael Verona (*Alberto*) 1976–79
Steve Viall (*Vince*) 1991
James Victor (*Dr. Simmons*) 1980

James Victor (*Rick*) 1994
Paula Victor (*Mrs. Haggerty*) 1975
Paula Victor (*Mrs. Stoner*) 1980–82
Jean Paul Vignon (*Jacques*) 1994
Fred Vincent (*Allen Quinn*) 1976
Victor Vitartas (*Eddie*) 1979
Mike Vitullo (*Dr. Miceli*) 1988–89
Tom Vize (*Dr. Evans*) 1966
Erik Von Detten (*Nicholas Alamain*) 1992–93
Lark Voorhies (*Wendy Reardon*) 1993–94
Caitlin Wachs (*Jeannie Donovan*) 1992
Christina Wagoner (*Samantha Brady*)
    1990–92
Gregory Wagrowski (*Jake Sellers*) 1985–87
Marged Wakely (*Sally Jamison*) 1977
Keith A. Walker (*Adam Blake*) 1979
Robert Walker (*Dr. Collins*) 1986
Rock Walker (*Sam*) 1992
Casey Wallace (*Little Kimmie*) 1992
David Wallace (*Tod Chandler*) 1985–86
George Wallace (*Miles Wentworth*) 1974
Chuck Walling (*Benny Lowman*) 1992
Donna Walsh (*Nurse*) 1968
Mimi Walters (*Nurse*) 1968
Denise Wanner (*Mystery Girl*) 1986
B. J. Ward (*Sylvie*) 1985
Caryn Michelle Ward (*Latoya Preston*) 1985
Lynn Ward (*Nurse*) 1967
Skip Ward (*J.R.*) 1975
Harlan Warde (*Dr. Mark Larson*) 1972
Billy Warlock (*Frankie Brady/François Von
    Leuschner*) 1986–88; 1990–91
Astrid Warner (*Sandy Horton*) 1967
Jim Warren (*Bartender Jim*) 1986–87
Mike Warren (*Jerry Davis*) 1976
Kirt Washington (*Jimmy*) 1972
Susanne Wasson (*Judge Elaine Bedford*) 1985
Barry Watson (*Randy*) 1990
Timothy Wayne (*Intern Craig*) 1985
Patty Weaver (*Trish Clayton Banning*)
    1974–82
Troy Weaver (*Joe "Iron Man" Steele*) 1992
Richard Webb (*General Rawlings*) 1977
Dean Webber (*Mr. Broderick*) 1992
Paul Anthony Weber (*Police Officer*) 1990
Kimberly Joy Weber (*Baby Hope*) 1974–75
Byron Webster (*Guthrie*) 1988
Diana Webster (*Livinia Peach*) 1985–86
Vernon Weddle (*Bruce Fischell*) 1989
Michael T. Weiss (*Dr. Michael Horton*)
    1985–90
Charles Welch (*Father Francis*) 1994
Nelson Welch (*Amos Franklin*) 1976
James Wellman (*Mr. Tucker*) 1970
James Wellman (*Dr. Hightower*) 1972–73
William Wellman (*Dr. Denason*) 1986
William Wellman (*Dr. Frances Briggs*) 1992

Aarika Wells (*Miss Harris*) 1986
Ashley Wells (*Elaine Forrest*) 1975
Danny Wells (*Sticky Foot Slim*) 1983
David Wells (*Mr. Bartlett*) 1994
Jack Wells (*Desmond Towns*) 1979
Lars Wensen (*Bum*) 1973
Martin West (*Commissioner Samuels*) 1988
Joanna Wexler (*Young Hope*) 1994
Robert Wexler (*Lester Hall*) 1979–80
Joseph Whipp (*Thug*) 1981
Bernie White (*Snake Selejko*) 1983
Betty White (*Nurse/Teacher*) 1988
Bill White (*Dr. Levittson*) 1981
Donn White (*Jerry Jones*) 1986
Frank Whiteman (*Mr. Coates*) 1978
Anne Whitfield (*Barbara Harris*) 1965
Zetta Whitlow (*Janet*) 1984
Nancy Wickwire (*Phyllis Anderson*) 1972–73
George Wilbur (*Ike*) 1992
Mary Wilcox (*Janene*) 1969
Kathryn Wilde (*Bus Passenger*) 1978
Ron Wilder (*Mike at 18*) 1970
Donna Wilkes (*Pamela Prentiss*) 1982–83
Jim Wilkey (*Goon*) 1992
Brett Williams (*Joe Fisher*) 1980
Brett Williams (*Tod Chandler*) 1980
Brian Williams (*Student*) 1991
Jeffrey Williams ("*Brad*"/*David Banning*)
    1970–73
Kiarra Williams (*Tashi*) 1988
Lisa Williams (*Lady Joanna*) 1985
Lisa Williams (*Lisa*) 1992–
Mark Williams (*Drum Player*) 1985
Robert Williams (*Gym Manager Steve*) 1994
Sherry Williams (*Irene Lansing*) 1984
Tom Williams (*Minister*) 1983
Tom Williams (*Priest*) 1990
Tom Williams (*Judge Whittaker*) 1992
Tom Williams (*Mitch, voice only*) 1993
Tony Williams (*Harbor Master*) 1993
Mikki Willis (*Head Coach*) 1992
Mikki Willis (*Scott Rydel*) 1992
Sheila Wills (*Lexie Brooks*) 1989
Terry Wills (*Lawyer Miller*) 1993
Cheryl–Ann Wilson (*Megan Hathaway*)
    1984–85
Brian Wimmer (*Dean*) 1987
Cory Winch (*Teen-age Nicholas Alamain*)
    1992
Kenya Winchell (*Janice*) 1984
Brian Wing (*Naguchi Baby*) 1975
Jason Wingreen (*Ralph Newton*) 1977
Jane Windsor (*Emma Donovan Marshall*)
    1985–87
Tammy Windsor (*Court Stenographer*) 1965
Chris Winfield (*Butler*) 1990
David Winn (*Alan Scholes*) 1985

Sally Winn (*Mrs. Foster*) 1967
Mary Winsor (*Franny*) 1983
Craig Winter (*Guard #1*) 1990
Anthony Winters (*Anthony*) 1988
Anthony Winters (*Stage Manager*) 1990
Mark Withers (*Coach Locke*) 1986–87
Steve Witmer (*Mystery Jack*) 1994
Ray Wise (*Hal Rummley*) 1982
Howard Witt (*Lieutenant Joe Burke*) 1980
Karin Wolfe (*Rita*) 1968
Karin Wolfe (*Miss Hicks*) 1972
Karin Wolfe (*Mary Anderson*) 1972–75
Gary Wood (*Ralph*) 1986
Janet Wood (*Young Mother*) 1971
Janet Wood (*Virginia Stanhope*) 1976
Lynn Wood (*Miss Graham*) 1969
Lynn Wood (*Miss Frasier*) 1970
Lynn Wood (*Miss Edwards, R.N.*) 1970
Lynn Wood (*Miss Dunn*) 1972
Lynn Wood (*Telephone Operator*) 1972
Lynn Wood (*Therapist*) 1975
Charlayne Woodard (*Desiree McCall*)
    1991–92
Heather Woodruff (*Nurse*) 1966
Jeff Woods (*Dean*) 1984
Leslie Woods (*Dorothy Kelly*) 1978
Robert S. Woods (*Paul Stewart*) 1986–87
Kate Woodville (*Marie Horton*) 1977
Morgan Woodward (*Phillip Colville*)
    1987–88
Harry Woolf (*Moving Company Manager*)
    1991
Dan Woren (*Organ Grinder*) 1984
Dan Woren (*Sheldon*) 1987–90
Wendall Wright (*Lloyd Preston*) 1985
Kai Wulff (*Petrov*) 1983–84; 1986; 1991
Meg Wylie (*Mrs. Thompson*) 1966
Meg Wyllie (*Mrs. Bishop*) 1975
Meg Wyllie (*Mrs. Flora Chisholm*) 1980
H. M. Wynant (*Orby Jensen*) 1982–84
Gina Yardum (*Baby Lewis*) 1977
Claire Yarlett (*Dr. Whitney Baker*) 1990
Amy Yasbeck (*Olivia*) 1986–87
Howard Yearwood (*Guitar Player*) 1983
Don Yesso (*Tony Becker*) 1993
Evelyn Yezek (*Nurse Jamie*) 1986
Merritt Yohnka (*Joey*) 1984–90
Francine York (*Lorraine Temple*) 1978
Gerald York (*Sam Blake*) 1971–72
Gerald York (*Police Officer*) 1977
Gerald York (*Ted Dale*) 1978
Gerald York (*Louie*) 1981
Charles Young (*Bruno*) 1990
Sallee Young (*Angel*) 1981
Paul Zachary (*Shawn Douglas Brady*) 1990
Carman Zapata (*Judge*) 1986
Gregory Zarian (*Brent*) 1986

Lawrence Zarian (*Union Soldier*) 1989
John Zee (*Nickerson*) 1984–85
John Zenda (*Dominic*) 1978
Suzanne Zenor (*Margo Horton*) 1977–80
Kate Zentall (*Dr. Bader*) 1994

Helbi Ziroe (*Woman Patient*) 1975
Dan Zubovic (*Fernando Torres*) 1991–92
Bill Zuckert (*Warden*) 1970
Bill Zuckert (*Judge Klein*) 1982

APPENDIX C

MAIN CHARACTERS

(*in alphabetical order*)

Lawrence Alamain: Michael Sabatino 1990–93

Leopold Alamain: Avery Schreiber 1990

Nicholas Alamain: Erik Von Dettan 1991–93

Vivian Alamain: Louise Sorel 1992–; Marj Dusay 1992–93

Bob Anderson: Mark Tapscott 1972–80; Dick Gittings 1978

Linda Phillips Anderson: Elaine Princi 1984–85; Margaret Mason 1970–72; 1975–80; 1982

Mary Anderson: Melinda Fee 1981–82; Barbara Stanger 1975–81; Kim Durso 1975–76; Susan Keller 1980; Carla Borelli 1975; Nancy Stephens 1975; Karin Wolfe 1972–75; Brigid Bazlen 1972

Phyllis Anderson; Corinne Conley 1973–82; Elizabeth MacRae 1977; Nancy Wickwire 1972–73

Madeline Armstrong: Lynn Clark 1990–92

Larry Atwood: Fred Bier 1977–78

J.J. Bagwood: Patti Johns 1989–90

Jill Bailey: Deborah Hobart 1990–91

David Banning: Gregg Marx 1981–83; Richard Guthrie 1975–81; Steve Doubet 1975; Jeffrey Williams 1970–73; Chad Barstad 1968–70

Scott Banning: Ryan MacDonald 1971–73; Robert Hogan 1970–71; Mike Farrell 1968–70; Robert Carraway 1968

Scotty Banning: David Hearst 1989–90; Dick Billingsley 1981–83; Erick Petersen 1978–80

Trish Clayton Banning: Patty Weaver 1974–82

Dr. Jordan Barr: George McDaniel 1979–80

Brady Black: Eric & Brandon Billings 1994–; Max & Alex Lucero 1992–94

John Black: Drake Hogestyn 1986, 1991–

Peter Blake: Jason Brooks 1993–

Calliope Jones Bradford: Arleen Sorkin 1984–90; 1992

Eugene Bradford: John DeLancie 1982–86; 1989

Letitia Bradford: Ruth Buzzi 1983

Trista Evans Bradford: Barbara Crampton 1983

Bo Brady: Robert Kelker–Kelly 1992–95; Peter Reckell 1983–87; 1990–91; 1995–

Caroline Brady: Peggy McCay 1983; 1985–; Barbara Beckley 1984–85; Jody Carter 1984

Carrie Brady: Tracey Middendorf 1991–92; Christie Clark 1986–90; 1992–; Andrea Barber 1982–86

Eric Brady: Bradley Hallock 1986–92; Edwood Palma 1986; Jesse Davis 1985–86; Rory Beauregard 1984

Frankie Brady (François Von Leuschner): Billy Warlock 1986–88; 1990–91

Hope Williams Brady: Kristian Alfonso 1983–87; 1990; 1994–; Tammy Taylor 1981; Natasha Ryan 1975–80; Kimberly Joy Weber 1974–75; Kristina Osterhaut 1974

Isabella "Belle" Brady: Brianna & Chalice Fischette 1993–

Max Brady: Ryan Brennan 1987–88; 1990–92; Adrian Arnold 1987

Marlena Evans Craig Brady: Deidre Hall 1976–87; 1991–

Roman Brady: Drake Hogestyn 1986–91; Wayne Northrop 1981–84; 1991–94

Samantha Brady: Alison Sweeney 1992–; Christina Wagoner 1990–92; Tiffany Nicole Palma 1986; Jessica Davis 1985–86; Lauren Ann Bundy 1985; Ronit Aronoff 1984

Shawn Brady: Frank Parker 1983–84; 1985–89; 1990–; Frank MacLean 1989–90; Lew Brown 1984–85

Shawn Douglas Brady: Collin O'Donnell 1995–; Scott Groff 1990–95; Paul Zachary 1990; Noel Bennett Castle 1987

Molly Brinker: Shannon Sturges 1991–92

Byron Carmichael: Bill Hayes 1979

Rosie Carlson: Fran Ryan 1976–79

Gail Carson: Patrice Chanel 1989

Abe Carver: James Reynolds 1981–90; 1991–

Jonah Carver: Thyme Lewis 1993–; Bumper Robinson 1987–88

Lexie Brooks Carver: Renee Jones 1993–; Shellye Broughton 1993; Angelique Francis 1992; Angelique de Windt 1989–90; Sheila Wills 1989; Cindy James Gossett 1988–89

Theo Carver: Rusty Candieff 1985

Chief Richard Cates: Rod Arrants 1985–86

Brent Cavanaugh: Frank Ashmore 1981; Perry Bullington 1980–81

Celeste: Tanya Boyd 1994–

Kellam Chandler: Bill Joyce 1980–81

Sunny Chandler: Jody Gibson 1984; Sandy Elliott 1980

Tod Chandler: David Wallace 1985–86; Paul Keenan 1980–81; Brett Williams 1980

Jack Clayton: Jack Denbo 1974–77

Jeri Clayton: Kaye Stevens 1974–79

Philip Collier: Richard Burgi 1992; Doug Larson 1992

Johnny Collins: Paul Henry Itkins 1975–77

Diana Colville: Genie Francis 1987–89

Phillip Colville: Morgan Woodward 1987–88

Serena Colville: Valerie Karasek 1987–88

Johnny Corelli: Antony Alda 1990–91

Nick Corelli: George Jenesky 1981; 1984; 1986–90

Amelia Craig: Loretta Fury 1978–79

Don Craig: Jed Allan 1971–85

Don Craig, Jr. ("D.J."): Matthew Paul Bischof 1980

Donna Temple Craig: Tracey E. Bregman 1978–80

Gwen Davies: Ann-Marie Martin 1982–85

Anjelica Deveraux Curtis: Judith Chapman 1989–90; Shelley Taylor Morgan 1989; Jane Elliot 1987–89

Liz Chandler Curtis: Gloria Loring 1980–86

Nathan Curtis: Tom Brown 1975–76

Dr. Neil Curtis: Joe Gallison 1974–91; Ben Archibek 1973

Noel Curtis: Samantha Barrows 1984–86; 1988; Christina Maisano 1983

Pete Curtis: Meegan King 1978–79

Dave, the waiter: Don Frabotta 1973–93

Ginger Dawson: Roberta Leighton 1991–92

Abigail Johanna Deveraux: Paige & Ryanne Kettner 1994–; Meghan & Michael Nelson 1992–94

Harper Deveraux: Joseph Campanella 1987–88; 1990–92

Jack Deveraux: Mark Valley 1994–; Matthew Ashford 1987–93; James Acheson 1987; Joseph Adams 1987

Jennifer Rose Horton Deveraux: Melissa Brennan Reeves 1985–; Jennifer Petersen 1977–78; Maren Stephenson 1976–77

Anna Brady DiMera: Leann Hunley 1982–86

Count Anthony DiMera: Thaao Penghlis 1981–86; 1993–

Benjy DiMera: Darrell Utley 1988–89; 1990

Daphne DiMera: Madlyn Rhue 1982–84

Kristen Blake DiMera: Eileen Davidson 1993–

Stefano DiMera: Joseph Mascolo 1982–85; 1988; 1993–

Monty Dolan: Jay Robinson 1988–89

Andrew Donovan: Brian Davila 1991–92; Bradley Pierce 1990–91; Justin Page 1989–90; Skye Rumph 1989; Brian Amber 1988–89; Robert Elliot Cauko 1986–88

Eve Donovan: Charlotte Ross 1987–91

Jeannie Donovan: Gabriella Massari 1992; Caitlin Wachs 1992; Emily Luann & Alicia Nichole Pillatzke 1991–92; Hannah Taylor Simmons 1991

Kimberly Brady Donovan: Ariana Chase 1992–93; Anne Howard 1990; 1991; Patsy Pease 1984–90; 1990–92; 1991–92; 1994

Shane Donovan: Charles Shaughnessy 1984–92

Arthur Downey: John Calvin 1989–90

Rebecca Downey: Tracey Kolis 1989–90

Dragon: Lawrence Trimble 1985

Lee Dumonde: Brenda Benet 1979–82

Renee Dumonde: Philece Sampler 1980–84

Yvette Dupres: Lori Hallier 1989

Ellen: Pamela Brull 1988

Britta Englund: Amy Stock 1986

Lars Englund: Ken Jezek 1986–87

Samantha Evans: Andrea Hall Lovell 1977–80; 1982

Jessica Blake Fallon: Jean Bruce Scott 1980–82

Joshua Fallon: Scott Palmer 1981–82; Stephen Brooks 1980–81
Carlo Forenza: Don Diamont 1984–85
Gillian Forrester: Camilla More 1986–87
Grace Forrester: Camilla More 1987; Carey More 1987
Glenn Gallagher: Rob Estes 1986–87
Lisanne Gardner: Lynn Herring 1992
Danny Grant: Roger Aaron Brown 1981–85; Hazzan Shaheed 1976; Michael Dwight-Smith 1975–78
Helen Grant: Ketty Lester 1975–77
Paul Grant: Lawrence Cook 1975–76
Valerie Grant: Diane Sommerfield 1981–82; Rose Fonseca 1977–78; Tina Andrews 1975–77
Ian Griffith: Darby Hinton 1985–86; Harrison Douglas 1985
Brooke Hamilton: Eileen Barrett 1978–80; Adrienne LaRussa 1975–77
Adele Winston Hamilton: Dee Carroll 1975–76
Alan Harris: Paul Kersey 1993–
Maxwell Hathaway: Tom Hallick 1984
Megan Hathaway: Cheryl-Ann Wilson 1984–85
Howard Alston Hawkins: Ray Stricklyn 1991–92
Howard Alston "Hawk" Hawkins III: J. Eddie Peck 1991–92
Henderson: Ron Leath 1987–
Howie Hoffstedder: Stanley Brock 1983–86
Kate Honeycutt, R.N.: Elinor Donahue 1984–86
Alice Horton: Frances Reid 1965–
Dr. Bill Horton: Christopher Stone 1987–88; 1994; Edward Mallory 1966–80; 1991; 1992; Bill Carr 1965–66
Kitty Horton: Regina Gleason 1967–69
Dr. Laura Spencer Horton: Jamie Lynn Bauer 1993–; Rosemary Forsyth 1976–80; Susan Oliver 1975–76; Susan Flannery 1966–75; Floy Dean 1966
Maggie Simmons Horton: Suzanne Rogers 1974–84; 1985–
Margo Horton: Suzanne Zenor 1977–80
Marie Horton: Lanna Saunders 1979–85; Kate Woodville 1977; Maree Cheatham 1965–68; 1970–73; 1994
Dr. Michael Horton: Roark Critchlow 1994–; Michael T. Weiss 1985–90; Paul Coufos 1981–82; Wesley Eure 1974–81; Stuart Lee 1973; Dick DeCoit 1973; John Armour 1971–73; Alan Decker 1970–71; Bobby Eilbacher 1970; Eddie Rayden 1970; Brian Andrews 1970; Craig Bond 1969; Wade Holdsworth 1969; Kyle Puerner 1968–69

Mickey Horton: John Clarke 1965–
Sandy Horton: Pamela Roylance 1983–84; Martha Smith 1982; Heather North 1967–71; Astrid Warner 1967
Sarah Horton: Alli Brown 1991; Aimee Brooks 1990; Shauna Lane-Block 1989; Lisa Brinegar 1985–89; Katie Krell 1982; Anthony Seaward 1981–82; Colin Lewis 1981
Dr. Tom Horton: MacDonald Carey 1965–94
Dr. Tommy Horton: John Lupton 1967–72; 1975–79
Amanda Howard: Mary Frann 1974–79
Dianne Hunter: Jane Kean 1965–66
Dr. Marcus Hunter: Richard Biggs 1987–92
Eli Jacobs: S. Marc Jordon 1986–87; 1989
Jeremy Jacobs: Jeremy Allen 1989
Robin Jacobs: Derya Ruggles 1985–87; 1989
Leslie James: Dianne Harper 1980–81
Barney Jannings: Michael Dante 1984
Charlie Jannings: Tommy House 1985
Ivy Selejko Jannings: Holly Gagnier 1985–86
Melissa Anderson Jannings: Camilla Scott 1990–91; Lisa Trusel 1983–88; 1994; Debbie Lytton 1978–80; 1982; Kim Durso 1976; Joseph Trent Everett 1971
Pete Jannings: Michael Leon 1983–86
Tess Jannings: Melonie Mazman 1984
Maxwell Jarvis: Charles Bateman 1980–81
Jasmine: Jolina Collins 1984–85
Grace Jeffries: Sandra Canning 1989–90
Colonel Jericho: Steve Eastin 1989–90
Duke Johnson: James Luisi 1987; 1990–92
Earl Johnson: James Luisi 1989
Jo Johnson: Marilyn McIntyre 1993; Joy Garrett 1987–93
Kayla Brady Johnson: Mary Beth Evans 1986–92; Rhonda Aldrick 1989; Catherine Mary Stewart 1982–83
Marina Toscano Johnson: Hunter Tylo 1989
Stephanie Kay Johnson: Amanda and Jessica Gunnarson 1990–92
Stephen "Patch" Johnson: Stephen Nichols 1985–90
Mitch Kaufman: Philip Levien 1986
Dr. Veronica Kimball: Lenore Kasdorf 1983
Woody King: Lane Caudell 1982–83
Adrienne Johnson Kiriakis: Judi Evans 1986–91
Alexander Kiriakis: Jonathan Thornton 1989–91
Baby Victor Kiriakis: Candace Mead 1990; Jacob Iorio 1990
Joey Kiriakis: Loren Mead 1990; Benjamin Iorio 1990
Justin Kiriakis: Wally Kurth 1987–91
Victor Kiriakis: John Aniston 1985–
Amy Kositchek: Robin Pohle 1978–79

Chris Kositchek: Josh Taylor 1977–86; 1987
Jake Kositchek: Jack Coleman 1981–82 René Lamart 1981
Stanislaus Kositchek: Thomas Havens 1979
Dr. Chip Lakin: Jay Pickett 1991–92
Rebecca North LeClere: Brooke Bundy 1975–77
Dougie LeClere: Mikey Martin 1979–80
Robert LeClere: Robert Clary 1972–73; 1975–80; 1981–83; 1986
Gretchen Lindquist: Bonnie Burroughs 1991
Jesse Lombard: Tony Rhodes 1992
Roger Lombard: Mark Drexler 1992
Stella Lombard: Elaine Bromka 1992
Maid Janet: Dale Kristien 1985–86
Dr. Carly Manning (Katerina Von Leuschner): Crystal Chappell 1990–93
Ivan Marais: Ivan G'Vera 1991–
David Martin: Clive Clerk 1966–67; Steve Mines 1966
Helen Martin: K.T. Stevens 1966–67; 1969
John Martin: Robert Brubaker 1966–71; Ed Prentiss 1966
Oliver Martin: Shawn Stevens 1982–83
Susan Hunter Martin: Bennye Gatteys 1973–76; Denise Alexander 1966–73
Alex Marshall: Quinn Redeker 1979–87
Emma Donovan Marshall: Jane Windsor 1985–87
Marty, the piano player: Marty Davich 1979–93
Taylor McCall: J. Cynthia Brooks 1992–93
Craig Merritt: Craig McLean 1965–67; Harry Lauter 1966
Tony Merritt: Ron Husmann 1966–67; Don Briscoe 1966; Richard Colla 1965–66
Rebecca Morrison: Dani Minnick 1992–93
Nico: Lorenzo Caccialanza 1988–91
Glynnis O'Connor: Felecia Bell 1990–91
Olivia: Amy Yasbeck 1986–87
Ben Olson: Robert Knapp 1965
Steve Olson: Stephen Schnetzer 1978–80; James Carroll Jordan 1972; Flip Mark 1965
Orion: Sandy McPeak 1988
Orpheus: George Deloy 1986–87
Diane Parker: DeAnna Robins 1984; Cindy Fisher 1984; Dana Kimmel 1983–84
Kelly Parker: Kim Morgan Greene 1990
Gabrielle Pascal: Karen Moncrieff 1987–88
Lavinia Peach: Pamela Kosh 1986–91; Diana Webster 1985–86
Peggy: Peggy Reyna 1989; 1990
Little Anne Peters: Elizabeth Hoy 1975–76; Lisa Lynch 1974; Andreana Marie Chutuk 1972–73
Mrs. Anne Peters: Jeanne Bates 1972–75

Eric Peters: Stanley Kamel 1972–76; John Lombardo 1971
Dr. Greg Peters: Peter Brown 1972–79
Jim Phillips: Victor Holchak 1971; 1974–75
Jimmy Potterfield: Ron Kuhlman 1984–85
April Ramirez: Lisa Howard 1988–91
Emilio Ramirez: Billy Hufsey 1988–90
Julio Ramirez: Michael Bays 1988–89
Rosa Ramirez: Silvana Gallardo 1988
Benjamin Reardon: Ashaneese & Nasharin Holderness 1994–
Wendy Reardon: Tammy Townsend 1994–; Lark Voorhies 1993–94
Austin Reed: Austin Peck 1995–; Patrick Muldoon 1993–95
Billie Holiday Reed: Lisa Rinna 1993–
Curtis Reed: Nick Benedict 1993
Ethan Reilly: Joe Colligan 1987–88
Kate Roberts: Deborah Adair 1993–95
Lucas Roberts: Bryan Dattilo 1993–
Sasha Roberts: Yvette Napier 1987; Danielle Brisebois 1987; Julie Jeter 1986
Porter Rollins: Anthony Peck 1990
Dan Ryan: David Ruprecht 1990–92
Sheila Salsbury: Kim Morgan Greene 1990
Brian Scofield: Robert Mailhouse 1990–92
Cassie Scofield: Melissa Baum 1990–91
Tanner Scofield: Michael Easton 1990–92
Vern Scofield: Wayne Heffley 1988–93
Adam Scott: Randy Reinholz 1989
Snake Selejko: Bernie White 1983
Speed Selejko: Tom Everett 1985; Robert Romanus 1983–85
Simmons: Gerry Gibson 1986–92
Danielle Stevens: Deborah Moore 1991–92
Barbara Stewart: Betsy Burr 1986–87
Paul Stewart: Robert S. Woods 1986–87; Gregory Mortensen 1986
Chief Tarrington: Ron Barker 1988–92
Faith Taylor: Mindy Clarke 1989–90
Rev. Saul Taylor: James Hampton 1989
Lorraine Temple: Francine York 1978
Fernando Torres: Dan Zubovic 1991–92
Jose Torres: Scott Colomby 1988
Miguel Torres: Al Ruscio 1988
Rafi Torres: David Ciminello 1991–92
Ernesto Toscano: Eric Mason 1990; Charles Cioffi 1990; Terrance Beasor 1989
Isabella Beatrice Toscano: Staci Greason 1989–92
Loretta Toscano: Katherine Bates 1990
Trent: Charles Van Eman 1988
Nikki Wade: Renee Jones 1982–83
Chad Webster: Kirk Geiger 1990
Larry Welch: Andrew Masset 1983–85
Dr. Evan Whyland: Lane Davies 1981–82

Stuart Whyland: Robert Alda 1981

Savannah Wilder: Shannon Tweed 1985–86

Addie Horton Olson Williams: Patricia Barry 1971–74; Pat Houston 1965–66

Doug Williams: Bill Hayes 1970–84; 1986–87; 1993; 1994

Julie Olson Banning Anderson Williams: Susan Seaforth Hayes 1968–84; 1990–93; 1994;

Cathy Ferrar 1967–68; Catherine Dunn 1967; Charla Doherty 1965–66

Kim Williams: Helen Funai 1971–72; 1976–77

Cal Winters: Joseph Bottoms 1991; Wortham Krimmer 1989–90

Stephanie Woodruff: Eileen Barrett 1978–80

EMMY NOMINEES AND WINNERS

(† *denotes winner*)

LIFETIME ACHIEVEMENT AWARD FOR DAYTIME TELEVISION
†1994/95   Ted and Betty Corday

OUTSTANDING DAYTIME DRAMA SERIES
1994/95   *Days of Our Lives*. Ken Corday, Executive Producer; Tom Langan, Co-Executive Producer; Stephen Wyman, Supervising Producer; Jeanne Haney, Sr. Coordinating Producer; Janet Spellman Rider, Coordinating Producer.

1984/85   *Days of Our Lives*. Al Rabin, Betty Corday, Executive Producers; Ken Corday, Shelley Curtis, Producers.

1983/84   *Days of Our Lives*. Mrs. Ted Corday, Executive Producer; Al Rabin, Supervising Executive Producer; Ken Corday, Shelley Curtis, Producers.

1982/83   *Days of Our Lives*. Mrs. Ted Corday, Executive Producer; Al Rabin, Supervising Executive Producer; Patricia Wenig, Supervising Producer; Ken Corday, Producer.

1978/79   *Days of Our Lives*. Betty Corday, H. Wesley Kenney, Executive Producers; Jack Herzberg, Producer.

†1977/78   *Days of Our Lives*. Betty Corday and H. Wesley Kenney, Executive Producers; Jack Herzberg, Producer.

1976/77   *Days of Our Lives*. Mrs. Ted Corday, Executive Producer; H. Wesley Kenney and Jack Herzberg, Producers.

1975/76   *Days of Our Lives*. Mrs. Ted Corday, Executive Producer; Jack Herzberg and Al Rabin, Producers.

1974/75   *Days of Our Lives*. Mrs. Ted Corday, Executive Producer; Ted Corday, Irna Phillips and Allan Chase, Creators; Jack Herzberg, Producer.

1973/74   *Days of Our Lives*. Betty Corday, Executive Producer; Ted Corday, Irna Phillips, and Allan Chase, Creators; H. Wesley Kenney, Producer.

OUTSTANDING LEAD ACTOR IN A DRAMA SERIES
1987/88   Stephen Nichols as *Steven (Patch) Johnson*

OUTSTANDING ACTOR IN A DRAMA SERIES

1978/79	Jed Allan (*Don Craig*)
1978/79	John Clarke (*Mickey Horton*)
1975/76	Macdonald Carey (*Dr. Tom Horton*)
1975/76	Bill Hayes (*Doug Williams*)
†1974/75	Macdonald Carey (*Dr. Tom Horton*)
1974/75	Bill Hayes (*Doug Williams*)

BEST ACTOR IN DAYTIME DRAMA

†1973/74	Macdonald Carey (*Dr. Tom Horton*)

OUTSTANDING LEAD ACTRESS IN A DRAMA SERIES

1986/87	Frances Reid as *Alice Horton*
1985/86	Peggy McCay as *Caroline Brady*

OUTSTANDING ACTRESS IN A DRAMA SERIES

1984/85	Deidre Hall (*Dr. Marlena Evans Brady*)
1983/84	Deidre Hall (*Dr. Marlena Evans*)
1978/79	Susan Seaforth Hayes (*Julie Williams*)
1977/78	Susan Seaforth Hayes (*Julie Williams*)
1975/76	Susan Seaforth Hayes (*Julie Olson*)
†1974/75	Susan Flannery (*Dr. Laura Horton*)
1974/75	Susan Seaforth (*Julie Olson*)

OUTSTANDING SUPPORTING ACTOR IN A DRAMA SERIES

1988/89	Joseph Campanella as *Harper Deveraux*
1978/79	Joe Gallison (*Dr. Neil Curtis*)

OUTSTANDING SUPPORTING ACTRESS IN A DRAMA SERIES

1988/89	Arleen Sorkin as *Calliope Bradford*
1988/89	Jane Elliot as *Anjelica Curtis*
1987/88	Arleen Sorkin as *Calliope Jones Bradford*
1986/87	Peggy McCay as *Caroline Brady*
†1985/86	Leann Hunley as *Anna DiMera*
1979/80	Deidre Hall (*Dr. Marlena Evans*)
†1978/79	Suzanne Rogers (*Maggie Horton*)
1978/79	Frances Reid (*Alice Horton*)

OUTSTANDING JUVENILE MALE IN A DRAMA SERIES

1988/89	Darrell Utley as *Benjy*

OUTSTANDING YOUNGER LEADING MAN IN A DRAMA SERIES

†1987/88	Billy Warlock as *Frankie Brady*
1986/87	Billy Warlock as *Frankie Brady*

OUTSTANDING YOUNGER ACTRESS IN A DRAMA SERIES

1991/92	Melissa Reeves as *Jennifer Horton Deveraux*
1990/91	Charlotte Ross as *Eve Donovan*

OUTSTANDING JUVENILE FEMALE IN A DRAMA SERIES

1989/90	Charlotte Ross as *Eve Donovan*

OUTSTANDING INGENUE/WOMAN IN A DRAMA SERIES

1984/85	Kristian Alfonso (*Hope Williams*)
1984/85	Lisa Trusel (*Melissa Anderson*)

OUTSTANDING GUEST/CAMEO APPEARANCE IN A DRAMA SERIES

†1979/80   Hugh McPhillips (*Hugh Pearson*)

OUTSTANDING DRAMA SERIES DIRECTING TEAM

1992/93   Susan Orlikoff Simon, Director; Stephen Wyman, Director; Herb Stein, Director; Sheryl Harmon, Associate Director; Roger W. Inman, Associate Director.

OUTSTANDING DRAMA SERIES DIRECTING TEAM (ASSOCIATE DIRECTORS)

1987/88   Joe Behar, Susan Orlikoff Simon, Herb Stein, Stephen Wyman, Directors; Becky Greenlaw, Gay Linvill, Sheryl Harmon, Associate Directors.

1986/87   Joseph Behar, Susan Orlikoff, Herb Stein, Stephen Wyman, Directors; Becky Greenlaw, Gay Linvill, Sheryl Harmon, Associate Directors.

1985/86   Susan Orlikoff Simon, Joseph Behar, Herb Stein, Stephen Wyman, Directors; Gay Linvill, Sheryl Harmon, Becky Greenlaw, Associate Directors.

OUTSTANDING DIRECTING IN A DRAMA SERIES (ASSOCIATE DIRECTORS)

1984/85   Al Rabin, Joseph Behar, Susan Orlikoff Simon, Stephen Wyman, Herb Stein, Directors; Gay Linvill, Sheryl Harmon, Becky Greenlaw, Associate Directors.

OUTSTANDING DIRECTING IN A DRAMA SERIES

1978/79   Al Rabin, Joe Behar, Frank Pacelli

OUTSTANDING INDIVIDUAL DIRECTOR FOR A DRAMA SERIES OR SINGLE EPISODE

1977/78   Al Rabin; February 21, 1978
1976/77   Al Rabin; Julie and Doug's Wedding
1976/77   Joseph Behar
1974/75   Joseph Behar; November 20, 1974.

BEST INDIVIDUAL DIRECTOR FOR A DRAMA SERIES

†1973/74   H. Wesley Kenney

OUTSTANDING DRAMA SERIES WRITING TEAM

1993/94   James E. Reilly, Headwriter; Maura Penders, Associate Headwriter; Dena Higley, Associate Headwriter; Ethel M. Brez, Associate Headwriter; Mel Brez, Associate Headwriter; Marlene Clark Poulter, Associate Headwriter; Dorothy Ann Purser, Associate Headwriter; Fran Myers, Dialogue Writer; Maralyn Thoma, Dialogue Writer; Peggy Schibi, Dialogue Writer; Michelle Poteet Lisanti, Dialogue Writer.

1986/87   Leah Laiman, Sheri Anderson, Thom Racina, Headwriters; Anne M. Schoettle, Dena Breshears, Richard J. Allen, Associate Head Writers; M.M. Shelley Moore, Penina Spiegel, Associate Writers.

OUTSTANDING WRITING IN A DRAMA SERIES HEAD WRITERS(S), BREAKDOWN WRITER(S), ASSOCIATE WRITER(S)

1984/85   Sheri Anderson, Headwriter; Leah Laiman, Margaret De Priest, Maralyn Thoma, Dana Soloff, Anne Schoettle, Michael Robert David, Leah Markus, Thom Racina.

OUTSTANDING WRITING IN A DRAMA SERIES

1983/84   Margaret De Priest, Sheri Anderson, Maralyn Thoma, Michael Robert
            David, Susan Goldberg, Bob Hansen, Leah Markus, Dana Soloff.

1978/79   Ann Marcus, Michael Robert David, Raymond E. Goldstone, Joyce Perry,
            Elizabeth Harrower, Rocci Chatfield, Laura Olsher.

1977/78   William J. Bell, Kay Lenard, Bill Rega, Pat Falken Smith, Margaret Stew-
            art

1977/78   Ann Marcus, Ray Goldstone, Joyce Perry, Michael Robert David, Laura
            Olsher, Rocci Chatfield, Elizabeth Harrower.

1976/77   William J. Bell, Pat Falken Smith, William Rega, Kay Lenard, Margaret
            Stewart.

†1975/76   William J. Bell, Kay Lenard, Pat Falken Smith, Bill Rega, Margaret
            Stewart, Sheri Anderson and Wanda Coleman; Series.

1974/75   William J. Bell, Pat Falken Smith and Bill Rega; November 21, 1974.

OUTSTANDING ORIGINAL SONG

1993/94   Song: "Don't Make Me Too Young." Ken Corday, Composer; Tom Langan,
            Lyricist/Composer.

OUTSTANDING MUSIC DIRECTION AND COMPOSITION FOR A DRAMA SERIES

1994/95   Amy Burkhard, Music Director; Stephen Reinhardt, Music Director; Ken
            Heller, Composer; Ken Corday, Composer; Cory Lerios, Composer; John
            D'Andrea, Composer; Dominic Messinger, Composer; D. Brent Nelson,
            Composer.

OUTSTANDING ACHIEVEMENT IN MUSIC DIRECTION AND COMPOSITION FOR A DRAMA SERIES

1993/94   Stephen Reinhardt, Music Director; Amy Burkhard, Music Director/Com-
            poser; David Leon, Music Supervisor; Ken Corday, Composer; D. Brent
            Nelson, Composer; Marty Davich, Composer; Cory Lerios, Composer;
            John D'Andrea, Composer; Ken Heller, Composer; Dominic Messinger,
            Composer.

†1989/90   Marty Davich, Music Director/Composer; Amy Burkhard, Music Supervi-
            sor; Ken Corday, Composer.

1988/89   Marty Davich, Music Director/Composer; Ken Corday, Composer; Amy
            Burkhard, Music Supervisor.

OUTSTANDING ACHIEVEMENT IN COSTUME DESIGN FOR A DRAMA SERIES

1989/90   Lee Smith, Costume Designer
†1987/88   Lee H. Smith
1986/87   Lee H. Smith
1985/86   Lee H. Smith

OUTSTANDING MAKEUP FOR A DRAMA SERIES

1994/95   John Damiani, Makeup Artist; Gail J. Hopkins, Makeup Artist; Nina
            Wells, Makeup Artist; Lucia Bianca, Makeup Artist.

OUTSTANDING ACHIEVEMENT IN MAKEUP FOR A DRAMA SERIES

1992/93   Carol Brown, Head Makeup Artist; Keith Crary, Makeup Artist; Lucia
            Bianca, Makeup Artist; Gail Hopkins, Makeup Artist; Nina Wells,
            Makeup Artist; Robert Sloan, Makeup Artist.

†1991/92   Carol Brown, Head Makeup Artist; Keith Crary, Gail Hopkins, Lucia
            Bianca, Robert Sloan, Makeup Artists.

†1990/91   Carol Brown, Head Makeup Artist; Keith Crary, Robert Sloan, Gail Hopkins, Lucia Bianca, Makeup Artists.

1989/90   Carol Brown, Head Makeup Artist; Keith Crary, Gail Hopkins, Robert Sloan, Lucia Bianca, Makeup Artists.

1988/89   Carol Brown, Head Makeup Artist; Keith Crary, Robert Sloan, Gail Hopkins, Lucia Bianca, Makeup Artists.

†1987/88   Carol Brown, Head Makeup Artist; Keith Crary, Robert Sloan, Gail Hopkins, Lucia Bianca, Makeup Artists.

1985/86   Carol Brown, Makeup Supervisor; Keith Crary, Robert Sloan, Gail Hopkins.

OUTSTANDING HAIRSTYLING FOR A DRAMA SERIES
†1994/95   Zora Sloan, Head Hairstylist; Terrie Velazquez, Hairstylist.

OUTSTANDING ACHIEVEMENT IN HAIRSTYLING FOR A DRAMA SERIES
1992/93   Zora Sloan, Head Hairstylist; Janet Medford, Hairstylist; Michelle Jennings, Hairstylist.

1991/92   Zora Sloan, Head Hairstylist; Sandra Rubin, Michele Jennings, Hairstylists.

1990/91   Zora M. Sloan, Head Hairstylist; Diane Shinneman, Voni Hinkle, Hairstylists.

†1987/88   Zora Sloan, Pauletta Lewis

1985/86   Zora Sloan

OUTSTANDING ACHIEVEMENT IN GRAPHICS AND TITLE DESIGN
1993/94   Wayne Fitzgerald, Title Designer; Judy Loren, Title Designer.

OUTSTANDING TECHNICAL DIRECTION AND ELECTRONIC CAMERAWORK — DAYTIME
1973/74   Gordon C. James, Technical Director; George Simpson, George Meyer, and John Kullman, Cameramen; July 20, 1973.

OUTSTANDING ACHIEVEMENT IN LIGHTING DIRECTION FOR A DRAMA SERIES
1988/89   Jeff Barr, John Nance, Lighting Directors

1987/88   John Nance, Art Busch, Carl Pitsch

OUTSTANDING LIGHTING DIRECTION — DAYTIME
1973/74   Alan E. Scarlett; July 20, 1973

OUTSTANDING ACHIEVEMENT IN LIVE AND TAPE SOUND MIXING AND SOUND EFFECTS FOR A DRAMA SERIES
1986/87   Frank Jackson, Davey Cone, John Machea, Production Mixers; Bob Mott, Sound Effects Mixer.

1985/86   Tom Ruston, Frank Jackson, Dave A. Cone, Production Mixers; Bob Mott, Sound Effects Technician.

OUTSTANDING SOUND MIXING — DAYTIME
†1973/74   Ernest Dellutri; July 20, 1973.

ACHIEVEMENT IN DESIGN EXCELLENCE FOR A DRAMA SERIES
1978/79   *Days of Our Lives*, Design Team

PROGRAM ACHIEVEMENT IN DAYTIME DRAMA
1972/73   *Day of Our Lives*. Betty Corday, Executive Producer; H. Wesley Kenney, Producer.

OUTSTANDING ACHIEVEMENT BY INDIVIDUALS IN DAYTIME DRAMA
1972/73   Macdonald Carey, Performer, Series
1972/73   H. Wesley Kenney, Director, March 6, 1973

OUTSTANDING ACHIEVEMENT IN DAYTIME PROGRAMMING — INDIVIDUAL
1967/68   Macdonald Carey as *Dr. Tom Horton*

SOAP OPERA AWARD WINNERS

(The First Annual Soap Opera Awards Show was broadcast in 1984. Prior to that the awards were broadcast intermittently, and the awards were referred to as "Soapys." See page 218.)

OUTSTANDING DAYTIME SHOW

1993/94	*Days of Our Lives*
1992/93	*Days of Our Lives*
1991/92	*Days of Our Lives*
1990/91	*Days of Our Lives*
1989/90	*Days of Our Lives*
1987/88	*Days of Our Lives*
1986/87	*Days of Our Lives*
1985/86	*Days of Our Lives*
1984/85	*Days of Our Lives*
1983/84	*Days of Our Lives*

BEST LOVE STORY

1990/91	*Jack and Jennifer* (Matthew Ashford and Melissa Brennan Reeves)

BEST WEDDING

1990/91	*Jack and Jennifer* (Matthew Ashford and Melissa Brennan Reeves)

HOTTEST FEMALE STAR

1992/93	Melissa Reeves (*Jennifer Deveraux*)
1991/92	Crystal Chappell (*Carly Manning*)

HOTTEST MALE STAR

1993/94	Drake Hogestyn (*John Black*)
1992/93	Drake Hogestyn (*John Black*)

HOTTEST SOAP COUPLE

1993/94	Robert Kelker-Kelly and Lisa Rinna (*Bo Brady and Billie Reed*)

OUTSTANDING ACTOR — DAYTIME
1992/93	Robert Kelker-Kelly (*Bo Brady*)
1986/87	Stephen Nichols (*Stephen "Patch" Johnson*)
1985/86	John Aniston (*Victor Kiriakis*)
1984/85	Peter Reckell (*Bo Brady*)
1983/84	Peter Reckell (*Bo Brady*)

OUTSTANDING ACTRESS — DAYTIME
1993/94	Deidre Hall (*Marlena Evans*)
1985/86	Patsy Pease (*Kimberly Brady Donovan*)
1984/85	Deidre Hall (*Dr. Marlena Evans*)
1983/84	Deidre Hall (*Dr. Marlena Evans*)

OUTSTANDING SUPPORTING ACTOR — DAYTIME
1991/92	Richard Biggs (*Marcus Hunter*)
1985/86	Stephen Nichols (*Stephen "Patch" Johnson*)
1984/85	John De Lancie (*Eugene Bradford*)
1983/84	John De Lancie (*Eugene Bradford*)

OUTSTANDING SUPPORTING ACTRESS — DAYTIME
1992/93	Deborah Adair (*Kate Roberts Kiriakis*)
1987/88	Joy Garrett (*Jo Johnson*)
1984/85	Arleen Sorkin (*Calliope Bradford*)
1983/84	Lisa Trusel (*Melissa Anderson*)

OUTSTANDING ACTOR IN A MATURE ROLE — DAYTIME
1984/85	Macdonald Carey (*Dr. Tom Horton*)
1983/84	Macdonald Carey (*Dr. Tom Horton*)

OUTSTANDING ACTRESS IN A MATURE ROLE — DAYTIME
1984/85	Frances Reid (*Alice Horton*)
1983/84	Frances Reid (*Alice Horton*)

OUTSTANDING YOUTH ACTOR — DAYTIME
1984/85	Brian Autenreith (*Zach Parker*)

OUTSTANDING YOUTH ACTRESS — DAYTIME
1984/85	Andrea Barber (*Carrie Brady*)
1983/84	Andrea Barber (*Carrie Brady*)

OUTSTANDING YOUNG LEADING MAN — DAYTIME
1985/86	Peter Reckell (*Bo Brady*)

OUTSTANDING CHILD ACTOR
1992/93	Scott Groff (*Shawn-Douglas Brady*)

OUTSTANDING NEW ACTOR — DAYTIME
1984/85	Charles Shaughnessy (*Shane Donovan*)
1983/84	Michael Leon (*Pete Jannings*)

OUTSTANDING NEW ACTRESS — DAYTIME
1984/85	Arleen Sorkin (*Calliope Bradford*)
1983/84	Kristian Alfonso (*Hope Williams*)

OUTSTANDING SUPER COUPLE — DAYTIME
1989/90	Melissa Brennan Reeves (*Jennifer Horton*) and Matthew Ashford (*Jack Deveraux*)

1987/88	Mary Beth Evans (*Kayla Brady Johnson*) and Stephen Nichols (*Stephen "Patch" Johnson*)
1985/86	Patsy Pease (*Kimberly Brady Donovan*) and Charles Shaughnessy (*Shane Donovan*)
1983/84	Kristian Alfonso (*Hope Brady*) and Peter Reckell (*Bo Brady*)

OUTSTANDING HERO — DAYTIME
| 1987/88 | Stephen Nichols (*Stephen "Patch" Johnson*) |

OUTSTANDING VILLAIN — DAYTIME
1993/94	Jason Brooks (*Peter Blake*)
1987/88	Matthew Ashford (*Jack Deveraux*)
1985/86	John Aniston (*Victor Kiriakis*)
1984/85	Joseph Mascolo (*Stefano DiMera*)
1983/84	Joseph Mascolo (*Stefano DiMera*)

OUTSTANDING VILLAINESS
| 1988/89 | Jane Elliot (*Anjelica Deveraux Curtis*) |
| 1984/85 | Cheryl Ann Wilson (*Megan Hathaway*) |

OUTSTANDING VILLAIN/VILLAINESS
| 1992/93 | Louise Sorel (*Vivian Alamain*) |

OUTSTANDING COMIC PERFORMANCE, MALE — DAYTIME
1991/92	Matthew Ashford (*Jack Deveraux*)
1990/91	Robert Mailhouse (*Brian Scofield*)
1986/87	Michael T. Weiss (*Dr. Michael Horton*)

OUTSTANDING COMIC PERFORMANCE, FEMALE — DAYTIME
| 1986/87 | Arleen Sorkin (*Calliope Bradford*) |
| 1985/86 | Arleen Sorkin (*Calliope Bradford*) |

OUTSTANDING MALE NEWCOMER
| 1992/93 | Patrick Muldoon (*Austin Reed*) |

OUTSTANDING FEMALE NEWCOMER
| 1992/93 | Lisa Rinna (*Billie Reed*) |

OUTSTANDING CONTRIBUTION BY AN ACTOR/ACTRESS TO THE FORM OF CONTINUING DRAMA WHO IS CURRENTLY ON A DAYTIME SERIAL
| 1985/86 | Deidre Hall (*Dr. Marlena Brady*) |

OUTSTANDING FEMALE SCENE STEALER
| 1993/94 | Louise Sorel (*Vivian Alamain*) |

FAVORITE SONG
| 1991/92 | "One Dream" |

OUTSTANDING MUSICAL ACHIEVEMENT
| 1992/93 | *Days of Our Lives* |

FAVORITE STORYLINE
| 1992/93 | "Who Fathered Marlena's Baby?" |

EDITORS' AWARD FOR THEIR OUTSTANDING
CONTRIBUTION TO THE MEDIUM
1988/89   Frances Reid (*Alice Horton*) and Macdonald Carey (*Dr. Tom Horton*)

SOAPY WINNERS

FAVORITE SOAP OPERA
1979   *Days of Our Lives*
1978   *Days of Our Lives*
1977   *Days of Our Lives*

FAVORITE ACTOR
1979   Jed Allen (*Don Craig*)
1978   Jed Allen (*Don Craig*)
1977   Bill Hayes (*Doug Williams*)

FAVORITE ACTRESS
1983   Deidre Hall (*Marlena Evans Brady*)
1982   Deidre Hall (*Marlena Evans*)
1977   Susan Hayes (*Julie Williams*)

FAVORITE NEWCOMERS
1979   Tracey Bregman (*Donna Temple*)
1978   Josh Taylor (*Chris Kositchek*)
1978   Andrea Hall-Lovell (*Samantha Evans*)

FAVORITE MATURE ACTOR
1979   Macdonald Carey (*Tom Horton*)
1978   Macdonald Carey (*Tom Horton*)

FAVORITE MATURE ACTRESS
1979   Frances Reid (*Alice Horton*)
1978   Frances Reid (*Alice Horton*)

FAVORITE VILLAIN
1983   Quinn Redeker (*Alex Marshall*)

BIBLIOGRAPHY

Books

Adams, Maryjo. "An American Soap Opera: As the World Turns 1956-1978." Ph.D. dissertation, University of Michigan, 1980.

Alfaro Moreno, Rosa Maria. *De la conquista a la Apropiacion de la Palabra*. Lima: Tarea, 1987.

Allen, Robert C. *Speaking of Soap Operas*. Chapel Hill: University of North Carolina Press, 1985.

Almeida, Dalmer Pacheco de. *Telenovela*. Brasil: Editora da Universidade Federal do Rio de Janeiro, 1987.

Angel, Velma. *Those Sensational Soaps: How Soap Operas Affect You Emotionally, Physically, Spiritually*. Brea, Calif.: Uplift Books, 1983.

Babrow, Austin Scott. "Extending and Refining an Expectancy-Value Theory of Media Gratifications: Two Studies in the Domain of Soap Opera Watching." Ph.D. dissertation, University of Illinois at Urbana-Champaign, 1986.

Biella, Peter. *The Logic of Irony: An Analysis of Mary Hartman*. Philadelphia, Pa.: Dept. of Anthropology, Temple University, 1978.

Biracree, Tom. *Soap Opera Mania: Love, Lust, and Lies from Your Favorite Daytime Dramas*. New York: Prentice Hall General Reference, 1994.

Bond, Mitzi Dale. "Soap Operas and Liberal Education Values." Ed.D. dissertation, University of North Carolina at Greensboro, 1980.

Bonderoff, Jason. *Daytime TV 1977*. New York: Manor, 1976.

____. *Soap Opera Babylon*. New York: Perigee Books, 1987.

Breen, M.P. and J.T. Powell. *Why College Students Watch Soap Operas*. Paper presented at the annual meeting of the Broadcast Education Association, Las Vegas, 1980. ERIC, ED 185627.

Brooks, Tim and Earle Marsh. *The Complete Directory to Prime Time Network Television Shows 1946 to Present*. New York: Ballantine, 1979. Revised and enlarged 1981, 1985.

Brown, Les. *Les Brown's Encyclopedia of Television*. New York: New York Zoetrope, 1982.

Brown, Mary Ellen. *Soap Opera and Women's Talk: The Pleasure of Resistance*. Thousand Oaks, Calif.: Sage Publications, 1994.

Buckman, Peter. *All for Love: A Study in Soap Opera*. Salem, N.H.: Salem House, 1985.

____. *All for Love: A Study in Soap Opera*. London: Secker & Warburg, 1984.

Cambridge, Vibert Compton. "Mass Media Entertainment and Human Resources Development: Radio Serials in Jamaica from 1962." Ph.D. dissertation, Ohio University, 1989.

Cantor, Muriel, and Suzanne Pingree. *The Soap Opera*. Beverly Hills, Calif.: Sage Publications, 1983.

Carey, Macdonald. *Beyond That Further Hill*. Columbia, S.C.: Univ. of South Carolina Press, 1989.

____. *A Day In the Life*. New York, N.Y.: Coward, McCann & Geoghegan, 1982.

____. *That Further Hill*. Los Angeles: Bombshelter Press, 1987.

Cassata, Mary, and Thomas Skill, eds. *Life on Daytime Television: Tuning-in American Serial Drama*. Norwood, N.J.: Ablex, 1983.

Colbert, Bath Lynn. "Assessing Soap Opera Value Themes." M.S. thesis, San Jose State University, 1989.

Cole, Barry G., ed. *Television*. 4th ed. New York: Free Press, 1973.

Compesi, Ronald J. "Gratifications of Daytime Television Serial Viewers: An Analysis of Fans of the Program 'All My Children.' Ph.D. dissertation, University of Oregon, 1976.

Compte, Carmen Emily. "Using Soap Opera Structure for Aural French Comprehension." Ph.D. dissertation, New York University, 1985.

Comstock, G., S. Chaffee, N. Katzman, M. McCombs and D. Roberts. *Television and Human Behavior*. New York: Columbia University Press, 1978.

Days of Our Lives Celebrates 25 Years of Romance. Fort Lee, New Jersey: Soap Opera Update Magazine, 1990.

Days of Our Lives Celebrity Cookbook. Sherman Oaks, Calif.: G. Loring, 1981.

"Days of Our Lives scripts, 1965-1988." TMs. Theater Arts Library, University of California, Los Angeles.

Denis, Paul, ed. *Daytime TV's Star Directory*. New York: Popular Library, 1976.

____. *Inside the Soaps*. Secaucus, N.J.: Citadel Press, 1985.

Dent, Karen. *The Soaps: Scene Stealing Scenes for Actors*. Colorado Springs, Colo.: Meriwether, 1989.

Downing, Mildred Harlow. "The World of Daytime Television Serial Drama." Ph.D. dissertation, University of Pennsylvania, 1974.

Edmondson, Madeleine and David Rounds. *From Mary Noble to Mary Hartman: The Complete Soap Opera Book*. New York: Stein & Day, 1976.

____. *The Soaps: Daytime Serials of Radio and TV*. New York: Stein and Day, 1973.

Elliott, Joyce Charlotte. "Images of Older Adult Characters on Daytime Television Serial Drama." Ed.D. dissertation, Columbia University Teachers College, 1981.

Emmy Awards Directory. North Hollywood: Academy of Television Arts and Sciences, 1975.

Examen del Genero Telenovela. Caracas: Despacho de la Ministro de Estado para la Participacion de la Mujer en el Desarrollo, 1983.

Falk, Irving A. "An Analysis of the Radio Network Daytime Serial Drama 'Vic and Sade' from 1932 to 1942 as Representative of Mid-Western American Humor." Ph.D. dissertation, New York University, 1971.

Fernandes, Ismael. *Memoria da Telenovela Brasileira*. Sao Paulo: Proposta Editorial, 1982.

____. *Memoria da Telenovela Brasileira*. Sao Paulo: Editora Brasiiense, 1987.

Fine, Marlene Gail. "A Conversation and Content Analysis of Interpersonal Relationships in Selected Television Soap Operas." Ph.D. dissertation, University of Massachusetts, 1980.

Frentz, Suzanne, ed. *Staying Tuned: Contemporary Soap Opera Criticism*. Bowling Green, Ohio: Bowling Green State University Popular Press, 1992.

Friends & Lovers: Both to Each Other: From the NBC TV Series The Days of Our Lives. Words and music by Paul Gordon and Jay Gruska, Gloria Loring & Carl Anderson. Secaucus, N.J.: Warner Brothers Publications, 1986.

Garaycochea, Oscar. *Narracion Audiovisual en Venezuela, (1973-1983)*. Caracas, Venezuela: Fondo de Fomento Cinematografico, 1986.

Geraghty, Christine. *Women and Soap Opera: A Study of Prime Time Soaps*. Cambridge: Polity, 1991.

Gilbert, Annie. *All My Afternoons: The Heart and Soul of the TV Soap Opera*. New York: A & W Publishers, 1979.

Goldsen, Rose. *The Show and Tell Machine: How Television Works and Works You Over*. New York: Dial, 1977.

Greenberg, Bradley S. *Life on Television*. Norwood, N.J.: Ablex, 1982.

Gross, Edward. *Dark Shadows: A 20th Anniversary Tribute: the Dark Shadows Files*. San Bernardino, Calif.: Borgo Press, 1987, c. 1986.

Groves, Seli. *Soaps: A Pictorial History of America's Daytime Dramas*. Chicago: Contemporary Books, 1983.

Hearts Past Reason. Days of Our Lives, vol. 2. Rocky Hill, Conn.: Pioneer Communications Network, 1986.

Heffley, Wayne. *Television As a Career*. New York: Macfadden-Bartell, 1964.

Higby, Mary Jane. *Tune in Tomorrow; or How I Found the Right to Happiness with Our Gal Sunday, Stella Dallas, John's Other Wife, and Other Sudsy Radio Serials*. New York: Cowles, 1968.

Hobson, Dorothy. *Crossroads: The Drama of a Soap Opera*. London: Methuen, 1982.

Inside the Soaps. Secaucus, N.J.: Citadel, 1985.

Intintoli, Michael James. "Soap Opera Production: An Ethnographic Case Study." Ph.D. dissertation, Temple University, 1983.

James, Cathy L. "Soap Opera Mythology & Racial-Ethnic Social Change: An Analysis of African American, Asian/Pacific, & Mexican/Hispanic American Storylines During the 1980s." Ph.D. dissertation, University of California, San Diego, 1991.

Kay, Graeme. *Coronation Street: Celebrating 30 Years*. London: Boxtree in Association with Granada Television, 1990.

Kilborn, R. *Television Soaps*. London: Batsford, 1992.

Kingsley, Hilary. *Soap Box: The Papermac Guide to Soap Opera*. London: Papermac, 1988.

Klagsbrunn, Marta Maria. *Brasiliens Fernsehserien*. Mettigen: Institut dur Brasilienkunde Verlag, 1987.

Kutler, Jane and Patricia Kerney. *Super Soaps*. New York: Grosset and Dunlap, 1977.

Lackmann, Ron. *Soap Opera Almanac*. New York: Berkeley, 1976.

LaGuardia, Robert. *From Ma Perkins to Mary Hartman*. New York: Ballantine, 1977.

____. *Soap World*. New York: Arbor House, 1983.

____. *The Wonderful World of TV Soap Operas*. New York: Ballantine, 1974. Revised 1977.

Laub, Bryna, ed. *Official Soap Opera Annual*. New York: Ballantine, 1977.

Lazarsfeld, Paul F., and Frank N. Stanton, eds. *Radio Research: 1942–1943*. New York: Essential Books, 1944.

Lemay, Harding. *Eight Years in Another World*. New York: Atheneum, 1981.

Love's Shattered Dreams. Days of Our Lives, vol. 1. Rocky Hill, Conn.: Pioneer Communications Network, 1986.

Lowery, Shearon Anne. "Soap and Booze in the Afternoon: An Analysis of the Portrayals of Alcohol Use in the Daytime Serial." Ph.D. dissertation, Washington State University, 1979.

MacDonald, J. Fred. *Don't Touch That Dial: Radio Programming in American Life from 1920 to 1960*. Chicago: Nelson-Hall, 1979.

Matelski, Marilyn J. *The Soap Opera Evolution: America's Enduring Romance with Daytime Drama*. Jefferson, N.C.: McFarland, 1988.

Mattelart, Michele. *Carnival of Images: Brazilian Television Fiction*. New York: Bergin & Garvey, 1990.

McNeil, Alex. *Total Television: A Comprehensive Guide to Programming from 1948–1980*. New York: Penguin, 1980. Revised, 1984.

Medina Cano, Federico. *La Telenovela: el Milagro del Amor*. Medellin, Colombia: Editorial U.P.B., 1989.

Melo, Jose Marques de. *As Telenovelas da Globo*. Sao Paulo: Summus Editorial, 1988.

Messmore, Francis B. "An Exploratory Investigation of Below-the-Line Cost Components for Soap Opera Production in New York City." D.PS. dissertation, Pace University, 1988.

Meyers, Richard. *The Illustrated Soap Opera Companion*. New York: Drake Publishers, 1977.

Modleski, Tania. *Loving with a Vengeance: Mass-Produced Fantasies for Women*. Hamden, Conn.: Archon Books, 1982.

____. "Popular Feminine Narratives: A Study of Romances, Gothics, and Soap Operas." Ph.D. dissertation, Stanford University, 1980.

Nariman, Heidi Noel. *Soap Operas for Social Change*. Westport, Conn.: Praeger, 1993.

Newcomb, Horace. *TV: The Most Popular Art*. New York: Anchor, 1974.

Nochimson, Martha. *No End of Her: Soap Opera and the Female Subject*. Berkeley: University of California Press, 1992.

Ornelas, Kriemhild Conee. "The Depiction of Sexuality in Daytime Television Melodrama (Soap Opera)." Ph.D. dissertation, Bowling Green State University, 1987.

Ortiz, Renato. *Telenovela: Historia e Producao*. 2nd ed. Sao Paulo: Editora Brasiliense, 1991, c. 1988.

Prelgovisk, Jacquelyn Sue. "Stereotypical Sex-role Characterization as Portrayed in Daytime Television Commercials." M.A. thesis, California State University, Fullerton, 1976.

Puga, Josefina. *Las Telenovelas, Valores y Anti–valores.* Santiago: Centro Bellarmino, Departamento de Investigaciones Sociologicas, 1982.

Rogers, Lynne. *The Loves of Their Lives.* New York: Dell, 1979.

Rossler, Patrick. *Dallas und Schwarzwaldklinik.* Munchen: R. Fischer, 1988.

Rouverol, Jean. *Writing for Daytime Drama.* Boston: Focal Press, 1992.

____. *Writing for the Soaps.* Cincinnati, Ohio: Writer's Digest Books, 1984.

Schemering, Christopher. *Guiding Light: A 50th Anniversary Celebration.* New York: Ballantine, 1987, c1986.

____. *The Soap Opera Encyclopedia.* New York: Ballantine, 1988, c1987.

Schihl, Robert J. *Studio Drama Processes and Procedures.* Boston: Focal Press, 1991.

Schreiber, Elliot Steven. "Comparative Assessments of Characters of Different Ages in Four Daytime Television Serials by Viewers of Varying Ages." Ph.D. dissertation, Pennsylvania State University, 1977.

Seiter, Ellen Elizabeth. "The Promise of Melodrama: Recent Women's Films and Soap Operas." Ph.D. dissertation, Northwestern University, 1981.

Shaikh, Farah. "Soap Opera Viewing Motivations of College Students and the Cultivation Effect." M.S. thesis, San Jose State University, 1989.

Silj, Alessandro. *East of Dallas: The European Challenge to American Television.* London: BFI Pub., 1988.

Siniawsky, Shelley J. "Television Soap Opera and Traditional Ethics: A Content Analysis." M.A. thesis, University of Florida, 1981.

Sirota, David Robert. "An Ethnographical, Ethnomethodological Study of Soap Opera Writing." Ph.D. dissertation, Ohio State University, 1976.

Skill, Thomas D. "Segmenting the Soap Opera Audience." Ph.D. dissertation, State University of New York at Buffalo, 1984.

Soap Opera Digest. New York: S.O.D. Publishing, vol. 1, Dec. 1975.

Soap Opera Digest Scrapbook. Chicago: Contemporary Books, 1984.

Soap Opera Update. New Jersey: Soap Opera Update Magazine, vol. 1, 1988.

Soap Opera Weekly. New York: News America Publishing, vol. 1, no. 1, Nov. 21, 1989–.

Soap Operas. Produced and directed by Kit Laybourne. 30 min. New York: Time-Life Video, 1982. Videocassette.

Soares, Manuela. *The Soap Opera Book.* New York: Harmony Books, 1978.

Sobre la Telenovela. Lima, Peru: Universidad de Lima, Facultad de Ciencias de la Comunicacion, Facultad de Ciencias Humanas, 1993.

Stedman, Raymond William. "A History of the Broadcasting of Daytime Serial Dramas in the United States." Ph.D. dissertation, University of Southern California, 1959.

____. *The Serials: Suspense and Drama by Installment.* Norman, Ok.: University of Oklahoma Press, 1971. Revised, 1977.

Television y Melodrama: Generos y Lecturas de la Telenovela en Colombia. Bogota, Colombia: Tercer Mundo Editores, 1992.

Terrace, Vincent. *The Complete Encyclopedia of Television Programs 1947–1976.* Cranbury, N.J.: A.S. Barnes, 1976.

____. *Television 1970–1980.* La Jolla, Calif.: A.S. Barnes, 1981.

Thomas, Sari. "The Relationship Between Daytime Serials and Their Viewers." Ph.D. dissertation, University of Pennsylvania, 1977.

Timberg, Bernard Mahler. "Daytime Television: Rhetoric and Ritual." Ph.D. dissertation, University of Texas at Austin, 1979.

Townley, Rod. *The Year in Soaps.* New York: Crown, 1984.

Tuchman, Paula Susan. "A Comparative Analysis of American and Mexican Daytime Serials." Ph.D. dissertation, University of California, Irvine, 1984.

Tucker, David Earl. "A Multivariate Analysis of Soap Opera Viewers." Ph.D. dissertation, Bowling Green University, 1977.

Uribe Diaz, Maximo. *Asi Se Escribe una Telenovela.* Colombia: s.n., 198-?

Valentin, Oliver. *Lindenstrasse: Modernes Marchen oder Wirklichkeit?* Frankfurt am Main: Haag + Herchen, 1992.

Variety's Directory of Major U.S. Show Business Awards. New York: Bowker, 1989.

Vink, Nico. *The Telenovela and Emancipation: A Study on Television and Social Change in Brazil.* Amsterdam, Netherlands: Royal Tropical Institute, 1988.

Wakefield, Dan. *All Her Children.* New York: Avon, 1976.
Walter, Norman and Rita Walter with Pam Proctor. *No Shadow of Turning.* Garden City, N.Y.: Doubleday, 1980.
Whitley, Dianna and Ray Manzella. *Soap Stars: America's 31 Favorite Daytime Actors Speak for Themselves.* Garden City, N.Y.: Doubleday, 1985.
Williams, Carol T. *It's Time for My Story: Soap Opera Sources, Structure, and Response.* Westport, Conn.: Praeger, 1992.
Workman Zahnd, Phyllis. "The Relationship Between Loneliness and Viewing Daytime Serial Dramas in Adolescent Females." Ph.D. dissertation, Fordham University, 1988.
Zahn, Susan Brown. "Media Generations: The Soap Opera as a Point of Comparison." Ph.D. dissertation, University of Texas at Austin, 1986.

Articles

Adler, R. "Afternoon Television: Unhappiness Enough and Time." *New Yorker*, 12 February 1972, 79-82.
Africano, L. "Soap Bubbles." *National Review*, 1 August 1975, 836-838.
Alexander, Alison. "Soap Opera Viewing and Relational Perceptions." *Journal of Broadcasting and Electronic Media* 29 (Summer 1985): 295-308.
Alfonso, Kristian. "Candidly Speaking…Bringing Back the Magic of Hope." *Soap Opera Update*, 16 July 1990, 16-18.
"All In A Days Work." *Soap Opera Digest*, 1 September 1992, 71.
"Always A Bride—Ever A Wife? Will Days' Jennifer Be Saved By Jack…Again?" *Soap Opera Weekly*, 2 October 1990, 5.
Anderson, Susan. "The Darling Women of Days." *Soap Opera Magazine*, 10 March 1992, 29.
"April Love: Or Is Mike Fooling Himself?" *Soap Opera Update*, 7 November 1988, 12.
"April Fools: Days of Our Lives: Dr. Carly Manning." *Soap Opera Digest*, 13 April 1993, 104.
Arcella, Lisa. "Black Jack, the Dark Knight Is Portrayed by Matthew Ashford." *Soap Opera Update*, 5 September 1988, 33-34.
"Are Matt Ashford's Days Numbered?" *Soap Opera Digest*, 15 October 1991, 35.
"Are Soaps Only Suds?" *New York Times Magazine*, 28 March 1943, 19, 36.
Armstrong, Lois. "Can Sally Sussman Find Happiness with Her Own Soap Opera? Only Time—and Generations—Will Tell." *People Weekly*, 17 April 1989, 113-114.
Armstrong, Sue. "South African Soap Aids the Health of the Nation." *New Scientist*, 27 August 1994, 5.
Ashford, Matthew. "Hit the Road Jack: In an SOU Exclusive, Matthew Ashford Writes Directly to You About the Future." *Soap Opera Update*, 30 September 1991, 18-20.
"Ashford Speaks Out on Days Exit." *Soap Opera Digest*, 17 August 1993, 5.
"Ask Matt Ashford." *Soap Opera Weekly*, 29 October 1991, 24-26.
Astrachan, A. "Life Can Be Beautiful/Relevant: Social Problems and Soap Opera." *New York Times Magazine*, 23 March 1975, 12-13, 54-64.
"Autograph Please! Patrick Muldoon." *Soap Opera Weekly*, 3 May 1994, 56.
"AW and Days Stars Turn Out for a Swinging Time for Charity." *Soap Opera Magazine*, 27 July 1993, 34-35.
Babb, J. "Grief: The Human Response to Man's Mortality." *Daytime Serial Newsletter*, November 1977, 4-5.
Babrow, Austin S. "Audience Motivation, Viewing Context, Media Content, and Form." *Communication Studies* 41 (Winter 1990): 343-361.
____. "An Expectancy-value Analysis of the Student Soap Opera Audience." *Communication Research* 16 (April 1989): 155-178.
"Backstage at *Days of Our Lives*." *Soap Opera Update*, 30 September 1991, 11-13.
Backus, Lisa. "Biggs on Acting." *Soap Opera Weekly*, 4 September 1990, 27.
____. "Days Goes Live from the Greek Theater." *Soap Opera Weekly*, 21 May 1991, 27.
____. "Funny Lady." *Soap Opera Weekly*, 20 November 1990, 27.

____. "Hoofin' It with Hufsey." *Soap Opera Weekly*, 10 April 1990, 27.

____. "Mac Sends a Message." *Soap Opera Weekly*, 15 December 1992, 28.

____. "Mental Health Program to Be Named After Macdonald Carey." *Soap Opera Weekly*, 16 March 1993, 27.

____. "Poetry in Motion: Macdonald Carey Expresses His Thoughts in Verse." *Soap Opera Weekly*, 2 October 1990, 27.

____. "Shape Up with Shaughnessy." *Soap Opera Weekly*, 24 September 1991, 28.

____. "The Write Stuff: Head Writers Reveal the Stories Behind Your Favorite Stories." *Soap Opera Weekly*, 17 April 1990, 40-41.

"Bad News Bradys: Roman's Return; Kayla Kidnapped." *Soap Opera Weekly*, 22 October 1991, 6.

"Bad Times Behind Her, Days's Kimberly Returns to Salem." *Soap Opera Digest*, 7 July 1992, 30.

"Bad Times for Days' Brady Bunch." *Soap Opera Weekly*, 21 May 1991, 5.

"Bad to the Bone: Soaps' Nastiest Villains: Vivian Alamain, Days of Our Lives." *Soap Opera Digest*, 25 May 1993, 100.

Bailey, Diane. "After School Special: Days' Alison Sweeney Gets Twice the Homework of Ordinary Kids, but She Makes the Grade." *Soap Opera Digest*, 20 July 1993, 26-29.

____. "Designated Hunk: Patrick Muldoon." *Soap Opera Digest*, 5 January 1993, 32-36.

____. "J. Eddie Peck: Don't Peg Me As a Hick." *Soap Opera Digest*, 21 January 1992, 24-27.

____. "Survival of the Fittest: Days of Our Lives' J. Cynthia Brooks." *Soap Opera Digest*, 11 May 1993, 38-40.

Baker, Russell. "Modern-day Gloom." *New York Times Magazine*, 24 May 1987, 16.

____. "Paradise for Pentagon." *New York Times*, 26 January 1991, 19(N), 25(L).

Baldwin, Kristen. "On the Attack: Days' Paul Kersey." *Soap Opera Weekly*, 31 May 1994, 33.

Baltera, L. "Designers Rap Fashions on Daytime TV Soapers." *Advertising Age*, 6 August 1973, 20, 22.

Barbatsis, Gretchen and Yvyette Guy. "Analyzing Meaning in Form: Soap Opera's Compositional Construction of 'Realness.'" *Journal of Broadcasting & Electronic Media* 35 (Winter 1991): 59-74.

Bednarz, Stella. "Behind the Love and Laughter: Interview, Matthew Ashford and Melissa Reeves." *Soap Opera Digest*, 25 June 1991, 12-13.

____. "Bo and Hope." *Soap Opera Digest*, 10 March 1987, 12-15.

____. "Days's Hot New Storylines." *Soap Opera Digest*, 16 April 1991, 6-9.

____. "Days of Our Lives: Wacky, Wild and Utterly Watchable." *Soap Opera Digest*, 30 August 1994, 34-37.

____. "Family Ties: Charles and David Shaughnessy." *Soap Opera Digest*, 18 February 1992, 52-53.

____. "5 of the Best Days Weddings." *Soap Opera Digest*, 17 November 1987, 14-19.

____. "Friends and Lovers: The Romance of Shane and Kimberly." *Soap Opera Digest*, 5 May 1987, 9-14.

____. "Frankie and Eve—Days's Next Super Couple?" *Soap Opera Digest*, 19 February 1991, 31.

____. "From Cruz and Eden to Jack and Jenn: Costume Designer Richard Bloore Segues from SB to Days." *Soap Opera Digest*, 7 August 1990, 57-58.

____. "Happy Anniversary! Days of Our Lives Turns 25." *Soap Opera Digest*, 13 November 1990, 66-78, 114-115.

____. "He Doesn't Have a Last Name, But This Days Character Has Been Around for Seventeen Years." *Soap Opera Digest*, 10 July 1990, 57-58.

____. "Home Alone: The Inside Story: When a Popular Couple Splits, What Happens to the Partner Left Behind? Charles Shaughnessy." *Soap Opera Digest*, 1 October 1991, 14.

____. "Look Out For Days' Christie Clark…" *Soap Opera Digest*, 6 October 1987, 94-95.

____. "The Making of a Super Couple." *Soap Opera Digest*, 5 May 1987, 16-17.

____. "Missing in Action: Patsy Pease Sets the Record Straight About Why She Left Days and What Happened to Her Baby." *Soap Opera Digest*, 22 January 1991, 22-25, 36.

____. "Nick of Time: They Went Down with the Cruise of Deception, But Drake Hogestyn & Staci Greason Are Back on Course—Thanks to Another Super Couple." *Soap Opera Digest*, 10 December 1991, 6-10.

____. "Once Patch Was 'Nothing' and Barbara Was a 'Doormat' Until the Headwriters at Days and ATWT Changed Everything." *Soap Opera Digest*, 22 September 1987, 96-101.

____. "Opposites Attract: The Love Story of Days's Jack and Jennifer." *Soap Opera Digest*, 7 August 1990, 20-25.

____. "The Romance of Shane and Kimberly." *Soap Opera Digest*, 5 May 1987, 9-14.

____. "Step Into My Parlor: Thyme Lewis." *Soap Opera Digest*, 6 July 1993, 75.

____. "The Ups and Downs of Playing Jack: Days' Matthew Ashford Is Enjoying the Ride." *Soap Opera Digest*, 17 April 1990, 96-97.

____. "'We Have to Have You Back:' Days Made Deidre Hall an Offer She Couldn't Refuse." *Soap Opera Digest*, 20 August 1991, 18-19.

Bednarz, Stella and Roberta Caploe. "Ride 'Em, Cowboy: Days's Jack and Jennifer Tie the Knot, Western Style." *Soap Opera Digest*, 17 September 1991, 128-130.

"Behind Closed Doors! Days Stars Give You a Private Tour of Their Dressing Rooms." *Soap Opera Update*, 2 November 1993, 18-21.

Belkin, Lisa. "Soap-opera Cliffhangers Trim Casts." *New York Times*, 28 April 1987, 27(N), C18(L).

Berle, Milton. "A Tribute to Macdonald Carey." *Soap Opera Weekly*, 19 July 1994, 15.

"The Best 'Days of Our Lives' Supercouple of All Time: Jack and Jennifer." *Soap Opera Update*, 19 November 1990, 18.

"The Best of Everything: Days of Our Lives, Salem Place Mall." *Soap Opera Digest*, 17 August 1993, 101.

"Betty Corday." *Variety*, 25 November 1987, 134.

Bevans, M.J. "Super Witches." *Us*, 6 January 1981, 42-47.

"Beyond Bliss: The Wedding of Steve and Kayla." *Soap Opera Update*, 5 September 1988, 14-15.

Bialkowski, Carol. "Behind the Scenes: Lost at Sea 'Days of Our Lives' Characters Jump Ship." *Soap Opera Digest*, 18 September 1990, 120-121.

"Big Changes at Days: Charles Shaughnessy Speaks Out About the Shane/Kayla/Kim Triangle." *Soap Opera Digest*, 17 September 1991, 33-34.

"The Big Picture: Drake Hogestyn." *Soap Opera Update*, 5 May 1992, 32-33.

"The Big Picture: Matthew Ashford." *Soap Opera Update*, 2 June 1992, 32-33.

Birnbach, L. "Daze of Our Lives (College Students and Soap Operas)." *Rolling Stone*, 1 October 1981, 33.

Birnbaum, Jesse. "A Soap Goes Black and White: NBC Unveils an Interracial Daytime Serial, Generations." *Time*, 27 March 1989, 85.

"Birthday Boy! Charles Shaughnessy." *Soap Opera Digest*, 19 February 1991, 43.

"Birthday Boy! Joe Gallison." *Soap Opera Digest*, 19 March 1991, 43.

"The Bittersweet Days of Izzy & John." *Soap Opera Update*, 20 October 1992, 20-21.

Black, Linda A. "Bill and Susan Hayes on Why They Left 'Days of Our Lives' and the Chances of Their Returning." *Soap Opera Digest*, 9 October 1984, 100-103, 139.

"Blacks in the Soaps." *Ebony*, March 1978, 32-34, 36.

Blau, Eleanor. "Soap Opera Magazines Fight for Fans' Hearts and Dollars." *New York Times*, 24 October 1988, 32(N), D10(L).

Blessing, Angela. "They Won't Win Any Scarlet Letters, but the Kids of UCLA's Campus Soap Opera Are in a Class by Themselves." *People Weekly*, 29 February 1988, 79-80.

"Bo and Carly Crisis: Tough Days Ahead." *Soap Opera Digest*, 27 October 1992, 36.

"Bo Is Shot! (But Parties on, Dude)." *Soap Opera Weekly*, 17 March 1992, 5.

"Bo Keeps the Truth About Victor's Deed from Carly." *Soap Opera Weekly*, 5 November 1991, 3.

Bodovitz, Sandra. "At 50, 'Guiding Light' Retains Early Themes." *New York Times*, 30 June 1987, 21(N), B6(L).

Boland Gianopulos, Kate. "Backstage at 'Days of Our Lives'." *Soap Opera Digest*, 5 April 1988, 20-26.

Bonderoff, Jason. "Countdown at the Chapel." *Soap Opera Digest*, 8 December 1992, 4-6.

____. "Dawn of a New Days." *Soap Opera Digest*, 22 June 1993, 20-22.

____. "How Days Gave Roman's Face a Bum Wrap." *Soap Opera Digest*, 14 April 1992, 54.

____. "Just What the Doctor Ordered." *Soap Opera Digest*, 3 March 1993, 86.

____. "Last Chance for Romance: What Will Happen to Bo and Carly if Peter Reckell Leaves Days?" *Soap Opera Digest*, 12 November 1991, 16, 104-106.

____. "Nobody Wants to Be a Jealous Lover but..." *Soap Opera Digest*, 10 July 1990, 65-69, 111.

____. "Roman Invasion: Are Two Romans Better Than One?" *Soap Opera Digest*, 1 October 1991, 6-8, 33-34.

____. "Set Sail for Salem!" *Soap Opera Digest*, 29 September 1992, 28-29.

____. "Super Couple, Super Trouble." *Soap Opera Digest*, 23 June 1992, 6-8.

____. "Threads 'R' Us: Days's Designer Kids." *Soap Opera Digest*, 5 January 1993, 70.

Bonderoff, Jason and Roberta Caploe. "Danger Signals: Is Days' Jennifer Making a Big Mistake Cuddling Up to Peter?" *Soap Opera Digest*, 2 August 1994, 26-28.

____. "What's Next in the Nursery?" *Soap Opera Digest*, 10 November 1992, 4-7.

____. "Who Killed Curtis Reed?" *Soap Opera Digest*, 29 March 1994, 22-24.

Bordewich, F.M. "Why Are College Kids in a Lather Over TV Soap Operas?" *New York Times*, 20 October 1974, II, 31:1.

Bosworth, P. "How to Be a Soap-Opera Writer: A Close-up (N. Franklin)." *Working Woman*, 6 May 1981, 150.

Botto, L. "That Family Sure Has Its Share of Problems; Daytime Serials." *Look*, 7 September 1971, 64-65.

Bowes, Elena. "Unilever Backs Pan-Euro Soap." *Advertising Age*, 7 January 1991, 29.

"The Brady Family Album: Days of Our Lives." *Soap Opera Digest*, 13 October 1992, 26-27.

Braxton, Greg. "As World Turns on Simpson Case, Soap Opera Fans Are Upset." *Los Angeles Times*, 8 July 1994, A25.

"Brenda Benet, Actress, Called Suicide Victim." *New York Times*, 9 April 1982, 16(N), B6(LC), 2.

Breslauer, Hope S. "Hit...Jack & Jenn's Wedding on Days." *Soap Opera Weekly*, 20 August 1991, 31.

"Broadcast Serial Audiences Not Types." *Broadcasting*, 26 April 1943, 19.

Broeske, Pat H. "Lisa Trusel Just Wants to Have Fun." *Soap Opera Digest*, 4 December 1984, 8-11.

Brown, Kitty. "Days of Our Lives Gala Anniversary Celebration." *Soap Opera Digest*, July 1978, 59-64.

____. "Days of Our Lives: On the Set." *Soap Opera Digest*, January 1978, 23-31.

____. "Deidre Hall's Fight to Save the Seals." *Soap Opera Digest*, August 1978, 101, 122-127.

____. "Joe and Melisa Gallison Believe Their Dogs Make Cosmic Contributions." *Soap Opera Weekly*, 20 February 1990, 31.

____. "Judi Evans and Her Garden of Animal Delights." *Soap Opera Weekly*, 24 July 1990, 32-33.

Brown, Meredith. "Behind the Smiles: Drake Hogestyn." *Soap Opera Digest*, 4 November 1986, 24-27, 30, 32-34.

____. "The Deidre Hall Interview." *Soap Opera Digest*, 3 June 1986, 20-24, 26-27.

____. "Facing Life: How and Why Macdonald Carey Fought His Addiction to Alcohol." *Soap Opera Digest*, December 1986, 20-23.

____. "Falling in Love on the Soaps." *Soap Opera Digest*, 14 February 1984, 31, 108.

____. "Peter Reckell, Why She's Leaving Days, and the Real Story About the Man She Will Marry—Kristian Alfonso Tells All!" *Soap Opera Digest*, 10 March 1987, 17-20.

____. "The Rise and Shine of Kristian Alfonso." *Soap Opera Digest*, 20 November 1984, 8-13.

____. "The Romance to End All Romances: Days of Our Lives Marlena and Roman Tie the Knot." *Soap Opera Digest*, 29 March 1983, 24-28.

____. "Stars from 'Days of Our Lives' and 'Young and the Restless' Bombard Canada." *Soap Opera Digest*, 22 November 1983, 112-113.

____. "Tough Cookie? Shannon Tweed Has Been a Model, a Centerfold and on Her Own Since She Was Fifteen. No One Tells Her What to Do." *Soap Opera Digest*, 11 March 1986, 8-12.

____. "Why Wayne Northrop Is Leaving and Why You're Going to Miss Him...Bad!" *Soap Opera Digest*, 25 September 1984, 8-14.

Brown, Paul B. "Soaps and Serials." *Inc.*, January 1987, 15-17.

Brown, Rich. "Stay Tuned for the Soap Channel." *Broadcasting*, 7 September 1992, 24.

Brown, William J. and Michael J. Cody. "Effects of a Prosocial Television Soap Opera in Promoting Women's Status." *Human Communication Research* 18 (September 1991): 114-142.

Bruckner, D.J.R. "El Galan de la Telenovela." *New York Times*, 27 October 1994, C17(L).

Brunt, Rosalind. "Don't Fade Away." *New Statesman & Society*, 14 July 1989, 53-54.

"Bryan Dattilo, Days of Our Lives' Lucas Roberts." *Soap Opera Update*, 23 August 1994, 23-25.

Buerkel-Rothfuss, Nancy L., and Sandra Mayes. "Soap Opera Viewing: The Cultivation Effect." *Journal of Communication* 31 (Summer 1981): 108-115.

Burch, Jeanne. "The Lazy Days of Days." *Soap Opera Weekly*, 1 May 1990, 44.

Burns, C. and D. Gritten. "Soaps' Sexy New Stars Prove Primetime Passions Aren't a Match for Lust in the Afternoon." *People*, 16 June 1980, 81-84.

Butler, J.G. "I'm-not-a-doctor-but-I-play-one-on-TV: Characters, Actors and Acting in Television Soap Opera." *Cinema Journal* 30 (Summer 1991): 75-91.

Byron, Ellen. "Deidre Hall: Happily Ever After..." *Soap Opera Digest*, 4 August 1992, 16-20.

____. "Don't Make Waves: Roberta Leighton." *Soap Opera Digest*, 17 March 1992, 68-71.

____. "Enter Laughing: Days's Offbeat Leading Man Is Winning Hearts Through Humor: Robert Mailhouse." *Soap Opera Digest*, 11 June 1991, 118-121.

____. "'I'm A Recovering Alcoholic:' Days's Macdonald Carey Confronts His Drinking Problem." *Soap Opera Digest*, 15 October 1991, 28-32, 129.

____. "Keeping Her Cool: Shannon Sturges." *Soap Opera Digest*, 3 September 1991, 114-121.

____. "Louise Sorel: Drama Queen." *Soap Opera Digest*, 24 November 1992, 28-31.

____. "Melissa Reeves: Golden Girl." *Soap Opera Digest*, 25 June 1991, 6-10.

____. "The Phoenix Keeps Rising: Joseph Mascolo Is Back (Again) on Days, But Will It Be the Last Time?" *Soap Opera Digest*, 26 April 1994, 40-42.

____. "Putting it Together: After a Troubled Start in Life, Bryan Dattilo Is Taking Charge." *Soap Opera Digest*, 28 September 1993, 50-52.

____. "A Tough Act to Follow: Days's Peter Reckell Says It's Tough Living in Bo Brady's Shadow." *Soap Opera Digest*, 21 August 1990, 114-118.

"Calliope's Days Talk Show: Could This Be the Start of Something Lasting?" *Soap Opera Digest*, 1 September 1992, 43.

"Can Days of Our Lives Continue to Shine in the Ratings? *Soap Opera Update, News Digest*, 5 October 1993, 12.

Canary, Daniel J. and Brian H. Spitzberg. "Loneliness and Media Gratifications." *Communication Research* 20 (December 1993): 800-822.

Cantor, Muriel G. "Our Days and Nights on TV." *Journal of Communication* 29 (Autumn 1979): 66-74.

Cantwell, Mary. " 'Days' Together: Sharing a Soap, Sharing Lives." *New York Times*, 26 January 1989, B1(N), C2(L), 1.

____. "When TV Soaps Wash Away the Real-life Grit." *New York Times*, 23 November 1989, B5(N), C2(L), 1.

"Capital Cities/ABC Closing Its Magazine for Soap-opera Fans." *Wall Street Journal*, 13 May 1993, A7(W), B12(E).

Caploe, Roberta. "Al Rabin Speaks Out on the Fab Four." *Soap Opera Weekly*, 10 December 1991, 10.

____. "Behind the Scenes at the Days Cover Shoot." *Soap Opera Digest*, 13 November 1990, 120-121.

____. "Behind the Scene: Crash and Splash, Days of Our Lives Stages a Flood and a Building Collapse." *Soap Opera Digest*, 26 June 1990, 104-105.

____. "Behind the Scenes: Night Sins: Days of Our Lives Stays Up Late." *Soap Opera Digest*, 16 March 1993, 28-29.

____. "Blind Faith: Days Gives New Meaning to the Phrase, 'Get Me to the Church on Time.'" *Soap Opera Digest*, 26 October 1994, 24-26.

____. "A Brand-new Dee." *Soap Opera Digest*, 27 April 1993, 18-20.

____. "Day by Day." *Soap Opera Digest*, 30 March 1993, 80-81.

____. "Days' Divas Dish." *Soap Opera Digest*, 22 November 1994, 38-41.

____. "Days' Fluffy: Not Just Another Pretty Face." *Soap Opera Digest*, 28 May 1991, 98-99.

____. "Days' Mary Beth Evans Faces 'Life Without Patch.'" *Soap Opera Digest*, 16 October 1990, 36.

____. "Hear My Song." *Soap Opera Digest*, 19 January 1993, 108.

____. "He's Tall, Dark, Handsome—and Very Italian." *Soap Opera Digest*, 16 October 1990, 62.

____. "Hope Opera." *Soap Opera Digest*, 13 September 1994, 50-54.

____. "John Black, This Is Your Life." *Soap Opera Digest*, 8 December 1994, 102-103.

____. "Lights, Camera...Attraction: Days's Peter Reckell and Crystal Chappell Turn Up the Steam As Bo and Carly, but Does the Temperature Level Drop When They Walk Offstage?" *Soap Opera Digest*, 23 July 1991, 6-10.

____. "Make Me an Offer." *Soap Opera Digest*, 28 April 1992, 6-11.

____. "The Naked Truth: Actress Eileen Davidson Hits Days with Ease." *Soap Opera Digest*, 9 November 1993, 50-54.

____. "No Hope for Bo & Billie." *Soap Opera Digest*, 7 June 1994, 22-24.

____. "The Real Marlena." *Soap Opera Digest*, 8 December 1992, 56.

____. "Scar Face." *Soap Opera Digest*, 25 May 1993, 70-71.

____. "Scott and Melissa Reeves Will Spend Valentine's Day with Their Happy, Little...Home Improvement." *Soap Opera Digest*, 16 February 1993, 26-27.

____. "Sign of the Times: Thaao Penghlis Reflects on the Changing Days of His Life." *Soap Opera Digest*, 27 December 1994, 32-34.

____. "Three of Hearts: Scott and Melissa Reeves." *Soap Opera Digest*, 15 February 1994, 22-24.

____. "The Tower of Bauer." *Soap Opera Digest*, 29 March 1994, 46-50.

____. "The Unsinkable Patsy Pease." *Soap Opera Digest*, 21 January 1992, 6-11, 61.

Cappozzoli, Mike, Jr. "Drake Hogestyn: Baseball, a Picket Fence & John Black." *Soap Opera Magazine*, 21 April 1992, 6-7.

"Carey, Macdonald." *Facts on File*, 24 March 1994, 220.

Carmody, Deirdre. "Soap Operas Attract a Fan on Wall Street." *New York Times*, 8 June 1992, C1(N), D1(L).

Carlson, Katie. "Soap Bitch: Nichols and Evans: Wasting Away?" *Soap Opera Weekly*, 7 August 1990, 40-41.

Carson, Tom. "Don't Try This at Home. (MTV's Television Series 'The Real World.')" *Rolling Stone*, 25 November 1993, 99-101.

Carswell, Julia. "A Bridge to Days' Deidre Hall." *Soap Opera Weekly*, 22 June 1993, 19.

Carter, Alan. "Luke and Laura: It Was the Wedding America Couldn't Resist." *TV Guide*, 6 May 1989, 24-25.

Carveth, Rodney and Alison Alexander. "Soap Opera Viewing Motivations and the Cultivation Process." *Journal of Broadcasting and Electronic Media* 29 (Summer 1985): 259-273.

Cassata, Mary B., P. Anderson and T.D. Skill. "The Older Adult in Daytime Serial Drama." *Journal of Communication* 30 (Winter 1980): 48-49.

Cassata, Mary B., T.D. Skill and S.O. Boadu. "In Sickness and in Health." *Journal of Communication* 29 (Autumn 1979): 73-80.

"CBS-TV Dominates Emmy Nominations of Daytime Shows." *Variety*, 13 May 1987, 90.

"Celebrating with Stars: Roark Critchlow." *Soap Opera Update*, 29 November 1994, 24-25.

Champagne, Christine. "Driven to Succeed: James Reynolds." *Soap Opera Weekly*, 6 July 1993, 12-14.

____. "Star Quality: Crystal Chappell." *Soap Opera Weekly*, 8 June 1993, 24-26.

Chappell, Crystal. "My 58 Favorite Things." *Soap Opera Update*, 23 March 1993, 54.

"Charles Shaughnessy, Shane, Days of Our Lives." *Soap Opera Update*, 3 March 1992, 30-31.

Chester, Jody. "Exotic Cooking Made Easy with Gregg Marx." *Soap Opera Digest*, 8 November 1983, 112-113.

"A Chip Off the Old Patch." *Soap Opera Weekly*, 6 March 1990, 47.

"Christie Clark, Carrie, Days of Our Lives." *Soap Opera Weekly*, 8 November 1994, 36.

Chunovic, Louis. "The World Turns for Dack Rambo." *Advocate*, 28 January 1992, 63.

Church, David. "Bill's Back." *Soap Opera Digest*, 1 July 1986, 92-94.

____. "A Conversation with Daytime's Favorite (and Only) Robot!" *Soap Opera Digest*, 1 March 1983, 106-111.

____. "Dumb Like a Fox: Gwen Davies." *Soap Opera Digest*, 5 June 1984, 128-132.

____. "Expect the Unexpected from Days of Our Lives Peggy McCay." *Soap Opera Digest*, 25 March 1986, 102-104, 124.

____. "The Godfather Comes to Daytime." *Soap Opera Digest*, 7 December 1982, 38-39, 134-136.

____. "His 'Days' Aren't Numbered: Wesley Eure." *Soap Opera Digest*, 16 February 1982, 14-19, 102.

____. "Is Leann Hunley a Sly and Sultry Seductress?" *Soap Opera Digest*, 13 September 1983, 140-144.

____. "Josh Taylor: the Gregarious Loner." *Soap Opera Digest*, 5 August 1980, 128-134.

____. "Josh Taylor—Rebel with a Cause." *Soap Opera Digest*, 10 April 1984, 140-144.

____. "Keeping Up with Quinn Redeker." *Soap Opera Digest*, 6 November 1984, 8-12.

____. "Leave 'Em Laughing." *Soap Opera Digest*, 30 June 1987, 128-131.

____. "Mr. Innocence in the Big City: Peter Reckell." *Soap Opera Digest*, 13 March 1984, 8-14.

____. "My Day on 'Days of Our Lives.'" *Soap Opera Digest*, 18 January 1983, 15-22.

____. "New and Improved: Josh Taylor's Life Is Taking a Different Direction." *Soap Opera Digest*, 8 April 1986, 8-11.

____. "A New Day Dawning for Days of Our Lives." *Soap Opera Digest*, 19 August 1980, 38-45.

____. "On the Razor's Edge with Thaao Penghlis." *Soap Opera Digest*, 24 April 1984, 8-12.

____. "Pollyanna Rides Again: Pamela Roylance." *Soap Opera Digest*, 8 May 1984, 30-31, 33-34.

____. "The Reluctant Daytimer." *Soap Opera Digest*, 15 March 1983, 120-125.

____. "The Return of Gloria Loring." *Soap Opera Digest*, 25 October 1983, 20-24.

____. "The Sixth Marx Brother: Gregg Marx." *Soap Opera Digest*, 19 January 1982, 130-135.

____. "Stephen Brooks: Climbing the Comeback Trail." *Soap Opera Digest*, 3 March 1981, 128-134.

____. "Still Crazy (About Each Other) After All These Years." *Soap Opera Digest*, 27 January 1987, 22-27.

____. "Susan and Bill Hayes' Significant Kisses." *Soap Opera Digest*, 10 May 1983, 20-26.

____. "Teenage Sex on the Soaps: A More Responsible Attitude Is Emerging on Days Of Our Lives and The Young and the Restless." *Soap Opera Digest*, 24 February 1987, 96-98, 135.

____. "Thaao Penghlis' Greek Christmas." *Soap Opera Digest*, 4 January 1983, 132-137.

____. "Tying the Knot on Days of Our Lives." *Soap Opera Digest*, 7 June 1983, 124-127.

Clark, Jennifer. "All Italy Has a Buzz for the Fiction Business." *Variety*, 23 March 1992, 54.

Clarke, Steve. "Oz Net Buys 50 Segs of U.K. Sudser." *Variety*, 17 October 1994, 156.

"Clash of the Romans: What the Return of Deidre Hall & Wayne Northrop Means for Days." *Soap Opera Weekly*, 25 June 1991, 3.

"Cliffhanger." *Life*, March 1989, 120-121.

Cochran, Beth. "Catching Up with Days' Charles Shaughnessy." *Soap Opera Magazine*, 24 May 1994, 39.

"The Code of Sudsville." *Time*, 20 March 1972, 93-94.

Coe, Steve. "NBC Cans 'Santa Barbara,' Gives Back Time." *Broadcasting*, 5 October 1992, 26.

Cohan, John. "The Soap Seer: Charles Shaughnessy." *Soap Opera Weekly*, 30 October 1990, 42.

____. "The Soap Seer: Deidre Hall Should Return to Days." *Soap Opera Weekly*, 16 April 1991, 45.

____. "The Soap Seer: Peter Reckell." *Soap Opera Weekly*, 28 August 1990, 45.

____. "The Soap Seer: Stephen Nichols." *Soap Opera Weekly*, 25 December 1990, 22.

____. "The Soap Seer: Susan Seaforth Hayes." *Soap Opera Weekly*, 1 January 1991, 45.

"College Fest Fiesta: NBC Soap Stars Go Back to School at UCLA." *Soap Opera Weekly*, 23 November 1993, 47.

Collins, Jackie and Ellen Byron. "Why Do We Love the Queens of Evil?" *Redbook*, February 1987, 62-64.

Collymore, Terrie. "Hot Off the Rack with Days' Patrick Muldoon." *Soap Opera Digest*, 12 April 1994, 88-89.

____. "In Therapy with Days of Our Lives." *Soap Opera Digest*, 6 August 1991, 50-51.

Compesi, Ronald J. "Gratifications of Daytime Serial Viewers." *Journalism Quarterly* 57 (1980): 155-58.

"Coming Home: Can Marlena and Roman Rekindle Their Love?" *Soap Opera Weekly*, 27 August 1991, 6.

"Coming Together & Falling Apart on Days." *Soap Opera Weekly*, 15 January 1991, 2.

Convisser, Julie. "And in Zaire, Prevention by Soap Opera." *Washington Post*, 17 November 1991, C5.

Cooper, Mary Ann. "Bo and Hope—Lovers in the Storm." *Soap Opera Update*, 26 September 1988, 30-31.

____. "Shane & Kim's Curtain Call?" *Soap Opera Magazine*, 4 August 1992, 7.

____. "Steve's Special Angel." *Soap Opera Update*, 4 July 1988, 13-14.

Cooper, Mary Ann, Richard Spencer and Allison J. Waldman. "Top Ten Couples: The Most: Days' Steve and Kayla." *Soap Opera Update*, 9 January 1989, 27.

____. "Top Ten Couples: The Most Beautiful: Days' Roman and Diana." *Soap Opera Update*, 9 January 1989, 36.

____. "Top Ten Couples: The Most Romantic: Days' Justin and Adrienne." *Soap Opera Update*, 9 January 1989, 34.

Cooperman, Daniel and Michael Logan. "The Envelope Please...." *TV Guide*, 13 January 1990, 8-9.

"Cop Out: Days' Taylor Off the Show." *Soap Opera Digest*, 11 May 1993, 6.

Copeland, R. "Confessions of a Soap Addict." *New York Times*, 26 June 1977, II, 1:1.

"Corday Sees Brighter Days." *Soap Opera Digest*, 31 August 1993, 5.

Cornell, James. "Science Soaps." *Technology Review*, October 1989, 12-13.

Costantinou, Marianne. "Soap Opera Fans Are Seeing Stars." *New York Times*, 7 February 1982, D31(N), D31(LC).

Coughlan, Sean. "Soap and Glory." *Times Educational Supplement*, 15 March 1991, 41.

_____. "Soap Power." *Times Educational Supplement*, 16 August 1991, 28.

"Crazy for You, Soaps' Nuttiest Couples: The Years of Living Dangerously: Days of Our Lives Jack and Jennifer." *Soap Opera Digest*, 12 November 1991, 31.

Crothers, Tim. "Splashed." *Sports Illustrated*, 31 August 1992, 114.

Danahy, Michael. "My Behavior Needed an Overhaul." *TV Guide*, 13 June 1987, 12-14.

"Dangerous Love: Bo's Boat Blows!" *Soap Opera Weekly*, 10 September 1991, 2.

Davis, Igor. "Deidre Hall." *Los Angeles Magazine*, March 1987, 16.

Davison, Valerie. "How to Marry a Soap Star: Lissa Layng and Days' James Reynolds." *Soap Opera Weekly*, 22 November 1994, 38.

_____. "John De Lancie." *Soap Opera Weekly*, 8 June 1993, 30.

_____. "A Place in Her Days: Deborah Adair." *Soap Opera Weekly*, 11 October 1994, 32.

_____. "Viva Mexico! Days of Our Lives Found It Hard to Say 'Hasta la Vista' to Chichen Itza." *Soap Opera Weekly*, 12 May 1992, 32-34.

"A Days' All Night Bash!" *Soap Opera Update*, 5 June 1989, 57.

"Days' Anniversary Party, November 9, 1992." *Soap Opera Update*, 29 December 1992, 25-26.

"Days Applauded for Environmental Storyline." *Soap Opera Weekly*, 22 October 1991, 2.

"Days' Carly & John Find Kin." *Soap Opera Weekly*, 12 May 1992, 4.

"Days' Caroline Is Vivian's Next Victim." *Soap Opera Weekly*, 6 July 1993, 4.

"Days' Carrie Switch: Tracy's Out, Christie's Back." *Soap Opera Digest*, 22 December 1992, 33-34.

"Days Celebrates 7000!" *Soap Opera Update Supplement*, 18 May 1993, 42-43.

"Days Confirms Return of Deidre Hall." *Soap Opera Weekly*, 23 July 1991, 2.

"Days Demotes Joe Gallison: Is Neil Getting a Raw Deal?" *Soap Opera Digest*, 17 September 1991, 36.

"Days Digs Up Passion and Danger Among the Ruins in Mexico." *Soap Opera Digest*, 26 November 1991, 33-35.

"Days' Explosive Finale: John Is About to Lose Everything." *Soap Opera Update (Digest)*, 14 June 1994, 2-3.

"Days' Fan Club Days." *Soap Opera Magazine*, 16 June 1992, 10-11.

"Days Fans Love to See Their Stars at Night." *Soap Opera Update: Inside Soaps*, 3 March 1992, 5.

"Days Feud: Chappell Tells Her Side." *Soap Opera Digest*, 31 August 1993, 4.

"Days' Hawk Flies the Coop...And Looks for a New Gig." *Soap Opera Digest*, 18 February 1992, 33-34.

"Days' Hidden Agendas: Will Austin Share the Truth with Carrie; Will Lacey Make Kimberly Kill." *Soap Opera Update (Inside Soaps)*, 22 September 1992, 3-5.

"Days Honcho Retires." *Soap Opera Digest*, 12 May 1992, 39.

"Days in the Sun: After Working Hard All Year, Days of Our Lives' Cast & Crew Pulled Out All the Stops at the Annual Company Picnic." *Soap Opera Weekly*, 13 November 1990, 46-47.

"Days' Jack Tries and Tries to Win Back Jennifer." *Soap Opera Weekly*, 28 January 1992, 5.

"Days' Kayla Says Good-Bye...Will Shane Be the Next to Leave?" *Soap Opera Digest*, 12 May 1992, 36.

"Days' Kim Exits." *Soap Opera Digest*, 5 January 1993, 10.

"Days' Kimberly in Crisis—Again." *Soap Opera Weekly*, 28 July 1992, 8.

"Days' Lisanne and Lynn: A Portrait in Contrasts." *Soap Opera Magazine*, 21 July 1992, 29.

"Days' Marlena Flies to London to Avoid John." *Soap Opera Digest*, 8 June 1993, 7.

"Days' Marlena: Is Her Life Still the Pits?" *Soap Opera Digest*, 2 February 1993, 10.

"Days' Matt Ashford Signs a New Deal Just in Time." *Soap Opera Digest*, 29 October 1991, 37-38.

"Days' Mother & Child Reunion." *Soap Opera Weekly*, 17 September 1991, 6.

"Days' Musical Mystery Tour." *Soap Opera Update*, 5 March 1991, 6.

"Days' New Kim Takes Over in a Hurry." *Soap Opera Digest*, 19 January 1993, 10.

"Days' New Teen Mother." *Soap Opera Digest*, 27 April 1993, 10.

"Days Nighttime Special to Air in January." *Soap Opera Weekly*, 24 December 1991, 2.

"The Days of Murder & Mystery: Victor Breathes His Last…or Has He?" *Soap Opera Weekly*, 12 November 1991, 4.

"Days of Our Lives' Bo & Carly Are in Love—But Will They Get Married?" *Soap Opera Update*, 6 April, 34-35, 37.

"Days of Our Lives Bo Knows…Now What?" *Soap Opera Update (Inside Soaps)*, 29 December 1992, 4.

"Days of Our Lives Celebrates the Holidays in Style." *Soap Opera Digest*, 13 March 1984, 130-131.

"Days of Our Lives Celebrates 17 Years on the Air!" *Soap Opera Digest*, 30 August 1983, 96-98.

"Days of Our Lives' Crystal Chappell on the Problems of Bo & Carly." *Soap Opera Update*, 18 March 1991, 34-35.

"Days of Our Lives: Daytime Writers Describe How Their World Turns." *Journal of the Writers Guild of America, West*, June 1992, 12-20.

"Days of Our Lives Family Tree." *Soap Opera Digest*, 6 December 1983, 136-137.

"A Days of Our Lives Fan Has Her Dream Come True." *Soap Opera Digest*, 9 March 1993, 55-57.

"A Days of Our Lives' FAN-tasy!" *Soap Opera Update*, 13 July 1993, 28-31.

"A Days of Our Lives Field Trip." *Soap Opera Update (Inside Soaps)*, 9 February 1993, 43.

"Days of Our Lives' Jack Deveraux: Autobiography of a Character." *Soap Opera Weekly*, 24 April 1990, 18.

"Days of Our Lives' Matthew Ashford and Melissa Brennan on Jack & Jennifer's Current Problems." *Soap Opera Update*, 18 March 1991, 36-37.

"Days of Our Lives' Michael Sabatino, Lawrence Alamain." *Soap Opera Update*, 4 February 1991, 34-35.

"Days of Our Lives Mourns the Death of Joy Garrett." *Soap Opera Update (Inside Soaps)*, 23 March 1993, 14.

"Days of Our Lives Preview." *Soap Opera Update (Inside Soaps)*, 23 March 1993, 2-5.

"Days of Our Lives: Stars Relax Between Scenes." *Soap Opera Digest*, 16 February 1982, 142-144.

"Days of Thunder: Producers Lower the Boom—and the Fans Bolt!" *Soap Opera Weekly*, 17 August 1993, 15.

"Days' Papa Problems." *Soap Opera Weekly*, 17 December 1991, 2.

"Days' Patrick Muldoon: Absolutely Free!" *Soap Opera Magazine*, 11 August 1992, 30.

"Days' Picnic in the Park." *Soap Opera Magazine*, 20 October 1992, 10-11.

"Days Plans a New Spin-off…But Will Deidre Hall Star?" *Soap Opera Digest*, 12 November 1991, 37.

"Days's Prime-Time Special: A Kiss-and-tell Report from a Star Villain." *Soap Opera Digest*, 21 January 1992, 35.

"Days Revolving Door." *Soap Opera Weekly*, 17 September 1991, 2.

"Days' Robert Kelker Kelly: A New, Brawny Bo." *Soap Opera Magazine*, 21 July 1992, 24-25.

"Days Shake-Ups: Writers' Reversal, Evans's Exit and Those Persistent Nichols Rumors." *Soap Opera Digest*, 26 May 1992.

"Days' Sarah Learns the Truth About Her Roots." *Soap Opera Weekly*, 4 June 1991, 7.

"Days' Star Hospitalized." *Soap Opera Digest*, 16 February 1993, 10.

"Days Stars Light Up the Night." *Soap Opera Update (Digest)*, 27 December 1994, 41-43.

"Days' Stars Score Big with the Fans." *Soap Opera Magazine*, 25 August 1992, 10-11.

"Days Throws a Picnic for Themselves." *Soap Opera Digest*, 1 December 1987, 134-137.

"Days to Become First Interactive Daytime Drama." *Soap Opera Weekly*, 21 June 1994, 8.

"Days To Remember: Days of Our Lives Celebrates a Milestone—25 Years on TV." *Soap Opera Digest*, 22 January 1991, 134-138.

"Days to Watch." *Soap Opera Update*, 9 February 1993, 38-47.

"Days Update: Rebecca Out; Melissa In." *Soap Opera Weekly*, 30 January 1990, 2.

"Days' Vivian Gets a Taste of Her Own Medicine." *Soap Opera Weekly*, 18 January 1994, 8.

"Days' Vivian Turns to Murder." *Soap Opera Weekly*, 8 June 1993, 9.

"Daytime." *TV Guide*, 9 September 1989, 20-23.

"Daytime." *TV Guide*, 1 October 1988, 18-21.

"Daytime's Best Moms: Everymom: Alice Horton, Days of Our Lives." *Soap Opera Digest*, 14 May 1991, 106.

"Dear Days: We Want More of Steve & Kayla. And We Want it Now. Signed, the Fans." *Soap Opera Weekly*, 7 August 1990, 40-41.

"Death in Small Doses: The Virus Takes Its Toll." *Soap Opera Weekly*, 23 July 1991, 3.
"Deborah Adair Comes to Days." *Soap Opera Digest*, 16 March 1993, 4.
"December Days of Danger." *Soap Opera Weekly*, 10 December 1991, 8.
"Deidre Hall Shares Her Wedding Photos." *Soap Opera Update (Inside Soaps)*, 3 March 1992, 44-45.
De Lacroix, Marlena. "The Days of Our Lives Report." *Soap Opera Weekly*, 4 June 1991, 46.
____. "Days of Our Lives: The Sands of Change." *Soap Opera Weekly*, 31 August 1993, 18.
____. "Days: Popcorn, Thrills and Chills." *Soap Opera Weekly*, 12 April 1994, 31.
____. "Days' Prime-Time Specials: From Crass to Class." *Soap Opera Weekly*, 30 March 1993, 18.
____. "Days' Winter Heat: Oxymoron a Go-go." *Soap Opera Weekly*, 8 March 1994, 38.
____. "Marlena on Marlena." *Soap Opera Weekly*, 24 September 1991, 31.
____. "Stefano's Kinky House of Games." *Soap Opera Weekly*, 5 July 1994, 18.
____. "We've Got Them Under Our Skin, Postmark: Salem: Macdonald Carey." *Soap Opera Weekly*, 19 April 1994, 18.
____. "When Days of Our Lives Was Sex Ed 101." *Soap Opera Weekly*, 13 November 1990, 23.
De Losh, Lara. "Alan's Get-Out-of-Jail-Free Card on Days." *Soap Opera Weekly*, 13 December 1994, 5.
____. "And They Call It Puppy Love: Days' Carrie Has the Hots for Austin." *Soap Opera Weekly*, 4 August 1992, 2.
____. "Billie Blows Her Chance." *Soap Opera Weekly*, 3 November 1992, 3.
____. "Billie Makes Tracks on Days." *Soap Opera Weekly*, 29 November 1994, 5.
____. "Bo Bolts, Carly Cries." *Soap Opera Weekly*, 22 December 1992, 5.
____. "Boo, Bo! Just Who Is the Wildcat on Days?" *Soap Opera Weekly*, 8 November 1994, 5.
____. "Brady Women in Peril on Days." *Soap Opera Weekly*, 15 February 1994, 7.
____. "Brian Heidik Takes a Gamble." *Soap Opera Weekly*, 13 October 1992, 10.
____. "Carrie's Love for Austin Is Put to the Acid Test on Days." *Soap Opera Weekly*, 9 March 1993, 5.
____. "Carrie On." *Soap Opera Weekly*, 13 April 1993, 24-26.
____. "Chicago Washed Out by Flood, But How Did Bo React to Carly's Secret?" *Soap Opera Weekly*, 12 May 1992, 8.
____. "Crazy Like a Fox: Elaine Bromka Turned a Short Stint as Days' Stella into a Full-time Job." *Soap Opera Weekly*, 3 November 1992, 10.
____. "Curiosity May Kill Rebecca's Love Life on Days." *Soap Opera Weekly*, 15 June 1993, 2.
____. "Days' Alan Gets Carrie-d Away." *Soap Opera Weekly*, 30 August 1994, 8.
____. "Days' Alan Takes on a Witness for the Prosecution." *Soap Opera Weekly*, 27 September 1994, 5.
____. "Days' Billie & Bo Board the Love Train." *Soap Opera Weekly*, 6 December 1994, 5.
____. "Days' Billie Bares All." *Soap Opera Weekly*, 22 March 1994, 3.
____. "Days' Bo & Billie in Beverly Hills." *Soap Opera Weekly*, 28 September 1993, 38.
____. "Days' Bo Chooses Gina." *Soap Opera Weekly*, 20 September 1994, 7.
____. "Days' Bon Amis: Peggy McCay and Joseph Mascolo." *Soap Opera Weekly*, 23 August 1994, 27.
____. "Days' Carrie and Austin: At Long Last Love." *Soap Opera Weekly*, 26 April 1994, 5.
____. "Days' Carrie Rejects Her Knight in Shining Armor." *Soap Opera Weekly*, 20 April 1993, 4.
____. "Days: The Confession." *Soap Opera Weekly*, 22 February 1994, 44.
____. "Days' Curtis Attacks Billie and Gets His Just Desserts." *Soap Opera Weekly*, 16 November 1993, 5.
____. "Days: Dealing with Mom." *Soap Opera Weekly*, 29 March 1994, 2.
____. "Days: Hanging Tough." *Soap Opera Weekly*, 25 October 1994, 2.
____. "Days' Jack and Jennifer: Infanticipating." *Soap Opera Weekly*, 13 October 1992, 3.
____. "Days' John and Kristen Find a Port in Their Storm." *Soap Opera Weekly*, 7 September 1993, 3.
____. "Days' John & Marlena Bring Back that Lovin' Feeling." *Soap Opera Weekly*, 9 February 1993, 5.
____. "Days' John Presses Paternity Issue." *Soap Opera Weekly*, 29 June 1993, 7.
____. "Days' Jonah Arrives Just in Thyme." *Soap Opera Weekly*, 16 February 1993, 7.
____. "Days' Kimberly Learns About Lacey." *Soap Opera Weekly*, 27 October 1992, 8.
____. "Days' Kristen: Like Father, Like Daughter?" *Soap Opera Weekly*, 21 September 1993, 6.

____. "Days' Lisa Rinna: Billie's Gruff." *Soap Opera Weekly*, 8 December 1992, 44.

____. "Days' Lucas Calls a Halt to His Military Career." *Soap Opera Weekly*, 22 June 1993, 6.

____. "Days' Mother-and-Child Reunion." *Soap Opera Weekly*, 26 April 1994, 36.

____. "Days of Fear and Compassion." *Soap Opera Weekly*, 28 June 1994, 3.

____. "The Days of His Life: Horton Patriarch Remembered." *Soap Opera Weekly*, 5 July 1994, 5.

____. "Days' Roman Loves Marlena, Who's Dreaming of John." *Soap Opera Weekly*, 26 January 1993, 6.

____. "Days' Sami Is Battling More Than the Bulge." *Soap Opera Weekly*, 20 July 1993, 6.

____. "Days' Sami Tells Lucas She Was Raped." *Soap Opera Weekly*, 26 July 1994, 6.

____. "Days' Stefano Sidelines John & Marlena." *Soap Opera Weekly*, 24 May 1994, 6.

____. "Days' Taylor Plays Both Sides of the Law." *Soap Opera Weekly*, 30 March 1993, 8.

____. "Days' Tony and Kristen Have an Explosive Wedding." *Soap Opera Weekly*, 22 February 1994, 5.

____. "Days' Vivian Lets Carly Be Buried Alive." *Soap Opera Weekly*, 27 July 1993, 5.

____. "Days' Vivian Sent Up the River." *Soap Opera Weekly*, 19 October 1993, 5.

____. "Death on Days." *Soap Opera Weekly*, 24 November 1992, 19.

____. "A Familiar Face in a Familiar Place: Arleen Sorkin Sails Back into Salem." *Soap Opera Weekly*, 1 September 1992, 9.

____. "Glory Days." *Soap Opera Weekly*, 26 October 1993, 2-3.

____. "Good Time Charley: Days' 'Hotshot' Lawyer Sets Down in Salem with a Bang!" *Soap Opera Weekly*, 5 May 1992, 14.

____. "Growing Up Brady: Allison Sweeney Hurries onto Days as a Fast-Sprouting Teenager." *Soap Opera Weekly*, 9 February 1993, 45.

____. "Heart-Stopping Excitement on Days." *Soap Opera Weekly*, 3 November 1992, 3.

____. "Honoring a Man in Blue: Peggy McCay." *Soap Opera Weekly*, 23 June 1992, 27.

____. "In-laws in Lust on Days." *Soap Opera Weekly*, 22 November 1994, 5.

____. "J. Cynthia Brooks Books into Town." *Soap Opera Weekly*, 13 October 1992, 10.

____. "Joe Mascolo: Days' Phoenix Rises Again." *Soap Opera Weekly*, 5 October 1993, 6-7.

____. "John's Past Determines Kristen's Future on Days." *Soap Opera Weekly*, 1 February 1994, 5.

____. "Kate's Past Revealed on Days." *Soap Opera Weekly*, 8 March 1994, 5.

____. "The Key to Kate's Past on Days." *Soap Opera Weekly*, 16 March 1993, 8.

____. "Laura's Days of Awakening." *Soap Opera Weekly*, 11 January 1994, 6.

____. "Life with Mike: Days' Roark Critchlow." *Soap Opera Weekly*, 7 June 1994, 30.

____. "Lucas' Not-so Golden Gloves on Days." *Soap Opera Weekly*, 25 January 1994, 5.

____. "Marlena Discovers She's Pregnant on Days." *Soap Opera Weekly*, 27 April 1993, 6.

____. "Make Room for Daddy." *Soap Opera Weekly*, 10 August 1993, 5.

____. "Miss...Days Disses Its Departing." *Soap Opera Weekly*, 7 December 1993, 46.

____. "Miss...Days' Financial Faux Pax." *Soap Opera Weekly*, 30 June 1992, 19.

____. "Molly Attacked by Gavin." *Soap Opera Weekly*, 30 June 1992, 2.

____. "Movie Look for Days." *Soap Opera Weekly*, 26 January 1993, 4.

____. "MTV Host Rocks Salem." *Soap Opera Weekly*, 1 June 1993, 7.

____. "No More Days of Deceit." *Soap Opera Weekly*, 5 April 1994, 9.

____. "Peter & Jennifer Find Southern Comfort on Days." *Soap Opera Weekly*, 7 June 1994, 3.

____. "Rating the Replacements: Kimberly Brady, Days of Our Lives." *Soap Opera Weekly*, 20 April 1993, 19.

____. "Reed-united on Days." *Soap Opera Weekly*, 3 August 1993, 9.

____. "Sami Gets Carrie-d Away on Days." *Soap Opera Weekly*, 1 November 1994, 2.

____. "Sister for Sale on Days." *Soap Opera Weekly*, 21 December 1993, 7.

____. "Tim Is No Angel." *Soap Opera Weekly*, 22 September 1992, 6.

____. "Too Close for Comfort: Pit Prisoners John & Marlena Re-Examine Their Past on Days." *Soap Opera Weekly*, 15 December 1992, 2.

____. "Torture for 2." *Soap Opera Weekly*, 30 November 1993, 3.

____. "What's In a Name? Days' Thyme Lewis." *Soap Opera Weekly*, 12 October 1993, 24-26.

____. "Will Stella's Death Mean the End of Marlena on Days?" *Soap Opera Weekly*, 1 December 1992, 6.

____. "Will the Truth Cost Days' Vivian Her Life?" *Soap Opera Weekly*, 10 November 1992, 4.

De Losh, Lara and Gretchen Keene. "Sitting Pretty: As Days' Chip, Newcomer Jay Pickett Is Right Where He Wants to Be." *Soap Opera Weekly*, 14 January 1992, 19.

De Losh, Lara and Jonathan Reiner. "Days Cliff-Hanger: Kristen Falls for John." *Soap Opera Weekly*, 23 November 1993, 7.

De Losh, Lara and Mark McGarry. "The Night the Lights Went Out in Salem." *Soap Opera Weekly*, 23 August 1994, 5.

____. "Days' Hortons Say Hello and Goodbye." *Soap Opera Weekly*, 26 July 1994, 12.

Demeuth, Philip and Elizabeth Barton. "Soap Gets in Your Mind." *Psychology Today*, July 1982, 74-78.

DeNatale, Barbara. "It's a Tough Job, But Somebody's Got to Kiss Peter Reckell." *Soap Opera Digest*, 19 March 1991, 30-32.

____. "The Other Alda." *Soap Opera Digest*, 2 April 1991, 114-117.

____. "Suzanne Rogers: Sometimes Nice Girls Finish First." *Soap Opera Digest*, 3 July 1984, 26-31, 139.

____. "Untamed Heart: Robert Kelker-Kelly." *Soap Opera Update*, 18 May 1993, 42-44.

____. "When Lisa Met Billie." *Soap Opera Update*, 10 August 1993, 18-21.

Dennison, Merrill. "Soap Opera." *Harper's*, April 1940, 498-505.

Denloe, Darlene. "A Soap For Us: Generations." *Essence Magazine*, June 1989, 32.

De Palma, Anthony. "Soap Opera from Past with Fears from Present." *New York Times*, 16 July 1994, 4(N), 4(L).

Devine, Elizabeth. "Their Most Popular Heroines: A Laundromat Attendant and a Cleaning Woman; English Soaps are Different." *TV Guide*, 14 February 1987, 44-45.

Di Lauro, Janet. "After Seven Months as Days' Hawk, J. Eddie Peck Is Flying the Coop." *Soap Opera Weekly*, 4 February 1992, 24-26.

____. "All American Girl: Alison Sweeney." *Soap Opera Weekly*, 30 August 1994, 24-26.

____. "Anderson Out as Co-Head Writer." *Soap Opera Weekly*, 13 April 1993, 10.

____. "Anjelica Axed?! Chapman's Days Are Numbered." *Soap Opera Weekly*, 2 January 1990, 2.

____. "Anne Howard Bids Adieu to Days." *Soap Opera Weekly*, 14 August 1990, 5.

____. "Another Days Weekend to Remember." *Soap Opera Weekly*, 23 June 1992, 32-33.

____. "Another Memorial Day of Days." *Soap Opera Weekly*, 22 June 1993, 36-37.

____. "Appeasing Patsy!" *Soap Opera Weekly*, 6 March 1990, 3.

____. "Are the Days of Staci Greason Numbered?" *Soap Opera Weekly*, 30 June 1992, 2-3.

____. "Are Bo and Billie's Future Hopes Dashed on Days?" *Soap Opera Weekly*, 21 June 1994, 3.

____. "Ariana Chase's New Days as Kimberly." *Soap Opera Weekly*, 12 January 1993, 8.

____. "Ashford & Days in Negotiation Deadlock." *Soap Opera Weekly*, 13 August 1991, 2.

____. "Ashford and Wife Release Cassette." *Soap Opera Weekly*, 5 May 1992, 27.

____. "Ashford Makes His Mark in Video." *Soap Opera Weekly*, 6 August 1991, 27.

____. "At the Days of Our Lives Fan Gatherings." *Soap Opera Weekly*, 18 June 1991, 13.

____. "Back to the Future: Writer Sheri Anderson Plans to Spice up Days of Our Lives by Borrowing from the Past." *Soap Opera Weekly*, 14 July 1992, 12-14.

____. "Backstage at Days of Our Lives." *Soap Opera Weekly*, 28 November 1989, 23-25.

____. "Bad Is Better: John Aniston Loves Playing Villains, But He Confines His Evil to Salem." *Soap Opera Weekly*, 8 October 1991, 31-33.

____. "The Best Days of Their Lives: Lynn Herring and Wayne Northrop." *Soap Opera Weekly*, 5 May 1992, 24-26.

____. "Bill & Susan do Dick & Liz as George and Martha." *Soap Opera Weekly*, 31 December 1991, 23-25.

____. "Bill & Susan Seaforth Hayes: Consider Yourself at Home." *Soap Opera Weekly*, 20 July 1993, 30.

____. "Bonding with Days' Mysterious Danielle, Deborah Moore." *Soap Opera Weekly*, 3 March 1992, 14.

____. "Boy, oh, Boyd!" *Soap Opera Weekly*, 4 October 1994, 45.

____. "Brady Siblings Rival Over Shane." *Soap Opera Weekly*, 12 February 1991, 3.

____. "Breaking in with the Brady Bunch: Tracy Middendorf Makes Her TV Debut on Days." *Soap Opera Weekly*, 17 March 1992, 26.

____. "Bridesmaids' Hell in Cancun." *Soap Opera Weekly*, 10 December 1991, 8.

____. "Brooks Blooms." *Soap Opera Weekly*, 25 December 1990, 29.

____. "Bryan Dattilo Joins Days as Lucas Roberts Junior Titan." *Soap Opera Weekly*, 25 May 1993, 40.

——. "Bye Bye Biggs? Days Star Set to Leave Salem." *Soap Opera Weekly*, 8 September 1992, 9.

____. "Calendar Boy! Patrick Muldoon." *Soap Opera Weekly*, 23 August 1994, 31.

____. "California Dreaming: Behind the Scenes with Days' Billie and Bo." *Soap Opera Weekly*, 7 September 1993, 24-26.

____. "Camilla Croons." *Soap Opera Weekly*, 21 August 1990, 28.

____. "Can Brian & Ginger Be Saved?" *Soap Opera Weekly*, 11 August 1992, 8-9.

____. "Can Days Redeem Lawrence Alamain, King of Torment?" *Soap Opera Weekly*, 11 December 1990, 5.

____. "Carey Hosts Volunteer Video." *Soap Opera Weekly*, 17 March 1992, 27.

____. "Carly Falls Victim to Victor." *Soap Opera Weekly*, 8 October 1991, 3.

____. "Charlotte Ross and Antony Alda Make Beautiful Music Together." *Soap Opera Weekly*, 18 June 1991, 27.

____. "Chilling Out: Billy Warlock Is Back on Days with a Relaxed Attitude and a Hot Storyline." *Soap Opera Weekly*, 19 February 1991, 12-14.

____. "Crystal Chappell Counts Down Her Last Days in Salem." *Soap Opera Weekly*, 14 September 1993, 6.

____. "Crystal Chappell's Surgery Puts Carly on Crutches." *Soap Opera Weekly*, 6 April 1993, 9.

____. "Crystal Clear." *Soap Opera Weekly*, 20 November 1990, 12-14.

____. "Czech Mate: Ivan G'Vera." *Soap Opera Weekly*, 18 January 1994, 19.

____. "Dateline: Salem." *Soap Opera Weekly*, 17 May 1994, 2-3.

____. "Days' Deborah Moore Stars with Anthony Michael Hall & Michael Pare in Into the Sun." *Soap Opera Weekly*, 3 March 1992, 31.

____. "Days' Doug & Julie Reunite for Susan Seaforth Hayes' Last Show." *Soap Opera Weekly*, 2 February 1993, 8.

____. "Days' Drake Hogestyn Up for Film Role." *Soap Opera Weekly*, 22 June 1993, 8.

____. "Days Drops Sabatino and Ashford; Chappell Quits." *Soap Opera Weekly*, 20 July 1993, 2.

____. "Days Drops Veteran Producer." *Soap Opera Weekly*, 7 September 1993, 9.

____. "Days Fan Weekend Report." *Soap Opera Weekly*, 28 April 1992, 27.

____. "Days Fans Unite, Again." *Soap Opera Weekly*, 23 April 1991, 27.

____. "Days' Final Reunion." *Soap Opera Weekly*, 13 April 1993, 27.

____. "Days Gives Jack a New Lease on Life." *Soap Opera Weekly*, 23 June 1992, 5.

____. "Days Goes Prime Time...the Sequel." *Soap Opera Weekly*, 2 March 1993, 3.

____. "Days Halloween Murder Victim One of Three." *Soap Opera Weekly*, 23 October 1990, 2-3.

____. "Days in Cancun." *Soap Opera Weekly*, 19 November 1991, 5.

____. "Days' Isabella Diagnosed with Cancer." *Soap Opera Weekly*, 1 September 1992, 2.

____. "Days' Joy Garrett Dead at 47." *Soap Opera Weekly*, 9 March 1993, 7.

____. "Days' Kimberly Is Going Hollywood." *Soap Opera Weekly*, 7 January 1991, 4.

____. "Days' Lori Hallier Is Free to Be...Whatever She Wants!" *Soap Opera Weekly*, 26 December 1989, 18.

____. "Days Penghlis 'Counts' His Blessings." *Soap Opera Weekly*, 9 November 1993, 8.

____. "Days' Rabin Retires! Again." *Soap Opera Weekly*, 28 April 1992, 3.

____. "Days Recycles Its Storylines—Literally!" *Soap Opera Weekly*, 28 September 1993, 9.

____. "Days Shocker: The Other Side of Alice." *Soap Opera Weekly*, 9 April 1991, 2.

____. "Days Spin-off Poised for NBC Go-ahead...With a New Name." *Soap Opera Weekly*, 12 May 1992, 7.

____. "Death Takes a Holiday: Bo Lives! But Will It Be Happily Ever After?" *Soap Opera Weekly*, 13 August 1991, 3.

____. "Deborah Adair on Salem Days and Melrose Place Nights." *Soap Opera Weekly*, 9 March 1993, 8.

____. "Deidre Hall Back on Days...Maybe." *Soap Opera Weekly*, 18 June 1991, 2-3.

____. "Despite Unbelievable Obstacles, Days' John and Isabella Marry." *Soap Opera Weekly*, 19 May 1992, 3.

____. "Dining with Deidre." *Soap Opera Weekly*, 22 March 1994, 27.

____. "Don Frabotta Is a Hollywood Helper." *Soap Opera Weekly*, 11 May 1993, 28.

____. "Don't Give Up Your Day Job: Jamie Lynn Bauer." *Soap Opera Weekly*, 8 March 1994, 16-18.

____. "Drake Hogestyn: To Catch a Thief." *Soap Opera Weekly*, 8 September 1992, 2.

____. "Easton & Sabatino Win 'World Series': Donate Winnings to Homeless." *Soap Opera Weekly*, 3 December 1991, 9.

____. "Eileen Davidson: Her Role on Days Hits Very Close to Home." *Soap Opera Weekly*, 25 May 1993, 8.

____. "Emergency Leave for Dr. Mike." *Soap Opera Weekly*, 6 March 1990, 5.

____. "Evans Noted for Nursing Style." *Soap Opera Weekly*, 23 April 1991, 7.

____. "Every Parent's Nightmare: Days' Jack and Jennifer Struggle with Their Daughter's Grave Illness." *Soap Opera Weekly*, 17 August 1993, 2-3.

____. "A Fair to Remember: Days Halloween Carnival Was Filled with More Thrills Than Chills." *Soap Opera Weekly*, 2 November 1993, 7.

____. "The Family Business: With a Name Like Antony Alda, Days' Johnny Was Destined to Be an Actor." *Soap Opera Weekly*, 2 October 1990, 34-35.

____. "Fan-fare!" *Soap Opera Weekly*, 28 August 1990, 27.

____. "Fellowship Nixed; Now Garrett's Miss Mona." *Soap Opera Weekly*, 16 July 1991, 28.

____. "Final Exit: Matthew Ashford Tells His Version of His Split with Days." *Soap Opera Weekly*, 17 August 1993, 12-14.

____. "First-time Fathers: David Wallace, Doug Davidson, Charles Shaughnessy." *Soap Opera Weekly*, 19 December 1989, 12-14.

____. "Four's a Crowd: Days Finally Gets it Right with Jack, Eve, Jennifer and Frankie." *Soap Opera Weekly*, 7 May 1991, 3.

____. "From Days to Dayo." *Soap Opera Weekly*, 5 May 1992, 27.

____. "From Slimeball to Saint: George Jenesky Has Run the Gamut on Days." *Soap Opera Weekly*, 6 February 1990, 24-26.

____. "From the Mouths of Days Fans." *Soap Opera Weekly*, 20 July 1993, 8.

____. "Gallison Off Days Contract Status." *Soap Opera Weekly*, 3 September 1991, 2.

____. "Gatherings Get Good Reviews." *Soap Opera Weekly*, 16 October 1990, 27.

____. "George Jenesky Bids a Fond Farewell." *Soap Opera Weekly*, 13 November 1990, 5.

____. "The Girl Next Door: Melissa Brennan Is Almost Too Good to Be True." *Soap Opera Weekly*, 3 July 1990, 24-26.

____. "Golden Boy: Days' Patrick Muldoon Has Never Had to Fight for His Success." *Soap Opera Weekly*, 23 February 1993, 24-26.

____. "A Grand Night for Days: 25 Years Worth of Stars Celebrate a Milestone Anniversary." *Soap Opera Weekly*, 11 December 1990, 46-47.

____. "His Blue Heaven: Scott & Missy's First Home." *Soap Opera Weekly*, 18 February 1992, 24-26.

____. "Hit...No More Sweetness of Days." *Soap Opera Weekly*, 6 August 1991, 31.

____. "Hit...Roman Does Hazel." *Soap Opera Weekly*, 9 June 1992, 26.

____. "Holiday Happenings on Days: Jennifer Gives Jack a 'Yes' for Xmas; New Year's Eve Murder." *Soap Opera Weekly*, 1 January 1991, 5.

____. "Home Is Where the Heart Is: Behind the Closed Doors of His Charming House, Billy Hufsey Finds True Happiness." *Soap Opera Weekly*, 11 December 1990, 12-13.

____. "Horror on the Cob: Christie Clark in Children of the Corn II." *Soap Opera Weekly*, 23 February 1993, 27.

____. "House of Cards: The Stakes Are High for Carly, Bo, Lawrence and Billie When They Play for Their Futures on Days." *Soap Opera Weekly*, 13 April 1993, 2-3.

____. "How Ashford and Reeves Cope with Abby's Illness." *Soap Opera Weekly*, 17 August 1993, 2.

____. "Howard & Alda Count Down Their Last Days." *Soap Opera Weekly*, 16 April 1991, 3.

____. "Identity Crisis: Drake Hogestyn Tells the History of His Character from Pawn to Priest." *Soap Opera Weekly*, 13 September 1994, 32-35.

____. "I'm Moving In! An Obsessed Lisanne Plots to Make Days' Lawrence Her Own." *Soap Opera Weekly*, 18 August 1992, 2-3.

____. "In a League of His Own: Drake Hogestyn." *Soap Opera Weekly*, 4 May 1993, 24-26.

____. "In the Comfort of His Arms." *Soap Opera Weekly*, 13 August 1991, 2.

____. "It's a Home Run! With Two Strikes on Her, Staci Greason Finally Scored with the Role of Isabella on Days." *Soap Opera Weekly*, 10 April 1990, 44-45.

_____. "It's About Thyme (Lewis)." *Soap Opera Weekly*, 16 March 1993, 37.

_____. "Izzy the Bride: Pretty in Peach." *Soap Opera Weekly*, 19 May 1992, 3.

_____. "Jack and Jennifer Go Wild!" *Soap Opera Weekly*, 3 July 1990, 3.

_____. "Jack Gets Psyched Out." *Soap Opera Weekly*, 4 September 1990, 2.

_____. "Jack Stands Up for Steve." *Soap Opera Weekly*, 6 February 1990, 3.

_____. "Jamie Lynn Bauer: On Bringing Laura Horton Back to Life." *Soap Opera Weekly*, 9 November 1993, 8.

_____. "Jennifer Finds Jack & Eve in Bed & Wed." *Soap Opera Weekly*, 19 February 1991, 2.

_____. "The Joke's on Melissa Reeves." *Soap Opera Weekly*, 4 June 1991, 5.

_____. "John Black Collared!" *Soap Opera Weekly*, 13 September 1994, 2-3.

_____. "Joy Garrett in Fellowship." *Soap Opera Weekly*, 25 June 1991, 28.

_____. "Jump Street Jumps Ahead with Michael Bays." *Soap Opera Weekly*, 26 December 1989, 28.

_____. "Ken Corday Continues the Family Traditions: Conducting Days' Dynasty." *Soap Opera Weekly*, 22 May 1990, 12-14.

_____. "A Kinder, Gentler Kelker-Kelly Takes on Bo." *Soap Opera Weekly*, 10 March 1992, 2.

_____. "Kiss My Cheek! Thaao Penghlis." *Soap Opera Weekly*, 5 April 1994, 24-26.

_____. "Last Days in Salem for Justin and Adrienne." *Soap Opera Weekly*, 22 January 1991, 5.

_____. "The Last Days of Staci Greason." *Soap Opera Weekly*, 28 July 1992, 9.

_____. "Leave Eve? Not This Year. Charlotte Ross Decides to Stay on Days as Salem's Head Witch." *Soap Opera Weekly*, 29 January 1991, 32-33.

_____. "A Life Ends, a Life Begins on Days." *Soap Opera Weekly*, 20 October 1992, 6.

_____. "Lifestyles of the Not Quite Rich, but Famous: At Home with Days' Michael Sabatino." *Soap Opera Weekly*, 7 April 1992, 23-25.

_____. "Lisa Rinna: Lady Sings the Blues." *Soap Opera Weekly*, 22 September 1992, 6.

_____. "Look Who's Talking About Her Baby-to-be: Melissa Reeves." *Soap Opera Weekly*, 12 November 1991, 8.

_____. "Mac Loves Letters." *Soap Opera Weekly*, 12 January 1993, 28.

_____. "Macdonald Carey, 81, Film Star and Days Patriarch...Remembering Mac." *Soap Opera Weekly*, 12 April 1994, 8.

_____. "Macdonald Carey Honored by Karate Association." *Soap Opera Weekly*, 12 November 1991, 27.

_____. "Macdonald Carey Recuperating." *Soap Opera Weekly*, 1 October 1991, 7.

_____. "The Making of Lacey and Clare." *Soap Opera Weekly*, 24 November 1992, 2.

_____. "Mary Beth Evans Named Slim Fast Spokesperson." *Soap Opera Weekly*, 19 March 1991, 27.

_____. "Mary Beth Evans on Her Final Days." *Soap Opera Weekly*, 2 June 1992, 7.

_____. "Matt Ashford: Going, Going, Gone from Days?" *Soap Opera Weekly*, 20 August 1991, 2.

_____. "Matthew Ashford's Family and Fan Reunion." *Soap Opera Weekly*, 17 September 1991, 27.

_____. "Matthew Ashford Is on Quantum Leap." *Soap Opera Weekly*, 24 March 1992, 28.

_____. "Mr. & Mrs. Black (not boring)." *Soap Opera Weekly*, 19 May 1992, 2.

_____. "A Memorable Days Weekend." *Soap Opera Weekly*, 26 April 1994, 27.

_____. "Memorial Days Delight." *Soap Opera Weekly*, 21 June 1994, 34-36.

_____. "Muldoon Hosts Ball." *Soap Opera Weekly*, 31 August 1993, 28.

_____. "Nasty as He Wants to Be: Days' Michael Easton Addresses the Rumors About His Attitude, Backstage Antics and Reputation for Being Surly." *Soap Opera Weekly*, 18 August 1992, 24-26.

_____. "New Writing Team to Revamp Days." *Soap Opera Weekly*, 12 May 1992, 7.

_____. "New Year's Eve Murder." *Soap Opera Weekly*, 1 January 1991, 5.

_____. "News from Days." *Soap Opera Weekly*, 23 January 1990, 7.

_____. "Nick Benedict Returns to Daytime as Curtis Reed." *Soap Opera Weekly*, 3 August 1993, 9.

_____. "The Night of Their Lives." *Soap Opera Weekly*, 2 March 1993, 2-3.

_____. "No Holds Barred: Melissa Reeves." *Soap Opera Weekly*, 30 November 1993, 12-14.

_____. "Official Fan Club Launched." *Soap Opera Weekly*, 13 April 1993, 10.

_____. "On Her Own: Mary Beth Evans Faces Days Without Her 'Husband' and Best Friend, Stephen Nichols." *Soap Opera Weekly*, 13 November 1990, 44-45.

_____. "On the Avenue I'm Taking You To...Bill and Susan Hayes In '42nd Street.'" *Soap Opera Weekly*, 28 August 1990, 27.

_____. "One Man and a Baby?" *Soap Opera Weekly*, 27 February 1990, 7.

____. "Part Tomboy, Part Siren, Days' Lisa Rinna Is a Two-Faced Woman." *Soap Opera Weekly*, 18 May 1993, 23-25.

____. "Parting Words from Days: Camilla Scott." *Soap Opera Weekly*, 4 June 1991, 6.

____. "Parting Words from Days: Charlotte Ross." *Soap Opera Weekly*, 4 June 1991, 6.

____. "A Pat on Days' Back: Patrick Muldoon Jazzes Up Salem." *Soap Opera Weekly*, 18 August 1992, 11.

____. "Paternity Row: Days' Sami Goes to Extremes to Keep Her Family Intact." *Soap Opera Weekly*, 7 December 1993, 2-3.

____. "Patsy Pease Returning to Days." *Soap Opera Weekly*, 16 June 1992, 3.

____. "The Phoenix Has Risen...Again! Days' Joe Mascolo on Stefano's Return." *Soap Opera Weekly*, 25 January 1994, 32-33.

____. "Play Misty for Me: Days' Charley Lang Directs a Video." *Soap Opera Weekly*, 28 April 1992, 30.

____. "The Play's the Thing: Behind Lock and Key: Wayne Heffley in Prisoners." *Soap Opera Weekly*, 21 April 1992, 27.

____. "Poetry in Motion: Michael Easton." *Soap Opera Weekly*, 19 November 1991, 24-26.

____. "Poker 101." *Soap Opera Weekly*, 13 April 1993, 3.

____. "Practically Perfect: Drake Hogestyn's Life Couldn't Be in Better Shape." *Soap Opera Weekly*, 20 February 1990, 23-25.

____. "Prescription for Evil: Days' Michael Sabatino Has Finally Learned to Love to Be Loathed." *Soap Opera Weekly*, 16 July 1991, 34-35.

____. "Queen Dee: Deidre Hall, One of Daytime's Greatest Treasures, Returns to Her Glory Days." *Soap Opera Weekly*, 1 October 1991, 23-25.

____. "Red Hot & Blue: Robert Kelker-Kelly Is Glad to Be Steaming Up the Screen as Days' Bo, but True Happiness Still Eludes Him." *Soap Opera Weekly*, 18 August 1992, 23-26.

____. "Real Life Love in the Afternoon: Susan Seaforth Hayes and Bill Hayes." *Soap Opera Weekly*, 14 April 1992, 28.

____. "Reeves' Early Maternity Leave." *Soap Opera Weekly*, 30 June 1992, 2-3.

____. "Renee Jones: Lady Cop." *Soap Opera Weekly*, 16 March 1993, 36.

____. "Rhodes Taken: Days' Jesse Sails into Salem." *Soap Opera Weekly*, 16 June 1992, 18.

____. "Richard Biggs Takes the Lead in Fanon's People." *Soap Opera Weekly*, 19 November 1991, 27.

____. "Roberta Leighton Forsakes Paris; Lands on Days." *Soap Opera Weekly*, 27 August 1991, 5.

____. "Roman Was Right—Isabella Did It!" *Soap Opera Weekly*, 17 April 1990, 2.

____. "Roommate Roulette." *Soap Opera Weekly*, 13 April 1993, 2-3.

____. "Round and Round and Round They Go...and Where Bo's Heart Will Stop Nobody Knows—Yet!" *Soap Opera Weekly*, 11 October 1994, 2-3.

____. "Sabatino Balks at a Lawrence/Carly/Bo Triangle." *Soap Opera Weekly*, 18 August 1992, 3.

____. "Salem Place: Days' Outside Set." *Soap Opera Weekly*, 7 July 1992, 9.

____. "Salem Shuffle: After 25 Years Not Much Has Really Changed. So Are the Days of Our Lives." *Soap Opera Weekly*, 13 November 1990, 11-14.

____. "Salem Sparkles: Days of Our Lives—26 and Counting!" *Soap Opera Weekly*, 3 December 1991, 16-17.

____. "Sami Brady Sneaks Back into Town." *Soap Opera Weekly*, 2 February 1993, 8.

____. "Sami's Deadly Secret." *Soap Opera Weekly*, 3 August 1993, 18-19.

____. "Send in the Clown: Robert Mailhouse Has Added a Much-needed Dose of Humor to Days of Our Lives." *Soap Opera Weekly*, 11 June 1991, 24-26.

____. "Sequins & Studs: Days Celebrates Its 27th Anniversary in Several Styles." *Soap Opera Weekly*, 8 December 1992, 46-47.

____. "Sex, Drugs and Edgar Allan Poe: George Jenesky in Seed of Darkness." *Soap Opera Weekly*, 24 April 1990, 27.

____. "Sexy Lexie." *Soap Opera Weekly*, 18 October 1994, 23-25.

____. "Shades of Gray: With Pen in Hand, Matthew Ashford Reveals a Lighter Side and a Hidden Talent." *Soap Opera Weekly*, 26 June 1990, 34-35.

____. "Shane Does Schtick." *Soap Opera Weekly*, 7 April 1992, 27.

____. "Shaughnessy Lands Pilot Lead." *Soap Opera Weekly*, 10 March 1992, 28.

____. "Shaughnessy Set to Leave Days." *Soap Opera Weekly*, 4 August 1992, 8.

____. "Sheri Anderson: SB's Loss Is Days' Gain." *Soap Opera Weekly*, 10 July 1990, 5.

____. "Sins of the Past, Days of the Future." *Soap Opera Weekly*, 12 April 1994, 2-3.

____. "60 Stormy Minutes of Days at Night." *Soap Opera Weekly*, 14 January 1992, 3.

____. "Sniper Attack at Steve and Kayla's Wedding." *Soap Opera Weekly*, 14 August 1990, 2.

____. "So Long, Sweetness? Mary Beth Evans' Days Future in Question." *Soap Opera Weekly*, 5 May 1992, 3.

____. "Something Fishy at Days." *Soap Opera Weekly*, 10 September 1991, 6.

____. "S.O.S., Save Our Salem: A Return to the Days of the Past Could Bring New Life to Today's Days of Our Lives." *Soap Opera Weekly*, 16 July 1991, 20-21.

____. "South of the Border: Highlights & High Jinks from Days' Mexican Remote." *Soap Opera Weekly*, 26 November 1991, 36-38.

____. "S. S. Hayes Sails Out of Salem." *Soap Opera Weekly*, 29 December 1992, 8.

____. "Stephen Nichols' Days Are Numbered." *Soap Opera Weekly*, 31 July 1990, 3.

____. "Stephen Nichols: Family Focus." *Soap Opera Weekly*, 9 June 1992, 28.

____. "Steve & Kayla's Wedding Journal." *Soap Opera Weekly*, 21 August 1990, 23-25.

____. "Sturges & Easton: Why They Are Leaving Days." *Soap Opera Weekly*, 11 August 1992, 9.

____. "The Survivors: 25 Years on the Job with Days of Our Lives' Frances Reid, Macdonald Carey and John Clarke." *Soap Opera Weekly*, 20 November 1990, 20-22.

____. "Susan Seaforth Hayes Brings Julie Back to Days Sassier and Sexier Than Ever." *Soap Opera Weekly*, 27 February 1990, 34-35.

____. "Susan Seaforth Hayes: Her Turn." *Soap Opera Weekly*, 17 May 1994, 28.

____. "Take 2: If Wally Kurth Can Start a New Chapter in His Life...Why Can't Justin?" *Soap Opera Weekly*, 13 November 1990, 32-36.

____. "Thank Heaven for Little Girls: Despite the Dirty Diapers and Sleepless Nights, Two Days Stars Dote on Their Darling Daughters." *Soap Opera Weekly*, 7 August 1990, 32-35.

____. "The Three Faces of Kimberly." *Soap Opera Weekly*, 24 November 1992, 2-3.

____. "Three, Three, Three Roles in One." *Soap Opera Weekly*, 24 November 1992, 3.

____. "Trial by Fire: Dani Minnick Tackles Her First Real Soap Role on Days." *Soap Opera Weekly*, 26 January 1993, 40.

____. "Turning Carrie into Scarface." *Soap Opera Weekly*, 6 April 1993, 9.

____. "29 and Holding: Days Anniversary Is a Car-lossal Success." *Soap Opera Weekly*, 29 November 1994, 15.

____. "Virginia Is For Ashford Lovers." *Soap Opera Weekly*, 31 August 1993, 27.

____. "The Vulnerable Side of Days' Vivian." *Soap Opera Weekly*, 29 September 1992, 8.

____. "Wally Kurth Releases Album." *Soap Opera Weekly*, 17 April 1990, 5.

____. "The Way We Were: Bo and Hope." *Soap Opera Weekly*, 9 August 1994, 2-3.

____. "Wayne's Back on Days." *Soap Opera Weekly*, 13 August 1991, 2.

____. "Wet, Wild & Wonderful! Soap Opera Weekly Goes On-location with Days for Jack & Jennifer's Slapstick Wedding." *Soap Opera Weekly*, 9 July 1991, 33-35.

____. "What About Me? Days' Staci Greason Speaks Out for Herself and the Beleaguered Isabella." *Soap Opera Weekly*, 21 April 1992, 24-26.

____. "Whew! Days Re-signs Ashford." *Soap Opera Weekly*, 15 October 1991, 3.

____. "Who Rubbed Out Nick? Days' Killer Revealed." *Soap Opera Weekly*, 16 April 1991, 3.

____. "Winter Heat." *Soap Opera Weekly*, 8 February 1994, 2-3.

____. "Winter Heat: Jennifer and Peter." *Soap Opera Weekly*, 8 February 1994, 5.

____. "The Wonder Years: Eileen Davidson." *Soap Opera Weekly*, 14 June 1994, 24-26.

Di Lauro, Janet and Caelie M. Haines. "Days' Isabella Survives...But Can Her Relationship with John Do the Same?" *Soap Opera Weekly*, 21 January 1992, 3.

"A Disappointed Billy Warlock Leaves Days for Baywatch; Charlotte Ross Waves Goodbye Too." *Soap Opera Digest*, 25 June 1991, 29-30.

Dobbs, Michael. "Moscow Turns to Mexican Soap Opera." *Washington Post*, 11 September 1992, A1.

"Does Afternoon Drama Sell Magazines?" *Folio* 20 (December 1, 1991): 5.

Dolan, Carrie, "Labor of Love: Watching the Soaps Is a Calling for Some." *Wall Street Journal*, 17 December 1992, A1(W), A1(E).

Douglas, Joanne. "Days of Our Lives Anniversary Party: 13 Is a Very Lucky Number." *Soap Opera Digest*, 4 September 1979, 30-35.

____. "Eileen Barnett's Singing Debut!" *Soap Opera Digest*, 19 February 1980, 122-128.

____. "Jed Allen: Don't Call Me a Soap Opera Actor." *Soap Opera Digest*, 6 November 1979, 22-25.

____. "Lanna Saunders: This Is the Happiest Time of My Life." *Soap Opera Digest*, 1 April 1980, 21-26.

____. "Peggy McCay Speaks Out for Animal Rights." *Soap Opera Weekly*, 28 November 1989, 31.

____. "Quinn Redeker: Bring Love to Every Moment." *Soap Opera Digest*, 11 November 1980, 14-22.

____. "Sabatino's Secret Agent." *Soap Opera Magazine*, 10 March 1992, 39.

____. "A Setside Visit to 'Days of Our Lives.'" *Soap Opera Digest*, January 1978, 23-31.

____. "Wesley Eure: Change Is Always Exciting." *Soap Opera Digest*, 3 June 1980, 38-41, 139.

Douglas, Joanne and Ellen Howard. "The Lighter Side of 'Days of Our Lives.'" *Soap Opera Digest*, 13 May 1980, 32-37.

Downing, Mildred. "Heroine of the Daytime Serials." *Journal of Communication* 24 (Spring 1974): 130-137.

"Drake Hogestyn Answers His Fan Mail." *Soap Opera Update*, October 22, 1990, 12.

"Drake Hogestyn: Days of Our Lives' John Black." *Soap Opera Update*, 29 November 1994, 33-35.

Drake, R. "Soap Opera Chemistry." *TV Guide*, 28 October 1972, 18-20.

Dresner, Sue. "Paradise Lost: Days Writers Fumble with Jack and Jennifer." *Soap Opera Weekly*, 23 April 1991, 32.

Duke, Tabitha and Stacey Totty. "Fantastic Encounter: The Best Days of Our Lives!" *Soap Opera Weekly*, 5 March 1991, 14.

Dullea, Georgia. "Luke Still Loves Laura. Do the Fans?" *New York Times*, 29 November 1993, B4(N).

____. "Will Love Conquer All?" *New York Times*, 28 November 1993, V1(L).

Dunning, Jennifer. "Real Live Soap Opera? A Crisis? Stay Tuned." *New York Times*, 3 August 1983, 18(N), C23(L).

Durdeen-Smith, J. "Daytime TV: Soft Soaping the American Woman." *Village Voice*, 8 February 1973, 19.

Dwyer, Victor. "Seducing Youth: the U.S. Networks Pursue Hip, Young Viewers." *Maclean's*, 31 August 1992, 40-41.

"Dynamic Duos: Sami Brady and Lucas Roberts Find Friendship (and Maybe More!) on Days of Our Lives." *Soap Opera Digest*, 11 October 1994, 74-75.

Easton, Michael. "A Touch of the Poet: Michael Easton, Days' Tough Tanner, Reveals a Tender Side in His Verse." *Soap Opera Weekly*, 10 March 1992, 34-35.

Ebert, Roger. "Suds and Sympathy." *Film Comment* 12 (Summer 1976): 38-39.

Edmondson, M. "Confessions of a Soap Addict." *Newsweek*, 22 August 1977, 3.

Efron, E. "The Soaps—Anything but 99 44/100 Percent Pure." *TV Guide*, 13 March 1965, 6-11.

____. "When Soap Opera Characters Die." *TV Guide*, 17 April 1971, 16-18.

____. "The Soap Opera Nurses." *TV Guide*, 19 February 1972, 24-25.

____. "The Great Male Secret: Men Watch Soap Operas Too." *TV Guide*, 10 May 1975, 4-7.

Eisler, Bill. "Master Marcus of Hunter, Sorcerer Extraordinaire Is Portrayed by Richard Biggs." *Soap Opera Update*, 5 September 1988, 35-36.

Elin Hammer, Linda. "Izzy B Good!" *Soap Opera Update*, 24 March 1992, 58-60.

Elliott, Stuart. "Elaborate Promotion for Taster's Choice." *New York Times*, 18 May 1992, C7(N), D9(L).

____. "From the Company that Invented the Soap Opera, a Call to Embrace New Media Technology." *New York Times*, 13 May 1994, C14(N), D16(L).

Elmore, S. "Confessions of a Soap-Opera Veteran." *TV Guide*, 5 October 1974, 14.

"Enemies by Day...Days of Our Lives' John & Tony." *Soap Opera Update*, 4 October 1994, 21.

"Engaging Days Ahead." *Soap Opera Weekly*, 20 August 1991, 5.

Epstein, Gloria. "On the Couch: Can Days' Jack Deveraux Really Change?" *Soap Opera Update*, 18 December 1989, 64.

____. "On the Couch: Is Days of Our Lives Kayla Too Good?" *Soap Opera Update*, 12 February 1990, 40.

____. "On the Couch: Jack Deveraux." *Soap Opera Update*, 9 April 1990, 24.

____. "On the Couch: What Makes Days of Our Lives' Justin Kiriakis Unable to Make..." *Soap Opera Update*, 6 November 1989.

Estep, Rhoda and Patrick T. MacDonald. "Crime in the Afternoon: Murder and Robbery on Soap Operas." *Journal of Broadcasting and Electronic Media* 29 (Summer 1985): 323-331.

Estrin-Mendelzon, Joyce. "Jean Bruce Scott: You'll Never Guess Where She Was Discovered." *Soap Opera Digest*, 29 September 1981, 126-131.

Evans, Judi. "Adrienne Says Good-bye to Days of Our Lives...Candidly Speaking." *Soap Opera Update*, 24 December 1990, 62-65.

Evans, Mary Beth. "One From the Heart." As told to Rosemary Rossi. *Soap Opera Update*, 8 October 1990, 9-10.

"Everything You Always Wanted to Know about Drake Hogestyn." *Soap Opera Update*, 26 July 1994, 16-17.

"Ex-AW Hunk Survives Audition and Becomes Days's New Bo." *Soap Opera Digest*, 17 March 1992, 33-34.

Facter, Sue. "His 'Days' Behind Him, 'Knots Landings' Peter Reckell Looks Ahead." *Soap Opera Update*, 2 May 1988, 36-37.

Falk-Kessler, J. and K.M. Froschauer. "The Soap Opera: A Dynamic Group Approach for Psychiatric Patients." *American Journal of Occupational Therapy* 32 (May-June 1978): 317-319.

"Fall Preview: Days of Our Lives." *Soap Opera Update*, 9 September 1992, 21.

"Family Tree: Days of Our Lives' Brady Family." *Soap Opera Digest*, 30 April 1991, 10-11.

"A Fan Goes Too Far: Days Devotee Pens Anti-Carly Campaign." *Soap Opera Digest*, 23 June 1992, 37.

"Fans to Days: Keep Brian and Ginger Alive." *Soap Opera Digest*, 4 August 1992, 34.

Farber, Stephen. "Soap Opera Formula Re-evaluated." *New York Times*, 8 April 1985, 15(N), C16(L).

"Fashion Focus: Days." *Soap Opera Update*, 12 July 1994, 44-45.

"The Fax on Fame." *Soap Opera Update*, 29 January 1990, 25.

Feast, Sandra M. "Fantastic Encounters: One of Those (Great) Days!" *Soap Opera Weekly*, 7 May 1991, 21.

Fellman, A.C. "Teaching With Tears: Soap Opera as a Tool in Teaching Women's Studies." *Signs* 3 (Summer 1978): 909-911.

"Fifteen Shocking Secrets About Days of Our Lives." *Soap Opera Update*, 31 May 1994, 22-24.

"Finally, All in the Black Family." *Newsweek*, 27 March 1989, 63.

Fine, Marilyn G. "Soap Opera Conversations: The Talk That Binds." *Journal of Communication* 31 (Summer 1981): 97-107.

Fisher, Sandy. "Baby Boom! A Days and Y&R Exclusive." *Soap Opera Update*, 21 April 1992, 56-61.

____. "Molly Would Never Approve!" *Soap Opera Update*, 5 May 1992, 40-42.

____. "10 Questions for Days of Our Lives' Supervising Producer Francesca James." *Soap Opera Update (Inside Soaps)*, 20 October 1992, 20.

Fissinger, Laura. "Beauty and the Beast: Robert Kelker-Kelly." *Soap Opera Weekly*, 21 June 1994, 24-26.

"The Five Best- and Worst-Dressed in the Soaps: Here's Mr. Blackwell's Guide to the Sharp and the Shapeless." *TV Guide*, 4 November 1989, 28-31.

Flans, Robyn. "Against the Grain: Jason Brooks." *Soap Opera Weekly*, 3 May 1994, 24-26.

____. "Coming to America: Ivan G' Vera." *Soap Opera Weekly*, 27 September 1994, 24-26.

____. "Life of Bryan." *Soap Opera Weekly*, 1 March 1994, 24-26.

"Flash Fax: Dancing into Each Other's Hearts: Matthew Ashford and Melissa Brennan." *Soap Opera Update*, 29 April 1991, 24-25.

"Flash Fax: Days of Our Lives' Matthew Ashford." *Soap Opera Update*, 24 September 1990, 46-47.

"Flash Fax: Days' Steve and Kayla." *Soap Opera Update*, 4 June 1990, 44-45.

"Flash Fax: Looking Back at Jack." *Soap Opera Update*, 5 October 1993, 52-53.

Forkan, James P. "Can Nets, Sponsors Still Find Happiness in Daytime TV? *Television-Radio Age*, 28 November 1988, 45-49.

Forsyth, Kate. "Where Are They Now? If You've Been Wondering Whatever Happened to Days of Our Lives Favorites Catherine Mary Stewart, Wesley Eure and Michael Leon, Read On." *Soap Opera Digest*, 13 November 1990, 116-118.

Fortenberry, Charlene and Nancy Burgess. "Matthew Ashford: A Jack of His Trade." *Soap Opera Weekly*, 18 September 1990, 27.

"Fox Stations Roll the Dice with 'Tribes.'" *Broadcasting*, 7 May 1990, 32-33.

Frakes, Gary C. "Fantastic Encounter: Reckell to the Rescue." *Soap Opera Weekly*, 20 August 1991, 18.

Fraser, C. Gerald. "Fans Mourn Soap Opera Cancellation." *New York Times*, 5 March 1991, B3(N), C11(L).

Frutkin, Alan. "MTV's Real Gay World." *Advocate*, 12 July 1994, 56-57.

Furlong, W.B. "You Have to Give the Soaps Credit (College Courses on Soap Operas)." *TV Guide*, 14 May 1977, 20.

Gade, E.M. "Representation of the World of Work in Daytime Television Serials." *Journal of Employment Counseling* 8 (March 1971): 37-42.

Garvey, R. "Would I Lie to You, Mr. Nielsen?" *TV Guide*, 14 November 1970, 8-10.

_____. "Soap Operas Are Naughty, But Nobody Has Fun." *TV Guide*, 12 August 1972, 39-40.

Gaylin, Alison Sloane and Jason Bonderoff. "Days Crazed." *Soap Opera Digest*, 21 June 1994, 42-45.

"'Generations' Soap Opera Debuts with Large Cast of Blacks." *Jet*, 3 April 1989, 60-62.

Genovese, John Kelly. "Critics Corner: Days of Our Lives." *Soap Opera Digest*, 6 May 1986, 16, 18-19, 140.

_____. "Critics Corner: Days of Our Lives." *Soap Opera Digest*, 2 August 1983, 134-135.

_____. "The Great Families of Daytime Drama: The Hortons of 'Days of Our Lives.'" *Soap Opera Update*, 23 May 1988, 59-61.

Gerbino, Teresa. "Carrie Is Confused." *Soap Opera Update*, 19 May 1992, 36.

_____. "Fade to Black: The Key to the Past: Deborah Moore." *Soap Opera Update*, 24 March 1992, 60.

_____. "Renaissance Rebel: Michael Easton." *Soap Opera Update*, 10 December 1991, 42.

_____. "Runaway with the Rich and Famous: Robert Mailhouse." *Soap Opera Update*, 14 July 1992, 50-51.

_____. "Vivian Is Vindictive." *Soap Opera Update*, 19 May 1992, 37.

_____. "You Don't Have to Forget Patch & Kayla." *Soap Opera Update*, 31 December 1991, 63.

Gerston, Jill. "A 'Soap Actress': Days of Her Life." *New York Times*, 7 March 1993, H1(N), H1(L).

_____. "Susan Lucci Proves Winning Isn't Everything." *New York Times*, 23 May 1993, H36(N), H36(L).

"Get the Facts: Soap Stars Come Clean!" *Teen Magazine*, October 1988, 50-51.

Gledhill, Christine. "Speculations on the Relationship Between Soap Opera and Melodrama." *Quarterly Review of Film and Video*, 14 (July 1992): 103-124.

"Going for the Silver: Days Celebrates 24 Years of Memories." *Soap Opera Update*, 29 January 1990, 28-29.

"Going to the Chapel: But Are Days' Victor and Carly Really Going to Get Married?" *Soap Opera Weekly*, 7 May 1991, 5.

Gold Levi, Vicki. "A Stephen Nichols Fan Bids Him a Fond Farewell." *Soap Opera Update*, 8 October 1990, 10,65.

Goldberg, Adrian. "Beyond the Corner Shop: Will Britain's First Asian Soap Opera Prove as Popular as Its White Neighbours? Can It Kill Off TV's Ethnic Stereotypes?" *New Statesman & Society*, 28 June 1991, 28-29.

Goldman, Kevin. "It May be a Pilot for a New Soap to Be Called, 'All My Chairmen.'" *Wall Street Journal*, 23 October 1991, B1(W), B1(E).

Goldman, Marla. "Do the Stars Dress Like Their Characters?" *Soap Opera Update*, 6 April 1993, 22-25, 59-60.

_____. "Taylor Made." *Soap Opera Update*, 12 January 1993, 42-43.

Goldsen, Rose. "Throwaway Husbands, Wives and Lovers." *Human Behavior* 4 (December 1975): 64-69.

Goldstein, Seth. "ABC Lines Up Busy Schedule for 1st Quarter." *Billboard*, 11 December 1993, 119-120.

Goldstein, Toby. "Person to Person: Veleka Gray and Deidre Hall." *Soap Opera Digest*, 14 February 1984, 32-38.

"Good-Bye, Julie: Days's Hayes Gets the Ax." *Soap Opera Digest*, 5 January 1993, 9.

"Goodbye, My Friends: Farewell to Two NBC Fan Faves." *Soap Opera Weekly*, 12 October 1993, 7.

"Good Life of the Soaps (Soap Opera Housewives Are Always Happy, While Career Women Are Frustrated)." *Human Behavior* 3 (January 1974): 62.

Goodman, Dottie. "Deidre Hall's Lunchbreak: Fun and Fantasy Fulfilled for Days of Our Lives Fans." *Soap Opera Digest*, 14 August 1984, 20-23, 93.

Goodman, Walter. "The Soaps: In Reality, It's Another World." *New York Times*, 27 April 1989, B1(N), C26(L).

Goodwin, Lee. "A Reader's View: In Defense of Roman Brady." *Soap Opera Weekly*, 28 May 1991, 18.

Gootee, Lloyd, Jr. "A Reader's View: Salem Solutions." *Soap Opera Weekly*, 22 October 1991, 34-35.

Gordon, Ruth J. "A Conversation with Days of Our Lives' Robert Clary." *Soap Opera Digest*, December 1977, 32-34.

_____. "Ill-fated Romance: Val and David." *Soap Opera Digest*, November 1977, 108-109, 114-115.

_____. "Patty Weaver: No One's Seen This Side of Me." *Soap Opera Digest*, January 1978, 60-69.

_____. "Tracy Bregman: Success at Sixteen." *Soap Opera Digest*, 8 January 1980, 20-23.

Gordon, Susan. "Learn About Anger from the Stars: A Study Shows Soaps Depict Good and Bad Ways to Get Mad." *Woman's Day*, 14 April 1987, 21.

Grafton, S. "The Tearful World of Soap Operas." *TV Guide*, 12 August 1961, 9-11.

Graham, Judith. "NBC Gearing Up for 'Generations'; Plans Big Launch of New Soap Opera." *Advertising Age*, 27 February 1989, 3-4.

Grant, Linda. "The Mother of All Soaps: Agnes Nixon." *Los Angeles Times Magazine*, 25 August 1991, 30-32, 34, 66-67.

Gratton, John. "The Marlena Miracle: Just How Old Is Days' Good Doctor?" *Soap Opera Weekly*, 14 September 1993, 38.

_____. "Return of the One-Eyed Man: How Steve Johnson Will Return to Days." *Soap Opera Weekly*, 19 March 1991, 18.

_____. "Roman Holiday." *Soap Opera Weekly*, 19 July 1994, 23.

_____. "10 Dating Tips for the Man Who Has Everything but Love." *Soap Opera Weekly*, 8 October 1991, 32-33.

_____. "What Really Happened to Marlena & Roman." *Soap Opera Weekly*, 24 September 1991, 35.

"Great Returns: Billy Warlock." *Soap Opera Update*, 14 January 1991, 29.

"Great Returns: Peter Reckell." *Soap Opera Update*, 14 January 1991, 30.

"Great Returns: Susan Seaforth Hayes." *Soap Opera Update*, 14 January 1991, 31.

"Great Soap Opera Fan Letters; Excerpt from Letters from Soap Opera Fans; Complied by B. Adler." *Good Housekeeping*, March 1977, 76.

Greenberg, Bradley S., R. Abelman and K. Neuendorf. "Sex on the Soap Opera: Afternoon Delight." *Journal of Communication* 31 (1981): 83-89.

_____ and Dave D'Alessio. "Quantity and Quality of Sex in the Soaps." *Journal of Broadcasting and Electronic Media* 29 (Summer 1985): 309-321.

_____, K. Neuendorf, N.L. Buerkel-Rothfuss and L. Henderson. "What's on the Soaps and Who Cares?" *Journal of Broadcasting* 26 (Fall 1982): 519-536.

Greenspan, E. "The Clean Addiction—Soap Operas." *Self*, June 1981, 80-82.

Greisch, J.R. "Life's Sudsy Situations." *Christianity Today*, 9 November 1973, 18-19.

Griffith, Mary Alice. "Drake Takes the Cake." *Soap Opera Weekly*, 25 December 1990, 31.

Grimes, William. "Computer Networks Foster Cultural Chatting for Modem Times." *New York Times*, 1 December 1992, B1(N), C13.

Grinspoon, Elisabeth. "Beijing TV Loves New York—Sort of..." *Los Angeles Times*, 28 September 1993, H3.

Grunwell, Jeanne Marie. "Days Does Benefit in Baltimore." *Soap Opera Weekly*, 30 October 1990, 27.

Guillermoprieto, Alma. "Obsessed in Rio." *New Yorker*, 16 August 1993, 44-55.

Gunther, Marc. "Peter Reckell's a Big Star. That's the Problem..." *The Detroit News*, 16 March 1986, F1.

Gutcheon, B. "There Isn't Anything Wishy-Washy About Soaps." *MS.*, August 1974, 42-43, 79-81.

Gutterman, Steven. "Mexican Soap Star Has Russian Fans in a Lather." *Los Angeles Times*, 1 September 1992, H3.

Haberman, Clyde. "In Japan, 'Oshin' Means It's Time for a Good Cry." *New York Times*, 11 March 1984, H25(N), H25(L).

Haines, Caelie M. "Brother Marcus: Days' Good Doctor Takes a Troubled Jesse Under His Wing." *Soap Opera Weekly*, 28 April 1992, 5.

____. "Crime Does Pay: Life as a Kidnapper Has Been Very Profitable for Days' David Ciminello." *Soap Opera Weekly*, 31 March 1992, 19.

____. "Honest Abe: Can Roman Handle It When His Best Friend Becomes His Boss on Days?" *Soap Opera Weekly*, 5 May 1992, 5.

____. "I've Got a Secret: Hidden Truths Begin to Surface." *Soap Opera Weekly*, 10 March 1992, 3.

____. "Kim Zmeskal Flips for Days." *Soap Opera Weekly*, 18 August 1992, 45.

____. "Lawrence's Letter: Days Villain Learns About His Painful Past." *Soap Opera Weekly*, 11 June 1991, 2.

____. "Leah Laiman Comes Home to Days of Our Lives." *Soap Opera Weekly*, 7 May 1991, 7.

____. "Past Lives—Secrets Come Crawling Out of the Woodwork on Days." *Soap Opera Weekly*, 31 March 1992, 5.

____. "Reunited! Days' Jack Puts Himself on Trial for Jennifer's Love." *Soap Opera Weekly*, 4 February 1992, 2.

____. "Roman and Marlena's Reunion on Days." *Soap Opera Weekly*, 17 September 1991, 38.

____. "Sleuthing Salem-Style: Days' Newest Detective, Robert Mailhouse." *Soap Opera Weekly*, 15 January 1991, 31.

____. "Taking On Tanner: Days of Our Lives' Michael Easton." *Soap Opera Weekly*, 5 March 1991, 18.

____. "To Tell the Truth: Days' Carly Risks Her Future with Bo By Telling Him the Secrets of Her Past." *Soap Opera Weekly*, 14 April 1992, 3.

____. "Who Are You? Identity Mysteries Comes to Light on Days." *Soap Opera Weekly*, 14 April 1992, 2.

Haithman, Diane. "25 Years of Giving a Hoot About the Hortons." *Los Angeles Times*, 12 November 1990, F10.

Hall, Deidre. "To See and Hear Is to Know, but to Feel Is to Be Understood." *Soap Opera Digest*, 6 November 1979, 36-41.

____. "Why I Won't Wear a Red Ribbon." *Soap Opera Digest*, 8 June 1993, 77.

Hall-Lovell, Andrea. "Deidre Hall's New Look—Short and Sassy." *Soap Opera Digest*, 12 October 1982, 136-139.

____. "Phaedra Hall-Lovell: Days of Our Lives' Newest Cast Member." *Soap Opera Digest*, January 1979, 20-21.

Hallett, Lisa. "Bo Bares All." *Soap Opera Digest*, 27 October 1992, 4-6.

____. "Carried Away: Tracy Middendorf." *Soap Opera Digest*, 18 August 1992, 126-128.

____. "Every Picture Tells a Story: Richard Burgi." *Soap Opera Digest*, 27 April 1993, 56-60.

____. "From Geeky to Gorgeous: Staci Greason." *Soap Opera Digest*, 14 May 1991, 22-25.

____. "Julie Without Doug, What a Concept! After a Six-Year Absence, Susan Seaforth Hayes Makes a Solo Return to Days of Our Lives." *Soap Opera Digest*, 18 September 1990, 134-138.

____. "Rock Steady: Matthew Ashford." *Soap Opera Digest*, 16 March 1993, 22-26.

____. "Sweet Revenge: She Was Too Tubby to Make Her High School Cheerleading Squad, But Camilla Scott's Having the Last Laugh." *Soap Opera Digest*, 30 October 1990, 26-29, 112.

____. "Wayne's World." *Soap Opera Digest*, 2 February 1993, 46-49.

"Halloween at 'Days of Our Lives.'" *Soap Opera Digest*, January 1979, 32-33.

Hampton, Wilborn. "Confessions of a Soap-opera Extra." *New York Times*, 31 December 1989, H30(N), H30(L).

"Happy Days for Days.'" *Soap Opera Weekly*, 28 November 1989, 47.

"Harper Deveraux Returns to Salem." *Soap Opera Weekly*, 13 March 1990, 2.

Harvey, K. "Death on a Soap Opera." *TV Guide*, 21 June 1975, 16-18.

Harvey, Steve. "TV Film Crew Gives Fresno Day in the Sun." *Los Angeles Times*, 17 July 1986, 3.

Hastings, Julianne. "McCallum Re-emerges on Soap Opera." *Los Angeles Times*, 4 October 1983, VI:11.

"Haunted Honeymoon." *Soap Opera Weekly*, 16 July 1991, 5.

Hayes, Bill. "Days with the Hayes." *Soap Opera Digest*, 22 April 1980, 130-139.

____. "Days with the Hayes." *Soap Opera Digest*, 25 November 1980, 32-36.

____. "Days with the Hayes." *Soap Opera Digest*, 12 May 1981, 120-127.

____. "Days with the Hayes." *Soap Opera Digest*, 23 June 1981, 134-139.

Hayes, Bill and Susan Seaforth Hayes. "Hayes & Hayes: Workshop Takes Off Like a Rocket." *Soap Opera Digest*, 12 April 1983, 11-14.

Hayes, Susan Seaforth. "Candidly Speaking." *Soap Opera Update*, 23 April 1990, 18-19.

____. "Days with the Hayes." *Soap Opera Digest*, 29 January 1980, 120-127, 130.

____. "Days with the Hayes." *Soap Opera Digest*, 3 February 1981, 134-141.

____. "Days with the Hayes." *Soap Opera Digest*, 17 March 1981, 134-139.

____. "Days with the Hayes." *Soap Opera Digest*, 31 March 1981, 134-139.

____. "Days with the Hayes." *Soap Opera Digest*, 4 August 1981, 134-139.

____. "Days with the Hayes." *Soap Opera Digest*, 13 October 1981, 104-108.

____. "Doug and Julie Finally Make it to Portofino." *Soap Opera Digest*, April 1978, 26-29.

____. "The Wedding of the Wolf and the Rose." *Soap Opera Digest*, 31 March 1981, 30-31.

Hayes, Susan Seaforth and Bill Hayes. "Days with the Hayes." *Soap Opera Digest*, June 1978, 8-10.

____. "Days with the Hayes." *Soap Opera Digest*, July 1978, 112-115.

____. "Days with the Hayes." *Soap Opera Digest*, August 1978, 112-117.

____. "Days with the Hayes." *Soap Opera Digest*, 20 March 1979, 112-119.

____. "Days with the Hayes." *Soap Opera Digest*, 24 July 1979, 6-14.

____. "Days with the Hayes." *Soap Opera Digest*, 14 August 1979, 29-34.

____. "Days with the Hayes." *Soap Opera Digest*, 25 September 1979, 130-136.

____. "Days with the Hayes." *Soap Opera Digest*, 6 November 1979, 6-7, 10-14.

____. "Days with the Hayes." *Soap Opera Digest*, 18 December 1979, 127-135.

____. "Days with the Hayes." *Soap Opera Digest*, 3 June 1980, 130-134.

____. "Days with the Hayes." *Soap Opera Digest*, 15 July 1980, 25-31.

____. "Days with the Hayes." *Soap Opera Digest*, 2 September 1980, 31-38.

____. "Days with the Hayes." *Soap Opera Digest*, 30 September 1980, 35-41.

____. "Days with the Hayes." *Soap Opera Digest*, 23 December 1980, 23-29.

____. "Holiday Time at the Hayes." *Soap Opera Digest*, December 1977, 122-124.

____. "Susan and Bill's Holiday Fashion." *Soap Opera Digest*, December 1977, 8-9, 16.

"Heart to Heart: Days of Our Lives, Molly Brinker and Tanner Scofield." *Soap Opera Digest*, 18 February 1992, 68.

Heighton, E.J. "TV Ratings, Evolution, Revolution and Privacy." *Television Quarterly* 24 (1989): 31-39.

Heinzel, Ron S. "Now You Can 'Own' a Star of 'Dynasty' Soap Opera." *Los Angeles Times*, 10 February 1985, 6.

Henig, Robin Marantz. "In Britain, a Soap Opera's Unwitting Viewers." *Washington Post*, 26 July 1977, WH5.

Henneberger, Melinda. "As the World Has Turned, So Has Helen Wagner." *New York Times*, 29 May 1994, H28.

Hennessee, J.A. "The Whole Soap Catalogue: Love and Money in the Afternoon." *Action*, May-June 1978, 16-22.

"Here Comes the Bride and the Baby." *Soap Opera Weekly*, 26 May 1992, 6.

Herrick, Linda. "In Defense of Days." *Soap Opera Weekly*, 23 July 1991, 19.

"Herring Leaves Days, Sets Her Sights on GH." *Soap Opera Digest*, 27 October 1992, 36.

Hersch, Linda T. "At Long Last: Doug and Julie Remarry!" *Soap Opera Digest*, 7 July 1981, 138-145.

____. "A British Soap Star Visits Days." *Soap Opera Digest*, 31 August 1982, 96-97.

____. "Days of Our Lives Celebrates 15 Years." *Soap Opera Digest*, 31 March 1981, 128-129.

____. "Days of Our Lives Is Looking Good at 17!" *Soap Opera Digest*, 28 September 1982, 14-18.

____. "'Days' Renee, Philece Sampler, Is Showered with Gifts." *Soap Opera Digest*, 22 December 1981, 132-133.

____. "A Days Visit to Days of Our Lives." *Soap Opera Digest*, 27 October 1981, 122-127.

____. "Daytime's Ms. Popularity Plays an Important Role in the Lives of Her Fans." *Soap Opera Digest*, 12 October 1982, 14-18.

____. "Dick Billingsley: Success Hasn't Spoiled This Seven-Year-Old Soap Star." *Soap Opera Digest*, 31 August 1982, 36-40.
____. "Dr. Neil Curtis: The Lonesome Loser." *Soap Opera Digest*, 31 March 1981, 22-29, 130.
____. "Doug and Julie Marry at Last!" *Soap Opera Digest*, 18 August 1981, 30-33.
____. "Goodbye Salem Strangler." *Soap Opera Digest*, 17 August 1982, 130-133.
____. "James Reynolds Is Going Places." *Soap Opera Digest*, 21 December 1982, 128-132.
____. "Jessica and Joshua Marry!" *Soap Opera Digest*, 26 October 1982, 38-39, 134-136.
____. "Pat Falken Smith: 'General Hospital's' Ex-Head Writer Has High Hopes for Days of Our Lives." *Soap Opera Digest*, 8 June 1982, 126-130.
____. "Philece Sampler: Her Dream Come True." *Soap Opera Digest*, 16 March 1992, 127-132.
____. "Robert Clary: He's Not Singing the Blues." *Soap Opera Digest*, 26 May 1981, 22-27.
____. "Robert Clary Recalls the Tragic Past He Can Never Forget." *Soap Opera Digest*, 6 July 1982, 124-129.
____. "A Victorious Day in Their Lives." *Soap Opera Digest*, 24 November 1981, 128-129.
____. "What a Night!" *Soap Opera Digest*, 25 May 1982, 122-126.
Hickey, N. "The First Hour-Long Soap Opera." *TV Guide*, 8 February 1975, 10-12.
"Higher Education, Low Drama." *New York Times*, 9 December 1987, 20(N), B8(L).
Hinsey, Carolyn. "Days of Our Lives Report Card, 1993." *Soap Opera Digest*, 26 October 1993, 68-70.
____. "'Dazed' by the New Days of Our Lives." *Soap Opera Digest*, 19 January 1993, 32-36.
Hinton, Karen. "Mad About Marcy: Billy Warlock Is a Man in Love." *Soap Opera Digest*, 14 July 1987, 24-27.
Hisck, Bill. "Lather Louts." *Times Educational Supplement*, 23 April 1993, II.
Hogestyn, Drake. "Candidly Speaking...a Personal Opinion Written by Days' Roman, Drake Hogestyn." *Soap Opera Update*, 4 December 1989, 31.
Hogestyn, Drake (as told to Mimi Leahy). "Days of Our Lives Goes to Greece." *Soap Opera Digest*, 15 December 1987, 15-20.
"Ho-ho Hogestyns: Drake and His Family Have a Christmas Frolic at FAO Schwarz." *Soap Opera Weekly*, 31 December 1991, 47.
Hong, Lanxing. "New Female-Oriented TV Series." *Beijing Review*, 29 March 1993, 32.
Honig, Les. "Days' Catalina Girl: Roberta Leighton." *Soap Opera Magazine*, 30 June 1992, 24-25.
____. "Days' Crystal Chappell: Finding Inner Beauty." *Soap Opera Magazine*, 12 May 1992, 29.
____. "Days' Frank Parker: Staying Forever Young." *Soap Opera Magazine*, 16 June 1992, 29.
____. "Days' John Clarke and Wife Patty: Making This World a Better Place." *Soap Opera Magazine*, 26 May 1992, 36.
____. "Days' Tony Rhodes: Just Go for It!" *Soap Opera Magazine*, 7 July 1992, 12.
____. "Designing Days: An Interview with Costume Designer Richard Bloore." *Soap Opera Magazine*, 19 May 1992, 44-45.
____. "Going Against the Grain: Jay Pickett." *Soap Opera Magazine*, 24 March 1992, 24-25.
____. "John Aniston Likes to Play Villains." *Soap Opera Magazine*, 31 March 1992, 30.
____. "Labor of Love: Days & GH Stars Bring Down the House for a Good Cause." *Soap Opera Magazine*, 25 February 1992, 15.
____. "Rebel with a Cause: Peggy McCay." *Soap Opera Magazine*, 2 June 1992, 34.
____. "Richard Biggs: A Real Kid at Heart." *Soap Opera Magazine*, 28 July 1992, 34.
____. "Robert Kelker-Kelly: Stepping into Bo's Jeans." *Soap Opera Magazine*, 7 April 1992, 27.
____. "Salem's Sweetheart: 'Days of Our Lives" Melissa Brennan." *Soap Opera Update*, 24 April 1989, 30-31.
____. "Prime-time Cliffhangers? The Suspense Isn't Killing Us Any More." *TV Guide*, 16 April 1988, 8-12.
____. "With a Little Help from Her Fans: Susan Seaforth Hayes." *Soap Opera Magazine*, 14 April 1992, 44-45.
Hopkins, Ellen. "Endless Loves: Behind the Soapy Scenes of 'One Life to Live.'" *New York*, 18 May 1987, 70-83.
Horn, John and Jay Sharbutt. "Opinions Differ as to Strike Impact on Soaps." *Los Angeles Times*, 6 March 1985, VI, 1:5.
Horovitz, Bruce. "Reality: Soap Opera Digest Kills Campaign." *Los Angeles Times*, 12 July 1988, IV:6.

"The Hourglass Menagerie: Take a Look Back at Days of Our Lives' Classic Stories." *Soap Opera Digest*, 26 April 1994, 52-55.

"The House of DiMera: A Family History." *Soap Opera Weekly*, 21 September 1993, 6.

"How to Be as Romantic as Your Favorite Soap Couples: Tips from the Soap that Knows Romance Best...Days of Our Lives." *Soap Opera Update*, 7 April 1991, 30-33.

Howard, Ellen. "Days of Our Lives: The Final Chapter: Dr. Marlena Evans." *Soap Opera Digest*, 5 June 1984, 98-103.

____. "Days of Our Lives Young Lovers Wed!" *Soap Opera Digest*, 1 February 1983, 108-111.

____. "Frankly Eugene, They Don't Give a Damn!" *Soap Opera Digest*, 29 March 1983, 112-113.

____. "The History of Days of Our Lives, Part I. " *Soap Opera Digest*, 5 July 1983, 122-127, 135.

____. "The History of Days of Our Lives, Part II." *Soap Opera Digest*, 13 September 1983, 94-99.

____. "The History of Days of Our Lives, Part III." *Soap Opera Digest*, 11 October 1983, 100-104.

____. "The History of Days of Our Lives, Part IV." *Soap Opera Digest*, 8 November 1983, 100-104.

____. "The History of Days of Our Lives, Part V." *Soap Opera Digest*, 20 December 1983, 34-36.

____. "Leann Hunley Celebrates a Birthday!" *Soap Opera Digest*, 10 May 1983, 30-31.

____. "Whatever Happened to Wesley Eure." *Soap Opera Digest*, 6 December 1983, 33.

Huhn, Mary. "K-III Is Preparing to Launch Soap Opera and 'Checkout' Titles." *Mediaweek*, 8 June 1992, 3.

____. "Soap Book Goes Glossy." *Mediaweek*, 1 February 1993, 6.

Humphrey, Mark A. "The Lovely Little Things that Turned 'Days' into Years." *Hollywood Reporter*, 8 November 1990, S1-S16.

"'I Don't Like Acting': Why Greason Quit Days." *Soap Opera Digest*, 18 August 1992, 32.

"If She Can Make It Here...New York Will Be Marlena's Home When Days Spins Off." *Soap Opera Weekly*, 25 February 1992, 2-3.

"If You Ask Us...Those Incredible Shrinking Friends: Days of Our Lives." *Soap Opera Digest*, 8 June 1993, 104.

"In Answer to Your Question: Why Has 'Days of Our Lives' Reversed Their Decision and Given Steve Johnson His Patch Back?" *Soap Opera Update*, 20 November 1989, 11.

"In Memoriam: Days's Joy Garrett." *Soap Opera Digest*, 16 March 1993, 5.

"In Memoriam: Macdonald Carey." *Soap Opera Digest*, 5 July 1994, 96-97.

"In Search of Those Missing Daytime Viewers." *Broadcasting* 93 (November 1977): 34-35.

"In This Corner...Days' Austin." *Soap Opera Weekly*, 12 January 1993, 2.

"In Trousers: Who's Wearing the Pants This Fall? Everyone!" *Soap Opera Weekly*, 2 October 1990, 46-47.

"Injury, Illness Sideline Two Days Stars." *Soap Opera Weekly*, 10 August 1993, 7.

"Inseparable Lovers Who Can't Stay Apart: Days of Our Lives: Jack and Jennifer." *Soap Opera Digest*, 12 May 1992, 14.

"Interactive Plot Thickens." *Washington Post*, 30 May 1994, WB13.

Irving, Molly. "Daytime Soaps: the Best and the Brightest." *TV Guide*, 6 August 1988, 2-6.

"Is It Over for Jennifer and Peter?" *Soap Opera Update (Digest)*, 19 April 1994, 2-3.

"Is Love Better the Second Time Around? Days' Roman and Marlena Re-tie the Knot." *Soap Opera Digest*, 21 October 1986, 120-124.

"Is Love in the Cards for Days' Austin?" *Soap Opera Digest*, 17 August 1993, 7.

"Is Matthew Ashford Leaving Days?" *Soap Opera Digest*, 3 September 1991, 45.

"Is She Really the Girl Next Door? Melissa Reeves." *Soap Opera Update*, 23 August 1994, 18-20.

"'I Was Stunned!' Says Sabatino." *Soap Opera Digest*, 17 August 1993, 4.

"Jack and Jennifer Get a Belated Wedding Gift: A Mystery Man!" *Soap Opera Update (Inside Soaps)*, 22 July 1991, 8.

"Jack Herzberg, Former Days' Producer, Dies." *Soap Opera Weekly*, 19 May 1992, 8.

"Jack of All Trades: Days of Our Lives' Jack Deveraux (Matthew Ashford)—Or Is It?" *Soap Opera Update*, 4 February 1991, 58-59.

Jakubovic, Jordana. "Sweet & Sour: A Very Candid Interview With Kristian Alfonso." *Soap Opera Weekly*, 20 February 1990, 34-35.

"Jamie Lynn Bauer Cast as Days' Laura Horton." *Soap Opera Weekly*, 2 November 1993, 10.

"Jason Brooks, Days of Our Lives' Peter Blake." *Soap Opera Update*, 6 September 1994, 33-35.

Jefferson, Geri, "Mary Frann's Hollywood Hills Home." *Soap Opera Digest*, August 1977, 119-122.

"Jennifer's Dress." *Soap Opera Digest*, 25 June 1991, 11.

Johnson, David. "Achieving a Delicate Balance: 'Days of Our Lives' Patsy Pease." *Soap Opera Update*, 15 August 1988, 14-16.
____. "At the Cover Shoot! Days of Our Lives' Boys Night Out." *Soap Opera Update*, 4 December 1989, 3.
____. "Days' Sweetheart's Life of Bliss with a Restless Romeo." *Soap Opera Magazine*, 15 October 1991, 39.
____. "Jane Elliot: Her New Role on 'Days of Our Lives' and Her Best Role as a Single Mother." *Soap Opera Update*, 23 May 1988, 58.
____. "He's Just Jack: Matthew Ashford." *Soap Opera Update*, 4 December 1989, 9.
____. "Hope & Glory." *Soap Opera Weekly*, 17 May 1994, 24-26.
____. "Louise Sorel Snares Plum Role of Vivian Alamain." *Soap Opera Weekly*, 10 March 1992, 2-3.
____. "Mischievous Mike: Michael T. Weiss." *Soap Opera Update*, 4 December 1989, 6.
____. "Playing Patch: Stephen Nichols." *Soap Opera Update*, 4 December 1989, 5.
____. "Restless & Bold: Bill Bell, One of Daytime's Most Creative Forces, Looks Back on 35 Years of Success." *Soap Opera Weekly*, 18 February 1992, 32-34.
____. "Romantic Justin: Wally Kurth." *Soap Opera Update*, 4 December 1989, 7.
____. "Sensuous Shane: Charles Shaughnessy." *Soap Opera Update*, 4 December 1989, 8.
Johnson, Robin. "Childless by Choice." *Soap Opera Digest*, 10 December 1991, 80.
____. "Tired of Your Old Soap??? Check It Out: What You Have to Know to Watch Days of Our Lives." *Soap Opera Digest*, 18 September 1990, 66-71.
Johnson, S. "How Soaps Whitewash Blacks." *American Film*, March 1982, 36-37.
"Joy Garrett; Honored Soap Actress." *Los Angeles Times*, 13 February 1993, A28.
"Jump on the Save Jenesky Bandwagon." *Soap Opera Weekly*, 26 March 1991, 7.
"Just Who Is the Father of Isabella's Baby?" *Soap Opera Weekly*, 5 November 1991, 3.
Kahwaty, Donna Hoke. "Days of Our Lives: Life As It Would Like to Be." *Soap Opera Digest*, 29 October 1991, 10-14.
Kanner, Bernice. "Tune in Tomorrow." *New York*, 16 August 1993, 20-21.
Kaplan, F.I. "Intimacy and Conformity in American Soap Opera." *Journal of Popular Culture* 9 (Winter 1975): 622-625.
Kaplan, Peter W. "Judith Anderson Set for Soap Opera." *New York Times*, 11 June 1984, 20(N), C17(L).
Kastor, Elizabeth. "Fandom of the (Soap) Opera." *Washington Post*, 1 August 1983, C1.
"Kate's New Son on Days." *Soap Opera Digest*, 13 April 1993, 12.
Katzman, Natan. "Television Soap Operas: What's Been Going on Anyway?" *Public Opinion Quarterly* 36 (1972): 200-212.
Keeler, John. "Soaps: Counterpart to the 18th Century's Quasi-Moral Novel." *New York Times*, 16 March 1980, 34.
Kelker-Kelly, Robert. "58 Favorite Things." *Soap Opera Update*, 15 December 1992, 45.
Kellogg, Mary Alice. "She Told the Gorilla Her Troubles and He Carried Her Off to Safety." *TV Guide*, 17 January 1987, 36-39.
"Kenya Uses Soap Opera to Stem High Birth Rate." *Jet*, 31 August 1987, 62.
Kerr, J. "Confessions of a Soap-Opera Addict." *McCalls*, September 1977, 36+
Kerr, Nancy. "Not Such a Lark: Days' Lark Voorhies." *Soap Opera Weekly*, 13 July 1993, 20.
Khan, Naseem. "Soap in Our Eyes." *New Statesman*, 3 April 1987, 26.
Kielwasser, Alfred P. "The Appeal of Soap-Opera: An Analysis of Process and Quality in Dramatic Serial Gratification." *Journal of Popular Culture* 23 (Fall 1989): 111-124.
Kilguss, A.F. "Therapeutic Use of a Soap Opera Discussion Group with Psychiatric In-Patients." *Clinical Social Work Journal* 5 (Spring 1977): 58-65.
____. "Using Soap Opera as a Therapeutic Tool." *Social Casework* 55 (November 1974): 525-530.
"Kimberly and Philip Face Their Final 'Days.'" *Soap Opera Digest*, 22 June 1993, 4.
"Kimberly's Cohabitating: Days' Lawrence Gets a Roommate." *Soap Opera Weekly*, 14 May 1991, 6.
King, Thomas R. "Networks Find Ads for 'Soaps' a Hard Sell." *Wall Street Journal*, 26 March 1991, B4(W), B6(E).
Kinkead, Gwen. "Another World." *Savvy Woman*, April 1989, 58-61.
____. "Confessions of a Soap Fiend." *Savvy Woman*, April 1989, 62-63.

Kinzer, Nora Scott. "Soap Sin in the Afternoon." *Psychology Today*, August 1973, 46-48.
Klemesrud, J. "Stars of the Soap Operas Playing the Mall Circuit." *New York Times*, 24 March 1979, 44:5.
Kneale, Dennis. "Fans of TV Soaps Sour on Glitz, Get Tied Up in 'Knots.'" *Wall Street Journal*, 8 May 1989, A1(W), A1(E).
Knight, Bob. "Primetime Soaps Slip Away." *Variety*, 11 November 1987, 36-37.
Knopf, Terry Ann. "Daytime Money and Power on the Soaps." *Boston Globe TV Week*, 1 February 1981, 12.
____. "Politicians: New Soap Scoundrels." *Boston Globe TV Week*, 22 March 1981, 10.
Knutzen, Eirik. "The Future's So Bright with a Featured Days Role and an Upcoming Marriage, Tanya Boyd Has to Wear Shades." *Soap Opera Digest*, 25 October 1994, 46-49.
____. "It's All Greek (Or I$ It Green?) to Him: Why Outspoken Thaao Penghlis Returned to Days." *Soap Opera Digest*, 15 February 1994, 46-49.
____. "Return to Sender: Christie Clark." *Soap Opera Digest*, 13 April 1993, 58-61.
____. "Rhythm + Time = Thyme." *Soap Opera Digest*, 3 August 1993, 58-61.
____. "Screw-up Makes Good: Jason Brooks Adds Some Mystery to Days." *Soap Opera Digest*, 7 December 1993, 26-28.
____. "Slow Start, Fast Finish: After Some Tough Breaks, Days of Our Lives' Roark Critchlow Is Moving Full Speed Ahead." *Soap Opera Digest*, 16 August 1994, 48-52.
____. "You Can Go Home Again: It's 10 Years Later, and Renee Jones Is Back in Salem." *Soap Opera Digest*, 2 August 1994, 42-44.
"Konica Teams with 'All My Children.'" *Advertising Age*, 29 March 1993, 45.
Kovach, Bill. "Media's Chance to Interact with the Voters." *Neiman Reports* 46 (Fall 1992): 2-3.
Krause, Irene S. "The Days of Carey's Life." *Soap Opera Weekly*, 19 February 1991, 27.
____. "Days Memorial Weekend Mania." *Soap Opera Weekly*, 11 May 1993, 27.
____. "When Charlie Met Harry." *Soap Opera Weekly*, 5 February 1991, 27.
LaGuardia, Robert. "Soap Gets In Your Eyes." *Saturday Evening Post*, September 1977, 40-41+
Lampe, Joanne Douglas. "Arleen Sorkin Remembers Calliope's 'Designer,' Lee Smith." *Soap Opera Weekly*, 9 March 1993, 34-35.
Landry, Robert J. "The Soaps: Then and Now." *Variety*, 11 January 1984, 170.
LaPota, M. and B. LaPota. "The Soap Opera: Literature to Be Seen and Not Read." *English Journal* 62 (April 1973): 556-563.
Larson, Stephanie Greco. "Television's Mixed Messages: Sexual Content on 'All My Children.'" *Communication Quarterly* 39 (Spring 1991): 156-163.
"The Last Days of Summer." *Soap Opera Weekly*, 3 November 1992, 47.
Lazarus, H. R. and D. K. Bienlien. "Soap Opera Therapy." *International Journal of Group Psychotherapy* 17 (April 1967): 252-256.
Leahy, Mimi. "Cruising the Caribbean with the Stars of Days of Our Lives." *Soap Opera Digest*, 16 June 1987, 132-138.
____. "Judi Evans on Her New Days' Role and Her Departure from Guiding Light." *Soap Opera Digest*, 25 August 1987, 105-107, 125.
____. "Matthew Ashford: Risky Business." *Soap Opera Digest*, 20 September 1988, 131-135, 144.
____. "Peter Reckell At the Crossroads." *Soap Opera Digest*, 10 March 1987, 104-107.
Leahy, Mimi and Jody Reines. "Beauty and the Beast: The Love Story of Patch and Kayla." *Soap Opera Digest*, 12 July 1988, 19-27, 100.
"Leaving Salem: Days Marcus Gets Ready to Call It Quits." *Soap Opera Digest*, 9 June 1992, 32.
Lehman, R. "Give My Regards to Woodridge; or Kicking the Soap Opera Habit." *Los Angeles Magazine*, June 1965, 63-64.
Lemish, Dafna. "Soap Opera Viewing in College: A Naturalistic Inquiry." *Journal of Broadcasting and Electronic Media* 29 (Summer 1985): 275-293.
Lev, Michael. "Soap Opera Fans Taster's Choice Flame." *New York Times*, 19 March 1991, C15(N), D19(L).
Levin, E. "White Coffee and Danish Disappeared…(Auditioning for a New TV Soap Opera.)" *TV Guide*, 4 October 1975, 28.
____. "Stuffed Chicken…and Passion: Soap Opera Lovers Enjoy a Memorable Lunch with Their Idols." *TV Guide*, 4 March 1978, 32.
Levine, Joshua. "Le Soap." *Forbes*, 19 August 1991, 102-103.

Levinson, R.M. "Soap Opera Game: Teaching Aid for Sociology of the Family." *Teaching Sociology* 7 (January 1980): 181-190.

Levitt, Shelley and Lorenzo Benet. "Oh, Mamas! Deidre Hall." *People Weekly*, 28 September 1992, 68-75.

Lewis, Sharon. "Fantastic Encounter: Flying High with Days." *Soap Opera Weekly*, 27 August 1991, 31.

Lieberman, Bill. "Adrienne's Finding Days of Independence: Up Close with Judi Evans." *Soap Opera Update*, 12 March 1990, 28-29.

_____. "Black Like Roman: Drake Hogestyn." *Soap Opera Update*, 9 September 1991, 32-35.

_____. "Bo Stays, Peter Reckell Leaves." *Soap Opera Update*, 31 December 1991, 43-44.

_____. "Carly Who? Days of Our Lives' Bo Bounces Back with a New Woman and a New Attitude." *Soap Opera Digest*, 26 October 1993, 22-24.

_____. "Catching Up with...Days of Our Lives' Memorable Marlena." *Soap Opera Update*, 23 April 1990, 16.

_____. "Days' Cal: Wortham Krimmer Finds His Place in the Sun in Salem." *Soap Opera Update*, 29 January 1990, 36-37.

_____. "Days of Our Lives' Drake Hogestyn." *Soap Opera Update*, 29 April 1991, 32-35, 63.

_____. "Do You Know This Man? He's Drake Hogestyn, But Who He Plays on Days Is Still a Mystery." *Soap Opera Digest*, 12 April 1994, 36-40.

_____. "Flavor of the Month: For a Home-cooked Meal and Friendly Appeal, the Brady Pub Is Quite a Deal." *Soap Opera Digest*, 1 February 1994, 76-78.

_____. "Hall Or Nothing: Back on Her Own Terms, But for How Long?" *Soap Opera Update*, 30 September 1991, 14, 16.

_____. "Home Again...Naturally: Patsy Pease." *Soap Opera Weekly*, 28 July 1992, 52-53.

_____. "If Marlena Returns to Days..." *Soap Opera Update*, 18 March 1991, 62-64.

_____. "Isabella Loves Roman...He Can Call Her Anything He Wants." *Soap Opera Update*, 30 July 1990, 44-46.

_____. "A Jennifer by Any Other Name." *Soap Opera Update (Inside Soaps)*, 3 March 1992, 41-43.

_____. "Let's Hear It for...Days of Our Lives and Remembering Hope Brady." *Soap Opera Update*, 24 September 1990, 66.

_____. "The Men Who've Made Our Days: A Look at Some of Salem's Best." *Soap Opera Update*, 4 December 1989, 32-33.

_____. "School? Days? Alison Sweeney." *Soap Opera Update*, 9 August 1994, 22-24.

_____. "There Will be Days and Days and Days Like This: Salem's Newest Triangle Ignites." *Soap Opera Digest*, 18 January 1994, 22-25.

_____. "We Were Just Wondering...Did Marlena Stay Away Too Long?" *Soap Opera Update*, 4 November 1991, 60.

_____. "What Do French Onion Soup, Beatrix Potter and Jack Deveraux All Have in Common? Answer: Melissa Reeves, Part II with Days of Our Lives' Jennifer." *Soap Opera Update*, 24 March 1992, 44-45.

_____. "With 3 You Get Patsy." *Soap Opera Update*, 29 December 1992, 48-49.

Lieberman, Bill and Michael Maloney. "Back to Basics: Days' Jack and Jennifer Find Romance Over Troubled Water." *Soap Opera Digest*, 20 July 1993, 36-37.

Lieberman, Bill and Richard Spencer. "From the Outside Looking in With Matthew Ashford, Days' Jack." *Soap Opera Update*, 2 July 1990, 40-41.

"Lies, Lust and Deception: Bo and Billie." *Soap Opera Update*, 8 March 1994, 62-63.

"Lights, Camera, Action...a Backstage Visit to the Set of Days of Our Lives." *Soap Opera Update*, 3 March 1992, 52-55.

Lindsey, R. "Soap Operas: Men Are Tuning In." *New York Times*, 21 February 1979, IV, 1.

Lippman, John. "'Santa Barbara' Is 1 of 2 Daytime Casualities at NBC." *Los Angeles Times*, 30 September 1992, D2.

Lipton, J. "Soap Operas Are for Real." *TV Guide*, 14 February 1970, 11-16.

Littman, Susan. "When Knots Landing Turned Its Actors Loose Without a Script." *TV Guide*, 28 November 1987, 8-11.

Livingstone, Sonia M. "Interpreting a Television Narrative." *Journal of Communication* 40 (Winter 1990): 72-85.

_____. "Interpretative Viewers and Structured Programs: The Implicit Representation of Soap Opera Characters." *Communication Research* 16 (February 1989): 25-57.

Logan, Dan. "Stephen Nichols Unmasked." *Soap Opera Digest*, 23 February 1988, 29-32.
Logan, Michael. "All My Children Turns 20: Happy Anniversary." *TV Guide*, 30 December 1989, 16-20.
____. "Carey Recalls the Daze of His Life." *TV Guide*, 15 June 1991, 20.
____. "Days Conquers Controversy: How Mike and Robin's Interfaith Romance Won Viewers' Hearts." *Soap Opera Digest*, 7 April 1987, 20-23.
____. "Dead in the Water?" *TV Guide*, 4 July 1992, 22.
____. "DOOL Dreamboat Is Back on Board." *TV Guide*, 26 October 1991, 20.
____. "Five Years After Leaving Her Legendary Role as GH's Laura Spencer, Daytime's Darling Is Back—and Days Has Her." *Soap Opera Digest*, 29 December 1987, 28-33.
____. "Hayes on Days." *TV Guide*, 23 January 1993, 32.
____. "Michael Weiss: How Can They Groom Me When They Can't Get Me to Shave." *Soap Opera Digest*, 6 May 1986, 20-24.
____. "1992: The Worst in Soaps." *TV Guide*, 2 January 1992, 30.
____. "On Those Sexy Soaps, Anything Goes." *TV Guide*, 20 March 1993, 8-14.
____. "Out of Hiding and Into the Limelight: Days of Our Lives' Derya Ruggles Is No Longer Afraid to Be Alive." *Soap Opera Digest*, 15 July 1986, 8-11.
____. "Personally, I Like a Guy Who Shaves: Mary Beth Evans." *Soap Opera Digest*, 7 October 1986, 20-23.
____. "Rumors, Controversy, Gossip: They Seem to Follow Days of Our Lives' Jane Elliot (Anjelica Deveraux) Wherever She Goes." *Soap Opera Digest*, 28 July 1987, 90-93.
____. "Wally Kurth: Prince Charming." *Soap Opera Digest*, 17 November 1987, 34-37, 103.
"Look Like a Star: Melissa Reeves." *Soap Opera Update*, 8 March 1994, 42-43.
Lopate, C. "Daytime Television: You'll Never Want to Leave Home." *Radical America* 11 (January-February 1977): 33-51.
"Love After Marriage? Just Ask Days of Our Lives' John and Isabella." *Soap Opera Update*, 14 July 1992, 30-31.
"The Love Story of Jack & Jennifer..." *Soap Opera Update*, 30 July 1990, 5-9.
Lowery, S.A. "Soap and Booze in the Afternoon: An Analysis of Alcohol Use in Daytime Serials." *Journal of Studies on Alcohol* 41 (September 1980): 829-838.
Lowry, Dennis T., G. Love and M. Kirby. "Sex on the Soap Operas: Patterns of Intimacy." *Journal of Communication* 31 (1981): 90-96.
Lowry, Dennis T. and David E. Towles. "Soap Opera Portrayals of Sex, Contraception, and Sexually Transmitted Diseases. *Journal of Communication* 39 (Spring 1989): 76-83.
"Lunchbreak: A Gathering of Stars." *Soap Opera Digest*, 20 July 1982, 138-141.
Machalaba, Daniel. "Clues to Myrna Clegg's Obsession and Other Soap-Opera Neuroses." *Wall Street Journal*, 14 September 1982, 35(W), 35(E).
MacKay, Kathleen, Linda Kenner and Alan W. Petrucelli. "You Gotta Have Heart! 3 Profiles in Courage." *Redbook*, February 1988, 102-106.
MacKenzie, B. "When the Soap Bubble Burst." *TV Guide*, 9 February 1974, 26-28.
MacLean, Sherry. "Hot Off the Rack: Days of Our Lives." *Soap Opera Digest*, 11 May 1993, 74-75.
____. "Hot Off the Rack: Days' Christie Clark." *Soap Opera Digest*. 28 September 1993, 76-77.
MacVicar, B. "On the Edge of Each and Every Night." *Macleans*, 23 February 1981, 62-63.
Maggitti, Phil. "Peggy McCay: Days of Her Life." *Animal Rights Agenda*, January/February 1990, 10.
"Making Love & Other Troubles." *Soap Opera Weekly*, 26 November 1991, 7.
Mallory, Michael. "Anything Goes: Days's Lisa Rinna Thrives on Taking Risks." *Soap Opera Digest*, 3 March 1993, 24-27.
____. "The Chase Begins: Filling Patsy Pease's Shoes on Days Is a Job Fit for Ariana Chase." *Soap Opera Digest*, 25 May 1993, 40-43.
Maloney, Michael. "Behind the Scenes: Days' Bo & Billie Turn Up the Heat." *Soap Opera Digest*, 23 November 1993, 26.
____. "Behind the Scenes: Hang On, Kristen!" *Soap Opera Digest*, 4 January 1994, 24-25.
____. "Behind the Scenes: The Secret Storm." *Soap Opera Digest*, 5 July 1994, 40-41.
____. "Cindy, Get Your Gun." *Soap Opera Digest*, 11 May 1993, 83-84.
Mannes, M. "Everything's Up-to-Date in Soap Operas." *TV Guide*, 15 March 1969, 16-21.
____. "No Soap Hospital." *New Yorker*, 8 January 1979, 10.

Manly, Lorne. "Do Enquiring Minds Want More Soap?" *Mediaweek*, 9 September 1991, 2.

Mano, D. K. "Making Soaps." *National Review*, 10 December 1976, 1355-1356.

Manry, Flynn. "Dallas: the Habit—a Working Mother Confesses Her Friday Night Affair." *Texas Monthly*, April 1988, 93.

Manus, Willard. "Lindenstrasse: the Man Who Brought the Soaps to Germany." *Sight and Sound* 58 (Winter 1988): 6.

"March Is Not April's Month." *Soap Opera Weekly*, 26 March 1991, 6.

Marcus, David. "How a Soap Opera Shatters Taboos—and Politicians." *IPI Report* 42 (September 1993): 15-17.

Margolis, Mac. "Once-Censored Soap Opera Carves Niche in Everyday Brazilian Life." *Christian Science Monitor*, 9 December 1985, 25.

Marlatt, Andrew. "Soap Titles Having the 'Days of Their Lives.'" *Folio*, 1 January 1992, 19-20.

"Marlena Mystery: How Days Is Writing the Return of Deidre Hall." *Soap Opera Weekly*, 30 July 1991, 5.

Marshall, Brenda and Allison J. Waldman. "Two Faces of Steve." *Soap Opera Update*, 13 June 1988, 9-12.

Marty, Martin E. "Soap Gets in Your Eyes." *Christian Century*, 4 November 1992, 1015.

"Mary Beth Evans' Wedding Days." *Soap Opera Update*, 2 July 1990, 26-27.

Mason, Judi Ann. "I Wrote For the Soaps." *Essence Magazine*, August 1988, 58-61.

Mathews, Judith. "Hayeses of 'Days' Leave the Nest." *Los Angeles Times*, 26 April 1984, VI, 11:1.

Maxwell, Judy. "Days' Kimberly & Shane." *Soap Opera Magazine*, 13 April 1993, 22.

____. "Days' Patch and Kayla." *Soap Opera Magazine*, 16 February 1993, 34.

____. "From the Journal of Days' Kate Roberts." *Soap Opera Magazine*, 11 May 1993, 22.

____. "Victor Victorious: The Dossier on Days' Victor Kiriakis." *Soap Opera Magazine*, 27 October 1992, 34.

____. "Who Killed Days' Nick Corelli?" *Soap Opera Magazine*, 30 March 1993, 26.

Mazzurco, Dawn. "Bo & Hope: A Love Story." *Soap Opera Update*, 21 May 1990, 5-6.

____. "Catching Up with Billy Warlock: He's Riding the Big Wave of Success." *Soap Opera Update*, 25 September 1989, 50-51.

____. "Crystal Clear." *Soap Opera Update*, 29 April 1991, 28-29, 58.

____. "Family Ties: Deidre Hall." *Soap Opera Update*, 5 October 1993, 22-25.

____. "Good and Evil: Days' J. Eddie Peck Struggles to Keep Hawk on the Edge." *Soap Opera Update*, 19 November 1991, 31-35.

____. "Hunter Tylo: Days' Mysterious Marina." *Soap Opera Update*, 6 November 1989, 16.

____. "Keeping an Eye on Hunter Tylo: Days' Mysterious Marina." *Soap Opera Update*, 6 November 1989, 16.

____. "Keeping An Eye on Racy Rich Hearst: Days' Handsome Little Rascal Scott." *Soap Opera Update*, 23 October 1989, 16.

____. "Who Had the Better Wedding: Robert & Anna or Jack & Jennifer?" *Soap Opera Update*, 9 September 1991, 50-53.

McAdow, R. "Experience of a Soap Opera." *Journal of Popular Culture* 7 (Spring 1974): 955-965.

McClellan, Stephen. "'Swans' Soap." *Broadcasting*, 6 January 1992, 50.

____. "Television Targeting Teens." *Broadcasting*, 18 May 1992, 22-23.

McGarry, Mark. "Flashback: The Days of Their Lives." *Soap Opera Weekly*, 26 November 1991, 23.

____. "Flashback: Days' Sister Act." *Soap Opera Weekly*, 6 December 1994, 20.

____. "Flashback: Falling Down." *Soap Opera Weekly*, 2 November 1993, 20.

____. "Flashback: Isabella Dies on Days." *Soap Opera Weekly*, 18 October 1994, 20.

____. "Flashback: Night Sins." *Soap Opera Weekly*, 1 March 1994, 20.

____. "Flashback: One Stormy Night." *Soap Opera Weekly*, 12 January 1993, 44.

____. "Flashback: Rape in the Afternoon Revisited." *Soap Opera Weekly*, 12 November 1991, 45.

____. "Flashback: The Runway of Love." *Soap Opera Weekly*, 8 February 1994, 20.

____. "Flashback: The Wedding of Steve and Kayla." *Soap Opera Weekly*, 2 August 1994, 20.

____. "The Heat Is On for Days' Lexie and Jonah." *Soap Opera Weekly*, 16 August 1994, 6.

____. "Mike Is Haunted by a Woman from His Past." *Soap Opera Weekly*, 19 July 1994, 5.

____. "Stranded! Days' Bo Tracks Down Gina and Spends the Night with Her." *Soap Opera Weekly*, 12 July 1994, 5.

McCauley, Marnie Winston. "Charlotte Ross: Salem's Tragic Teen, Eve Donovan." *Soap Opera Update*, 20 February 1989, 52-53.

McCourt, J. "One Day of One Life." *Film Comment*, May 1977, 46-47.

McManus, John. "Afternoon Delight." *Mediaweek*, 18 February 1991, 21-22.

McWilliams, Michael. "Is It the End for TV's Prime-time Soaps?" *TV Guide*, 24 October 1987, 36-38.

"Memorial Days Vacation." *Soap Opera Digest*, 26 May 1992, 43.

"Memorial Days Weekend." *Soap Opera Weekly*, 25 June 1991, 46-47.

"Mexican Soap." *American Demographics* 11 (January 1989): 18.

Meyer, C. "Race for Daytime Dominance Speeds Up." *Television*, June 1968, 34-37.

"Michael Easton, Tanner Scofield, Days of Our Lives." *Soap Opera Digest*, 11 June 1991, 12-13.

"Michael Morrison, 33, CBS Soap Opera Actor." *New York Times*, 19 February 1993, C20(N), A19(L).

Milstead, Janey. "A Heart Full of Love Saved Margaret Mason's Life." *Soap Opera Digest*, 20 July 1982, 138-141.

_____. "Robert Alda: Cornerstone of a Three Generation Acting Family." *Soap Opera Digest*, 15 September 1981, 12-15, 126.

_____. "You Also Have to Get on with Living: Brenda Benet." *Soap Opera Digest*, 8 December 1981, 28-33.

Mitra, Ananda. "An Indian Religious Soap Opera and the Hindu Image." *Media, Culture & Society*, 16 (January 1994): 149-156.

"Monte Carlo or Bust?" *Economist*, 2 September 1989, 68-69.

Morello, Ted. "Good, Clean Fun: Soap Operas to Promote Family Planning in China." *Far Eastern Economic Review*, 2 December 1993, 27-28.

Morgan, Thomas. "'General Hospital' Celebrates Longevity at 6,000 Episodes." *New York Times*, 1 September 1986, 12(N), 38(L).

Moss, Robert F. "The Next Episode: Soap Operas as a Bridge to Improved Verbals Skills." *English Journal* 76 (January 1987): 35-41.

Nadel, G. "Try a Dose of Grief, Misery, and Woe (Using Soaps as Therapy for Mentally Disturbed)." *TV Guide*, 13 December 1975, 29.

Narine, Dalton. "Blacks on Soaps: From Domestics to Interracial Lovers." *Ebony*, November 1988, 92-95.

"NBC Drops 35-year-old Soap Opera." *New York Times*, 5 November 1986, C30(L).

"NBC Gets Tangled in a Storyline (Interracial Love)." *Broadcasting*, 6 June 1977, 38.

"NBC-TV Jettisons a Soap Opera, Plans Block of New Shows." *Wall Street Journal*, 23 November 1990, B4(W), B4(E).

"'Neighbors' in Nappies." *Economist*, 17 June 1989, 108-109.

Nelson, Robyn Anne. "Days Actors Charm Beantown." *Soap Opera Weekly*, 2 November 1993, 27.

"New Days Are Dawning: Marlena Gets a Spin-Off." *Soap Opera Digest*, 18 February 1992, 35.

"New 'Days' for Eileen Davidson." *Soap Opera Digest*, 8 June 1993, 8.

"A New Days Is Dawning." *Soap Opera Update*, 21 September 1993, 38-42.

"New Patriarch for Days—Peter MacLean." *Soap Opera Weekly*, 27 February 1990, 5.

"News Corp to Launch Soap Opera Magazine." *Wall Street Journal*, 14 September 1989, B6(W), B5(E).

Nichols, Stephen. "Candidly Speaking, the Patch Is Gone, But Not the Patchman." *Soap Opera Update*, 11 September 1989, 6-7.

_____. "Stephen Nichols Says Goodbye to Patch." *Soap Opera Update*, 8 October 1990, 6-8.

Nickens, Christopher. "Between Shane and Shaughnessy." *Soap Opera Update*, 2 May 1988, 27-29.

_____. "Days of Our Lives' Devilish Deveraux: Matthew Ashford." *Soap Opera Update*, 23 October 1989, 50-51.

_____. "The Enduring Love of Justin and Adrienne." *Soap Opera Update*, October 1988, 10-13.

_____. "Is the Honeymoon Over? 'Days of Our Lives' Mary Beth Evans Speaks Out!" *Soap Opera Update*, 28 November 1988, 15-16.

_____. "Keeping Kayla Special: Looking Into the Future With 'Days of Our Lives' Mary Beth Evans." *Soap Opera Update*, 19 December 1988, 38-39.

_____. "The Lover Beneath the Mask: Days of Our Lives' One of a Kind Romantic, George Jenesky." *Soap Opera Update*, 25 September 1989, 28-29.

"The 9 Most Provocative Women in Daytime: Lisa Rinna, Billie, Days of Our Lives." *Soap Opera Update*, 21 September 1993, 58.

"The 9 Most Provocative Women in Daytime: Melissa Reeves, Jennifer, Days of Our Lives." *Soap Opera Update*, 21 September 1993, 61.

Nixon, Agnes E. "Coming of Age in Sudsville." *Television Quarterly* 9 (1970): 61-70.

_____. "In Daytime TV, the Golden Age Is Now." *Television Quarterly* 19 (Fall 1972): 49-54.

_____. "They're Happy to Be Hooked." *New York Times*, 7 July 1968, II, 13:3.

"Now Appearing...Familiar Faces, New Places: Patsy Pease." *Soap Opera Update*, 14 January 1991, 47.

"Now Appearing...Familiar Faces, New Places: Stephen Nichols." *Soap Opera Update*, 14 January 1991, 44.

Nuwer, H. "Soaps Lure Male Viewers." *Saturday Evening Post*, November 1980, 78-81.

O'Connor, John J. "TV: Tears Flow Amid the Suds." *New York Times*, 20 July 1977, III, 18.

Odosso, Shirley. "Fantastic Encounter: Down-to-Earth Drake." *Soap Opera Weekly*, 7 April 1992, 35.

O'Leary, Mick. "Fun Databases: My Top Ten." *Database*, 15 (October 1992), 60-62.

Oliphant, R. "See 'Soaps,' Keep Ahead." *New York Times*, 18 August 1980, A, 23:2.

Oliver, Myrna. "'Days of Our Lives' Actor Macdonald Carey, 81, Dies." *Los Angeles Times*, 22 March 1994, B1.

"On the Cover: When Kim Phones Home for Christmas, Will Shane Put the Divorce on Hold?" *Soap Opera Digest*, 25 December 1991, 33-34.

"On Days of Our Lives: Has Brady Created Problems for John and Isabella?" *Soap Opera Update*, 11 August 1992, 54-56.

"One on One with Days of Our Lives' Christie Clark (Carrie) and Bryan Dattilo (Lucas)." *Soap Opera Update*, 16 November 1993, 46-47.

"On-screen and Off-screen Changes at Days." *Soap Opera Weekly*, 21 May 1991, 3.

"Oops: Shane & Kayla Didn't Do it!" *Soap Opera Weekly*, 10 September 1991, 7.

Orlean, Susan. "Intensive Care." *New Yorker*, 28 June 1993, 33.

O'Toole. "G. H. Syndrome." *Nutshell*, 1981/82, 109, 112.

Pare, Terence. "Getting Into the Act." *Fortune*, 20 June 1988, 113.

"Party; Soap Opera Festival." *People*, 5 June 1978, 90-91.

"Pastime Passions: Louise Sorel." *Soap Opera Digest*, 27 October 1992, 78-79.

"Pastime Passions: Michael Sabatino." *Soap Opera Digest*, 1 October 1991, 19.

"Pastime Passions: Roberta Leighton." *Soap Opera Digest*, 12 May 1992, 73.

"Pastime Passions: Susan Seaforth Hayes." *Soap Opera Digest*, 29 October 1991, 71.

Passalacqua, Connie. "The Hottest Love Stories on Daytime Soaps." *TV Guide*, 24 June 1989, 2-5.

_____. Review of *The Days of My Life*, by Macdonald Carey. *Soap Opera Weekly*, 14 May 1991, 27.

"Patrick Muldoon (Days of Our Lives' Austin)." *Soap Opera Update*, 18 October 1994, 33-35.

"Patsy Pease Out, Ariana Chase In." *Soap Opera Weekly*, 29 December 1992, 9.

Payne, Andrea. "Alex Marshall: A Man of Many Passions." *Soap Opera Digest*, 28 February 1984, 24-28, 125.

_____. "Days of Our Lives Dazzles New Orleans." *Soap Opera Digest*, 23 October 1984, 108-113.

_____. "Days of Our Lives: Joe Gallison Celebrates 20th Anniversary in Daytime." *Soap Opera Digest*, 22 May 1984, 6-7.

_____. "Days of Our Lives Mystery Is Solved: Almost!" *Soap Opera Digest*, 17 July 1984, 30-32.

_____. "For Lanna Saunders Happiness Is a Family of Actors." *Soap Opera Digest*, 30 August 1983, 102-107.

_____. "Going with the Flow: Matt Ashford's Learned There's Nothing Wrong with Being Trouble Free." *Soap Opera Digest*, 19 June 1984, 38-40.

_____. "Good-bye to All That: Why Suzanne Rogers Is Leaving 'Days.'" *Soap Opera Digest*, 6 November 1984, 18-19.

_____. "A Hair Story: Two Actresses Shear It Off!" *Soap Opera Digest*, 14 February 1984, 18-19, 106.

_____. "How Background Music on a Soap Opera Took the Nation by Storm." *Soap Opera Digest*, 13 January 1987, 132-135.

_____. "Living It Up on the High Seas with Days of Our Lives." *Soap Opera Digest*, 17 June 1986, 32-35.

_____. "The Saga of Liz and Neil." *Soap Opera Digest*, 3 July 1984, 105-107.

____. "What Gloria Loring Loved and Hated About Days of Our Lives and Why She Left." *Soap Opera Digest*, 13 January 1987, 133, 135, 144.

____. "Why Is Days of Our Lives So Hot?" *Soap Opera Digest*, 6 November 1984, 132-137.

____. "The Wild and Wacky Romance of Days of Our Lives Eugene and Calliope." *Soap Opera Digest*, 1 January 1985, 32-34.

Payne, Pam. "Celestial Cooking: Richard Guthrie." *Soap Opera Digest*, 24 June 1980, 116-119.

____. "Celestial Cooking: Rosemary Forsyth." *Soap Opera Digest*, 24 July 1979, 104-107.

____. "Diane McBain Talks About the Aftermath of Being Raped." *Soap Opera Digest*, 24 May 1983, 130-131, 134.

____. "I Prefer to Be Half of Twosome and Yet I've Always Been Independent: Melinda Fee." *Soap Opera Digest*, 27 October 1981, 22-26.

____. "Suzanne Rogers." *Soap Opera Digest*, July 1977, 77-79.

Pearlman, Jill. "The Lives of Deidre Hall Fans Made Bleak by Her Absence from the Soaps, Get a New Lease on Our House." *People Weekly*, 14 December 1987, 65-67.

Pearlstein, Jeffrey. "Adair's on Air." *Soap Opera Weekly*, 25 May 1993, 32-33.

____. "Days' Billy Hufsey Splits from Salem for Greener Pastures." *Soap Opera Weekly*, 4 December 1990, 5.

____. "Days' Louise Sorel: From Augusta to Vivian & Everything in Between." *Soap Opera Magazine*, 21 April 1992, 43.

____. "The Doc and the Cop: The Eternal Love of Roman and Marlena." *Soap Opera Update*, 7 November 1988, 14-15.

____. "John de Lancie: Remembering Eugene." *Soap Opera Magazine*, 9 June 1992, 47.

____. "Louise Sorel Sidelines; Marj Dusay Steps In." *Soap Opera Weekly*, 29 December 1992, 8.

____. "On the Road to Recovery: If SB's Augusta Is Louise Sorel's Illness, Days' Vivian Will Surely Provide the Cure." *Soap Opera Weekly*, 21 July 1992, 12-13.

Pease, Patsy. "Candidly Speaking…by Days' Patsy Pease," *Soap Opera Update*, 20 May 1991, 30-31, 60.

____. "You'll Be Seeing Me Sooner than You Think: Candidly Speaking." *Soap Opera Update*, 11 February 1992, 24-26.

Penzotti, John A. "She Had Hair for Days or…How to Do a Doo on DOOL." *Soap Opera Update*, 7 August 1989, 24.

Perloff, M. "Television: Soap Bubbles." *New Republic*, 10 May 1975, 27-30.

Perse, Elizabeth M. and Alan M. Rubin. "Audience Activity and Satisfaction with Favorite Television Soap Operas." *Journalism Quarterly* 65 (Summer 1988): 368-375.

____. "Chronic Loneliness and Television Use." *Journal of Broadcasting & Electronic Media* 34 (Winter 1990): 37-53.

Perse, Elizabeth M. and Rebecca B. Rubin. "Attribution and Parasocial Relationships." *Communication Research* 16 (February 1989): 59-77.

"Pesky Party Favors." *Soap Opera Weekly*, 11 February 1992, 4.

"Peter's Point." *Soap Opera Digest*, 17 December 1985, 16-21.

Phillips, Irna. "Every Woman's Life Is a Soap Opera; Editorial by H. Markel." *McCalls*, March 1965, 116-117+.

"Photoplay: Matthew Ashford." *Soap Opera Update*, 23 February 1993, 34-35.

Pierce, P. "Souping Up the Soap Operas." *McCalls*, June 1973, 39.

"Point/Counterpoint: Days' Carly and Lawrence: Beautiful Ending or Botched Storyline?" *Soap Opera Digest*, 12 October 1993, 38.

Polskin, Howard. "Casting for Guiding Light: Decisions! Decisions! Who Should Play the Sexy Teenager?" *TV Guide*, 28 January 1989, 12 15.

Potter, J. "The Soaps Face Real Life." *New York Times*, 20 March 1977, 1, 17:4.

"Quick-draw Nichols: The Patchman Goes West." *Soap Opera Update*, 3 April 1989, 5.

Raddatz, L. "Soap Operas Used to Be Fun." *TV Guide*, 15 October 1977, 18-19.

Ramsdell, M.L. "The Trauma of TV's Troubled Soap Families." *Family Coordinator* 22 (July 1973): 299-304.

"A Reader's View, Point/Counterpoint: Jack Deveraux: The Debate Continues." *Soap Opera Weekly*, 25 September 1990, 40-41.

"A Reader's View: Stop Treating Ashford Like A Door Matt." *Soap Opera Weekly*, 1 October 1991, 14.

"Real Drama in Daytime: The Network's Battle for Dominance." *Broadcasting*, 2 July 1973, 17-19.

"Real-Life Heroes: Who Says Nice Guys Have to Finish Last?" *Soap Opera Digest*, 15 October 1991, 112.

"The Real Story: How Days Lured Lucy Away from Port Charles." *Soap Opera Digest*, 17 March 1992, 35.

"The Real Story: Why Patsy Pease Left Days of Our Lives." *Soap Opera Digest*, 19 January 1993, 4-5.

Reckell, Peter. "Candidly Speaking..." *Soap Opera Update*, 21 May 1990, 8-9, 57.

Reddicliffe, Steven. "Is J.R. Shot?" *Texas Monthly*, April 1988, 90-101.

Reed, Jon-Michael. "Best and Worst of Daytime." *Los Angeles Times*, 25 February 1983, VI, 21:1.

____. "'Soap Studs' Gifts 'n' Other Goodies." *Los Angeles Times*, 15 December 1982, VI:9.

Reed, Julia. "As Soapdish Makes Light of Daytime Dramatics, Julia Reed Reveals Why She, for One, Is Dead Serious about Raven, Sky, Draper, April..." *Vogue*, June 1991, 80-82.

Reichardt, Nancy M. "ABC Videos Offer Daytime Hunks, Weddings and On-the-Set Scenes." *TV Times (Los Angeles Times)*, 27 February 1994, 22.

____. "First Impressions Count for Jamie Lyn Bauer." *TV Times (Los Angeles Times)*, 13 March 1994, 19.

____. "Jason Brooks' Surprise Announcement." *TV Times (Los Angeles Times)*, 3 April 1994, 63.

Rein, R.K., G. Birnbaum and B. Landine. "Soaps' New Teenage Sex Kittens Struggle to Lead Normal Lives Away from the Set." *People*, 27 October 1980, 80-82.

Reiner, Jonathan. "Days Sends Beth Nielsen Chapman Soaring Up the Charts." *Soap Opera Weekly*, 17 September 1991, 5.

____. "Hit...Sami's Angst on Days." *Soap Opera Weekly*, 14 September 1993, 18.

Reines, Jody. "Stephen Nichols Faces Life After Patch." *Soap Opera Digest*, 27 November 1990, 34.

"A Return For Steve and Kayla?" *Soap Opera Digest*, 31 August 1993, 5.

Richardson, Donald Charles. "Daytime TV Hunks." *Weight Watchers Magazine*, June 1988, 58-59.

Richmond, Ray. "I Can't Be a Teenager Forever...So What's Billy Warlock Doing Back on Days?" *Soap Opera Digest*, 19 February 1991, 24-30.

——. "A Solitary Man: Though He's Happily Married and Happy to Be on Days, Sometimes Michael Sabatino Has to Leave Them Both Behind." *Soap Opera Digest*, 16 April 1991, 10-15.

Rigg, Cynthia E. "Days' Places of Interest." *Soap Opera Magazine*, 11 October 1994, 54-55.

____. "Who's Who in Salem." *Soap Opera Magazine*, 4 October 1994, 54.

Rizzo, Tony. "Deidre Hall Throws a Party for Her Fans." *Soap Opera Digest*, 13 September 1983, 138-139.

____. "Hiking with Brenda Benet." *Soap Opera Digest*, 15 July 1980, 126-134.

____. "Jack Coleman: Being an Actor Is a Double-edged Sword." *Soap Opera Digest*, 13 April 1982, 136-141.

____. "Mark Tapscott: Devouring the Gifts of a New Life." *Soap Opera Digest*, 14 August 1979, 72, 97-99.

____. "Patty Weaver and Richard Guthrie...Mutual Admiration Society." *Soap Opera Digest*, 22 May 1979, 123-127.

____. "Rosemary Forsyth: Daytime's Wonder Woman." *Soap Opera Digest*, 14 August 1979, 18-23.

____. "Wayne Northrop: I've Never Considered Myself a Pretty Boy." *Soap Opera Digest*, 11 May 1982, 126-131.

"Roark Critchlow, Days of Our Lives Mike Horton." *Soap Opera Update*, 20 September 1994, 33-35.

"Roark Critchlow, Mike, Days of Our Lives." *Soap Opera Weekly*, 2 August 1994, 44.

Roberts, Ronee. "Josh Taylor: He's Not Only an Actor, He's a Lawyer." *Soap Opera Digest*, May 1978, 6-7.

Roberts, Roxanne. "In a Lather Over the Soaps; Bubbling with Enthusiasm, Fans Meet Their Favorite Daytime Celebrities." *Washington Post*, 23 August 1993, B1.

Robbins, Fred. "...And So Are the Days of His Life: During His 25 Years on Days, Macdonald Carey's Life Has Resembled a Soap Opera." *Soap Opera Weekly*, 18 June 1991, 34-35.

____. "You Don't Say: Deidre Hall." *Soap Opera Weekly*, 28 January 1992, 42.

"Robert Kelker-Kelly (Days of Our Lives' Bo Brady)." *Soap Opera Update*, 15 November 1994, 33-35.

"Robert Kelker-Kelly Is Days' New Bo." *Soap Opera Weekly*, 3 March 1992, 3.

"Rocky Days Ahead: Love and Tragedy Will Hit Salem." *Soap Opera Digest*, 1 September 1992, 42.

Rogers, Deborah D. "Daze of Our Lives: The Soap Opera as Feminine Text." *Journal of American Culture*, 14 (Winter 1991): 29-42.

____. "Guiding Blight: The Soap Opera and the 18th-Century Novel." *Centennial Review* 34 (Winter 1990): 73-91.

Rogers, Sheila. "U.K. Suds." *Rolling Stone*, 10 March 1988, 38.

"Roman Redux: Days' Roman Comes Face to Face with Himself." *Soap Opera Weekly*, 15 October 1991.

Romine, Damon. "A Face in the Crowd: An SOU Editor Spends a Day in Salem." *Soap Opera Update (Inside Soaps)*, 26 January 1993, 6-7.

____. "At Home in the White House: Scott, Emily, & Melissa Reeves." *Soap Opera Update*, 20 April 1993, 34-39.

____. "Candidly Crystal." *Soap Opera Update*, 29 June 1993, 18-21.

____. "Days' Jennifer Cuts Loose." *Soap Opera Update*, 5 October 1993, 70-71.

____. "Days to Remember: One Last Good-bye to 3 of Your Favorite Stars." *Soap Opera Update*, 7 September 1993, 18-23.

____. "Deborah Adair." *Soap Opera Update*, 1 June 1993, 28-29, 49.

____. "Devil in Disguise: Thaao Penghlis." *Soap Opera Weekly*, 25 January 1994, 48-49.

____. "Fabulous Foes: Laura and Kate." *Soap Opera Update*, 19 April 1994, 20-22.

____. "Family Man: Drake Hogestyn." *Soap Opera Update*, 5 April 1994, 22-25.

____. "First the Secrets, Then the Sizzle." *Soap Opera Update*, 27 July 1993, 60-63.

____. "Forget Everything You've Seen Before...There's a New Mike in Salem." *Soap Opera Update*, 31 May 1994, 52.

____. "Good vs. Good: The Days of Reckoning." *Soap Opera Update*, 25 January 1994, 60-62.

____. "Heartbreaker or Lovemaker: Eileen Davidson." *Soap Opera Update*, 15 June 1993, 42-45.

____. "Here Comes Trouble: Lisa Rinna." *Soap Opera Update*, 15 December 1992, 50-51.

____. "Hope Springs Eternal." *Soap Opera Update*, 14 June 1994, 38-39.

____. "How Far Will Marlena Go to Save John?" *Soap Opera Update*, 17 May 1994, 62-63.

____. "If Madonna Can Do It...So Can Days of Our Lives' New Kimberly." *Soap Opera Update*, 23 March 1993, 50-51.

____. "Is There Still Hope for Days?" *Soap Opera Update*, 16 November 1993, 58-59.

____. "Killer Charm: Patrick Muldoon." *Soap Opera Update*, 8 February 1994, 18-20.

____. "Let's Talk: Patrick Muldoon." *Soap Opera Update*, 24 August 1993, 44-46.

____. "Louise's Lair." *Soap Opera Update*, 20 September 1994, 22-24.

____. "A Man for All Seasons: Days of Our Lives' Michael Sabatino Prefers the Freedom of the Outdoors to the Confines of a Studio." *Soap Opera Update*, 30 June 1992, 50-53.

____. "Missy Bounces Back." *Soap Opera Update*, 14 December 1993, 22-25.

____. "Murder He Wrote: Matt Ashford Kicks Off a Fun-filled Days Weekend." *Soap Opera Update*, 4 May 1993, 32-35.

____. "Passion Play: Will Days' Roger Make a Move on Marlena?" *Soap Opera Update*, 3 November 1992, 47.

____. "Picture Perfect: Deborah Adair Is Living the Ideal Hollywood Life." *Soap Opera Update*, 30 November 1993, 18-21.

____. "Prime Time: Deidre Hall." *Soap Opera Update*, 29 November 1994, 48-49.

____. "Rebel with a Cause: Robert Kelker-Kelly." *Soap Opera Update*, 11 January 1994, 34-37.

____. "Redefining Family Values: Jack and Jennifer." *Soap Opera Update*, 26 January 1993, 60-63.

____. "The Secret Garden of Louise Sorel." *Soap Opera Update*, 22 September 1992, 22-25.

____. "SOU Readers Reunite the Most Romantic Couple of All Time!" *Soap Opera Update*, 22 September 1992, 40-41.

____. "Sweet Sixteen: Days of Our Lives' Alison Sweeney (Sami)." *Soap Opera Update*, 20 April 1993, 62.

____. "There's Always Hope." *Soap Opera Update*, 1 November 1994, 46-47.

____. "Two Together: Carrie and Austin." *Soap Opera Update*, 28 June 1994, 24-26.

____. "Will Jack and Jen Be Able to Save Their Baby?" *Soap Opera Update*, 1 June 1993, 60-61.

Rorke, Robert. "Executive Sweet: Deborah Adair." *Soap Opera Digest*, 6 July 1993, 38-41.

____. "A Fine Madness: Louise Sorel." *Soap Opera Weekly*, 16 August 1994, 12-14.

____. "Ivan the Not-so-terrible." *Soap Opera Digest*, 22 June 1993, 90.

____. "Seeing the Light of 'Days.'" *Soap Opera Digest*, 13 October 1992, 64.

____. "Two Heads Are Better than One: When Writing a Soap, Having a Partner Can Make the Difference." *Soap Opera Digest*, 7 August 1990, 62–64, 112.

____. "Which Woman Will be Days of Our Lives' Bo's Wife?" *Soap Opera Update*, 6 September 1994, 60-62.

____. "Why Everybody Loves Frances Reid." *Soap Opera Digest*, 5 January 1993, 64-65.

Rose, B. "Thickening the Plot." *Journal of Communication* 29 (Autumn 1979): 81-84.

Rose, Rick. "How to Become a Salem Nurse." *Soap Opera Update*, 16 June 1992, 41-43.

Rosenberg, Howard. "Ten Years After: In a Decade of 'Dallas' Clones and 'Infotainment,' Was Anything Real?" *American Film*, December 1988, 18-19.

Rosenthal, Sharon. "Dynasty's Sin: Bitch Goddess Alexis Goes Wimp." *Mediaweek*, 25 November 1991, 32.

____. "Soaps Are Like Morality Plays of the 16th Century." *Mediaweek*, 4 November 1991, 25.

"Ross & Warlock Leaving Days." *Soap Opera Weekly*, 28 May 1991, 2.

Rossi, Rosemary. "An Adam for Eve...or Kim? Days' Randy Reinholz Tunes In to Salem." *Soap Opera Update*, 5 June 1989, 37.

____. "Arleen Sorkin Says, 'Take Michael Weiss, Please.'" *Soap Opera Update*, 19 December 1988, 8-12.

____. "Days of Our Lives' Emilio Is Hot!" *Soap Opera Update*, 28 August 1989, 12.

____. "Days of Our Lives' Lisa Howard Tells the Truth About Mike and April." *Soap Opera Update*, 9 January 1989, 14-15,

____. "A Days of Our Lives Timely Fantasy: Creating a 1940s Manhattan Melodrama." *Soap Opera Update*, 1 January 1990, 48-49.

____. "The Eve Chronicles." *Soap Opera Update*, 25 February 1991, 60-62.

____. "Glimpsing Another Side of Days of Our Lives Stephen Nichols." *Soap Opera Update*, 18 June 1990, 8-9.

____. "Good Old Days Ahead!" *Soap Opera Update*, 12 February 1990, 24.

____. "Have I Got a Deal for You: Johnny Corelli Swindles Salem." *Soap Opera Update*, 18 March 1991, 42-44.

____. "He Ain't Heavy, He's My Brother: A Conversation with Days' Charles and Y&R's David Shaughnessy." *Soap Opera Weekly*, 31 March 1992, 12-13.

____. "Is Mary Beth Evans Leaving Days?" *Soap Opera Update*, 8 April 1991, 13-14.

____. "Mary Beth Evans' Day of Reckoning, Giving Birth to Katie." *Soap Opera Update*, 18 June 1990, 6-7.

____. "Mindy Clarke, Days of Our Lives New Found Faith." *Soap Opera Update*, 7 August 1989, 17.

____. "Motherhood, the Peggy McCay Way." *Soap Opera Update*, 15 May 1989, 50-51.

____. "Quick Takes with Our Lovers from the Cover." *Soap Opera Update*, 15 January 1990, 6-7.

____. "Sweetness—Mary Beth Evans." *Soap Opera Update*, 13 June 1988, 13-14.

____. "What Do You Get When You Cross Peter Sellers, Clark Kent and Columbo? Days of Our Lives' New Bumbling Detective Brian Scofield." *Soap Opera Update*, 25 February 1991, 12-13.

Rothman, Andrea. "Soap Opera Digest Ad Campaign Spoof Runs into Reality." *Wall Street Journal*, 23 June 1988, 34(W), 38(E).

Rubenstein, Leslie. "Confessions of a Soap Opera Addict." *McCall's*, March 1986, 84-90.

Rubin, Alan M. "Uses of Daytime Soap Operas by College Students." *Journal of Broadcasting and Electronic Media* 29 (Summer 1985): 241-258.

Rubin, T. I. "Psychiatrists' Notebook; Soap Operas." *Ladies Home Journal*, January 1976, 43.

Rule, Sheila. "Happy End or Turmoil? Soap Fans Thicken Plot." *New York Times*, 25 May 1989, B1(N), A4(L).

____. "Soundtrack for a Soap." *New York Times*, 16 February 1994, C17.

____. "To Cut Births, Kenya Turns to a Soap Opera." *New York Times*, 14 June 1987 7(N), 15(L).

Russell, D. "Deidre and Andrea: Actresses and Twins." *TV Guide*, 12 November 1977, 18-19.

"Sailing Back Into Salem: Days' Reunion Cruise." *Soap Opera Magazine*, 25 January 1994, 39.

"Salem Finally on the Map?" *Soap Opera Weekly*, 28 May 1991, 5.

"Salem's Outbreak of Odd Couples." *Soap Opera Weekly*, 2 April 1991, 5.

"Salem Shake-Up: The Days Are Numbered for Isabella, Ginger and Brian." *Soap Opera Digest*, 4 August 1992, 33-34.

Saltzman, J. "Tune in Tomorrow." *USA Today*, November 1980, 39.

Sammons, Mary Beth. "Dressed to Thrill: Soap Opera Bridal Fashions." *Soap Opera Digest*, 12 November 1991, 6-11.

Sandberg, Jared. "Melrose Place Inspires Passion in Cyberspace." *Wall Street Journal*, 20 May 1994, B1.

Schaffer, Kay. "'A Country Practice:' Motherhood, Surrogacy and the Price of Love." *Hecate* 19 (October 1993): 128-139.

Schalchlin, Steven M. "The Stay-Young Secrets of a Soap Opera Queen (Ruth Warrick)." *Weight Watchers Magazine*, August 1988, 58-59.

Scheier, Madeline. "Bill Hayes Finds His Roots." *Soap Opera Digest*, 17 September 1991, 135.

Schemering, Christopher. "This Week in Soap History: Days Tragedy, Ryan's Torment." *Soap Opera Weekly*, 10 April 1990, 39.

____. "This Week in Soap History: Days Please." *Soap Opera Weekly*, 19 December 1989, 21.

____. "This Week in Soap History: Salem's St. Valentine's Day Massacre." *Soap Opera Weekly*, 20 February 1990, 40.

Schmuckler, Eric. "Darkness on the Edge of Night: CBS Daytime Ratings Fall Precipitously; Network's Research Chief Blames O.J." *Mediaweek*, 7 November 1994, 3.

Schnaufer, Jeff. "Soap Opera Forum Focuses on Change." *Los Angeles Times*, 11 March 1994, B2.

Schoenstein, R. "I Was a Soap-Opera School Dropout." *TV Guide*, 9 October 1976.

____. "Watch It for Me, Daddy, Until I Get the Flu." *TV Guide*, 4 December 1976.

Schreiber, E. S. "The Effect of Age and Sex on the Perception of TV Characters: An Inter-Age Comparison." *Journal of Broadcasting* 23 (Winter 1979): 81-93.

Schultze, Quentin J. "The Never-Ending Story: Today's Soap Operas Seem to Be Going Nowhere, but a Christian View of Life Knows That Someday God Will Write, 'the End.'" *Christianity Today*, 17 April 1987, 26-29.

"Score or Snore: The Wedding of Days' John & Isabella." *Soap Opera Weekly*, 9 June 1992, 5.

"Seaforth Hayes and Gallison Tell Their Own Stories." *Soap Opera Weekly*, 26 November 1991, 8.

"The Search for Baby Isabella Rages On." *Soap Opera Update (Digest)*, 28 December 1993, 2-3.

"The Secret Alamain Plot to Destroy John." *Soap Opera Update*, 30 June 1992, 56-59.

Serwer, Andrew. "Lights! Camera! Cash Flow!" *Fortune*, 6 September 1993, 11.

"Seven Deadly Daytime Sins." *Time*, 8 April 1966, 61.

"Seven Sexist Soapers." *Us*, 24 November 1981, 13-14, 17-18, 22-23.

Severo, Richard. "Macdonald Carey, 81, Film Actor with a Soap Opera Career, Dies." *New York Times*, 22 March 1994, B15(N), B8(L).

"Sex and Suffering in the Afternoon." *Time*, 12 January 1976, 46-48, 51-53.

"Sex, Lies and Lucas." *Soap Opera Weekly*, 22 March 1994, 3.

Shader, Diane. "Your Continuing Success Story in Soap Opera Writing." *Writer's Digest*, December 1987, 41-45.

"Shadows." *New Yorker*, 26 June 1989, 28-29.

Shaffer, Louise. "Confessions of a Soap-Opera Star: How I Learned to Love Daytime Drama." *Glamour*, November 1988, 62-64.

Shaheen, Jack G. and Alan Bunce. "A Skewed Image of Arabs." *Christian Science Monitor*, 17 September 1990, 11.

"Shane's Final Days: Why Shaughnessy's Leaving Salem." *Soap Opera Digest*, 29 September 1992, 39.

Shaughnessy, Charles. "Candidly Speaking." *Soap Opera Weekly*, 8 October 1990, 32-33, 65.

Shenon, Philip. "Cliffhanger Down Under: Soap Opera Has Malaysia in a Huff." *New York Times*, 24 July 1991, A4(N), A10(L).

Sherwood, D. "All About Money-Counting Music and Other Soap Opera Times." *TV Guide*, 26 February 1972, 42-43.

"Should Days' Hortons Slug It Out?" *Soap Opera Digest*, 10 November 1992, 36.

Showalter, Elaine. "The Vampyr: A Soap Opera." *Times Literary Supplement*, 8 January 1993, 14.

Siegel, M. "Soap Opera Stars." *Good Housekeeping*, June 1976, 86+

Siegler, Bonnie. "Days' Crystal Chappell: Protecting the Environment and Dressing the Part." *Soap Opera Magazine*, 2 February 1993, 10-11.

____. "Days Dreamer." *Soap Opera Update*, 5 November 1990, 44-47.

____. "Days' Elusive Staci Greason: I Want the American Dream." *Soap Opera Magazine*, 25 February 1992, 10-11.

_____. "Days Would Be Different With…Charles in Charge." *Soap Opera Update*, 4 November 1991, 18-19.
_____. "Emilio, Days of Our Lives' Billy Hufsey." *Soap Opera Update*, 3 April 1989, 50-51.
_____. "Kristian Alfonso Has the Best Role of Her Life." *Soap Opera Update*, 14 January 1991, 6-10.
_____. "Mary Beth Evans On…" *Soap Opera Update*, 5 May 1992, 21-23.
_____. "The New & Improved Mary Beth Evans." *Soap Opera Update*, 4 November 1991, 16-18.
_____. "Shaping Up A Days of Our Lives Triangle." *Soap Opera Update*, 13 August 1990, 38-39, 64.
_____. "Stranger in His Native Land." *Soap Opera Update (Inside Soaps)*, 5 May 1992, 2-3, 41.
_____. "The Unsinkable Shannon Sturges." *Soap Opera Magazine*, 17 March 1992, 39.
_____. "A Visit to Matthew Ashford's Dressing Room." *Soap Opera Update*, 3 December 1990, 44-45.
_____. "Why There's No Hope for Days." *Soap Opera Update*, 9 September 1991, 58-60.
Sita, Barbara G. "Getting to Know Them: Luncheon with Josh and Deidre." *Soap Opera Digest*, January 1979, 30-31.
"Sixteen Things You Wanted to Know About a Leading Actor on Days of Our Lives Who's Romantic, Debonair, Handsome and So Much in Love with April Ramirez." *Soap Opera Update*, 12 March 1990, 31-32.
Slate, Libby. "As the Soaps Turn to Summer." *TV Times (Los Angeles Times)*, 21 June 1992, 79.
_____. "'Bold' Star's a One-man Agency." *Los Angeles Times*, 13 September 1994, F1.
_____. "For Soap Awards, A Nighttime 'Days'." *Los Angeles Times*, 10 January 1992, F27.
_____. "Getting Down and Dirty on Daytime." *TV Times (Los Angeles Times)*, 19 June 1994, 5-6.
_____. "Like a Beautiful Dance." *TV Times (Los Angeles Times)*, 2 January 1994, 5-6.
_____. "The Nights of Their Lives." *TV Times (Los Angeles Times)*, 21 February 1993, 84.
_____. "Return of the Count: Thaao Penghlis." *TV Times (Los Angeles Times)*, 2 January 1994, 6.
_____. "Soaps with a Mission." *Los Angeles Times*, 19 July 1992, F82, 85.
_____. "Summer Soaps Heat Up for the Young Audience." *TV Times (Los Angeles Times)*, 17 July 1990, 2-3.
_____. "Time of Their Lives." *Emmy*, April 1992, 58-63.
Sloane, Alison. "Sound Familiar?" *Soap Opera Digest*, 22 December 1992, 55.
Sloane, Stephanie. "Food for Thought." *Soap Opera Digest*, 7 July 1992, 52.
_____. "Flavor of the Month: For Down-Home English Fare, Brady's Pub on Days of Our Lives Is Salem's Coziest Eatery." *Soap Opera Digest*, 25 May 1993, 88-89.
_____. "Spotlight on Ivan G'Vera." *Soap Opera Digest*, 12 April 1994, 83.
_____. "Spotlight on Lark Voorhies and Miriam Parrish." *Soap Opera Digest*, 18 January 1994, 86-87.
Smith, Lillian. "Y&R's Scott Reeves and Days' Melissa Reeves: Prepared for Parenthood." *Soap Opera Magazine*, 23 June 1992, 10-11.
"Snake Charmers of the Soaps: Days of Our Lives, Peter Blake." *Soap Opera Update*, 9 August 1994, 28-29.
"Soaps' Most Exciting Newcomers: Bryan Dattilo." *Soap Opera Digest*, 20 July 1993, 107.
"So Long, Salem: Why Days Stars Keep Leaving." *Soap Opera Digest*, 18 August 1992, 31.
"Soap Bitch: Days of Whose Lives?" *Soap Opera Weekly*, 10 November 1992, 23.
"Soap Dish!" *People Weekly*, Summer 1989, 136-137.
"Soap Milestone." *People Weekly*, 8 January 1990, 7.
"Soap Opera." *Fortune*, March 1946, 119-124, 146-148, 151-152.
"Soap Opera Addiction: What's the Attraction?" *Teen Magazine*, March 1987, 36-38.
"Soap-opera Error with an Emmy." *New York Times*, 23 July 1986, 11(N), B4(L).
"Soap Operas: Men Are Tuning In." *New York Times*, 21 February 1979, 1 (3).
"Soap's Best Love Stories: Jack and Jennifer." *Soap Opera Digest*, 16 February 1993, 94.
"Soap's Luckiest Characters: Alice Horton." *Soap Opera Digest*, 16 March 1993, 102.
"Soaps' Most Preposterous Plots: Kim's Brain—the Last Frontier." *Soap Opera Digest*, 27 April 1993, 102.
"Soap's Most Romantic Weddings Ever! John and Isabella." *Soap Opera Digest*, 3 March 1993, 103.
"Soap's On." *Seventeen*, February 1980, 53.
"Soaperific Idea." *Playboy*, June 1974, 195.
"Soap Special: Stephen Nichols." *Teen Magazine*, August 1990, 84.
"Soapy Sales." *Video Review*, December 1989, 19.

Sobczak, Gene H. "Michael Easton: Born to Be Wild!" *Soap Opera Digest*, 20 August 1991, 14-17.
"Something Old, Something New: Camilla Scott Creates a New Melissa." *Soap Opera Weekly*, 13 March 1990, 30.
Sorel, Louise. "59 Favorite Things." *Soap Opera Update*, 3 May 1994, 25.
Sorkin, Arleen. "Double Take: Arleen Sorkin Interviews Herself." *Soap Opera Digest*, 18 November 1986, 30-32, 40.
_____. "Tribute: A Very Special Man: A Days Star Remembers Costume Designer Lee Smith." *Soap Opera Digest*, 18 February 1992, 136-137.
"A Southern Fete a la Maison des Secrets." *Soap Opera Weekly*, 7 June 1994, 6.
"Southern Hospitality: South Carolina Fans Give a Warm Welcome to Days." *Soap Opera Weekly*, 29 October 1991, 47.
Span, Paula. "The Queen of Daytime: Life in TV's Golden Ghetto." *Wall Street Journal*, 26 April 1984, 28(W), 26(E), 1.
_____. "Soap Opera Magazines, Cleaning Up." *Washington Post*, 19 June 1992, B1.
"The Spectator: Read All About It." *Soap Opera Digest*, 9 November 1993, 86-87.
Spencer, Richard. "Battle of the Supercouples." *Soap Opera Update*, 22 October 1990, 40-41.
_____. "Better Me than Kitty Kelley: Why Days' Macdonald Carey Wrote His Autobiography." *Soap Opera Update*, 30 September 1991, 17.
_____. "A Bundle of Joy for Izzy B." *Soap Opera Update (Inside Soaps)*, 19 May 1992, 2-3.
_____. "Carly Finds Her Son, but Will She Lose Bo?" *Soap Opera Update (Inside Soaps)*, 17 November 1992, 2-3.
_____. "Charles Tells on Patsy." *Soap Opera Update*, 15 August 1988, 15.
_____. "Chip Is Challenged." *Soap Opera Update*, 19 May 1992, 38.
_____. "The Days Ahead: A Happy New Year for Days' Romantic Couples." *Soap Opera Update*, 15 January 1990, 5-6.
_____. "The Days Ahead: What You Can Expect from Days of Our Lives' New Headwriter Gene Palumbo." *Soap Opera Update*, 22 July 1991, 46-47.
_____. "Days' Kirk Geiger: Don't Let Him Drive Your Car." *Soap Opera Update*, 24 September 1990, 49.
_____. "Days of Change: Familiar Faces and a Return to Romance at Days of Our Lives." *Soap Opera Update*, 26 February 1990, 18-19.
_____. "Days of Our Lives' According to Charles." *Soap Opera Update*, 4 July 1988, 29.
_____. "Days of Our Lives' New Headwriter, Anne Howard Bailey, Promises Lots of Laughs and Love." *Soap Opera Update*, 26 June 1989, 17.
_____. "Days of Our Lives' Wild Romantic: the Dossier on Wally Kurth." *Soap Opera Update*, 1 January 1990, 16.
_____. "Don't Ask Wayne Northrop to Love Hollywood." *Soap Opera Update*, 10 December 1991, 14-16.
_____. "Exactly What You Can Expect to See on NBC: An Interview with Vice President of Daytime Programming Jackie Smith." *Soap Opera Update*, 10 September 1990, 42-43.
_____. "Fade to Black: The Future Revealed." *Soap Opera Update*, 24 March 1992, 61.
_____. "Falcon Crest's Sheri Anderson from Days to Nighttime." *Soap Opera Update*, 6 November 1989, 50-51.
_____. "Huggable Julio: 'Days of Our Lives' Michael Bays." *Soap Opera Update*, 3 April 1989, 16.
_____. "Jack & Jennifer's Action-Packed Wedding." *Soap Opera Update*, 1 July 1991, 14-17.
_____. "Legendary Lovers: The Bittersweet Ballad of Days' Neil and Liz." *Soap Opera Update*, 26 March 1990, 38-39.
_____. "Michael T. Weiss Unveiled." *Soap Opera Update*, 9 October 1989, 30.
_____. "Nouveau Bo!" *Soap Opera Update*, 7 April 1992, 54-56.
_____. "Other Days Dilemmas." *Soap Opera Update (Inside Soaps)*, 17 November 1992, 4-5.
_____. "Please Call Him Patrick." *Soap Opera Update*, 25 August 1992, 48-49.
_____. "The Problems of Bo and Hope." *Soap Opera Update*, 21 May 1990, 7.
_____. "Sneak Preview of the Days of Our Lives Spinoff." *Soap Opera Update*, 7 April 1992, 42-43.
_____. "A Surprising Future for Days of Our Lives." *Soap Opera Update*, 22 February 1994, 42-44.
_____. "Superman: Drake Hogestyn." *Soap Opera Update*, 9 March 1993, 31-35.
_____. "That Was Then, This Is Now: Billy Warlock Has His Old Job Back on Days of Our Lives. But He Knows It Will Never Be the Same." *Soap Opera Update*, 5 November 1990, 64-65.

_____. "Triangle Trauma: Days of Our Lives Tells Us What's Ahead: Is There Hope for Bo and Carly?" *Soap Opera Update*, 29 April 1991, 40-42.

_____. "Wayne Northrop on Deidre Hall." *Soap Opera Update*, 19 November 1991, 18.

_____. "What the Future Holds for Days' Jack and Jen." *Soap Opera Update (Inside Soaps)*, 14 July 1992, 2-3.

_____. "Why Marlena Is Daytime's Strongest Character." *Soap Opera Update*, 30 September 1991, 15.

_____. "The Write Stuff: Days Fans Want to Know: Bo Without Hope? Kayla Without Patch? And What About Jack & Jennifer?! Days of Our Lives' Supervising Executive Producer Al Rabin Answers Those Questions and More." *Soap Opera Update*, 27 August 1990, 38-39.

Sperling, Caryn. "Jonah's Girl: Days' Tammy Townsend." *Soap Opera Weekly*, 19 July 1994, 22.

"Spring Fashion Fling: Shannon Sturges and Roberta Leighton." *Soap Opera Magazine*, 28 April 1992, 10-11.

"Star Desk: Deidre Hall." *Soap Opera Digest*, 25 November 1980, 72-73, 140.

"Starlit Christmas." *McCalls*, January 1990, 104-108.

"Stefano's Return Threatens John & Kristen's Future on Days!" *Soap Opera Update*, 19 October 1993, 60-61.

Stein, B. "Soap Operas." *Saturday Evening Post*, December 1974, 46-47+

"Step Into My Parlor: Thyme Lewis." *Soap Opera Digest*, 6 July 1993, 75.

"Stephen Nichols Lights One Fan's Fire." *Soap Opera Weekly*, 10 September 1991, 26.

"Stephen Nichols: No Daytime Return Planned." *Soap Opera Weekly*, 17 December 1991, 9.

"Stephen Nichols Returns to Daytime…Well, Sort Of." *Soap Opera Update*, 1 July 1991, 62-63.

Stern, Christopher. "ABC Cleans Up on QVC; 'All My Children' Merchandise Sales Reach $260,000 in One Hour." *Broadcasting & Cable*, 2 August 1993, 44.

"A Steve and Kayla Reunion on Days? Don't Hold Your Breath." *Soap Opera Digest*, 9 June 1992, 30.

"Storm Warning: Days' John and Kristen Fight Mother Nature and Tony's Rage." *Soap Opera Weekly*, 15 November 1994, 4.

"The Story Behind Billie's 'Pretty Woman' Fashion Show." *Soap Opera Update (News Digest)*, 21 September 1993, 44-45.

"Storyline Special Report: Will Days of Our Lives Keep Kim and Shane Apart?" *Soap Opera Update*, 25 February 1991, 64.

Sullivan, M.F. "Soap Opera in the Classroom." *Educational Leadership* 37 (October 1979): 78-80.

"Susan Seaforth Hayes Says Good-Bye." *Soap Opera Update (Inside Soaps)*, 9 March 1993, 38.

Susman, Linda. "Deidre Hall Stages On-Location Wedding." *Soap Opera Weekly*, 28 January 1992, 9.

_____. "It Looks Like Reckell's Leaving Days Again." *Soap Opera Weekly*, 19 November 1991, 2.

_____. "Izzy B's a Mom-to-be." *Soap Opera Weekly*, 1 October 1991, 5.

_____. "Lynn Herring Exits Days." *Soap Opera Weekly*, 6 October 1992, 4.

_____. "Risky Business: Throwing Caution to the Wind, Peter Reckell Leaves Days to Pursue His Dreams." *Soap Opera Weekly*, 10 December 1991, 12-15.

_____. "Storm Clouds Could Have Silver Lining for Days." *Soap Opera Weekly*, 31 December 1991, 8.

_____. "Straight Talk from NBC's Susan Lee." *Soap Opera Weekly*, 28 December 1993, 2-3.

Swanbrow, Diana. "As the Third World Turns: the Last Word In Contraceptive Devices: TV Soap Operas." *California*, June 1988, 18-19.

"Syndicators Testing the Waters with Teenage Soaps." *Broadcasting*, 16 October 1989, 31.

"Tammy Townsend: Wendy, Days of Our Lives." *Soap Opera Weekly*, 5 September 1994, 20.

Tarpley, Tami. "The Days of My Life." *Soap Opera Weekly*, 1 January 1991, 18.

Taylor, Clarke. "The Big Apple Captures Another Soap." *Los Angeles Times*, 24 June 1983, VI:22.

Taylor, Josh. "A Moving Tribute to Brenda Benet." *Soap Opera Digest*, 6 July 1982, 116.

Taylor, Rick. "Michael's Big Dive." *Soap Opera Magazine*, 9 June 1992, 24-25.

Tedesco, Tommy. "T.T On the TV Screen." *Guitar Player*, February 1987, 122.

Tel-A-Soap. "Putting Soaps on the Line." *Nation's Business*, August 1981, 72.

"Tempest in a Soap Dish." *Time*, 5 August 1991, 43.

"The Ten Hottest Lovers: Bo Brady." *Soap Opera Update*, 22 February 1994, 35.

"The Ten Hottest Lovers: John Black." *Soap Opera Update*, 22 February 1994, 41.

Tepper, A. "Stop Scoffing at the Soaps." *Seventeen*, July 1981, 24.

"Thaao Penghlis (Days of Our Lives' Tony DiMera)." *Soap Opera Update*, 1 November 1994, 33-35.

"That's Entertainment: James Reynolds." *Soap Opera Update*, 14 June 1994, 47.

"They're Back! What's Soap Life Like the Second Time Around? Days of Our Lives: Peter Reckell as Bo Brady; Susan Seaforth Hayes as Julie Williams." *Soap Opera Digest*, 5 March 1991, 119.

Thomas, Sari. "The Relationship Between Serials and Their Viewers." Ph.D. diss., University of Pennsylvania, 1977.

"3 Days of Days." *Soap Opera Update*, 12 July 1994, 52-53.

"Thumbs Down! Days of Our Lives: Don't Talk to Me!" *Soap Opera Digest*, 25 May 1993, 80-81.

"Thumbs Down! Is Beauty Skin-Deep? Days of Our Lives." *Soap Opera Digest*, 17 August 1993, 74-75.

"Thyme Lewis (Days of Our Lives' Jonah Carver)." *Soap Opera Update*, 4 October 1994, 33-35.

"Till Death Us Do Part: John and Isabella Black, Days of Our Lives." *Soap Opera Digest*, 22 June 1993, 104.

Timoney, Bill. "My Two Romans." *Soap Opera Weekly*, 29 October 1991, 18.

"Too Close for Comfort: Days's Sami Falls for Austin." *Soap Opera Digest*, 16 February 1993, 12.

Torchin, Mimi. "Black Family Shares Spotlight in a New Soap Opera." *New York Times*, 26 March 1989, H27(N), H27(L).

____. "Chris Evert: From Days in the Sun to Days of Our Lives." *Soap Opera Weekly*, 7 September 1993, 19.

Tormey, Carol. "Stephen Nichols Unmasked." *Soap Opera Weekly*, 12 December 1989, 12-14.

Tousignant, Marylou. "Alternative Days of Their Lives." *Washington Post*, 5 October 1992, C1.

Townley, R. "She Introduced a Stranger to the World of Soaps (Agnes Nixon, Creator of Several Soap Operas)." *TV Guide*, 3 May 1975, 12-16.

"Tragedy Hits Days's Carly: Will Her Love Survive?" *Soap Opera Digest*, 29 September 1992, 33-34.

Trank, Lisa. "Judi Evans: Getting Fit for the Best Days of Her Life." *Soap Opera Weekly*, 23 October 1990, 45.

"Trapped: Will Days's Doc Escape from the Pit?" *Soap Opera Digest*, 24 November 1992, 35.

"Trick or Treat: Days of Our Lives: Jack Deveraux." *Soap Opera Digest*, 20 October 1991, 74.

Trillin, Calvin. "Uncivil Liberties." *Nation*, 17 January 1987, 38.

"And Trouble Takes Three: Third Parties Bring Turmoil to Days' Favorite Couples." *Soap Opera Weekly*, 31 December 1991, 7.

Tuckman, Shara, and Irene Tuckman. "Fantastic Encounter: The Daze of Our Lives." *Soap Opera Weekly*, 24 March 1992, 42.

Tunnel, M. "Too Bad." *Us*, 6 January 1981, 49.

Turisi, Kim. "The Super Couple Equation." *Soap Opera Weekly*, 7 May 1991, 14-15.

Turk, Rose-Marie. "Petite Andrea Evans Is Long on Wit, Style." *Los Angeles Times*, 17 August 1984, V:12.

Turk, Stephen. "The Royal Family of Suds." *Los Angeles Magazine*, December 1987, 76-79.

Turrow, J. "Advising and Ordering: Daytime, Prime Time." *Journal of Communication* 24 (Spring 1974): 138-141.

"TV's Most Beautiful Women: Crystal Chappell." *Soap Opera Digest*, 8 June 1993, 57.

"TV's Most Romantic Stories: First Love: Tanner and Molly, Days of Our Lives." *Soap Opera Digest*, 18 February 1992, 6-7.

"TV's Romantic Villains: Lawrence Alamain, Days of Our Lives." *Soap Opera Digest*, 16 April 1991, 68.

"The 20th Anniversary Party for Days of Our Lives." *Soap Opera Digest*, 25 February 1986, 118-123.

"25 Photos to Celebrate Days of Our Lives' 25 Years." *Soap Opera Update*, 19 November 1990, 40-43.

"The Two Faces of Bo." *Soap Opera Digest*, 27 April 1993, 7.

"Two of a Kind: Actors Who Are Like Their Characters: Melissa Reeves." *Soap Opera Digest*, 30 March 1993, 101.

"The 2 Weeks That You Simply Can't Miss on Days of Our Lives." *Soap Opera Update*, 19 October 1993, 58-59.

"The 2 Weeks That You Simply Can't Miss: Days of Our Lives." *Soap Opera Update*, 3 May 1994, 22-24.

"The 2 Weeks That You Simply Can't Miss: Days of Our Lives." *Soap Opera Update*, 4 October 1994, 46-48.

Urhanska, Wanda. "Deidre Hall: At Home in Our House." *McCalls*, February 1988, 140-143.

Uhry, M. and R. Bricker. "As the World Turns, So Do the Lady Killing Louses Who Are Beefing Up the Soaps." *People*, 9 March 1981, 73-76.

"Valentine Fantasies from the Sexy Men of Daytime: Matthew Ashford." *Soap Opera Update*, 21 January 1992, 32-33.

"Valentine's Day Preview: Days of Our Lives." *Soap Opera Update*, 11 February 1992, 32-33.

Vine, Dorothy. "Anne Howard Extended on Days." *Soap Opera Weekly*, 10 April 1990, 4.

____. "Birth, Death and Everything In Between Will Fill Salem's Days." *Soap Opera Weekly*, 22 September 1992, 9.

____. "Cinderella Won't Be Going to the Ball: Peggy McCay Nabs Nighttime Emmy Nomination but You Won't See Her on TV." *Soap Opera Weekly*, 13 August 1991, 7.

____. "Days Signs Peggy McCay to Contract." *Soap Opera Weekly*, 20 February 1990, 2.

____. "An Eloquent Defender of Animals' Rights: Peggy McCay." *Soap Opera Weekly*, 31 July 1990, 27.

____. "Happy Days for Ken Corday." *Soap Opera Weekly*, 17 September 1991, 10.

____. "Here's to You, Bill Bell!" *Soap Opera Weekly*, 18 February 1992, 10.

____. "I'm Still Here! Despite What the Fates Have Thrown Her, Days' Roberta Leighton Is a Cheerful Survivor." *Soap Opera Weekly*, 24 March 1992, 12-14.

____. "Joe Gallison Renews His Contract with Days." *Soap Opera Weekly*, 13 March 1990, 4-5.

____. Michael O'Connor: Days' Villain-in-Training." *Soap Opera Weekly*, 1 October 1991, 10.

____. "Mother Courage: Patsy Pease Put Her Baby's Health Before Her Job; Now She's Happy to Be Back on Days." *Soap Opera Weekly*, 12 February 1991, 23-25.

____. "Peggy McCay Takes Home an Emmy." *Soap Opera Weekly*, 17 September 1991, 6.

____. "Sabatino Finds Immortality." *Soap Opera Weekly*, 12 November 1991, 10.

Von Dish, Diva. "TV's Best and Worst Mothers: The Best: Alice Horton." *Soap Opera Digest*, 12 May 1992, 123.

Viorst, Judith. "Soap Operas: The Suds of Time March On." *Redbook*, November 1975, 62+

Waggett, Gerald J. "Bill Hayes: Song and Dance Man." *Soap Opera Weekly*, 3 November 1992, 28.

____. "Busy Days Ahead for Daniel Pilon." *Soap Opera Weekly*, 21 July 1992, 28.

____. "Peter Reckell Makes Time for Cheryl Ladd." *Soap Opera Weekly*, 29 October 1991, 28.

____. "A Plea To the Soaps: 'Let's Stop Turning Rapists into Heroes.'" *TV Guide*, 27 May 1989, 10-11.

Wagner, Andrea. "Cruising on the Love Boat with Peter Reckell." *Soap Opera Digest*, 11 September 1984, 106-110.

Wakefield, Dan. "Why Soap Operas Are So Popular." *Family Circle*, July 1976, 92+.

Waldman, Allison J. "Building a Better Romance: The Days Way to Love." *Soap Opera Update*, 9 April 1990, 5-6, 57.

____. "A Check-Up with Dr. Mike—Michael T. Weiss Diagnoses 'Days of Our Lives.'" *Soap Opera Update*, October 1988, 58-59.

____. "Crime Time on Daytime: The Battle Between Days' DiMeras and Bradys." *Soap Opera Magazine*, 21 June 1994, 55.

____. "Days of Our Lives." *Soap Opera Update*, 17 July 1989, 30-31.

____. "Days of Our Lives' Mary Beth Evans Looking into the Future of Patch & Kayla." *Soap Opera Update*, 11 September 1989, 8-9.

____. "The Drakester Is Wild: Quick-Takes with Days' Roman." *Soap Opera Update*, 28 November 1988, 56-57.

____. "The Eternal Love of Robin & Mike." *Soap Opera Update*, 30 January 1989, 14-15.

____. "A Great Days Love Story from the Past: Diana & Roman." *Soap Opera Magazine*, 20 September 1994, 55.

____. "Happily Ever After…" *Soap Opera Update*, 15 August 1988, 10-11.

____. "Happy Anniversary Patch & Kayla." *Soap Opera Update*, 7 August 1989, 5.

____. "Happy Ending for Justin and Adrienne." *Soap Opera Weekly*, 25 December 1990, 5.

____. "Hey, Mike! Are You Staying on Days or What?" *Soap Opera Update*, 4 June 1990, 24-25.

____. "How Do I Love Thee? The Romance of Justin and Adrienne." *Soap Opera Update*, October 1988, 12-13.

____. "I Can Hear Music 'Days of Our Lives.'" *Soap Opera Update*, 11 April 1988, 62-63.

____. "Let's Hear It for…Chemistry from Days!" *Soap Opera Update*, 2 July 1990, 56-57.

____. "Let's Hear It for…Days of Our Lives." *Soap Opera Update*, 17 July 1989, 20-21.

____. "Let's Hear It for…Kayla! Days' Mary Beth Evans." *Soap Opera Update*, 29 January 1990, 48.

____. "Look Out April! Robin's Back! 'Days'' Derya Ruggles." *Soap Opera Update*, 15 May 1989, 6.

____. "Lord Roman, the Sheriff of Salemtown Is Portrayed by Drake Hogestyn." *Soap Opera Update*, 5 September 1988, 29-30, 62.

____. "The Man Behind the Romance: Days' Man in Charge, Al Rabin." *Soap Opera Update*, 9 April 1990, 7-8.

____. "Prince Michael of Mirth, Heir of Horton, Royal Jester Is Portrayed by Michael T. Weiss." *Soap Opera Update*, 5 September 1988, 31-32, 62.

____. "Reflections: Days' Charles Shaughnessy on the Twins." *Soap Opera Update*, 13 March 1989, 10-11.

____. "A Return to Traditional, Emotional Storytelling: Executive Producer Ken Corday Talks about Days." *Soap Opera Update*, 7 May 1990, 38-39, 57.

____. "Roman and Steve: Two Sides of the Coin." *Soap Opera Update*, 26 September 1988, 15-16.

____. "Salem's Beautiful Bradys." *Soap Opera Update*, 15 May 1989, 51.

____. "Salem's New Doctor Hides Mysterious Past." *Soap Opera Update*, 13 August 1990, 16.

____. "Steve and Kayla's First Christmas." *Soap Opera Update*, 9 January 1989, 1.

____. "The Storybook Lovers of 'Days of Our Lives.'" *Soap Opera Update*, 25 July 1988, 29-36.

____. "Swinging and Swaying to the Romantic Sounds of Nick & April's Love Story." *Soap Opera Update*, 26 February 1990, 40.

____. "Tantalizingly Tormented Triangle: Robin, Mike and April, 'Days.'" *Soap Opera Update*, 26 June 1989, 14-16.

Waldron, Robert. "The Continuing Days (and Nights) of Gloria Loring." *Soap Opera Weekly*, 10 April 1990, 27.

____. "Holding Out For A Hero: Peter Reckell Returns to His Ideal Role—Bo Brady." *Soap Opera Weekly*, 17 July 1990, 12-13.

____. "Kristian Alfonso: Everyone Loves a Lover." *Soap Opera Weekly*, 24 September 1991, 30.

____. "Marriages That Beat All Odds: Days' Tom & Alice Horton." *Soap Opera Magazine*, 16 February 1993, 45.

Waldrop, Judith and Diane Crispell. "Daytime Dramas, Demographic Dreams." *American Demographics* 10 (October 1988): 28-32.

Walley, Wayne. "ABC Data: Soaps Are Good Buy." *Advertising Age*, 23 October 1989, 91.

Walsh, Colleen. "Is Shane a Negative Role Model?" *Soap Opera Weekly*, 24 July 1990, 19.

Walsh, Kathryn. "Days' Co-head Writer Explains Jack's Reform Process." *Soap Opera Weekly*, 6 February 1990, 3.

____. "Days' Disasters: Art Director Chip Dox Has Been Busy Wrecking Havoc on Salem." *Soap Opera Weekly*, 24 April 1990, 43.

____. "Hit…Days Celebrates the Holidays." *Soap Opera Weekly*, 1 February 1994, 10.

____. "Hit…Jo and Jack on Days." *Soap Opera Weekly*, 2 February 1993, 23.

____. "Jack Nulls Nuptials." *Soap Opera Weekly*, 24 April 1990, 2.

____. "Jennifer Violated: Days' Innocent Heroine Victim of Rape." *Soap Opera Weekly*, 6 November 1990, 3.

____. "Just the Ten of Us' Brooke Theiss Doesn't Miss a Day of Days." *Soap Opera Weekly*, 12 December 1989, 18.

____. "Miss…The Wicked Witch of Salem." *Soap Opera Weekly*, 10 August 1993, 15.

____. "Pete and Repeat—It's the Same Old Stories in Salem." *Soap Opera Weekly*, 20 March 1990, 7.

____. "Seaforth Hayes Returns to Days." *Soap Opera Weekly*, 26 December 1989, 3.

____. "There's Hope (& Bo) for Days." *Soap Opera Weekly*, 10 April 1990, 3.

Walsh, Maureen. "Welcome to the Parrish." *Soap Opera Weekly*, 3 August 1993, 19.

Wander, P. "The Angst of the Upper Class." *Journal of Communication* 29 (Autumn 1979): 85-88.

Wang, Min, and Arvind Singhal. "Ke Wang, a Chinese Television Soap Opera with a Message." *Gazette*, 49 (May 1992): 177-92.

Warner, Chris. "Soap Opera Just Like NHL." *Sport*, June 1988, 12.

Warren, Elaine. "Love! Pain! Outrage! A Guide to the Hottest Triangles on Daytime Soaps." *TV Guide*, 1 August 1987, 26-29.

Warren, Jim. "Behind the Scenes at Days of Our Lives." *Soap Opera Weekly*, 27 April 1993, 36-38.

____. "Lynn Herring Leaves GH for Days." *Soap Opera Weekly*, 25 February 1992, 7.

____. "Meet Days' New Bad Boy: Brian Heidik." *Soap Opera Update (Inside Soaps)*, 20 October 1992, 19.

____. "Some Last Words from Days' Billy Warlock." *Soap Opera Weekly*, 25 June 1991, 2.

"Watch Out, Marlena: Stella's Anger Grows on Days." *Soap Opera Digest*, 13 October 1992, 37.

Waters, Harry F. "New Giant-Size Soaps; 90-Minute Specials." *Newsweek*, 18 February 1974, 18, 86.

____. "New Sins in Soapland." *Newsweek*, 9 December 1968, 100.

____. "New Varieties of Soap: Teens and Gays Push the Limits of the Genre." *Newsweek*, 26 February 1990, 60.

____. "Television's Hottest Show." *Newsweek*, 28 September 1981, 60-66.

Watson, L.E. "Soap Star Round-Up—Your Favorites on Daytime TV." *Teen*, August 1981, 27-30.

"Wayne Northrop Renews Contract with Days." *Soap Opera Update (Inside Soaps)*, 3 March 1992, 3.

"Wayne Northrop Returns to Days: Salem Will Be Overrun by Romans." *Soap Opera Digest*, 3 September 1991, 44.

"We Like Them, We Really Like Them! Drake Hogestyn." *Soap Opera Update*, 18 October 1994, 38.

Weinrub, Bernard. "Academics Analyze TV as If Soaps Were Opera." *New York Times*, 22 July 1988, 14(N), C26(L).

"Wedding Outtakes." *Soap Opera Update*, 5 September 1988, 65.

Wetzel, Gretchen. "Hola, Marlena and Roman!" *Soap Opera Digest*, 15 October 1991, 56-57.

"What They Did for Love: Soap Moms' Greatest Sacrifices: Jo Johnson." 11 May 1993, 108.

"What They're Really Watching in Salem." *Soap Opera Update*, 22 March 1994, 28-30.

"What's Ahead on Days of Our Lives!" *Soap Opera Update (Inside Soaps)*, 12 January 1993, 3-5.

"What's Next for Marlena on Days of Our Lives? The Future Looks Rocky for Roman and Isabella." *Soap Opera Digest*, 20 August 1991, 35.

"When Days' Billie Is Held Hostage, It's Bo to the Rescue." *Soap Opera Weekly*, 18 May 1993, 4.

"Where Oomph Has Gone; Daytime Dramas Attract Stars." *Newsweek*, 29 November 1965, 88.

"Which Man Really Saves Marlena?" *Soap Opera Update (Inside Soaps)*, 15 December 1992, 2-3.

"While Shane's Away, Kim's Easy Prey: Days Welcomes Back Another Villain." *Soap Opera Weekly*, 24 September 1991, 8.

White, Molly. "Days' Matthew Ashford Makes Her Birthday Dream Come True." *Soap Opera Update*, 21 January 1992, 58.

Whitley, Dianna. "An Intimate View of the House That Wayne and Lynn Northrop Love." *Soap Opera Digest*, 16 August 1983, 140-144.

"Who'll Be the Next Bo? Reckell Leaves Days, Role to Be Recast." *Soap Opera Digest*, 24 December 1991, 39-40.

"Who'll Co-Star On Marlena's New Spin-Off? Here's Days's Secret Wish List." *Soap Opera Digest*, 3 March 1992, 33-34.

"Who Killed Days' Curtis? Suspect #1." *Soap Opera Weekly*, 30 November 1993, 8.

"Who Killed Days' Curtis? Suspect #2." *Soap Opera Weekly*, 7 December 1993, 5.

"Who Killed Days' Curtis? Suspect #3." *Soap Opera Weekly*, 28 December 1993, 7.

"Who Killed Days' Curtis? Suspect #4." *Soap Opera Weekly*, 4 January 1994, 9.

"Who Killed Days' Curtis? Suspect #5." *Soap Opera Weekly*, 11 January 1994, 4.

"Who Killed Days' Curtis? Suspect #6. *Soap Opera Weekly*, 18 January 1994, 5.

"Who's Who? Days of Our Lives." *Soap Opera Digest*, 17 September 1991, 20-21.

"Why Days of Our Lives Made Eve and Jack Marry in Haste." *Soap Opera Digest*, 19 March 1991, 33.

"Why Patsy Pease Disappeared from Days of Our Lives: Anne Howard Replaces Pease Once Again." *Soap Opera Digest*, 6 August 1991, 32.

"Why 2 Days Stars Are Really Leaving: Michael Sabatino and Crystal Chappell." *Soap Opera Digest*, 14 September 1993, 38-40.

Wild, David. "'Melrose Place' Is a Really Good Show." *Rolling Stone*, 19 May 1994, 48-54.

"Will Hope Return to Days?" *Soap Opera Digest*, 16 February 1993, 8.

"Will 'The Phoenix' Rise Again in Salem?" *Soap Opera Digest*, 12 November 1991, 38.

Williams, Phyllis S. "Adios, Adrienne? Is Judi Evans Leaving Days?" *Soap Opera Weekly*, 21 August 1990, 2.

____. "Al Rabin Comments on Appeasing Patsy Pease." *Soap Opera Weekly*, 27 March 1990, 5.

____. "Anne Howard to the Rescue." *Soap Opera Weekly*, 27 March 1990, 5.

____. "Bo and Hope Return to Days of Our Lives." *Soap Opera Weekly*, 3 April 1990, 3.

____. "Stephen Nichols to Become Blues Man?" *Soap Opera Weekly*, 2 January 1990, 3.

Willis, F. "Falling in Love with Celebrities." *Sexual Behavior* 2 (1972): 2-8.

Wilows, Mark Edward. "Getting Personal with…Bryan Dattilo." *Soap Opera Update*, 28 December 1993, 60.

Wilson, Susan. "Rocking & Rolling Right to the Top." *Soap Opera Digest*, 17 July 1984, 30-32.

"Win A Trip to Days of Our Lives: Rate Salem's Sexy Men and You Could Spend a Day Behind the Scenes at Days." *Soap Opera Digest*, 14 April 1992, 6-9.

Winkel, Gabrielle. "Days Spin-Off Update." *Soap Opera Weekly*, 31 March 1992, 8.

____. "Kirk Geiger: Is Days' Chad Bad?" *Soap Opera Weekly*, 25 September 1990, 39.

Winsey, V. "How Soaps Help You Cope." *Family Health*, April 1979, 30-32.

"Witchboard." *Variety*, 21 January 1987, 20.

"Wolfman John: Days Gives Us More Clues in the John Black Mystery." *Soap Opera Weekly*, 24 December 1991, 7.

"The Woman You Would Most Like to Look Like Is…Melissa Reeves." *Soap Opera Update*, 17 November 1992, 36-39.

"Women Making Money; Scanning the Soaps." *Ladies Home Journal*, July 1975, 49.

"Women Who Love Too Much: Jennifer Deveraux, Days of Our Lives." *Soap Opera Digest*, 3 March 1992, 115.

"Write-Your-Own-Ending Soap Opera." *Los Angeles Magazine*, August 1975, 184.

"Write-Your-Own-Soap-Opera-Ending Ending." *Los Angeles Magazine*, October 1975, 182.

"The Young & the Restless' Ryan & Days of Our Lives' Jennifer." *Soap Opera Update*, 11 February 1992, 42-43.

Zenka, Lorraine. "Acid Hurled in Carrie's Face." *Soap Opera Magazine*, 9 March 1993, 8.

____. "Alfonso Returns to Days…Again!" *Soap Opera Magazine*, 17 May 1994, 5.

____. "At Home with Days' Alison Sweeney." *Soap Opera Magazine*, 1 February 1994, 24-25.

____. "At Home with Days' Jamie Lyn Bauer." *Soap Opera Magazine*, 5 July 1994, 30-31.

____. "At Last…Carrie and Austin Finally Make Love." *Soap Opera Magazine*, 19 April 1994, 8-9.

____. "Austin Wheels and Deals His Way to the Top." *Soap Opera Magazine*, 27 September 1994, 8-9.

____. "Behind the Scenes: Fire on the Days Set." *Soap Opera Magazine*, 15 February 1994, 34-35.

____. "Billie Fears Bo Will Learn the Truth." *Soap Opera Magazine*, 18 January 1994, 6-7.

____. "Billie Races to Find Bo and Gina in Time." *Soap Opera Magazine*, 22 November 1994, 8-9.

____. "Bring on Brian." *Soap Opera Magazine*, 3 November 1992, 28.

____. "Bryan Dattilo Gets His Kicks with Karate." *Soap Opera Magazine*, 13 September 1994, 49.

____. "California Dreamin': At Home with Days' John Aniston." *Soap Opera Magazine*, 9 March 1993, 44-45.

____. "Carrie and Austin Rekindle Romance." *Soap Opera Magazine*, 20 April 1993, 7.

____. "Carving Out a Niche for the Carvers." *Soap Opera Magazine*, 25 May 1993, 23.

____. "Catching Up with Days' Matt Ashford." *Soap Opera Magazine*, 2 August 1994, 51.

____. "Catching Up with Days' Peter Reckell." *Soap Opera Magazine*, 25 March 1994, 24.

____. "A Christmas Beginning for Days' Christie Clark and Patrick Muldoon." *Soap Opera Magazine*, 21 December 1993, 34.

____. "A Day at Days." *Soap Opera Magazine*, 13 April 1993, 44-45.

____. "Days' Ariana Chase: A Fast Takeover of Kim." *Soap Opera Magazine*, 2 March 1993, 32.

____. "Days' Beauties Grace the Grand Cotillion." *Soap Opera Magazine*, 7 June 1994, 54.

____. "Days' Bryan Dattilo: Home on the Range." *Soap Opera Magazine*, 15 March 1994, 14-15.

____. "Days: Carly Buried Alive by Vivian." *Soap Opera Magazine*, 11 January 1994, 30.

____. "Days' Deborah Adair: Doing Double Duty—And Loving It." *Soap Opera Magazine*, 15 June 1993, 12-13.

____. "Days' Drake Hogestyn and John Black: A Study in Contrasts." *Soap Opera Magazine*, 16 November 1993, 45.

____. "Days' Drake Hogestyn Goes Home to Indiana." *Soap Opera Magazine*, 4 October 1994, 26-27.

____. "Days' Eileen Davidson: Still Surfing After All These Years." *Soap Opera Magazine*, 21 September 1994, 12-13.

____. "Days' Eileen Davidson Throws a Great Beach Bash for Charity." *Soap Opera Magazine*, 13 September 1994, 14-15.

____. "Days' Erik Von Detten: Making Summertime Memories." *Soap Opera Magazine*, 10 August 1993, 42.

____. "Days' Frances Reid Recalls...a Few Fantastic First Times." *Soap Opera Magazine*, 18 October 1994, 52.

____. "Days' Frank Parker Reveals the Secret to Brady's Famous Chowder!" *Soap Opera Magazine*, 12 July 1994, 49.

____. "Days' Gang Gathers for a Fun-filled Family Picnic." *Soap Opera Magazine*, 1 November 1994, 54-55.

____. "Days' Harvest Festival Carnival." *Soap Opera Magazine*, 26 October 1993, 34-35.

____. "Days' Ivan G'Vera: Portrait of an Adventurous Soul." *Soap Opera Magazine*, 29 March 1994, 26-27.

____. "Days' J. Cynthia Brooks: Shooting." *Soap Opera Magazine*, 22 December 1992, 10-11.

____. "Days' Jamie Lyn Bauer: Injecting New Life into an Old Role." *Soap Opera Magazine*, 30 September 1993, 45.

____. "Days' Jim Reynolds: Committed to His Community." *Soap Opera Magazine*, 1 February 1994, 45.

____. "Days' Joe Mascolo: A Gentleman's Good Taste." *Soap Opera Magazine*, 7 June 1994, 30-31.

____. "Days' John Aniston Recalls Those Wonderful First Times." *Soap Opera Magazine*, 9 August 1994, 25.

____. "Days' John Clarke: Chasing Adventure on His Harley." *Soap Opera Magazine*, 28 June 1994, 49.

____. "Days' Lisa Rinna: Memories from Her Mother." *Soap Opera Magazine*, 30 August 1994, 45.

____. "Days' Lisa Rinna: Old-fashioned Values Shape Her Life." *Soap Opera Magazine*, 2 November 1993, 12-13.

____. "Days' Louise Sorel: Making Vivian a Madwoman Viewers Love to Hate." *Soap Opera Magazine*, 28 September 1993, 15.

____. "Days' Louise Sorel Remembering Those Fabulous Firsts." *Soap Opera Magazine*, 16 August 1994, 39.

____. "Days' Macdonald Carey Turns 80!" *Soap Opera Magazine*, 16 March 1993, 15.

____. "Days' Makeup Person Keith Crary: Applies the Artist's Touch." *Soap Opera Magazine*, 18 August 1992, 34.

____. "Days' Mark Drexler: A Very Happy Man." *Soap Opera Magazine*, 10 November 1992, 24-25.

____. "Days' Matthew Ashford: Taking Control of Jack." *Soap Opera Magazine*, 9 February 1993, 12.

____. "Days' Michael Sabatino and Crystal Chappell: Going Places Together." *Soap Opera Magazine*, 20 July 1993, 14-15.

____. "Days' Miriam Parrish Shows Us Easy Exercises You Can Do at Home." *Soap Opera Magazine*, 23 August 1994, 49.

____. "Days' Patrick Muldoon." *Soap Opera Magazine*, 1 June 1993, 24-25.

____. "Days' Patrick Muldoon Talks About Women...And Men." *Soap Opera Magazine*, 26 April 1994, 26-27.

____. "The Days Ratings Game: How Salem Moms Measure Up with Their Children." *Soap Opera Magazine*, 10 May 1994, 45.

____. "Days' Richard Burgi: Creative Inner Magic." *Soap Opera Magazine*, 15 September 1992, 27.

____. "Days' Robert Kelker-Kelly & Lisa Rinna." *Soap Opera Magazine*, 27 April 1993, 12.

____. "Days' Robert Kelker-Kelly: I Don't Like People to Lie to Me." *Soap Opera Magazine*, 7 December 1993, 45.

____. "Days' Sister Act." *Soap Opera Magazine*, 5 October 1993, 39.

____. "Days' Stars Shape Up at Salem's New Gym." *Soap Opera Magazine*, 19 July 1994, 52.

_____. "Days' Susan Seaforth Hayes: Telling It Like It Is." *Soap Opera Magazine*, 18 August 1992, 27.

_____. "Days' Suzanne Rogers: Looking for Love…and a Stronger Story." *Soap Opera Weekly*, 17 November 1992, 28.

_____. "Days' Suzanne Rogers Shares Her Cherished Memories." *Soap Opera Magazine*, 6 September 1994, 14-15.

_____. "Days' Thaao Penghlis: A Touch of Suave Sophistication." *Soap Opera Magazine*, 7 December 1993, 12-13.

_____. "Days' Three-way Love Affair: Bo, Carly and Lawrence." *Soap Opera Magazine*, 23 March 1993, 39.

_____. "Days' 27th Anniversary Extravaganza." *Soap Opera Magazine*, 1 December 1992, 44-45.

_____. "Days' Wayne Northrop: Keeping a Low Profile." *Soap Opera Magazine*, 7 September 1993, 42.

_____. "Days' Wesley Eure." *Soap Opera Magazine*, 2 February 1993, 34.

_____. "A Delightful Days' Fantasy: Carrie and Austin Enjoy a Picnic in the Park." *Soap Opera Magazine*, 31 August 1993, 24-25.

_____. "The DiMera Living Room on Days." *Soap Opera Magazine*, 6 December 1994, 30-31.

_____. "Dressing Up for Days: Behind the Scenes at Bo's Costume Ball." *Soap Opera Magazine*, 9 November 1993, 24-25.

_____. "Ed Mallory's Memories…of Days Gone By." *Soap Opera Magazine*, 29 September 1992, 15.

_____. "Executive Producer Ken Corday: What's Ahead for Days." *Soap Opera Magazine*, 4 August 1992, 6-7.

_____. "For Crystal Chappell and Michael Sabatino: A Final Curtain on Days." *Soap Opera Magazine*, 12 October 1993, 15.

_____. "For Days' Macdonald Carey…A Memorable Journey Through Life." *Soap Opera Magazine*, 31 May 1994, 38-39.

_____. "For Macdonald Carey: 'Days Has Gone Too Far.'" *Soap Opera Magazine*, 28 December 1993, 42.

_____. "For the Women of Days…Female Friendships Run Deep." *Soap Opera Magazine*, 3 May 1994, 52.

_____. "Frances Reid: Filling Her Days With Adventure." *Soap Opera Magazine*, 26 January 1993, 12.

_____. "Gloria Loring: Conquering Life Since Days." *Soap Opera Magazine*, 14 July 1992, 32.

_____. "A Great Love Story from the Past: Days' Julie and Doug." *Soap Opera Magazine*, 23 November 1993, 45.

_____. "Halloween Revelers Enjoy a High Time." *Soap Opera Magazine*, 8 November 1994, 30-31.

_____. "Happy 29th Anniversary, Days!" *Soap Opera Magazine*, 6 December 1994, 18.

_____. "Heroic Drake Nabs Crook." *Soap Opera Magazine*, 1 September 1992, 6.

_____. "He's Baaaaack! Days' Joe Mascolo." *Soap Opera Magazine*, 19 October 1993, 15.

_____. "It's a Tough Job! Christie Clark." *Soap Opera Magazine*, 23 March 1993, 32.

_____. "Jason Brooks Reveals What It's Like Working on Days." *Soap Opera Magazine*, 12 April 1994, 27.

_____. "Join the Fans at a Days Extravaganza." *Soap Opera Magazine*, 28 June 1994, 14-15.

_____. "Joy Garrett, 1945-1993." *Soap Opera Magazine*, 2 March 1993, 6.

_____. "The 'Joy' of Cooking." *Soap Opera Magazine*, 13 October 1992, 22.

_____. "Kim—Lacey—Claire." *Soap Opera Magazine*, 12 January 1993, 26-27.

_____. "Laura's Worst Fear About Peter and Jennifer Comes True." *Soap Opera Magazine*, 25 October 1994, 8-9.

_____. "Learning to Live the Single Life: Wayne Heffley." *Soap Opera Magazine*, 28 July 1992, 34.

_____. "Lisa Sings the Blues." *Soap Opera Magazine*, 3 November 1992, 28.

_____. "Louise Sorel Shows Us…Days' Changeable Vivian." *Soap Opera Magazine*, 2 August 1994, 52.

_____. "Lucas' Biggest Problem Is Sexual Frustration." *Soap Opera Magazine*, 29 November 1994, 39.

_____. "Meet Roark Critchlow: The New Michael Horton." *Soap Opera Magazine*, 3 May 1994, 7.

_____. "On the Set: Days' Cheatin' Heart." *Soap Opera Magazine*, 30 November 1993, 34-35.

_____. "180° of Separation: Days' Paul Kersey." *Soap Opera Magazine*, 20 September 1994, 48.

_____. "Patsy Pease Comes Home to Salem." *Soap Opera Magazine*, 21 July 1992, 44-45.

____. "Robert Kelker-Kelly: Finally Finding Happiness in Daytime." *Soap Opera Magazine*, 19 January 1993, 12.

____. "Rockin' On with Days' Patrick Muldoon." *Soap Opera Magazine*, 19 July 1994, 30-31.

____. "Salem's Burning Question: Who Killed Curtis?" *Soap Opera Magazine*, 14 December 1993, 6-7.

____. "Staci Greason: Leaving Days for…Everything." *Soap Opera Magazine*, 8 September 1992, 12.

____. "Star of the Week: Days' Alison Sweeney." *Soap Opera Magazine*, 27 September 1994, 24.

____. "Star of the Week: Days' Deidre Hall." *Soap Opera Magazine*, 10 May 1994, 52.

____. "Star of the Week: Days' Kristian Alfonso." *Soap Opera Magazine*, 12 July 1994, 24.

____. "Star of the Week: Days' Renee Jones, Thyme Lewis & Tammy Townsend." *Soap Opera Magazine*, 28 June 1994, 24.

____. "Star of the Week: Days' Wayne Northrop." *Soap Opera Magazine*, 22 March 1994, 25.

____. "Stars Galore at the Days' Fan Club Weekend." *Soap Opera Magazine*, 29 June 1993, 34-35.

____. "Stars Shine at Soap Spectacular." *Soap Opera Magazine*, 18 August 1992, 46-47.

____. "Tony Sees John and Kristen During an Emotional Moment." *Soap Opera Magazine*, 15 November 1994, 8-9.

____. "What's Ahead on Days: An Interview with Head Writer James Reilly." *Soap Opera Magazine*, 14 September 1994, 30.

INDEX

271